Beyond the New Public Management

NEW HORIZONS IN PUBLIC POLICY

General Editor: Wayne Parsons
Professor of Public Policy, Queen Mary and Westfield College,
University of London, UK

This series aims to explore the major issues facing academics and practitioners working in the field of public policy at the dawn of a new millennium. It seeks to reflect on where public policy has been, in both theoretical and practical terms, and to prompt debate on where it is going. The series emphasizes the need to understand public policy in the context of international developments and global change. New Horizons in Public Policy publishes the latest research on the study of the policy-making process and public management, and presents original and critical thinking on the policy issues and problems facing modern and post-modern societies.

Titles in the series include:

Innovations in Public Management
Perspectives from East and West Europe
Edited by Tony Verheijen and David Coombes

Beyond the New Public Management
Changing Ideas and Practices in Governance
Edited by Martin Minogue, Charles Polidano and David Hulme

Beyond the New Public Management

Changing Ideas and Practices in Governance

Edited by
Martin Minogue

Senior Research Fellow, Institute for Development Policy and Management, University of Manchester, UK

Charles Polidano

Lecturer in Public Sector Management, Institute for Development Policy and Management, University of Manchester, UK

David Hulme

Professor of Development Studies, Institute for Development Policy and Management, University of Manchester, UK

NEW HORIZONS IN PUBLIC POLICY

Edward Elgar
Cheltenham, UK • Northampton, MA, USA

Published by
Edward Elgar Publishing Limited
Glensanda House
Montpellier Parade
Cheltenham
Glos GL50 1UA
UK

Edward Elgar Publishing, Inc.
6 Market Street
Northampton
Massachusetts 01060
USA

A catalogue record for this book
is available from the British Library

Library of Congress Cataloguing in Publication Data
Beyond the new public management : changing ideas and practices in
governance / edited by Martin Minogue, Charles Polidano, David
Hulme.
        — (New horizons in public policy)
    Chiefly papers presented at Public Management for the Next
Century: an International Conference to Review Trends and Public
Management and Governance, held June–July 1997, University of
Manchester.
    1. Organizational change—Congresses.   2. Administrative agencies—
Reorganization—Congresses.   3. Civil service reform—Congresses.
I. Minogue, Martin.   II. Polidano, Charles, 1967–   .   III. Hulme,
David.   IV. Public Management for the Next Century: an International
Conference to Review Trends and Public Management and Governance
(1997 : University of Manchester)   V. Series.
JF1525.073 B49   1998
351—dc21   96–4035
                                                                                                CIP

ISBN 1 85898 913 2 (cased)

Typeset by Manton Typesetters, 5–7 Eastfield Road, Louth, Lincolnshire, LN11 7AJ, UK.
Printed and bound in Great Britain by Bookcraft (Bath) Ltd.

For Nick and Ben (Martin Minogue)
For Malcolm Norris (David Hulme)
To Catherine (Charles Polidano)

Contents

PART II CHANGING INSTITUTIONS AND PRACTICES IN
         PUBLIC MANAGEMENT AND GOVERNANCE

List of figures

List of tables

List of contributors

David Brown is a research fellow in the Forestry Programme at the Overseas Development Institute, London. He worked for OXFAM–UK in Francophone West Africa before joining the Agricultural Extension and Rural Development Department at Reading University where he was responsible for courses in rural social development. His current research focuses on the social dimensions of biodiversity conservation and forest management in the tropics.

Robert Chambers is a research associate of the Institute of Development Studies at the University of Sussex, UK. He has practical and research experience mainly in Sub-Saharan Africa and South Asia. His most recent books are *Challenging the Professions: Frontiers for Rural Development* (1993) and *Whose Reality Counts? Putting the First Last* (1997). His current work is on participatory methodologies and anti-poverty policies and practices.

Helen Chauncey is an assistant professor of Asian Studies at the University of Victoria. From 1994 to 1996 she served as Representative for the Vietnam field office of The Asia Foundation, a US-based policy and development organization. Recent monographs include *Schoolhouse Politicians: Locality and State During the Chinese Republic* (University of Hawaii Press, 1992). Her research interests cover the state, social policy, and public management in twentieth-century Vietnam and China.

Ian Christoplos is a researcher working at the Department of Rural Development Studies at the Swedish University of Agricultural Sciences. His studies focus on how local service institutions deal with turbulent situations in development, rehabilitation and emergency contexts. In recent years he has worked primarily in Vietnam and Angola, paying special attention to the roles of Red Cross branches and agricultural extension.

Richard Common is a research assistant professor in the Department of Public and Social Administration, City University of Hong Kong. Until summer 1997, he was a senior lecturer in the Business School, Leeds Metropolitan University. His current research interests include comparative public administration in the Asia–Pacific region and public sector management.

David P. Dolowitz is a lecturer in the Department of Politics at the University of Liverpool. He has written widely on the areas of policy transfer and welfare state reform. His most recent book is entitled *Learning From America: Policy Transfer and the Development of the British Workfare State* (1988).

David Hulme is Professor of Development Studies at the Institute for Development Policy and Management, University of Manchester. He has particular interests in public service provision for the poor in developing countries and on state–voluntary sector relationships. He is author of *Governance, Administration and Development: Making the State Work*, London: Macmillan (with M. Turner) and *NGOs, States and Donors: Too Close for Comfort?*, London: Macmillan (with M. Edwards).

Moses N. Kiggundu is Professor of Management, Strategy, and Human Resources at the School of Business, Carleton University, Ottawa–Ontario, Canada. His active research interests include international management and development, with a special focus on administrative theory and practice in developing and transition economies. He is the author of various publications, including *Managing organizations in developing countries* (Kumarian Press, 1989). He graduated from Makerere University, Kampala with a BA (Hons) and received a Ph.D. from the University of Toronto. For more details, visit: URL:http://www.business.carleton.ca

George A. Larbi is a researcher and associate lecturer with the Development Administration Group, School of Public Policy, University of Birmingham, UK. His research, teaching experience and interests are in the areas of new public management reforms, structural adjustment and civil service reforms, and governance and capacity building. He has previously done work in Ghana, Nigeria and Finland.

Maureen Mackintosh is Professor of Economics at the Open University. Her main research interest is in the economics and politics of public service reform both in Europe and in developing countries.

David Marsh is Head of Department and Professor of Politics in the Department of Political Science and International Studies at the University of Birmingham. He has published widely on political sociology, political economy, comparative politics, British politics and policy transfer. He is editor of the *British Journal of Politics and International Relations*.

Willy McCourt is a lecturer in Human Resource Management in the Institute for Development Policy and Management at the University of Manchester, having previously worked in British local government and adult education, and in higher education in Nepal. He is currently researching public sector pay and employment reform in developing countries, and is also developing a new model for personnel selection in organizations.

Martin Minogue is a senior research fellow at the Institute for Development Policy and Management, University of Manchester; and was from 1984 to 1996 Director of the University's International Development Centre. He has published extensively in the area of comparative public policy and development, and has undertaken consultancies for the United Nations Development Programme (UNDP), British Council, UK Department for International Development, and the Economic and Social Research Council (ESRC – UK).

Charles Polidano is Lecturer in Public Sector Management at the Institute for Development Policy and Management, University of Manchester. He has published papers on administrative reform and accountability in journals such as *Public Administration, Governance,* and *Public Policy and Administration,* and he is co-author of *Redrawing the Lines: Service Commissions and the Delegation of Personnel Management* (Commonwealth Secretariat, 1996).

Mark Robinson is a fellow of the Institute of Development Studies at the University of Sussex. His current research interests are the role of civic organizations in the provision of social services, political participation and public policy, and the contribution of foreign aid to the strengthening of civil society in Africa.

Mark Turner is Associate Professor in the Faculty of Management at the University of Canberra. He previously held positions at the Research School of Pacific and Asian Studies at the Australian National University and the Administrative College of Papua New Guinea. He has extensive research and consultancy experience in Asia and the Pacific. He has published widely on politics, public sector management and sociology in developing countries, especially in Southeast Asia and the Pacific. Among his publications are the books *Governance, Administration and Development: Making the State Work,* Macmillan, 1997 (with David Hulme); *Profiles of Government Administration in Asia,* Australian Government Publishing Service, 1995 (with John Halligan); *Papua New Guinea: the Challenge of Independence,* Penguin, 1990; and *Sociology and Development: Theories, Policies and Practices,* Harvester Wheatsheaf, 1990 (with David Hulme).

Gordon White was a professorial fellow at the Institute of Development Studies, University of Sussex. A political scientist, he worked on the form and functions of the state in developing societies, with particular emphasis on China and East Asia.

Abbreviations

AfDB	African Development Bank
ASEAN	Association of South East Asian Nations
CAPAM	Commonwealth Association for Public Administration and Management
CSR	Civil service reform
DANIDA	Danish International Development Agency
DFID	Department for International Development (UK)
ESCOR	Economic and Social Committee for Overseas Research (DFID, UK)
ESRC	Economic and Social Research Council (UK)
GATT	General Agreement on Tariffs and Trade
HRM	Human resource management
IDPM	Institute for Development Policy and Management (Manchester University, UK)
ILO	International Labour Organization
IMF	International Monetary Fund
NAO	National Audit Office (UK)
NGO	Non-governmental organization
NORAD	Norwegian Agency for International Development
NPM	New public management
ODA	Overseas Development Administration (UK)
OECD	Organization for Economic Cooperation and Development
PPA	Participatory poverty assessment
PRA	Participatory rural appraisal
RRA	Rapid rural appraisal
SAP	Structural adjustment programme
SIA	Sector institutional assessment
SIDA	Swedish International Development Authority
SOA	Special operating agency
SOE	State-owned enterprise
UNDP	United Nations Development Programme
UNESCO	United Nations Educational, Scientific and Cultural Organization
UNICEF	United Nations Children's Fund
USAID	US Agency for International Development

Preface

The 'new public management revolution' has sparked unprecedented interest in attempts to reshape and improve governance, defined as the array of ways in which the relationships between the state, society and the market is ordered. The radical public sector reform programmes of the 1980s that began in the UK, the USA, Australia and New Zealand have fostered a wave of reform in developed, developing and transitional countries, further fuelled by the collapse of the Iron Curtain and the notion that there are specific models of 'good governance' that have universal applicability.

This interest in public management and governance has had profound implications for the teaching, research and technical activities that staff at the Institute for Development Policy and Management (and more broadly across the University of Manchester) are engaged in. One particular issue that we found ourselves constantly confronting related to the question of the transferability of models of public management and governance, and especially the feasibility of exporting the 'British reform model' to other countries. We believed there was a need to explore and compare the theory and practice of 'improving governance' and to this end the Institute for Development Policy and Management convened a major international conference at the University of Manchester in June and July 1997 entitled 'Public Sector Management for the Next Century: An International Conference to Review Trends in Public Management and Governance'. This conference, and related publications, were generously supported by the Economic and Social Committee for Overseas Research (ESCOR) in the Department for International Development, and by the University of Manchester's Graduate School of Social Sciences.

It soon became clear not only that this topic had generated enormous interest (300 participants and 90 papers), but that 'governance' was very widely construed, with papers offered on new public management, good governance, local governance, decentralization of public services, gender and governance, public enterprise reform, government and structural adjustment, information technology and human resources management. Moreover, research material drew on cases spanning developed industrial countries, transitional economies and developing countries. The range of disciplines represented was a reminder that an interest in government goes well beyond the concerns of management studies; and the conceptual problems to which this breadth of interest gives rise are explored in the editorial introduction. Most – though not all – of the contributions in this volume were originally presented at the Manchester conference, and have been specifically revised for this publication. They were selected to draw out the enduring concern to clarify the relationships between ideas (or 'theory') and actual practice in the field of public management and governance as we move into the twenty-first century.

We owe many debts of gratitude, not least to the anonymous reviewers, whose careful comments and thoughtful advice helped us in our task of ordering and selecting from a substantial amount of material. Dymphna Evans, the commissioning editor at Edward Elgar, is to be congratulated for the speed and care with which the book was produced. Debra Whitehead ably led the Institute for Development Policy and Management team that provided superb administrative support for the original conference. But there might not have been a book at all without the calm competence with which Cath Baker handled the final transcript, and ensured that we met our deadline.

As this book went to press we heard of the death of Gordon White, joint author of Chapters 6 and 13. We take this opportunity to pay our respects to a colleague whose intellectual achievements were exceeded only by his great personal courage.

Martin Minogue
Charles Polidano
David Hulme

1. Introduction: the analysis of public management and governance

Martin Minogue, Charles Polidano and David Hulme

CHANGING IDEAS ABOUT PUBLIC ADMINISTRATION AND MANAGEMENT

A consistent thread running throughout the contributions to this book is a recognition of the need to define the dominant ideas about how to change government, and then to evaluate the impact (beneficial or otherwise) of these ideas as they are translated into practice. But it is not easy to maintain conceptual and analytical coherence in this enterprise, partly because conceptual models of government reform are themselves constantly in flux, and partly because they are applied across a diverse set of real governmental systems and economies. It is useful, therefore, in establishing the framework for the contributions which follow, to reflect further on the problems of definition and conceptualization which now arise in the fields of public management and governance.

What can confidently be stated is that the narrower approaches of the earlier literature on public administration and on management studies have been found wanting, and have in effect been ousted by broader conceptualizations of the field of government. This is, in part, a result of the expansion of state intervention into all areas of economic and social activity, since this in turn summoned up the interest and concern of people from many disciplines and sub-disciplines: economics, anthropology, sociology, politics, social policy, geography, planning, medicine, agricultural economy, and so on. In the field of public administration, the public administration or management specialist has become just one of a wide array of analysts. Correspondingly, anyone who hopes to gain a proper understanding of government and its interventions must be ready to master a diverse set of literatures. The failure to do so leads to the errors of blinkered analysis identified in Polly Hill's excoriating attack on development economists (Hill, 1986); while few disciplines are exempt from this kind of criticism, management specialists are more prone than most to ignore or dismiss the insights and findings of related disciplines such as political science or anthropology.

A second factor to explain the breadth which now characterizes the study of governance and management issues is rooted in the practice of reform. The past two decades have witnessed the apotheosis of neo-liberal thought, and the translation into practice of neo-liberal principles across the whole spectrum of reforms impinging on or directly involving the public sector. Economic reforms have focused on liberating the operations of the market from the distortions produced by government interventions; public sector reform followed the same logic, blurring the distinctions between 'public' and 'private', and seeking to reduce the size and activities of the state, while introducing private sector disciplines into the public sector. This application of a particular conception of political economy did further damage to the idea that the public sector comprised a narrow and specialized set of institutions with a unique identity. To examine government or the public sector was to examine the state in the context of its broad relations to society and economy; and following this logic, neo-liberal principles have been applied to areas of social policy as well as economic policy.

A related development was the appearance of the idea of 'good governance', based on a political conception of appropriate reforms. Rooted in the sudden 'collapse of socialism' in the former Soviet Union and some Eastern European countries, this idea took shape and substance from new policies of political conditionality applied by both multilateral and bilateral aid donors in their aid relationships with developing and transitional economies. A logical extension of the earlier strategy of economic conditionality associated with structural adjustment reforms, this new approach was ambiguous in conception and inconsistently practised (Stokke, 1995). More obviously controversial than economic interventions by aid donors, it raised awkward analytical questions as well as the hackles of those to whom these new political pressures were applied.

It is clear, then, that some attention must be paid to the changing terminology which has characterized analysis of the state and its activities over the past two decades or more. The central character of this analysis does not alter: the concern always is to examine the institutions and processes of government. But the changing labels which characterize this examination are significant, for they indicate changes of emphasis, both in the perception of government and in proposals for changing government. It will be useful here to define briefly the labels customarily in use: the study of public administration, of 'what governments do', is more complex than it initially seems (Minogue, 1993). As a field of study it is primarily a twentieth-century creation, reflecting the substantial expansion of the social and economic responsibilities of modern government. However, the orthodox forms of analysis, derived largely from the classic bureaucratic theory of the German sociologist, Max Weber, concentrate on the administrative system, and essentially consist of an examination of formal structures and institutions of government, in which a conceptual separation between 'administration' and 'politics' is maintained.

This analytical framework has been extended and criticized by two conceptual approaches, which may be designated as the public policy and the public management perspectives. The *public policy* perspective concentrates on the policy process (a constant stream of actions and activities), rather than on formal institutions. This approach has the intention of emphasizing:

- the political context in which public administration operates;
- the organizational and personal networks involved in the formulation and delivery of policies;
- the success, failure, and desirability of actual policies, so linking implementation mechanisms to results;
- the central concept of 'the state', essential to an understanding of the relationship between the administrative and political systems, and between politics, economy and society.

The *public management* perspective, shaped by neo-classical economic principles, has subjected to critical questioning the size, roles and structures of public sectors, including those in developing countries. It is asserted that in many countries the public sector has failed to be the engine of national development; in some countries it is even the main barrier to development. Public bureaucracies, it is claimed, are not capable of managing effectively utilities such as electricity supply or telecommunication; civil services are seen as too inflexible and rule-bound to respond to changing needs, so that, for example, industrial policy is more likely to obstruct enterprise development than promote it. Increasingly it is the private sector which is seen as having the managerial capacity, flexibility and competitive drive essential for the efficient and effective provision of many activities previously assumed to be the province of the public sector.

The governments of many countries, both developed and developing, are reviewing the roles of the civil service, local authorities and public enterprises. Many functions previously performed by public sector organizations are being privatized; the remaining public corporations are being required to compete with private firms or to become profitable. Local authorities are being forced to tender for work in competition with private suppliers.

These dramatic changes, driven by a seemingly global ideological consensus, present extremely complex, and in many countries largely unexplored, problems and challenges. Issues of institutional values, beliefs and norms, and of individual attitudes, led to a focus on organization culture and how this might be changed by policy makers and top managers (UNDP, 1995; Commonwealth Secretariat, 1993). Overall, the label 'public management' is regarded as accurately capturing the whole range of public–private sector relations. While this wave of reforms originated in developed economies, notably the UK (Gray and Jenkins, 1995) and the USA (Moe, 1994), it has been extended to both transitional and developing economies (World Bank, 1996; Collins, 1993).

Despite the 'privatizing' orientation of contemporary reforms in government, it is acknowledged that there remains a crucial role for government in developing countries in managing effective responses to the social and economic needs of their populations, in other words, development management (World Bank, 1997). Governments in these countries may reduce their levels of central economic direction, but they will continue to be responsible for the design and implementation of effective public policies, especially in relation to economic transformation, poverty reduction, improved agricultural performance, the provision of employment, the supply of better social services and environmental protection (UNDP, 1995). This is initially a matter of political will and leadership, but political leaders will continue to depend on well-trained and appropriately qualified advisers with a good grasp of development issues, and competence in the design of effective systems of policy design, analysis and advice.

The management and administration of development inevitably raises issues of policy design, implementation and evaluation. Development policies are a major responsibility of governments in developing countries, covering a wide range of economic issues (economic growth, trade, expenditure and fiscal policy, industrialization, agricultural production, employment), and social issues (income distribution, poverty reduction, health, education, social welfare, urban–rural relations). If we regard public managers as 'agents of development', then they must be resourced and equipped for this role (Dia, 1996; UNDP, 1995). The effective management of development also implies the effective development of management. Again, these issues are seen as germane in both transitional and developing economies; indeed, public sector reform is identified as a crucial component of reform programmes in both types of economy (World Bank, 1997; 1996).

FROM 'PUBLIC MANAGEMENT' TO 'GOVERNANCE'

The defining themes of recent public management reform have been the achievement of the objectives of economy and efficiency, in the context of relations between the state and the market, and an explicit emphasis upon the dominance of individual over collective preferences. But we need to recognize that modern government is about much more than efficiency; it is also about the relationship of accountability between the state and its people: people who are treated not merely as consumers or customers (as in the new public management approach) but as *citizens*, who have the right to hold their governments to account for the actions they take, or fail to take. Citizens do want efficient public services, and (ideally) low taxes; but they may simultaneously want to have their rights protected, to have their voices heard, to have their values and preferences respected. The ultimate sanction in the hands of a dissatisfied citizen is to eject from office those politically responsible for poor or inadequate public provisions. Containing costs, introducing competition, setting higher standards of quality may hit the right notes where there is a concern for competent management and efficient use of resources, but if these reforms result only in inadequate provision, fragmented organization and lower levels of public service, the citizen as voter might exact a political revenge. Such a response would undermine or limit the entrepreneurial model of government reform. On the other hand, the citizen as taxpayer might be willing to bear the possible costs of the entrepreneurial model in order to enjoy the benefits of lower direct taxation and increased choice between the providers of goods and services. But it is not easy to define where the boundary appropriately lies or how these contested choices might be resolved. At the level of service provision, the new managerial reforms may reduce accountability; at the level of governmental systems, institutions of accountability may be weak or non-existent. Issues of accountability, control, responsiveness, transparency and participation are, therefore, at least as important as issues of economy and efficiency. So, for citizens, are questions of law and order, which can only be guaranteed by a state – and a legitimate state.

The term 'governance' is intended to reflect these broader concerns, yet it is a term without precision or agreed usage, as we can see if we examine a range of definitions by different public agencies. The most overtly political definition is that used by the Department for International Development (formerly UK Overseas Development Administration) under the label 'good government' (ODA, 1993). This sets out four main components. *Legitimacy* implies that a system of government must operate with the consent of those governed, who must therefore have the means to give or withhold that assent: such legitimacy is seen in the British policy document as most likely to be guaranteed by pluralist, multi-party democracy. *Accountability* involves the existence of mechanisms which ensure that public officials and political leaders are answerable for their actions and use of public resources, and will require transparent government and a free media. *Competence* in making and executing appropriate public policies and delivering efficient public services is essential, while *respect for law and protection of human rights* should buttress the entire system of good government.

An alternative definition is provided by the United Nations Development Programme (UNDP, 1995), with the contrasting label of 'sound governance'. While similar principles are rehearsed, there are two significant variations of interpretation. First, UNDP places less emphasis on the assumed superiority of pluralist, multi-party, electorally oriented systems, recognizing that different forms of political authority may combine efficiency and accountability in different ways. Second, it recognizes that there is a problem about relative cultural values, that systems of governance may vary in response to different sets of values placed on economic, political and social relationships, giving different weights to such ideas as participation, individuality, order and authority.

A final example uses the World Bank's approach, which skips rather uneasily between the neutral label 'governance' and the trickier 'good governance': tricky for the World Bank in that its Articles of Agreement explicitly prohibit political interventions and require it to take into account only economic considerations. Accordingly, the World Bank documents (World Bank, 1992; 1994) emphasize open and predictable policy making, a professional policy and management capability, and the effective use of resources to achieve improved levels of social and economic development. Yet in its calls for a strong participatory civil society, operating clearly within the rule of law, the World Bank can scarcely avoid stepping into political (and controversial) territory; and almost half of its 'governance' lending in 1991–93 was to projects with these unavoidably political connotations (World Bank, 1994).

If we compare these definitions by major aid donors, we see at once that good governance aims to achieve much more than mere efficient management of economic and financial resources, or particular public services; it is also a broad reform strategy to strengthen the institutions of civil society, and make government more open, responsive, accountable and democratic. In this respect, 'public management' is a component of the broader strategy of 'good governance'; and it is in good governance that we see the efficiency concerns of public management combine with the accountability concerns of governance. It is no accident that these definitions are drawn from major aid donors, for it is through the aid mechanism that attempts are made to implement (some would say impose) these models of governance: there are considerable pressures on developing and transitional economies to adopt the whole range of governance reforms. Aid donors have always, to some degree, used economic conditionality to ensure the application of their preferred economic policies in recipient countries: now we see the use of political conditionality, which may involve limiting or withholding aid until political liberalization takes place in a recipient country, often in relation to the protection of human rights, or to processes of democratization (Stokke, 1995).

This raises a final question: if we can begin to identify a global model of efficiency (new public management), can we also identify a global model of accountability? If we can relate and integrate these two models (of efficiency and accountability) we might then be in touching distance of a holy grail: a global model of governance, with universal application.

The issues raised by the broader conceptions of governance, and the explicitly political debate to which they lead, cannot easily be confined within a survey of ideas and practice in public management reforms. Before the wider notion of good governance can be engaged with, we need to have a clear view of its component parts, of which public management is one. This book necessarily embraces this more limited perspective, yet will, it is hoped, provide ammunition in the wider war of ideas about governance.

CONCEPTUALIZING RECENT PUBLIC MANAGEMENT REFORMS

These categories of academic analysis, therefore, differ in their histories, conceptual preferences, and their perceptions of what constitute the significant areas of practice (this is true even of the orthodox approaches: we leave aside here the complications introduced by the paradigmatic conflicts which have generally bedevilled the social sciences). Yet the world of practice has increasingly come to be dominated by a particular model of governmental reforms now labelled 'the new public management' (NPM). Minogue (Chapter 2) outlines the origins and characteristics of this reform movement, summarizes the practical impact of these reforms in developed economies, and notes the mixed results of this reform practice, with claims of reduced accountability, damage to public services and disputed efficiency gains. In addition he identifies significant constraints on attempts by aid donors to foster the NPM model in the governmental systems of transitional and developing economies. While other globalizing tendencies promote a global model of governmental reform, variation and resistance in national systems may be persuading aid donors towards more flexible application of the model.

In this context a significant question is addressed both by Dolowitz and Marsh (Chapter 3) and Common (Chapter 4). How, and under what conditions, does the effective 'transfer' of institutional reforms occur between different administrative and political systems? Dolowitz and Marsh attempt to establish a general framework within which issues of policy and institutional transfer may be examined. They consider both voluntary transfer and coercive transfer (conditionality), and a range of key actors (notably a group labelled 'policy entrepreneurs'), who combine to produce transfers, between different systems, of policies, institutions, ideologies and attitudes. They also elaborate a range of constraints which inhibit, affect, or prevent institutional and policy transfer, that is, which help to explain transfers which 'fail'.

Common is concerned with a particular case of transfer: what are the agencies that can be identified as having promoted the transfer of new public management reform initiatives, which he takes to be characterized primarily by the adoption of market-type mechanisms to replace more traditional forms of public action? He suggests that multilateral aid donors have played a crucial role in this respect, and 'need to be understood both as facilitators of policy transfer and as a key source of pressure on governments to modernize their public sectors'. These pressures may be coercive, but often involve collaboration with national political élites anxious to secure the political benefits in a process labelled 'the politics of reinvention'. Common goes on to argue that NPM transfer exemplifies the integral relationship between the modernizing and democratizing tendencies associated with the globalization of an essentially Western model of political economy: international organizations appear to be instrumental in establishing such linkages. He uses privatization reforms as an example of a widespread strategy which can only be understood by taking into account the international environments that influence policy; and suggests that this internationalization of public management reforms may prevent national governments from innovating in 'ways suited to their own political and institutional contexts'.

All the following four chapters are, to some extent, concerned with the conceptual issues involved in the transfer of a global model of public management reform. A rather different issue is what might be called 'reception', that is, what are the characteristic responses of countries on the receiving end of the transfer process? To what extent do they genuinely embrace the NPM reform model? What degree of transformation of their institutions occurs? Does adaptation occur in ways which transmute the reform model itself, suggesting the need for revision or revaluation of the model? Or is there evidence that the reforms may be damaging or inappropriate, or are subject to resistance, providing the basis for an argument that the reform model is itself deeply flawed, and at best either impractical or irrelevant? These questions are addressed by most of the contributors to this volume, and especially in Part II, but receive the most critical formulation in Mackintosh (Chapter 5). This analysis notes that NPM thinking entails a cultural and organizational change in social provision, expressed in concepts of individualism; and that the effect of this is to create conditions of social exclusion, so that the reforms damage most those most in need of state provision and welfare safety nets: the poor and the vulnerable. Noting that studies from Tanzania and Thailand demonstrate the importance of government action in exacerbating or reducing social exclusion, Mackintosh focuses on the effects of government-led NPM reforms in the British context, using detailed cases from social policy. She concludes, on this basis, not only that NPM reforms can reinforce social exclusion, 'despite a rhetoric of decentralization and responsiveness', but 'may impede the design of a more inclusive public sphere' (a concern also addressed by Chauncey in her Vietnam-based study in Chapter 12).

A central tenet in Mackintosh's approach to public management is the need to design 'socially inclusive institutions'. This theme is elaborated in detail by White and Robinson in Chapter 6. They present the case for pursuing 'synergy', or the development of a range of inter-institutional relationships between state and non-state (or civic) organizations. The advantage of this approach, they argue, is that it plays to the strengths of both types of institution, while reducing the weaknesses to which each sector (public and civic) is prone. The path to effective reform in the provision of better and more inclusive public services, therefore, consists of the search for, and design of, 'complementarity' between state and civic spheres. The problems involved (organizational complexity, political resistance, deficiencies of appropriate skills and resources) are acknowledged, but the judicious conclusion is that 'the call to seek solutions through synergistic partnerships between state and civic providers appears to make eminently good sense': here, conceptualization is aimed firmly at realizable practice.

A similar, but conceptually more radical approach is proffered by Chambers (Chapter 7), who wants to see institutions of public service provision energized and made more responsive to social needs by insisting on the need to root them in effective mechanisms of participation. He sees current managerial reforms as flawed because they become yet another source of power and control for professional managers, who thereby strengthen their domination within the institutional framework of public service provision, particularly in the context of designing and delivering rural and agricultural development policies and programmes. He calls for procedures which will 'enable poor people themselves to analyse and articulate their priorities', and proposes a 'radical agenda' of institutional, professional and personal change which will produce a transformed system aimed at the achievement of a vision of 'responsible well-being' of all citizens, poor and wealthy: another path to social inclusion, rather than social exclusion.

This 'neo-populist' position is challenged by Brown (Chapter 8) on the grounds that it is ambiguous and over-optimistic about the ways in which professional élitism might be reduced; that it has an inadequate grasp of the political context of bureaucratic and professional operations; and that the proposed remedy of a 'new professionalism' scarcely frees itself from the constraints and dilemmas identified in the critique of 'normal professionalism'. Brown suggests that the great weakness of this approach is its relative silence on how the fundamental, structural bases of poverty may be overcome or transformed.

RELATING CONCEPTS TO PRACTICE

A concern which consistently emerges from these essays is the need, in the field of governance and public management, to connect theory to practice in a meaningful way. Ideally, each should contribute to the other: the concepts produced by theory should assist the formulation of new ideas about practice, while analysis of practice should not only demonstrate which conceptual models 'work' (and which do not), but also produce adjustments to the models. Ultimately, there should be a constant dialectic between theory and practice.

This idealized state is rarely achieved, for a variety of reasons. As indicated earlier, concepts in the field of governance and public management, with its primary political framework, are not neutral or objective. Since the concepts are contested, there is no agreement on what models should be derived, and put into effect. None the less, the past two decades have undoubtedly witnessed the domination of particular ideas (notably those of new public management), so that a clearly defined attempt to influence practice may be observed. As noted, complications then occur in relation to the attempt to transfer this working practice across cultural boundaries; and a significant task of research and analysis is to monitor this process of transfer.

Part II of this book reflects this task, examining the ways in which the concepts considered in Part I have been applied in practice. The cases are drawn mainly from developing countries, but have a manifest origin in the reforms introduced in more developed systems.

The first chapter (9) in Part II, by Kiggundu, provides an overview of civil service reform efforts in developing countries. Kiggundu distinguishes various facets of public management reform: inputs (funding, equipment, technical assistance), processes (consultations, meetings, seminars, preparation of policy statements), outputs (retrenchment, pay increases), outcomes (higher organizational capacity, greater accountability, better service delivery) and impacts (democratic development, better quality of life). If one focuses on inputs and processes, an impressive extent of activity reveals itself. But all this effort appears to fizzle out in the translation to outputs; and the impacts of reform are negligible.

The reasons for this are no mystery: the absence of a strategic framework for reform, the lack of political commitment, the inability to generate local 'ownership', the failure to enlist civil society in the cause of reform. They have been set out in report after report. However, says Kiggundu, 'There is yet little evidence that [the] lessons of experience have been translated into lessons learnt.'

Kiggundu argues that a fundamental change of direction is needed if reforms are to be more successful. He calls for a transformative model of reform that extends beyond narrow organizational concerns to encompass wider issues of governance, including the development of shared national values and the strengthening of indigenous institutions. In coming decades, he suggests, the adoption of such a model will be the key to a sharper differentiation between those countries that are successful in reform and those that are not: the 'winners' and the 'losers'.

McCourt (Chapter 10) also looks at the success or failure of reform, concentrating on what is often a central component: retrenchment. He analyses the experiences of Ghana and Uganda in comparison with the United Kingdom. Retrenchment is commonly seen as politically difficult, yet McCourt shows it need not be as problematic as is often supposed. A variety of measures can be taken to keep the number of involuntary dismissals to a relatively low proportion of all posts abolished. There are administrative as well as political obstacles to retrenchment: for example, a lack of coordination between central agencies, particularly the ministries of public service and finance, or an inability to 'plug' the multiple points of recruitment throughout government. Measures to provide transitional assistance to retrenchees can be particularly badly affected by problems of implementation. All three of the countries studied by McCourt succeeded in bringing civil service numbers down, though he notes that the record is much less impressive in other countries. But even in the successful cases, the decline in numbers was not matched by a drop in spending. This raises the issue of whether governments should seek to control staffing through numbers or costs: the latter is more in keeping with new public management philosophy than the former (implying that retrenchment cannot in itself be taken as a sign that a particular country is taking the NPM route to reform). The latter approach has its advantages, but its applicability to developing countries must be considered in the light of the general debate about the transferability of NPM. Larbi (Chapter 11) engages this debate with a case study of new public management reform in Ghana. He discusses organizational change in the Ministry of Health and the Ghana Water and Sewerage Corporation. Both organizations are undergoing a programme of management decentralization involving the devolution of authority from the central government to the organization and from upper to lower levels within the organization itself. Changes in the Ministry of Health are particularly ambitious: the ultimate aim is to carve a separate Ghana Health Service out of the ministry. Teaching hospitals are also being given a distinct organizational identity and a degree of managerial autonomy.

However, the reforms are a good example of the gap between inputs/ processes and outputs/outcomes as discussed by Kiggundu. Some of the changes have not been properly implemented, and line management is still subject to considerable central control. Larbi inquires why this is so. The reasons he identifies include inertia; vested interests on the part of senior officials; a failure to plan properly for implementation; legal constraints; and problems of institutional coordination within the central government. There is also a lack of management capacity in the line and performance monitoring capacity at the centre, implying that key elements of the NPM model may not be operable.

Chauncey (Chapter 12) is also concerned with the progress and effects of a particular case of sectoral public service reform: the impact on the educational system of Vietnam of the switch away from highly centralized 'socialist' planning towards a market-oriented system of educational provision. She is critical both of the internal lack of direction and clarity of purpose of Vietnamese educational reform, and of the misunderstandings and mixed motives associated with external donor interventions. Arguing the need to establish a relevant and socially inclusive public discourse as a basis for real progress attached to a genuinely local vision of what is appropriate for Vietnam, Chauncey also uses this case to reconsider conceptual positions linking state and civic society: she posits an intermediate perspective in which a 'political public' may act, through different forms of public discourse and state–civic relationships, to influence the decisions and actions of the state.

The ways in which these state–society relationships might be more precisely defined is illustrated by Robinson and White, in Chapter 13. Their second contribution to the book examines a wide range of types of civic organizations involved in the provision of public services, with particular reference to the health and education sectors. A comprehensive review of the empirical literature is used to elucidate the strengths and weaknesses of these organizations, concluding that while they play a significant role, notably in targeting disadvantaged groups, they also show serious deficiencies. The ways forward therefore seem to be in collaborative partnerships between state and non-state providers: the 'synergistic' approach presented in their conceptual analysis in Chapter 6. The dualistic approach of new public management, whereby the state makes wholesale transfers of responsibility to non-state providers, and simply serves as an 'enabler', is rejected as both impractical and undesirable.

Turner (Chapter 14) picks up the theme of institutional transfer as expressed through the importation of ideas of new public management and governance reforms into governmental systems in the countries of the Asia–Pacific region. He does so by employing the notion of 'convergence', that is, the extent to which the region exhibits 'increasingly similar politico-administrative systems modelled after Western democratic pluralism'. He concludes that while the 'language of reform undoubtedly shows convergence ... whether those speaking it actually mean the same thing is highly doubtful'. Moreover, his analyses of a range of reforms focused on the centralization–decentralization spectrum in Papua New Guinea, Bangladesh, Indonesia, the Philippines, Laos and Vietnam demonstrate that 'divergence rather than convergence is still the dominant theme in central–local relations'. But he identifies 'a universal concern with the subject ... [which] is mostly framed in a discourse of decentralization'; and finds that all are committed to the need for public sector reform. This gap between discourse and practice is explained in terms of 'a range of political structures, institutional frameworks, state–society relations and cultural distinctions'. This is the sort of empirical finding which might be anticipated from a reading of Dolowitz and Marsh (Chapter 3) and Common (Chapter 4).

In an interesting final paper (Chapter 15) Christoplos examines the vexed issue of service provision in collapsed states, with particular reference to the Angolan experience. Although many students of public management treat such contexts as abnormal, temporary phenomena in rare cases that do not merit analysis until normalcy returns, he reminds us that extended state collapse is increasingly common. Changes in the nature of conflict in the late twentieth century (UNDP, 1993) indicate that significant numbers of desperately weak states and collapsed states are likely to be an important feature of our 'New World Order' for decades to come. This is not only a developing country problem, as is well illustrated by events in former Yugoslavia and the former Soviet Union.

In such contexts attempts to provide basic services continue but are usually increasingly taken over by multilateral and non-governmental relief agencies. These are driven by a laudable humanitarian imperative but, as in the Angolan case, such external efforts are often very clumsy and may marginalize local efforts to meet local needs. Paradoxically, the short-term focus of what Christoplos terms 'internationalized public welfare' may actually retard the evolution of more sustainable service delivery systems and, at times (Afghanistan is the most obvious example), reduce the likelihood of peace. More locally, nuanced relief interventions that recognize the complexity and specificity of livelihoods in conflict situations (what Paul Richards, 1996, has conceptualized as 'smart relief') must be sought. These would not only make long-term basic service provision more likely but could also generate forms of associational life and local leadership that can ultimately play a positive role in peace building and the rehabilitation or reconstruction of a state.

In a concluding chapter, the editors draw on all these contributions to outline an agenda for future research and action in public management and governance, based on past ideas and practice, but looking ahead to a future in which the role of the state will continue to be debated and redefined.

REFERENCES

Collins, P. (1993), 'Civil service reform and retraining in transitional economies: strategic issues and options', *Public Administration and Development*, **13**, 323–44.

Commonwealth Secretariat (1993), *Administrative and Managerial Reform in Government*, London: Commonwealth Secretariat.

Dia, M. (1996), *Africa's Management in the 1990s and Beyond: Reconciling Indigenous and Transplanted Institutions*, Washington, DC: World Bank.

Gray, A. and Jenkins, W. (1995), 'From public administration to public management: reassessing a revolution', *Public Administration*, **73**, 75–99.

Hill, P. (1986), *Development Economics on Trial: the anthropological case for a prosecution*, Cambridge: Cambridge University Press.

Minogue, M. (1993), 'Theory and practice in the analysis of public policy and administration', in M. Hill (ed.), *The Policy Process: A Reader* (2nd edn), London: Prentice Hall/Harvester Wheatsheaf, pp. 10–29.

Moe, R.C. (1994), 'The reinventing government exercise: misinterpreting the problem, misjudging the consequences', *Public Administration Review*, **54** (2), 114–22.

ODA (1993), *Taking Account of Good Government*, London: UK Overseas Development Administration.

Richards, P. (1996), *Fighting for the Rain Forest: War, Youth and Resources in Sierra Leone*, London: James Currey.

Stokke, O. (1995), *Aid and Political Conditionality*, London: Frank Cass.

UNDP (1993), *Human Development Report, 1993*, London and New York: Oxford University Press.

UNDP (1995), *Public Sector Management, Governance, and Sustainable Human Development*, New York: United Nations Development Programme.

World Bank (1992), *Governance and Development*, Washington, DC: World Bank.

World Bank (1994), *Governance: the World Bank Experience*, Washington, DC: World Bank.

World Bank (1996), *World Development Report, 1996: From Plan to Market*, Oxford: Oxford University Press.

World Bank (1997), *World Development Report, 1997: The State in a Changing World*, Oxford: Oxford University Press.

PART I

Changing ideas about public management and
governance

2.   Changing the state: concepts and practice in the reform of the public sector

Martin Minogue

INTRODUCTION: CONCEPTUALIZING THE PUBLIC SECTOR

Reform is a journey, rather than a destination. (OECD, 1995)

This chapter focuses on attempts in the last two decades to achieve more efficient government, and the emphasis in these reforms is on reshaping the boundaries and responsibilities of the state, especially through privatization, the restructuring of public services, and the introduction of private market disciplines into public administration. Modern public administration is not just about efficiency; it also involves ideas of democratic participation, accountability and empowerment. There is therefore a constant tension between two main themes: making government efficient and keeping government accountable. There is a corresponding tension between the conception of people as consumers, in the context of relations between the state and the market; and the conception of people as citizens, in the context of relations between the state and society. The influential model of 'new public management' (NPM) promises to integrate these themes, linking efficiency and accountability together, and these reforms will be critically examined to judge the extent to which these promises have been delivered.

A MANAGERIALIST REVOLUTION?

Analysis of public management reforms must begin with the understanding that this is an area of 'contested' concepts. Criticism and exploration of what governments do well or badly always contain elements of prescription, indicating preferences about what governments *should* do, what public management *should* achieve, how public managers *should* behave. If the public sector may be seen as a battleground of contending concepts (and contending prescriptions or models for improving practice), can we identify winners and losers? Many commentators agree that something akin to a paradigm shift (or revolution) has taken place in the last two decades, with the older welfare assumptions about the state yielding to an entrepreneurial model of government and 'new public management' driving out the devalued currency of 'old public administration'. Associated with a spate of public sector critiques and reforms in the UK (Gray and Jenkins, 1995; OECD, 1995; Common, Flynn and Mellon, 1992), this entrepreneurial model, conceptualizing a move away from the market and towards the state, was summarized by Osborne and Gaebler (1992) in terms of the following ten principles:

1. Steer the ship, rather than row it.
2. Empower communities, rather than simply deliver services.
3. Encourage competition rather than monopoly.
4. Be mission driven rather than rule driven.
5. Fund outcomes rather than inputs.
6. Meet the needs of customers rather than the bureaucracy.
7. Concentrate on earning resources, not just spending.
8. Invest in prevention of problems rather than cure.
9. Decentralize authority.
10. Solve problems by making use of the marketplace rather than by creating public programmes.

The radical changes in existing practice needed to promote and achieve this transformed model of public management have been established by:

- restructuring of the public sector, particularly through privatization;
- restructuring and slimming down central civil services;
- introducing competition, especially through internal markets and contracting public services to the private sector;
- improving efficiency, especially through performance auditing and measurement.

The pursuit of these inter-related reforms would produce a different kind of public management, characterized by:

- a separation of strategic policy from operational management;
- a concern with results rather than process;
- an orientation to the needs of customers rather than those of bureaucratic organizations;

- a withdrawal from direct provision in favour of a steering or enabling role;
- a transformed bureaucratic culture.

WHY NPM?[1]

The somewhat tautological explanation often given for the dominance of the 'new public management' model, and its widespread adoption across divergent economic and political systems (Common, Chapter 4, this volume; see also Montgomery, 1996; Commonwealth Secretariat 1993, 1996; CAPAM, 1994), is that it is an idea that has met its time. Its precision as a future model is contested: while Osborne and Gaebler (1992) insist that there is an 'inevitable' and 'global' movement to a single NPM model, Dunleavy and Hood (1994, p. 13) assert that 'plausible futures in this area are multiple, not single'. What cannot be doubted is that a generic wave of reforms must have a generic stimulus: this we can find in the consistency and similarity across systems of the pressures for change (Common, Chapter 4, this volume).

Pressure 1: Finance

'Rising government expenditure coupled with poorer than anticipated economic performance has inspired a fundamental questioning of the effectiveness of large public bureaucracies' (Manning, 1996, p. 2). In the OECD countries government expenditure per capita almost doubled between 1980 and 1990 (OECD, 1995). For many developing countries, continued growth in public expenditure took place against a background of significant economic decline, while in some cases debt servicing rose to some 80 per cent of total GDP (Commonwealth Secretariat, 1995). Increasingly the view gained ground that government had become too big and too expensive; yet at the same time it would have to bear rising social burdens associated with unemployment and ageing populations (for example, the most recent UK projection shows an increase over the next 30 years of around 50 per cent in the 60–84 age group). Government would have to be reduced in size, or made more efficient, or both: it could not be afforded in its existing form, nor would its rising costs be tolerated by taxpayers. A significant component of new public management reforms is expenditure and cost reduction (often expressed in ways which disguise a reduction in output or services).

Pressure 2: Quality

In a world where the citizen is pre-eminently a consumer, the over-extended state has been castigated for its low level of performance, producing what Montgomery (1996) terms 'the annoyance factor'. As Manning (1996, p. 13) comments: 'In all countries, citizens increasingly define themselves as active customers of government services rather than active recipients.' Unflattering comparisons with the private sector are made, especially at the point of service provision. Concern with service delivery systems is beginning to appear in the literature on developing countries (Dia, 1996). The language used reflects these consumerist orientations (empowerment, stakeholders, access, redress, value for money), though these are essentially a reinterpretation of old labels.

Pressure 3: Ideology

The reform wave of new ideas itself constitutes a pressure for change not only because it represents a fundamental shift in public service values, but also because it offers an opportunity to policy makers searching for a solution to the conflicting pressures both to improve and reduce the state (Manning, 1996; Commonwealth Secretariat, 1993). An alternative view suggests that 'policy élites' see the new reforms as a means of entrenching and reinforcing their power at the centres, while distancing themselves from the uneasy problems of implementation at decentralized levels; they may also perceive opportunities for political or personal gain (Dunleavy and Hood, 1994). There is a risk in NPM reforms that individual and group interests will maximize the gains, while the public will bear the losses. This would be deeply ironic, since a major theme in the neo-liberal critique was that government allows self-interested politicians and bureaucrats to abuse publicly provided resources.

NPM STRATEGIES IN PRACTICE

If the pressures for managerial reforms are widespread, the extent of adoption has varied across groups of economies, and the types of response range from substantial transformation to mere rhetoric (Manning, 1996; OECD, 1995). This section reviews attempts to implement NPM strategies, concentrating on public sector restructuring (privatization); civil service reform; and the introduction of competitive disciplines into the provision of public services.

Restructuring the Public Sector

In broad terms, 'restructuring the public sector' can be conceived as systemic, that is, decentralized reforms; or as internal, that is, re-engineering forms of civil service organization, for example, the UK creation of new executive agencies. But in the debate on governance, this phrase usually refers to shifts in the boundary away from the state and towards the private sector, or privatization. According to a World Bank study (Galal and Shirley, 1994), privatization is now a fact of life almost everywhere in the world. A UNDP report (UNDP, 1995, p. 37) asserts that 'privatisation lies at the heart of the market-based approach to public management'. The World Bank's analysis of transitional economies declares openly that 'public provision must become the exception rather than the rule. State intervention is justified only where markets fail' (World Bank, 1996, p. 110). But these confident statements beg some vexed and unresolved questions. Propositions which emerge from existing research literature include:

1. In general, evidence for the superiority of private over public enterprise is mixed and inconclusive (Cook and Kirkpatrick, 1995).
2. The real issue is monopoly and its associated inefficiencies rather than ownership (Cook and Kirkpatrick, 1994).
3. The link between privatization and economic growth has not been demonstrated; privatization should rather be seen as one of a bundle of measures necessary to successful economic reform strategies (World Bank, 1996; Cook and Kirkpatrick, 1994).
4. Profitable and efficient public enterprises exist in all types of economy, and there is no reason why efficiency goals cannot be attained through the rehabilitation or corporatization of public enterprises, ensuring commercial operation under public ownership (UNCTAD, 1992).

It seems, then, that the general movement to privatize is driven by ideological enthusiasm rather than economic logic; moreover, if we examine figures on the incidence of privatization, we see that much of the enthusiasm is rhetorical rather than real. While more than 7000 enterprises have been privatized (Galal and Shirley, 1994), Cook and Kirkpatrick (1995) show that three quarters of asset sales in 1988–92 were in developed countries and that privatization in developing economies has been concentrated in a few countries: asset sales in Africa constitute only 1 per cent of the global total, and only 5 per cent for Asia–Pacific countries. These findings reinforce an earlier study (Adam, Cavendish and Mistry, 1992) showing that only in a handful of countries did privatization account for more than 1 per cent of GDP. Shirley (1996), a supporter of privatization, admits that the importance of the state-

owned enterprise (SOE) sector has on average remained substantially unchanged in developing countries.

While research findings clearly contradict some central assumptions about
privatization, its significance as a component of governance reforms is likely
to continue. It is important to note that while privatization technically means
divestment of public assets, in developing countries it is used to cover a
whole range of change in public–private sector relationships, including con-
tracting-out arrangements, joint ventures, and the financial and managerial
restructuring of existing public enterprises. In some countries (for example,
China, Vietnam, India) the very term 'privatization' is unacceptable to the
local political culture, yet changes in the public–private relationship are
being pursued. In Eastern Europe and the former Soviet Union, despite the
constant setbacks caused by the unforeseen effects of privatization programmes,
the priority accorded by aid donors to privatization as a fundamental component of transitional economic reform will ensure that it continues to occupy a
high place on the reform agenda (World Bank, 1996).

In relation to developing economies, especially in Africa, the political
factor is primary. The public enterprise sector is clearly in need of reform, but
the very characteristics which make reform of these enterprises necessary
(excessive staffing, large financial subsidies, corruption, inept management)
also constitute the basis for resistance to reform, for they are often integral to
local political structures and relationships. If privatization always produces
winners and losers, and the potential losers are a necessary part of a political
patronage system, then political will to sustain privatization reforms is likely
to be absent. In short, solutions which recognize the pre-eminence of political
factors need to be constructed: this points in the direction of rehabilitation of
public enterprises, rather than a restructuring of the public sector (Cook and
Minogue, 1990). A recent World Bank study (World Bank, 1995) explicitly
qualifies the optimistic and enthusiastic tone of most of its publications on
privatization by admitting the need to understand the differences between the
few countries that reformed successfully and the many that have not. While
claiming a link between changes in government ownership and improved
economic performance, the report identifies three political conditions necessary for successful reforms:

1.   Reform must be politically desirable to the leadership and its constituen-
     cies: political benefits must outweigh political costs.
2.   Reform must be politically feasible: leaders must be able to overcome
     opposition, either by compensating losers or compelling their compli-
     ance.
3.   Reforms must be politically credible to significant stakeholders (for ex-
     ample employees, investors).

One of the principal findings of the study is that 'political obstacles are the main reason that state-owned enterprise reform has made so little headway in the last decade' (Shirley, 1996, p. xi). Some proponents of privatization would argue that it is precisely because of such obstacles that it is necessary to get these enterprises out of the public sector altogether; but this is to disregard the significance of political structures in terms of their necessary contribution to social and economic stability (Cohen, 1993).

Restructuring the Public Service

The creation of more effective public management depends heavily on the creation of an efficient and effective system of central administration, which highlights both structure and performance, particularly of the central civil service.

An initial difficulty here is the way civil service reform is defined. A broad, 'constitutional' approach defines the civil service as an essential institution within a framework of the major responsibility for the functions of government, and even as essential to the survival of a governmental system (Glentworth, 1989). This view rests on a traditional conception of government which divides the political system from the administrative system, and characterizes the members of the administrative system (civil servants) as neutral, responsive, and accountable, both through the dominant political apparatus, and through a framework of law. In this model, problems of non-performance are often captured in the word 'overload': that is, there is nothing inherently wrong with the system; rather there is a mismatch between the objectives of the system and the resources (financial and human) available to ensure the achievement of systemic objectives. Moreover, in this view, public service reform must not be imposed in isolation, but should be linked to a comprehensive programme of institutional and political reform, recognizing that the weakness of the traditional model of public bureaucracy is a failure to recognize the significance of the political context in which public bureaucrats work. This model undoubtedly corresponds well with a broad governance concept.

A much narrower approach to public service reforms limits itself to the bread-and-butter issues of internal organization, size, recruitment, remuneration, career management and promotion (Nunberg and Nellis, 1995). While these have also been traditional concerns, it is an approach which fits more readily into the NPM paradigm, with its emphasis on cost cutting, efficiency, managerial autonomy, and performance appraisal and measurement. 'Improving the civil service' is overwhelmingly translated into 'making civil servants into enterprising modern managers'. The performance side of this new coinage will be considered in the next section; this part focuses on the structural or organizational side.

We may recall here that for Osborne and Gaebler (1992) 'reinventing government' requires structures which are mission-driven, decentralized and entrepreneurial. Gray and Jenkins (1995) note that this analysis has much in common with that of another American management guru, Rosabeth Moss Kanter (1989), whose model of successful organizations produces a small central core overseeing a flatter fragmented structure. These structures are regarded as more responsive to external forces and changes, as facilitating a more professional organizational culture, and as encouraging entrepreneurialism.

The NPM model of public service reform assumes that the existing system is inefficient (because it does not have those essential characteristics); that what has traditionally been positively valued (for example bureaucratic routines, public service ethics, professional codes of conduct) may have to be assessed as costs rather than benefits; that networks of organizations work better when fragmented; and that internal structures respond better to individualized incentives than to corporate values: 'thus, efficiency is valued over accountability, and responsiveness over due process' (Gray and Jenkins, 1995, p. 87).

The British experience with agency reforms ('next steps' agencies) has been a dramatic example of the structural changes involved in the introduction into the public service of this kind of model, and indicates too that fundamental reforms require a high degree of political will and commitment to overcome resistances. What is arguably the most far-reaching internal reform in modern British government has fragmented a hitherto unified public service organization into a series of free-standing agencies, though most are loosely related to smaller core ministries. There are now 130 such agencies, employing some 386 000 civil servants, or 75 per cent of the total; of 133 chief executives appointed so far, 90 have been recruited by open competition; approximately 25 per cent of the appointments are from outside the civil service (UK Cabinet Office, 1997). Agency and chief executive performances will be measured against output, financial and service quality targets set in five-year framework documents, and performance incentives will apply. Similar (if less radical) reforms have been introduced in Canada (Commonwealth Secretariat, 1994), where special operating agencies (SOAs) are part of a restructuring of government intended to promote cost-effective and client-centred services: SOAs apply private sector norms in the planning and delivery of services either to the public or to government departments, and delegate greater authority to individual managers and employees. The linchpin of New Zealand's radical transformation of the public sector since 1984 was the creation of new executive agencies whose outputs and performance were contractually monitored by ministers; this, notably, involved 'decoupling policy advice and policy implementation' (Manning, 1996, p. 14).

While commending this model, a review of it noted that the structure of the bureaucracy would necessarily seem messy (Boston et al., 1996).

The executive agency model of public service restructuring is still in its infancy; proper evaluation must await further research. But it is clear that the examples cited involve a direct attack on the traditional notion of a unified civil service. Government is regarded as too large to be managed as a unified institution, but rather is a collection of inter-related but separately functioning businesses (Nunberg, 1995). Reformers claim transformative effects on administrative culture, and efficiency gains (Mountfield, 1997). Yet British experience has proved controversial, with anxieties developing about public accountability. These agencies are an administrative, not a legislative creation; they have no independent legal personality, so cannot be subject directly to judicial review; some are allowed to operate as trading funds, a form of self-financing which increases their autonomy (Craig, 1994). Relations between agency chiefs, senior ministry staff and ministers have proved to be confused and often problematic (Polidano, 1997). The overall effect has been to create a central administration defended officially as 'unified, but not uniform', but said by critics to produce a 'hollow state'. It has yet to be established whether structural change has produced improvements in public services, or in the performance of public service organizations. Nunberg's study (1995, p. 41) asserts that this model of reform requires 'technological, and human resources skills beyond the present capacity of many reforming countries', and suggests that only the better endowed can hope to follow it.

There are no clear examples of agency reforms of this type in developing countries. The reason is doubtless that you cannot apply a decentralizing, fragmenting model of reform if you do not have a traditional unified public service to begin with. The objective for many developing and transitional countries is move towards the creation of such a permanent, unified, 'steel frame' bureaucracy, rather than towards its destruction. According to Nunberg (1995), the reform priorities in developing countries are the creation of strong centralized institutions of civil service management, and support for the institutionalization of recruitment and of establishment control, both essential to the creation of a professionalized and competent civil service. She further suggests that low priority should be given to the introduction of performance pay arrangements, not least since 'the benefits of performance pay need to be demonstrated in industrialised country public sectors' (Nunberg, 1995, p. 42).

Many recent studies of public management reforms in developing countries do not really take us any further forward, simply because they do not pay enough attention to the real-world factors which intervene between the undesirable problem and the tidy solution (for example, Adamolekun, 1989; Nunberg, 1990; World Bank, 1991). Both problem and solution are easily diagnosed; but turning the solution into a real outcome is another matter. There is a need to recognize the significant influence on reform outcomes of ideological and political positions; and of the problem that the condition of administrative underdevelopment is itself a primary obstacle to effective reforms, since those who benefit from existing systems are generally the most powerful members of them, and best placed to resist or sabotage reforms. It is the recognition of this political and cultural reality which moves some commentators to argue for gradualist reforms which identify and build on existing organizational and cultural characteristics, rather than seek to eliminate them, particularly in Africa (Dia, 1996; Cohen, 1993; Sandbrook, 1993; Blunt and Jones, 1992; Blunt, 1991).

How can these institutional and structural problems be alleviated? According to Dia (1996; 1993) a governance approach to civil service reform can overcome some of these obstacles: economic reform packages should be designed for the particular needs of the individual country, but there are some general stages an economic reform programme should follow to begin to resolve the problems identified above. These involve improving the institutional environment, better economic management and coherent civil service management, especially through pay and incentive systems linked to performance (but see Nunberg, 1995, quoted above). Ultimately, a strategy is required which changes the whole culture of the civil service, but innovative thinking is required: 'what works in the environment of developed countries cannot be literally transplanted into Sub-Saharan Africa' (Dia, 1993, p. 11). Dia is insistent that donors should undertake more explicitly political analysis of developing country requirements and characteristics. (Kiggundu, Chapter 9, this volume, also calls for a reconceptualization of civil service reform in the context of assessment of national political capacity and support.) A practical approach, Dia suggests (Dia, 1996), is to begin with sector institutional assessments, which assess client need, capacity and institutional endowment, as a basis for institutional investment and development programmes in each policy sector.

Making Public Management More Efficient

The new public management insists that structural reform is not an end in itself: the essential objective is that public services should be provided in the most appropriate and cost-effective way.

If managers are given greater freedom to manage, they must, correspondingly, be under an obligation of accountability for their performance. This means meeting specified targets within specified resources. This can only be done through a system of performance management, involving performance agreements and performance targets. Monitoring will require a system of performance measurement, using performance indicators, and can be the basis for performance rewards and incentives. The overall objective, central to new public management reforms, is to make working practices more efficient, and to obtain 'value for money' by using organizational and managerial changes to achieve a more efficient use of resources (Walsh et al., 1997).

In the UK, efficiency mechanisms have been successively promoted. This process began in the early 1980s with the so-called Rayner scrutinies, efficiency reviews intended to make senior managers more cost-conscious. The whole process was action-oriented: a scrutiny of a departmental activity had to be completed in 90 days, an action plan in three months, and an implementation report in two years. By 1986, 300 efficiency scrutinies had produced savings of £950 million. This led on to a financial initiative, delegating financial responsibility to lower levels, and making managers of cost centres accountable for their budget management. The 'next steps' (executive agencies) reforms also introduced performance agreements, service targets and performance measures.

A variation on this performance approach is to emphasize the degree of satisfaction or dissatisfaction with what the public organization provides. The model here is the citizen as customer. The organization should be responsive to the customer's needs, and care about the customer's perception of the service being provided. The creation of a standard quality of service at a high level should be a primary objective of the organization, and should be a significant motivating influence upon those working in the organization. It is important to be able to define and measure customer satisfaction, since this requires a match between expectations of the service and the service actually delivered. Clearly, any gap between expectation and actual delivery represents potential customer dissatisfaction. This can be the basis, along with an appreciation of available resources, for the establishment of a realistic standard of service provision to which the organization commits itself. The standard should include simple arrangements to receive and respond to customer complaints.

This may be done through citizen's charters, customer care programmes and quality management initiatives. In the UK, the citizen's charter programme encouraged public organizations to draw up, publish, and then work to a clear set of operating standards. The charter established a number of principles: the setting of *standards* for service delivery and the assessment of actual performance against those standards; *openness* as to how the services are run; *consultation* with service users; *choice* as to the services which are available; *value for money*; and *remedies* when things go wrong. Almost all public service organizations, and the privatized utilities, operate charters; 1400 managers have joined local charter networks; and 645 agencies hold the Charter Mark Award (indicating performance to high standards). A Citizen's

Charter Complaints Task Force has reviewed public complaints systems, recommending standard complaints procedures for every public organization. Supporters see this mechanism as a simple and effective method for empowering customers, and assisting managers to pursue quality improvement. The charter stimulated the introduction, into legislation affecting local authorities and public utilities, of provisions for performance standards and complaints systems (Craig, 1994). It might therefore be seen as an attempt to cure defects in privatization and contracting out (Willett, 1997).

Introducing Competition into Public Services

Clearly the principle of competition is the key to the entrepreneurial model of public management, with an assumption (not always justified) that privatization and contracting out will ensure the application of competitiveness. Where services are likely to remain with a public agency, the competitive principle is applied by a process of 'market testing', that is, activities must be continuously reviewed to establish whether in-house provision remains competitive with any alternative form of provision.

The claim for market testing of public services is that it will raise the supplier's awareness of the customer's demands, which in turn will increase the efficiency of converting taxpayers' money into good-quality services. Market testing will also increase the commercial awareness and entrepreneurial attitudes of public sector organizations. Quality and efficiency are then mutually supportive objectives. No targets are set, and many activities remain categorized as essential. Where market testing results in a private sector contract, in many cases the employment and conditions of service of existing employees are protected. The evaluation of bids must treat external and internal bidders on an equal basis. The successful bid will be the one which offers the best long-term value for money.

In the UK, these principles of competition were enshrined in a 'competing for quality' programme, established in 1992. Analysis of the UK market testing process has shown that the average saving of individual market tests is about 20 per cent of the pre-test cost of service, irrespective of whether the outcome of the test was transfer to a private contract or retention with the in-house team. By 1996 in-house teams had won 71 per cent of those bids for which in-house teams competed; £3.6 billion of public activities had been reviewed; and approximately one third of these activities had been transferred to private sector contractors. Since 1995, all departments must produce efficiency plans which record their application of these competitive principles (UK Cabinet Office, 1997).

While efficiency gains are a significant part of the NPM philosophy, another proclaimed objective is to achieve the more effective delivery of public services. Public organizations are identified as rigid bureaucratic cultures which are shaped by their own internal interests, and are therefore not responsive to the needs or preferences of those who receive public services: ordinary citizens. One solution to this is to introduce into public organizations the discipline of the market, that is, competition. The provider of services would succeed in the face of competitors only if the preferences of the market – whether internal or external – were observed. In this scenario, the preferred model is the citizen as consumer.

These varied arrangements (deregulation, contracting, market testing) have similar objectives: to reduce the direct costs of public service provision; to introduce competition into the service delivery system, ensuring value for money, while permitting greater consumer choice; and to convert government into an enabling rather than a providing system. In principle, contracts should always produce efficiency gains, simply by introducing the competitive discipline of the marketplace. Services can be precisely specified, efficiently priced, and their performance monitored against penalties. The purchaser retains overall control; the provider simply provides the specified service. Australia, New Zealand, Singapore, Malaysia and Trinidad are experimenting with some of these forms (Commonwealth Secretariat, 1995). But the UK has taken the greatest strides in the direction of the contract state, and has stimulated a considerable debate on the strengths and weaknesses of such arrangements, particularly in relation to the National Health Service and local government.

Since contracting for service is likely to gain ground in all types of economy, it is worth considering the critique of British experience. In British government, 'the concept of contract is as much a metaphor ... as (a) formal legal mechanism' (Deakin and Walsh, 1996, p. 33), and it is not difficult to see why it has become attractive across the political spectrum. It offers simultaneously to cut costs and contain expenditure; to set standards of performance and quality; and to strengthen both policy makers and managers by making a clear separation between the determination of services and their delivery. But on closer examination none of these promises is unproblematic, and there is a particular need to analyse the assumption that the contract model offers a direct, and superior, alternative to the traditional model of government.

The review of British practice (Deakin and Walsh, 1996) demonstrates that the reality of contracted public service provision is not so straightforward as the contract model. The first obvious problem is that the market is not always, or even often, able to provide the desired competition; a high proportion of local government contracts attracted not a single private sector bid. A number of competitive private bidders were rejected in favour of politically preferred in-house bidders. The argument then advanced is that the threat of competition has compelled direct service organizations to make internal efficiency gains through restructuring, labour reductions and reduced wages. While this argument clearly has some force, there are costs attached to this process in terms of internal organizational values and relationships, and reduced morale.

There is a clear link here from efficiency to accountability. Contract proponents claim that contracts make service providers accountable downwards to their consumers/users, rather than upwards through a hierarchy which is both bureaucratically and politically driven. The problem with this argument is that it takes too narrow a view of what constitutes a system of government. Efficiency is not the only value in government, which is also a mechanism for expressing and representing broader values, such as equity, community, democracy, citizenship and constitutional protection; none of these are values likely to be given much weight in a contract culture.

The traditional public service system, with its mix of political leadership and bureaucratic professionalism, is a careful balancing of interests, both internal and external. As with virtually all organizations, there is a deliberate generality about objectives, to permit the operation of a culture of 'sorting things out' (UK local government official, quoted in Deakin and Walsh, 1996). As Deakin and Walsh comment: 'Contracts deal poorly with ambiguity in the policy process' (1996, p. 37). One damaging aspect of internal client–contractor relationships is that these may render fragmented and conflictual what should be a cohesive organization.

In turn this raises a major question about what should be the principal values which inform a public service culture: values of efficiency, enterprise and economy do not always sit easily with values of equity and empowerment. The conventional literature, best represented by Handy (1985) assumes that while types of organizational culture may vary, the model is of the achievement of a unitary culture with shared values. More recent work criticizes this essentially normative model, mainly for omitting the link between dominant values and the distribution of powers inside organizations, and thereby failing to understand that real organizations will be characterized by conflicts over competing values, rather than the possession of shared values (Morgan, 1986; Painter, 1992). This lack of perception of the real dynamics of public service organizations is still prevalent in the literature on public management reform (for example, Commonwealth Secretariat, 1996; World Bank, 1995).

The Regulatory State

Regulation and deregulation are constantly recurring phrases in the public management reform literature. In one sense, *deregulation* is a key theme: managers must be freed from hierarchical and budgetary controls and allowed to manage; public services (through market-type mechanisms) must be freed from the orthodox command and control systems; the private sector must be able to operate in an environment free from regulations and controls. On the other hand the implementation of public management reforms has also required a need for new forms of *regulation*. Mechanisms for ensuring efficiency, for setting standards of service, and for exercising financial audit, act to regulate public management agencies and their outputs, and through performance contracts and incentives regulate the activities of public managers. Where significant industries and utilities are privatized, pressures arise for a regulatory regime to protect a continued and often vocal public interest.

Some commentators use the phrase 'the regulatory state' to encompass developments in forms of regulation. New institutional forms arise from the need for central government to 'steer' and 'enable' an increasingly wide range of actors responsible for service provision. The regulatory requirement also flows from the attempt to separate policy from operational management. This is notably the case in the UK with privatization, with executive agencies and with local government contracting.

The primary change is the appointment of free-standing regulators for the privatized industries (for example, OFGAS, OFWAT); but this also applies to regulators *within* government (eg National Audit Office; Office for Standards in Education). This institutional change also seems to involve more formal types of regulation (for example, detailed rules on contracting, executive agency framework agreements). Membership of the European Union is also a source of important new regulatory rules. The general view is that this new regulatory governance has increased transparency (Loughlin and Scott, 1997).

Meanwhile, deregulation has been deliberately pursued, in terms of policy (for example, the deregulation of bus transport services) and procedure (the creation of a deregulation unit in the Cabinet Office to oversee a deregulation initiative).[2] This initiative has seen the introduction of a requirement on central departments to estimate the compliance costs of any new law or regulation, and powers for ministers to modify burdensome legislation. Alternatives are offered in the USA, which has a rigorous cost–benefit impact assessment of proposed regulatory actions, and Germany, which has a checklist system intended to sensitize officials to regulatory costs (OECD, 1995).

The new regulatory forms represent a shift away from the traditional oversight values of probity and professionalism towards a primary concern with efficiency and value for money (Loughlin and Scott, 1997). The concern of governments everywhere is to establish a link between spending and performance. These developments now generally fall under the label of 'performance auditing' (OECD, 1996).

In the UK, the trend is most clearly seen in the development of public audits, mainly through the National Audit Office (NAO), established in 1983 as an independent external body which reports to Parliament its examinations of the financial accounts of central government (a separate Audit Commission audits the accounts of local authorities and the Health Service). The NAO remit goes well beyond traditional audit of fiscal regularity, into the field of value for money (VFM) audits. These involve recommendations on how public bodies can improve their performance and achieve better value for money in meeting their specified objectives. Key performance indicators have been those concerned with the relationship between costs and resources (economy); between resources and outputs (efficiency); and between outputs and outcomes (effectiveness). NAO reports have informed and sharpened public debate by identifying the financial costs and benefits of alternative working methods for the achievement of existing policy objectives. A crucial feature is that the NAO can select its own subjects for investigation. While creative recommendations may embarrass or offend existing organizational interests, the collaborative and informal process can be helpful to public service organizations anxious to improve their financial and management information systems. Moreover, an effective system of public audit provides for the dissemination of 'good practice'. VFM audits made efficiency savings of £256 million in 1994 (NAO, 1995). Performance auditing is, in future, likely to bring about closer working relationships between auditors and managers (OECD, 1996).

Ethical Issues

Questions of honesty and ethical behaviour have become a major concern for government everywhere; in turn, these produce a concern with transparency (World Bank, 1996). More generally, ideas of good governance incorporate democratic and participative values which give greater weight to accountability than efficiency, while recognizing that citizens want government to be efficient too. In developing countries, corruption has been a major issue for some time, and there is growing recognition of the costs of corruption to effective and legitimate government; it has been noted that rapid transition to a market economy appears to stimulate corruption (IDS, 1996; White, 1993); in developing countries, the reduced accountabilities linked to public management reforms have given rise to new anxieties about public service ethics.

In the long run, corruption will recede as government becomes more efficient and accountable; but in the short run governments and aid donors have found corruption difficult to target because of its political context, and because it all too often supplies the deficiencies of poor public management. Reforming governments have much more control over the internal characteristics of transparency and public ethics. In the UK, several high-profile cases created substantial public concern about declining standards of behaviour in public life. The result was the creation of a new Parliamentary Select Committee on Standards in Public Life, together with a Code of Conduct for MPs. Government had already published a new Civil Service Code in 1995; among other things this obliges civil servants to:

- assist the duly constituted government, of whatever political complexion;
- act with honesty, impartiality and integrity;
- ensure the proper use of public money;
- avoid using their official position to further their private interests;
- comply with restrictions on their political activities;
- avoid disclosure of confidential information;
- report evidence of criminal or unlawful activity by others.

Relevant also is the new (1994) Code of Practice on Open Government, which provides greater access to government information. More than 30 000 previously closed records have been released under this initiative, which also requires departments to provide more information about policy analysis, costs, targets, performance and complaints procedures Substantially more stringent requirements are expected under the new Labour administration.[3]

CONCLUSION

In developed states, the orthodox 'welfarist' model of improvement has largely been displaced by the 'new public management' revolution, which involves a major rethinking of the state and its relations with the market. The radical critique of the centralized, inefficient, unaccountable, over-extended state has produced a transformative conception, and intensive efforts to turn this conception into practice. But such managerialist conceptions of government are not neutral: they constitute an ideology, a set of beliefs (or preferences) about how government should work; an important factor in the rapid spread of NPM practices has been their utility and acceptability to dominant political élites.

The NPM model is comprehensive, but oriented more to the cost cutting, tax reducing concerns of northern states than the capacity building and developmental concerns of southern states. Clearly, it is a model which should not be inflexibly applied, but adapted to different administrative and political contexts.

Main lessons from existing practice appear to be that:

1. In developing countries privatization has more rhetoric than substance, because it sits so uneasily with local economic systems and political cultures.

2. Sophisticated reforms such as market testing and internal markets are unlikely to work outside developed economies.
3. However, improvement of public services delivery, a much neglected area, is badly needed, and both market-type mechanisms and user-oriented initiatives can play a part here.
4. There is a clear need to strengthen core administrative systems, and especially the strategic centre. This means working towards the creation of a well-resourced, professional, 'steel frame' civil service capable of managing both policy direction and operational delivery. Since there is no one ideal model, this is an area where local creativity and innovation are needed to reflect local political and institutional contexts. Above all, reform here must be pragmatic if realistic progress is to be made.
5. A related need is to build policy capacity, another neglected area. Many studies identify failures of policy capacity and design as a principal defect in government systems, especially in developing countries. Efforts in this area should be 'up-stream', concentrating on core policy capabilities (UNDP, 1995).
6. Effective use of human resources means attention to clarification of roles and responsibilities, both for organizations and individuals; and to the fostering of professional values and ethics. Training remains, in principle, a crucial mechanism for the transmission of new skills and values, and for the provision of internal analytic capacity.
7. Institutional creativity involves a willingness to consider new hybrid forms of public–private organization, through contracts and partnerships, and mutually supportive relations with the non-governmental and community bodies which are an important link between government and grassroots. Both efficiency *and* accountability gains are possible. There is much scope for institutional experiment, particularly in relation to local governance.

   While most people would agree that developing countries need to create greater efficiency in systems of government and in the provision of public services to citizens, there is much less agreement on what kind of state this implies: should we be seeking to reduce the size and scope of the state, or should we be seeking to strengthen state capacity and powers? It is interesting to note that the World Bank, for the past decade or more a proponent of NPM ideas, in its most recent Annual Report reaffirmed the significance of the state in achieving developmental objectives, asserted a clear relationship between 'good government' and levels of economic growth, and endorsed a strategy to 'raise state capability by reinvigorating public institutions' (World Bank, 1997, p. 3), while describing the minimalist state approach as 'an extreme view' (ibid., p. iii). If this call for a reinvigoration of the state is echoed by other aid donors, the millennium may see a return to the main idea of the 1960s: the developmental state.

NOTES

1. This section draws on an unpublished draft paper (1996) by N. Manning, then at the Commonwealth Secretariat.
2. The new Labour administration of 1997 has renamed this the Better Regulation Unit.
3. They propose a Freedom of Information Act in which ministers, government departments, quangos and other public bodies will be legally bound to open their files to the public, on demand, within 20 working days, though there will be specific exemptions. An Information Commissioner will be appointed with powers to order disclosure, and to ensure reasonable charges for the provision of information (*Guardian*, 7 January 1998).

REFERENCES

Adam, C., Cavendish, W. and Mistry, P.S. (1992), *Adjusting Privatisation: Case Studies from Developing Countries*, London: James Currey.

Adamolekun, L. (1989), *Issues in Development Management in Sub-saharan Africa*, Economic Development Institute, Washington, DC: World Bank.

Blunt, P. (1991), 'Organisational culture and development', *International Journal of Human Resource Management*, **2** (1), 55–41.

Blunt, P. and Jones, M. (1992), *Managing Organisations in Africa*, Berlin: Walter de Gruyter.

Boston, J., Martin, J., Pallot, J. and Walsh, P. (1996), *Public Management: the New Zealand Model*, Oxford: Oxford University Press.

CAPAM (Commonwealth Association for Public Administration and Management) (1994), *Government in Transition*, London: Commonwealth Secretariat.

Cohen, J. (1993), 'The importance of public service reform: the case of Kenya', in *Journal of Modern African Studies*, **3**.

Common, R., Flynn, N. and Mellon, E. (eds) (1992), *Managing Public Services: Competition and Decentralisation*, London: Butterworth/Heinemann.

Commonwealth Secretariat (1993), *Administrative and Managerial Reform in Government*, London: Commonwealth Secretariat.

Commonwealth Secretariat (1994), *Current Good Practices and New Developments in Public Service Management: Canada*, London: Commonwealth Secretariat.

Commonwealth Secretariat (1995), *From Problem to Solution: Commonwealth Strategies for Reform*, London: Commonwealth Secretariat.

Commonwealth Secretariat (1996), *Current Good Practice and New Developments in Public Service Management: the Commonwealth Portfolio*, London: Commonwealth Secretariat.

Cook, P. and Kirkpatrick, C (1994), 'Privatisation and enterprise reforms in transitional economies: a comparison of European and Asian experience', conference paper, Bradford, March.

Cook, P. and Kirkpatrick, C. (1995), *Privatisation Policy and Performance: International Perspectives*, London: Harvester Wheatsheaf.

Cook, P. and Minogue, M. (1990), 'Waiting for privatisation: towards the integration of economic and non-economic explanations', *Public Administration and Development*, **10** (4), 389–403.

Craig, P. (1994), *Administrative Law* (3rd edn), London: Sweet and Maxwell.

Deakin, N. and Walsh, K. (1996), 'The enabling state: the role of markets and contracts', *Public Administration*, **14**, 33–48.

Dia, M. (1993), 'A governance approach to civil service reform in subSaharan Africa', Washington, DC: World Bank Technical Paper No. 225.

Dia, M. (1996), *Africa's Management in the 1990s and Beyond: Reconciling Indigenous and Transplanted Institutions*, Washington, DC: World Bank.

Dunleavy, P. and Hood, C. (1994), 'From old public administration to new public management', *Public Money and Management*, **14** (3), 9–16.

Galal, A. and Shirley, M. (1994), *Does Privatisation Deliver?*, EDI Development Studies, Washington, DC: World Bank.

Glentworth, G. (1989), *Civil Service Reform in Sub-saharan Africa*, London: ODA.

Gray, A. and Jenkins, W. (1995), 'From public administration to public management: reassessing a revolution?', *Public Administration*, **73**, 75–99.

Handy, C.B. (1985), *Understanding Organisations* (3rd edn), London: Penguin.

IDS (1996), *Liberalisation and the New Corruption*, IDS Bulletin, **27** (2) April, Institute of Development Studies, University of Sussex, Brighton.

Kanter, R.M. (1989), *When Giants learn to Dance*, London: Unwin Hyman.

Loughlin, M. and Scott, C. (1997), 'The regulatory state' in P. Dunleavy et al., *Developments in British Politics*, London: Macmillan, pp. 205–18.

Manning, N. (1996), 'Improving the public service', unpublished paper, London: Commonwealth Secretariat.

Montgomery, J.D. (1996), 'Bureaucrat, heal thyself! Lessons from three administrative reforms', *World Development*, **24** (5), 953–60.

Morgan, G. (1986), *Images of Organisation*, London: Sage.

Mountfield, R. (1997), 'The British public management reform experience', paper presented at the international conference on Public Sector Management for the Next Century, University of Manchester, 29 June–2 July.

NAO (1995), *Annual Report*, London: National Audit Office.

Nunberg, B. (1990), 'Public sector management issues in structural adjustment lending', Washington, DC: World Bank Discussion Paper No. 99.

Nunberg, B. (1995), 'Managing the civil service: reform lessons from advanced industrialised countries', Washington, DC: World Bank Discussion Paper No. 204.

Nunberg, B. and. Nellis, J. (1995), 'Civil service reform and the World Bank', Washington: World Bank Discussion Paper No. 161.

OECD (1995), *Governance in Transition: Public Management Reforms in OECD Countries*, Paris: OECD.

OECD (1996), *Performance Auditing and the Modernisation of Government*, Paris: OECD.

Osborne, D. and Gaebler, R. (1992), *Reinventing Government*, Reading, MA: Addison-Wesley.

Painter, J. (1992), 'The Culture of Competition', *Public Policy and Administration*, **7** (1), 58–68.

Polidano, C. (1997), 'The bureaucrat who fell under a bus: ministerial responsibility, executive agencies and the Derek Lewis affair in Britain', Public Policy and Management Working paper No. 1, IDPM, University of Manchester.

Rhodes, R. (1997), *Understanding Governance: Policy Networks, Governance, Reflexivity and Accountability*, London: Open University Press.

Sandbrook, R. (1993), *The Politics of Africa's Economic Recovery*, London: Cambridge University Press.

Shirley, M. (1996), 'The Economics and Politics of Government Ownership', conference paper, Bradford, July.

UK Cabinet Office (1997), *Briefing on Civil Service Issues*, London: Cabinet Office.

UNCTAD (1992), *Design, Implementation and Results of Privatisation Programmes*, Geneva: UN Conference on Trade and Development.

UNDP (1995), *Public Sector Management, Governance, and Sustainable Human Development*, New York: UNDP.

Walsh, K., Deakin, N., Smith, P. and Thomas, N. (1997), *Contracting for Change: Contracts in Health, Social Care and other Local Government Services*, Oxford: Oxford University Press.

White, G. (1993), *Riding the Tiger: the Politics of Economic Reform in Post Mao China*, California: Stanford Press.

Willett, C. (ed.) (1997), *Public Sector Reform and the Citizen's Charter*, London: Blackstone Press.

World Bank (1991), *The Africa Capacity Building Initiative*, Washington, DC: World Bank.

World Bank (1995), *Bureaucrats in Business: the Economics and Politics of Government Ownership*, Oxford: Oxford University Press.

World Bank (1996), *World Development Report, 1996: From Plan to Market*, Oxford: Oxford University Press.

World Bank (1997), *World Development Report, 1997: The State in a Changing World*, Oxford: Oxford University Press.

3. Policy transfer: a framework for comparative analysis

David P. Dolowitz and David Marsh

WHAT IS POLICY TRANSFER? A FRAMEWORK FOR ANALYSIS

In recent years there has been a growing body of literature analysing policy transfer: the process by which knowledge of ideas, institutions, policies and programmes in one time and/or place is fed into the policy making arena in the development of policies and programmes in another time and/or place.[1]

There can be no doubt that policy transfer has always existed. For example, Moses Hada (1959) clearly illustrates the role that both voluntary and coercive policy transfer played in the spread of ideas, policies and programmes across Europe and the Middle East during the Hellenistic period. However, it is also indisputable that the rapid growth in communications of all types, when combined with the dramatic increase in the number and role of international organizations since the start of the twentieth century, has accelerated the process.

Not surprisingly, the increase in policy transfer has led to the development of interest in the topic among students of comparative politics, public policy, organizational sociology and, increasingly, political development. Two examples should suffice. First, Shamsul Haque (1996, pp. 206–7) argues that: 'among international agencies, the World Bank, IMF, the US Agency for International Development, and the British Overseas Development Administration have influenced Third World countries to adopt pro-market policies'. More recently, John Campbell (1997) demonstrated how the institutional legacies of Poland, Hungary and Czechoslovakia helped account for different national outcomes when the IMF attempted to impose neo-liberal policies on these countries as a condition for a loan guarantee.

The aim of this chapter is to develop a framework for the study of policy transfer. It is necessary to establish such a framework both because much of the existing literature lacks focus and because such a framework will provide an essential step towards the development of any theory of policy transfer. The framework presented here highlights a series of questions (Table 3.1):

Table 3.1   Policy transfer: a framework for analysis

When does transfer occur?	Why transfer? Continuum			Who is involved in transfer?	What is transferred?	From where?			Degrees of transfer	Restrictions/ facilitators
	Want to...... Voluntary	Mixtures	Have to...... Coercive			Past	Within a nation	Cross-national		
Regular policy cycle (mixtures)	Problems/ dissatisfaction	Perceptions of falling behind	Direct imposition	Elected officials	Policies	Internal	International organizations	International organizations	Copying	Policy complexity
Crisis (copying)	Cyclical events	International consensus	Supra-national institutions	Bureaucrats Administrators Professionals	Institutional structures	Global	Regional State Local governments	Regional State Local governments	Emulation	Past policies
	Political conflict	Externalities	Inter-governmental organizations	Entrepreneurs/ consultants	Ideology				Mixtures	Structural/ institutional
	Legitimate conclusions already reached		Trans-national corporations	Political parties	Ideas				Inspiration	Feasibility • ideology • cultural • proximity • technology • economic • bureaucratic
				Pressure groups/non-governmental organizations	Negative lessons					
				Think tanks						
				International organizations	What not transferred					Language
				Networks						
				Issue						
				Advocacy						
				Epistemic						Past relations Symbols

Source: Adapted from Dolowitz (1997), *Learning From America.*

- Why and when do actors engage in policy transfer?
- Who transfers policy?
- What is transferred?
- From where are lessons drawn?
- Are there different degrees of transfer?
- When do actors engage in policy transfer and how does this affect the process?
- What restricts policy transfer?

Overall, this chapter has two aims: first, it will demonstrate the utility and use of the concept of policy transfer; second, and more important, it will show that using this framework helps provide a greater understanding of the content and development of public policy in various settings.

WHY AND WHEN DO ACTORS ENGAGE IN POLICY TRANSFER?

When studying policy transfer we need to know what drives actors to engage in the process. This information helps explain why policy makers look to particular models and nations rather than others. More important, knowing why actors turned to policy transfer can help explain why they occasionally appear to be adopting policies or programmes inappropriate to a given country or situation. It is crucial to make a distinction between voluntary and coercively driven policy transfer. Voluntary transfer implies that rational, calculating actors desire a change and actively seek policies to satisfy their needs. Coercive transfer, or conditionality, occurs when policy makers are forced by the actions of outsiders to engage in transfer.[2] In our view it is best to see these categories as lying at opposite ends of a continuum ranging from wanting to engage in policy transfer, to having to. Furthermore, any case of policy transfer can contain both voluntary and coercive elements but, as a general rule, one will dominate. Finally, in the case of voluntary policy transfer how a lesson is used often depends upon the audience addressed.

Voluntary Transfer

The primary catalyst of voluntary transfer is some form of dissatisfaction or problem with the *status quo*. When engaging in voluntary transfer, agents of change are unlikely to begin looking for lessons until a problem arises. This is because, before the emergence of a problem, established routines provide the best means of policy making, because they tend to require actors to expend the least amount of resources. It is only when routines stop providing solutions that it becomes necessary to search for new policies or programmes. In the search for new solutions, actors turn to policy transfer when they perceive the process as providing an easier solution than the adaptation of the existing policy or the development of an original one. Of more importance, actors may also resort to policy transfer if they believe they can justify the development of the policy or programme with the argument that since it works in one system it will also work when imported.

Cyclical political events, particularly elections and annual addresses, also drive actors to engage in policy transfer. Valerie Bunce demonstrates the importance of elections in the creation of new public policies, concluding: 'What counts in succession ... is not so much the appearance of new faces, but rather the fact that these new faces may do new things' (Bunce, 1981, p. 14). Political conflict often acts as a catalyst for voluntary policy transfer because supporters and opponents of change actively seek lessons which they can use to advance their positions. In this process, the same lessons can even be used to different ends by supporters and opponents of change.

Voluntary policy transfer also occurs when agents of change need to legitimate or justify decisions they have already reached. For example Henig et al. (1998) documented how the international spread of privatization policies and programmes is partially attributable to governments using lessons to legitimate conclusions arising out of neo-liberal economic policy.

Finally, while voluntary policy transfer would logically appear to lead to incremental policy change, policy makers can use policy transfer to introduce and justify fundamental change. For example, while describing the changes in welfare policies in Hungary and Czechoslovakia, Cox (1993, p. 351) argues that: 'Borrowing may promote non-incremental policy change because policy makers think that radical change is possible, or that some change in circumstances may soon make radical change possible, or simply because they desire to propose change.'

The Middle Ground

While voluntary forces are often the primary catalyst for policy transfer, there are many situations in which policy transfer is driven by a combination of more or less voluntary and coercive forces. One of the primary catalysts for policy transfer lying towards the centre of the continuum is when key actors within the policy making process perceive their country to be falling behind its primary competitors.[3] A prime example of this motivation can be seen in Zambia's decision to pursue an aggressive privatization programme (Fundanga and Mwaba, 1997, p. 5).

Another catalyst driving policy transfer is in effect the converse of the previous category: the emergence of an international consensus. When there is general international agreement upon the definition of a problem or a solution, nations not adopting this definition or solution will face increasing pressure to join the international community in implementing similar programmes or policies. For example, it has been argued that the current debates within Norway in respect of the adoption of a national workfare programme stem from the perceived need to catch up with the international consensus forming around the adoption of workfare systems, rather than indigenous political or economic need.[4]

Actors can also be pushed toward policy transfer if they believe that this action will make their system internationally recognized or acceptable. Thus, John Campbell (1997, p. 5) found that 'some [post-communist countries] sought to harmonize their tax structures with those of their West Europe neighbors in an effort to appear westernized and legitimate thereby increasing their chances of being accepted into various international organizations and accords'.

Moving towards the coercive end of the continuum, policy transfer can also be driven by actors in one setting who feel that they have to engage in transfer as a result of the actions of external actors or events. One of the most common forms of indirect coercion occurs when the policies of one state produce externalities detrimental to another. While the most observable form of such transfer is environmental regulation, labour market regulations can also drive actors to engage in transfer. A classic example was provided by the British Prime Minister, Tony Blair, while addressing the Socialist Leaders' Congress in Malmo, Sweden on 6 June 1997. He argued that Britain and Europe must retain a flexible labour market policy within the employment chapter because of the economic challenge presented by the tiger economies of Southeast Asia.

Coercive Transfer: Conditionality

Coercive transfer occurs when agents of change are forced into action. The most direct method of coercive policy transfer is when one government forces another to adopt a policy. For example, after World War II the American government drafted the Japanese constitution and was heavily involved in the development of various sections of the German constitution (Majone, 1991).

Since the reconstruction period after World War II and the end of direct colonialism, the imposition of a policy on one country by another has been rare. However, international organizations, particularly lending agencies such as the International Monetary Fund (IMF) and the World Bank, act as agents of coercive transfer by attaching certain conditions to loans. For example, John Campbell (1997) has documented how during the 1980s and 1990s the

IMF coerced many post-communist governments into implementing neo-liberal economic and social policies as a precondition for any form of financial assistance. In particular, Campbell demonstrates that lending agencies demanded that Poland, Hungary and Czechoslovakia reduce their rate of inflation and budget deficits by introducing specific measures to decrease private and corporate taxes; eliminate subsidies to state enterprises; and restrict the size and scope of their welfare service. More specifically, it has been the policy of the IMF and the World Bank to force many developing nations into adopting privatization programmes as a condition of their loans. This is clearly demonstrated by Fundanga and Mwaba (1997, p. 1), of the African Development Bank, who argue: 'Privatization now frequently features ... in conditionalities from donors. The past decade has ... seen the World Bank and other donors get increasingly involved in lending operations towards parastatal sector reforms that included privatization components.'

International lending organizations gain coercive powers through the conditions attached to loans because: '[their] loans are much more attractive than private loans ... but there is a catch. To qualify for an IMF loan, nations must in practice surrender a degree of control over their economic policies. The IMF will stipulate certain economic policies that have to be implemented if the loan is to be granted' (Hague et al., 1992, p. 129).

Agents of coercive transfer worth mentioning are transnational corporations (TNCs). As Hague et al. (1992, p. 106) argue: 'In their relations with national governments, the TNCs hold the ace card of mobility.' While the extent to which capital mobility and truly global operational bases exist is questionable, there is no doubt that TNCs may act as a driving force for policy transfer. In the drive to attract inward investment, this perceived need to do so can play a significant role in encouraging a government, even in countries classified as having an advanced industrial economy, to adopt policies against its wishes. A prime example of this is provided by Fundanga and Mwaba (1997, p. 24), who note:

> Heinz's offer to take a stake in a Zambian parastatal in the food processing industry was rejected on the basis that the offer was low. Heinz quickly moved to a neighbouring country where a similar offer was accepted. Heinz not only buys and processes farm produce (and exports) in that country, but the company helps the suppliers with advanced farming practices to get the best yields [technology transfer].

WHO TRANSFERS POLICY?

It is not enough to understand why policy makers engage in policy transfer; one must also identify the key people and groups involved in the process. In any specific case of transfer more than one category of actor is likely to be involved at various stages of the process and in performing various roles.[5] Moreover, the actors involved in the process of policy transfer will reside in different countries and regions, interacting through a series of policy networks or epistemic communities and a plethora of non-governmental organizations.

Elected Officials

In most, but not all, policy areas, the principal actors involved in policy transfer are elected officials, because 'their values give direction to public policy and their endorsement is needed to legitimate the adoption of programs' (Rose, 1993, p. 52). Elected officials are also important because they set the boundaries of acceptable policy during their administrations. As discussed by the African Development Bank (Fundanga and Mwaba, 1997), while Zambia began a process of privatization under President Kaunda, the true impetus driving the Zambian privatization programme came from his successor, President Chiluba.

Bureaucrats/Administrators/Professionals

Associated with politicians are professionals, administrators and civil servants. In the process of policy transfer these groups may be as important as politicians in the policy development stage and more important during the implementation stage. This is because 'almost every agency of modern government has a stake in some aspect of international relations and maintains direct contact ... with its opposite numbers' (Haas, 1980, p. 357). This provides them with the knowledge and resources necessary to transfer policies. While discussing the role of bureaucratic élites in Turkey and Ghana Mosley et al. (1991, p. 173) argue that it was this bureaucratic or technocratic élite which forced through 'a liberalisation programme on terms more or less consistent with what the World Bank was asking for'.

Entrepreneurs/Consultants

Increasingly, there has been an emphasis on the role policy entrepreneurs play in the policy making process. Specifically, entrepreneurs are people with an interest in a particular substantive area of policy and who are willing to 'invest their resources, time, energy, reputation, and sometimes money, in the hope of a future return' (Kingdon, 1984, p. 129). Policy entrepreneurs are important to policy transfer because of their advocacy of lessons and because of their national and international contacts. These contacts are the basis of new ideas and lessons. It is often difficult to distinguish between policy entrepreneurs and politicians or bureaucrats performing their regular duties. However, we can suggest possible criteria for distinguishing entrepreneurs. They are likely to demonstrate an extensive history of involvement in the policy being examined; use personal time; and use personal finances in pursuit of the implementation of a desired policy or programme. For example, *The Economist* reported that Michael Porter of the Harvard Business School "'has been asked by governments from Portugal to Colombia to do for them what he and his kind have done for private enterprise''' (cited in Common, Chapter 4, this volume).

Closely associated with entrepreneurs are paid consultants, or individuals and firms who are hired by international organizations and national governments to act as experts or discussants in an effort to transform some existing policy, system or practice. As Bevan et al. (1997, pp. 3–4) argue:

> Most consultants to developing and transitional governments are contracted by donors; their consultancies are usually part of a larger donor programme over which they have no control. The lead ... is usually taken by the international financial institutions (IFIs), particularly the World Bank, who currently exert considerable leverage through the conditionalities attached to their Structural Adjustment Loans. However, other international organizations (eg UNDP, the EU, the African Development Bank) and bilateral donors (eg ODA/DfID, NORAD, SIDA, etc) can take different lines, or try to modify the IFI approach, and they may do this through consultancies.

As this quotation demonstrates, one of the unique features of consultancy is that different organizations can hire different consultants in their efforts to exert pressure on national governments. Not only does this pit different agencies and consultants against one another, but means that national governments have room to manoeuvre as they can pick and choose amongst the consultants' suggestions.

Political Parties

Only individual agents of policy transfer have been discussed so far, but groups and organizations can also be involved in the process. The first key group involved in the process of policy transfer is political parties. Political parties are constantly engaging in policy transfer because they need new ideas and policies to increase their electoral appeal or appease party activists. However, it must be noted that, within the process of policy transfer, parties tend to use lessons selectively either to defend or promote ideas and policies which advance their ideological beliefs and electoral chances.

Interest Groups

Interest groups are also involved in policy transfer as their main concern is to influence the policy making process. Moreover, many interest groups keep in contact with groups in other nation-states, exchanging ideas and drawing lessons from each other's experience. This information is then fed into the policy making process through governmental contacts and public pressure. While examining the impact of American environmental pollutants and regulations on Canada, Hoberg (1991, p. 127) stresses the importance of pressure groups.

Linked to domestic pressure groups are international non-governmental organizations (NGOs). Over the past 50 years there has been an explosion in the number of non-governmental organizations operating at both the national and international level. As with domestic pressure groups, while their organization, issues and level of influence will vary across countries and policy area, there is no denying their importance in the global spread of ideas and information. Sally Gear (1997) illustrates the importance of NGOs in the transfer of policies, not only from one country to another but also from the developing world to Britain:

> Oxfam have recently decided to develop their programme to include poverty alleviation in the UK. They have found that groups working on poverty in the UK can benefit from the experience Oxfam has gained from working with community organisations overseas. For example they have visits from practitioners working with slum dwellers in India to come the Britain to share their working methods with practitioners working on housing issues in Britain. (p. 8)

Think Tanks

In developing a framework for analysing the process of policy transfer it is also important to discuss the role of institutions. During the 1980s think tanks, particularly neo-liberal think tanks, were extremely influential in the spread of ideas and policies both within and between countries. As institutions designed to influence the development of public policy, think tanks are extremely important in the policy transfer process because their ideas are often presented as the basis and justification for new ideas and policies.[6] The role of free market think tanks has been particularly important in the development and spread of neo-liberal ideas and programmes around the globe, as can be seen from opening the pages of the World Bank's 1997 *World Development Report*, which argues:

> Far from supporting a minimalist approach to the state, these examples have shown that development requires an effective state, one that plays a catalytic,

facilitating role, encouraging and complementing the activities of private business and individuals. Certainly, state-dominated development has failed. (World Bank, 1997, p. III)

International Organizations

Supranational organizations and regimes are also involved in policy transfer, particularly transfer based on conditionality. Organizations such as the OECD (Organization for Economic Cooperation and Development) and the United Nations are devoted to the spread and coordination of ideas and policies across the globe. More importantly, many of these organizations are staffed, in large part, by individuals drawn from the public services of their member states. As such, these organizations form powerful networks of individuals devoted to the generation of policy advice used in the development of policies not only within the organization but within all nations affected by these organizations.

Usui's work provides a specific example of the role of an international organization in the spread of ideas. After studying the role and policies of the International Labour Organization (ILO), Usui (1994, p. 259) argued that supranational collectives have a 'demonstrable influence over participating nations toward their own social insurance legislation'. Martin Senti (1997, p. 2) has expanded upon this research to argue that the ILO has generated a

> broad system of Labour Standards to which nations are expected – but not forced – to conform. Member states are obligated to submit standards adopted by the tripartite ILO-Conference to national legislative authorities. The ILO therefore has an important agenda-setting function which must not be underestimated.

International organizations often use international conferences to spread information and policies around the globe. Currently, many of these conferences and meetings are designed to familiarize Third World and post-communist governments with Western practices and neo-liberal economic and social policies. As John Campbell (1997, p. 5) notes:

> The IMF, World Bank, OECD and a variety of other institutions convened a plethora of conferences designed to familiarize postcommunist scholars, experts and officials with typical western taxation, spending and fiscal policy practices. Often the proceedings of these conferences were published and disseminated widely, thus providing vehicles for the diffusion of a potentially isomorphic set of norms regarding the appropriate or legitimate way to organise postcommunist fiscal systems.

Policy Networks

To influence policy decisions, individuals and groups must gain access to the government's decision making process. Not all interests have equal access to this decision making process. Rather, institutionalized relationships develop between government officials and broader societal interests within a given policy domain. The actors involved within these policy domains enjoy close, continual, and often privileged, access to key government officials. These formalized contacts exist as national and international policy networks. Such networks may be international in nature; if they are, they can clearly be one of the primary mechanisms for the spread of information amongst various actors on a global scale. More important, such networks can play a crucial role in placing information on the governing agenda. As John Barlow (1997, p. 5) observed when analysing the development of local authorities in Hungary, 'there are well developed policy networks and policy communities of professionals ... and local politicians, meeting at conferences or as members of a local authority national association. Fashionable new ideas of management are taken up and circulated with great speed.'

What is Transferred?

What is transferred clearly varies from situation to situation. However, five broad categories can be established: policies; institutions; ideologies/justifications; attitudes; and negative lessons. At present, the last category is hardly addressed but clearly researchers should consider lessons not transferred and examine why actors choose to transfer from a particular place or time rather than from other places or times.

Policies

One of the first things actors can transfer from one unit of government to another, or from one system to another, is a public policy. It should be stressed that, when transferring a policy, agents of change are not obliged to transfer the entire policy but can pick and choose amongst a policy's goals, contents, instruments and substance without transferring the entire policy. For example, after studying American and British inner city regeneration policies, Wolman (1992, p. 41) argued: 'In many cases a specific policy idea ... may be borrowed, but the specific design or structure through which this occurs in the original country may not be.'

Institutions

The institutions used to implement policy can also be transferred, although this is not as straightforward or easy as the transfer of policies. This happened when the Thatcher Government began developing the British welfare-to-work system. More specifically, the Thatcher Government transferred the structure, programmes, and even the name, of American Job Clubs directly into the British welfare-to-work system (Dolowitz, 1997).

Ideologies/justifications
When ideologues enter office they often look for rhetoric to justify their policy preferences and/or programmes. In this vein, President Reagan and Prime Minister Thatcher adopted each other's ideas, ideological rhetoric and justifications to defend and spread political programmes based upon New Right principles. More directly, Richard Common (Chapter 4) has observed:

> The reform measures promoted in the 1980s appear to mirror the effects and efforts of some governments in the West ... The headquarters of the international organizations, based in the United States, were unlikely to remain immune in the 1980s from a local political climate charged by the New Right, armed with public choice theory ... Mosley et al.'s (1991, p. 65) remark that conditionality, 'the vehicle which the Bank chose as a means of changing the economic policies of LDC governments', is 'designed to ensure the execution of a *contract*' smacks of public choice theory.

Attitudes
While the transfer of a programme or an institution may not be possible, actors often attempt to transfer the attitudes underlying a programme or institution from one system to another. Often this type of transfer is used to shift the political climate or to win a political battle. Just such a situation occurred in the transfer of the American Urban Development Action Grant system to Britain:

> Participants frequently talked about the value of learning about different concepts and approaches rather than specific policy designs. Thus, public–private partnerships, local capacity building, citizen empowerment, and deregulation all featured as concepts which attracted British policymakers to the American experience. (Wolman, 1992, p. 41)

Negative lessons
While policy transfer is normally associated with the drawing of positive lessons, by examining foreign policy models, policy makers can learn what not to do or expect: they can draw negative lessons. Salazar's (1997) study of Latin American health care reform provides a particularly good example. After tracing the development of British, Swedish, Ecuadorian and Chilean reforms, he concludes that:

> it seems that these two Latin American countries have taken as read the distinct and cumulative development of the health care systems in European countries:

and that on-going reform initiatives could not alone achieve the complementary but essential goals of equity and comprehensiveness in the provision of health services ... [these countries learned that] market-oriented innovation should be supported or supplemented with appropriate incentives and infrastructure ... in order to achieve major goals (pp. 13–14).

FROM WHERE ARE LESSONS DRAWN?

When developing a framework for analysing the process of policy transfer it is not enough to understand who is involved, what is involved, and why actors engage in policy transfer. The framework must also identify the levels of governance to which actors look for lessons. We focus on five levels: the international level; the national level; the regional level, both within a federal system and groups of states; the state level within federal nations; and, finally, the local level. In addition, policy makers can also look to both their own past and the global past when searching for lessons.

Regional, State and Local Units of Government

Within a nation, actors engaging in policy transfer can and do draw lessons from other political systems or units within their own country. This is particularly useful, and likely, if a nation's constitutional structures create a series of similar sub-national units of government. This process is further enhanced when there exists a relatively homogeneous political culture across the nation. Not only can sub-national units of government draw lessons from each other, but the national government can draw lessons from lower levels of government. This is particularly likely in federal systems for states can, and do, act as laboratories for future federal legislation (Dolowitz, 1996).

Policy transfer within a nation is not only possible within federal states; it also happens in unitary systems. As noted by Barlow (1997, p. 5), 'There is undoubtedly tremendous scope for lesson drawing in local government within a particular country as professionals move from one authority to another as part of their natural career development.'

Cross-National

Although constraints exist, it is common for governments and agents to transfer policies from one nation to another. The basic assumption involved in drawing lessons across national boundaries is that 'Similarities are greater within a given program across national boundaries than among different programs within a country' (Rose, 1988, pp. 227–8). As Table 3.1 illustrates, when drawing lessons from other nations actors are not limited to looking at national governments but can look to other sub-national levels and units of government. Moreover, national governments can look to regional governing institutions in the search for new ideas, programmes or even institutions. Moreover, even local units of government can engage in cross-national policy transfer. In fact, this is the stated purpose of the British Know How Fund. This fund establishes projects in which British local governments are twinned with a foreign counterpart in order to provide technical assistance in institutional and programme development (Barlow, 1997).

International Level

When developing a framework for the analysis of policy transfer we must consider not only transfers between national and sub-national actors, but also the international policy domain. In this process, international organizations such as the International Monetary Fund (IMF), United Nations, European Union and even the African Development Bank (AfDB) are key players, often acting as stores of information to be drawn upon. More importantly, these institutions bring together policy makers from various polities where ideas are shared and policy proposals and documents disseminated. When examining the role of the international level in the process of policy transfer, international conventions and protocols must also be considered.

The Past

While the previous categories have all involved different physical locations, the first place agents of change can search for lessons in the process of policy transfer is in past policies and institutions. In this process, although actors can examine the global past, it is more common for them to search their own nation's past. This type of search has the advantage of saving resources, both political and economic, associated with cross-national policy transfer. More importantly, from the perspective of policy makers, searching the past has the added advantage of reducing the insecurities associated with cross-national policy transfer.

While searching for lessons in the past has the advantage of saving time and resources, it involves subjective evaluation, for although history is constant, it is open to many interpretations. This is a particular concern when searching another nation's past. A current situation may not be truly analogous to a past situation, especially when it is another nation's. Indeed, when drawing lessons, actors might not truly understand the past or its relation to the present. All this increases the possibility that the lessons transferred will fail to achieve the goal for which they were transferred.

DEGREES OF TRANSFER

Policy transfer is not an all-or-nothing process. While any particular instance of policy transfer may involve a combination of processes and agents, there are basically four different degrees of transfer, or ways in which agents of change can adopt a policy or institution based upon information transferred from another time or setting: copying; emulation; mixtures; and inspiration.

Copying

While copying is probably the least common form of policy transfer, it occurs when one country adopts a programme previously used, or in use, elsewhere without making any changes. The easiest way to prove that copying has occurred is to examine the wording of the paper or legislative bill authorizing the programme.

Emulation

Policy transfer can also occur as emulation, as when policy makers base a policy, programme or institution upon a single foreign model but do not copy it in every detail. So, although many post-communist governments accepted the model of neo-liberalism presented by the IMF, they consistently adapted the programmes the IMF was pushing to fit their particular situation.

Mixtures

While emulation involves only a single model, mixtures involve combining elements of policies and/or programmes found in two or more countries to develop a policy best suited to the emulator. It should be noted that in this process it is generally difficult for researchers to establish the influence of various policies and programmes involved in the development of a mixed programme or policy.

Inspiration

Finally, policy transfer can, and often does, provide the inspiration for new thinking and procedures, although this is extremely difficult to demonstrate without the use of intensive interviewing.

Not only are there different ways to utilize lessons in the creation of new policies, but lessons can be put to different uses at different stages during the policy process. More important, different types of lessons are likely to emerge depending on who is engaging in policy transfer, and whether they use lessons within the agenda setting, policy formulation, policy adoption or implementation stages of the policy process. So, while the IMF and the World Bank often impose policies upon nations before granting them loans, it is often the case that the receiving nation is able to alter these policies to fit existing institutional structures and prevailing conditions during the implementation stage. Likewise, policies which emerge during the regular policy cycle are more likely to involve emulation or mixtures of policies than those emerging at times of political crisis. For example, during a war or the reconstruction period immediately following a war, policy transfer is far more likely to lead to direct copying of the original policy, because governments on the losing side will have policies imposed upon them.

RESTRICTIONS ON, AND FACILITATORS OF, POLICY TRANSFER

Any account of policy transfer must consider the constraints faced by actors engaging in the process. This is particularly important because it helps explain why some policies are transferred while others are not. Moreover, it helps explain why policies are transferred from some systems rather than others. While this discussion will stress how various aspects of policy, institutional and societal structure act as restrictions on policy transfer, each of these can also act as a facilitator for policy transfer. There are six broad categories to consider in the development of a policy transfer framework: policy complexity; interactive effects; institutional constraints; feasibility constraints; language constraints; and past relationships.

Policy Complexity

The first possible constraint upon an agent's ability to engage in policy transfer involves questions of policy complexity. Specifically, it is likely that the more complex a policy or programme, the harder it will be to transfer.

Interactive Effects

Obviously, past policies constrain what can be transferred, what agents look for and which agents engage in policy transfer. For example, in the development of the American 1988 Family Support Act, Congress, the Reagan Administration, and even external pressure groups, were constrained by the existence of the Work Incentive Program, the welfare-to-work programmes initiated in response to the 1981 Omnibus Budget Reconciliation Act, and the job search programmes initiated in the 1982 Tax Equity and Fiscal Responsibility Act. Overall, these programmes were so influential in the development of the 1988 legislation that it was little more than an incremental development of previous programmes (GAO, 1987, pp. 37–8).

Institutional Constraints

Institutional and structural constraints can also prevent transfer. If the institutional structures of two systems are too dissimilar, the possibilities of transfer are severely restricted. In contrast, some structures can greatly facilitate transfer. More directly, the structure and procedures found within individual government departments and agencies can assist or restrict transfer. Departments with well-developed hierarchies and reporting procedures can help the process of policy transfer, as programmes and ideas have established paths for advancing into the policy domain. Conversely, these same hierarchies can act as a restraint on policy transfer, as juniors must submit proposals and ideas to managers who can prevent the information from ever reaching the policy agenda. Along these same lines, policy transfer is more likely to develop within departments in which there is a relatively harmonious culture, especially when there is a positive working relationship between ministers and senior civil servants, as both sides are likely to listen to the advice being provided by the other.

The structures of existing legislation and policies also shape the boundaries of policy transfer. For example, by establishing the Aid to Families with Dependent Children (AFDC) programme as a joint federal–state programme, the American Congress restricted the ability of future policy makers to alter it. Here, the structure of the programme shaped how policy makers perceived the problems of the programme, the acceptable solutions, and the acceptable modifications (Dolowitz, 1997).

The relationships between two political systems further encourage or deter agents from engaging in transfer. Past or existing relationships can both help and prevent agents from looking to a different system or time for solutions. Even within a federal system, sub-units which have a traditionally antagonistic relationship with the central government will rarely have their policies or ideas accepted or even examined. On the other hand, systems having a tradition of harmonious relationships both within and across national boundaries will have established the lines of communication necessary for effective policy transfer and may thus act as a model more often than other systems. These generalizations also hold true for policy transfer of a more coercive nature. Under these conditions nations having good relationships with the imposing institution, particularly an international institution, are less likely to attempt to change the policy at the implementation stage or through the delegation of responsibilities to sub-national political institutions, than are countries having antagonistic relationships with the transferring institution.

Feasibility Constraints

The political, bureaucratic, technological and economic resource similarities between systems also influence where actors look for policies, and what policies are or are not transferred. Political ideology plays an important, if not dominant, role in determining where actors look for policies and what policies they accept and reject. For example, the neo-liberal ideology of the American and British governments inclined the Thatcher Government to look towards American programmes in the development of the British welfare-to-work system. As King (1992, p. 239) argues, 'The Conservatives turned to the US model because its stress upon the contractual obligations of the citizen receiving public funds fitted their ideology and policy objectives.'

Closely associated with political ideologies are societal values, or cultural proximity. When engaging in policy transfer, agents are constrained by the prevailing values in society. If these values are too dissimilar, the possibilities of transfer are severely restricted. At the same time, transfer is facilitated by an extensive degree of cultural proximity.

Obviously, even desirable programmes will not be transferred if implementation is beyond a nation's technological abilities. For example, in the development of health care institutions and policies the technology used in the American health system is unavailable in most countries, particularly ex-communist and developing countries, and where it is available, it tends to be on a limited basis. This considerably constrains the ability of agents to transfer any aspect of the American health system dependent upon these technologies.

Associated with technological restrictions are fiscal resource limitations. As Rose (1993, p. 96) argues, 'Money matters, for programs vary greatly in what they cost, and it is hard to apply lessons learned from programs beyond the fiscal means of a public agency.' In fact, it is often a combination of economic and technological restrictions which prevents Third World and post-communist governments from adopting Western programmes and policies, rather than the lack of political desire or knowledge.

Language

Although perhaps not a major constraint on policy transfer, the role of language is not negligible. In the development of policies the ability to access documentation and discuss policies directly with individuals in a foreign system enhances the attractiveness of some systems over others. Additionally, with a shared language, there is a tendency to assume that actors understand the meanings contained within the language and implementation of policies and programmes. The assumption that understanding accompanies language similarities can often help to explain why policies which appear to be working in one system fail when implemented in another. This often happens when language similarities mask cultural or political differences upon which success in the originating system depends. This said, the assumption that agents of transfer understand the meanings associated with the wording of legislation, policies and institutions in similar language systems further adds to their attractiveness as a model for policy development.

CONCLUSION

Policy transfer refers to the process by which actors borrow programmes and policies from one setting to develop programmes and policies within another. It is an important area to study because, as this chapter clearly indicates, policy transfer is a common phenomenon. As such, it is important to develop a framework for analysing the process in order to understand its growth. Here, we have developed and applied such a framework, concentrating upon a series of critical questions which will help focus future research. In our view, those interested in political development are most likely to be interested in the role of coercive transfer; the links between coercive and voluntary transfer; the way in which the internal dynamics of a political and social system act to modify the transfer of policies and programmes; and the extent to which, and the way in which, policies and programmes resulting from either voluntary or coercive transfer fail as a result of features of the process of policy transfer rather than as a result of the nature of the policy or programme itself.

NOTES

1. Within the political science literature, lesson drawing, emulation and convergence all refer to the process we term policy transfer. A similar body of literature can also be found within organizational sociology. These studies emphasize the importance of the global environment in generating a range of legitimate policies that nation states gradually adopt, thus becoming isomorphic. In this literature the three key driving forces of this process are coercive, where nations are cajoled into policy transfer; normative, where interaction leads to transfer; and mimetic, where uncertainty leads to copying. For more information see DiMaggio and Powell (1991), Dolowitz and Marsh (1996); Bennett (1992); Rose (1993).
2. Note that while voluntary transfer is a process which applies equally to any actor wishing to change the system, coercive transfer, or conditionality, will generally only apply to policy makers operating within a government or a government operating under imperial domination.

3. It should be stressed that, under conditions of comparative inadequacy it is often the appearance of new actors and/or agendas which leads to policy transfer, not the emergence of a new issue or the sudden realization that the actor's system is lagging behind its competitors'.
4. Information conveyed to the author during the 1997 ECPR joint workshops, Bern, Switzerland, 27 March–4 April 1997.
5. This is not an exhaustive list; rather it is offered as a framework within which to organize the analysis found within this book. Almost any person or group involved at the design stage of the policy making process can act as an agent for policy transfer.
6. For more information on the role and concept of think tanks see Stone (1996); Blackstone and Plowden (1988); Cockett (1994); James (1993).

REFERENCES

Barlow, J. (1997), 'Policy transfer: the management of change in a Hungarian local authority', unpublished paper, international conference on Public Sector Management for the Next Century, University of Manchester, 29 June – 2 July.

Bennett, C. (1992), 'What is policy convergence and what causes it?', *British Journal of Political Science,* **21**, 215–33.

Blackstone, T. and Plowden, W. (1988), *Inside the Think Tank: Advising the Cabinet, 1971–1983*, London: Heinemann.

Bunce, V. (1981), *Do New Leaders Make a Difference?*, Princeton, NJ: Princeton University Press.

Campbell, J. (1997), 'A comparative analysis of fiscal reform in post communist Europe', unpublished paper, conference on Globalization: Critical Perspectives, University of Birmingham, 14–16 March.

Cockett, R. (1994), *Thinking the Unthinkable: Think-Tanks and the Economic Counter-Revolution, 1931–1983*, New York: HarperCollins.

Cox, R. (1993), 'Creating welfare states in Czechoslovakia and Hungary: why policymakers borrow ideas from the West', *Environment and Planning* C, 11, pp. 349–64.

DiMaggio, P. and Powell, W. (1991), 'The iron cage revisited: institutional isomorphism and collective rationality in organizational analysis', in W. Powell and P. DiMaggio (eds), *The New Institutionalism in Organizational Analysis*, Chicago: Chicago University Press.

Dolowitz, D. (1996), 'Towards a Model of Policy Transfer: An Examination of the British and American Welfare-to-Work Systems: Developments of the 1980s', University of Strathclyde, unpublished Ph.D. Thesis.

Dolowitz, D. (1997), *Learning From America: Policy Transfer and the Development of the British Workfare State*, Oxford: Sussex.

Dolowitz, D. and Marsh, D. (1996), 'Who learns what from whom? A review of the policy transfer literature', *Political Studies,* **44**, 343–57.

Fundanga, C. and Mwaba, A. (1997), 'Privatizaton of public enterprises in Zambia', unpublished paper, international conference on Public Sector Management for the Next Century, University of Manchester, 29 June – 2 July.

GAO (1987), *Work and Welfare: Current AFDC (Aid to Families With Dependent Children), Work Programs and Implications For Federal Policy*, US General Accounting Office, Washington, DC: Government Printing Office.

Gear, S. (1997), 'Social development and "those inner cities"', unpublished paper, international conference on Public Sector Management for the Next Century, University of Manchester, 29 June–2 July.

Haas, E. (1980), 'Why collaborate? Issue-linkage and international regimes', *World Politics*, **32** (3), 357–406.

Hada, M. (1959), *Hellenistic Culture: Fusion and Diffusion*, New York: Columbia University Press.

Hague, R., Harrop, M. and Breslin, S. (1992), *Comparative Government and Politics*, Basingstoke: Macmillan.

Henig, R., Hamnett, C. and Feigenbaum, H. (1988), 'The politics of privatization: a comparative perspective', *Governance*, **1** (4), 442–68.

Hoberg, G. (1991), 'Sleeping with an elephant: the American influence on Canadian environmental regulation', *Journal of Public Policy*, **11**, 107–32.

James, S. (1993), 'The idea brokers: the impact of think tanks on British government', *Public Administration*, **71** (4), 491–506.

King, D. (1992), 'The establishment of work–welfare programs in the United States and Britain: politics, ideas and institutions', in S. Steinmo, K. Thelen and F. Longstreth (eds), *Structuring Politics: Historical Institutionalism in Comparative Analysis*, Cambridge and New York: Cambridge University Press, pp. 217–50.

Kingdon, J. (1984), *Agendas, Alternatives, and Public Policies*, United States: HarperCollins.

Majone, G. (1991), 'Cross-national sources of regulatory policymaking in Europe and the United States', *Journal of Public Policy*, **11**, 79–106.

Mosley, P., Harrigan, J. and Toye, J. (1991), *Aid and Power: the World Bank and policy-based lending*, London: Routledge.

Rose, R. (1988), 'Comparative policy analysis: the program approach', in M. Dogan (ed.), *Comparing Pluralist Democracies*, Boulder, CO: Westview Press, pp. 219–36.

Rose, R. (1993), *Lesson Drawing in Public Policy*, New Jersey: Chatham House.

Salazar, A. (1997), 'Health care reform in European countries: what are the lessons and opportunities for Latin America?', unpublished paper to international conference on Public Sector Management for the Next Century, University of Manchester, 29 June – 2 July.

Senti, M. (1997), 'Welfare state development in an international context: diffusion of social policy program adoption', unpublished paper presented at the 25th ECPR joint sessions, Bern, Switzerland, 27 February – 4 March.

Shamsul Haque, M. (1996), 'Public service under challenge in the age of privatization', *Governance*, **9** (2), 186–216.

Stone, D. (1996), *Capturing the Imagination: Think Tanks and the Policy Process*, London: Frank Cass.

US Government (1988), *1988 Family Support Act*, Washington, DC: Government Printing Office.

Usui, C. (1994), 'Welfare state development in a world system context', in T. Janoski and A. Hicks (eds), *The Comparative Political Economy of the Welfare State*, Cambridge, MA: Harvard University Press, pp. 254–77.

Wolman, H. (1992), 'Understanding cross national policy transfer: the case of Britain and the US', *Governance*, **5** (1), 27–45.

World Bank (1997), *World Development Report*, Oxford: Oxford University Press.

4. The new public management and policy transfer: the role of international organizations

Richard Common

INTRODUCTION

One 'of the most conspicuous trends in modern government' is 'the internationalization of public management reform' (Metcalfe, 1994, p. 272). Public administration across the world is supposedly converging around a new paradigm of public management. Why should we be surprised at this particular trend? It is possible to argue that since the development of modern bureaucracy, the nature and role of public administration, when examined country by country, has always appeared similar. The aim of this chapter is to highlight the analytical problems confronted when attempting to account for the internationalization of public policies. The focus here is on the emergence of new public management (NPM) as the new global paradigm for public administration, and on how international organizations have acted as 'policy transferors' of NPM-type reforms to developing countries. The chapter places in context the internationalization of NPM within the wider debates on globalization, modernization and democratization. Also, it examines the nature of the policies being transferred and questions their appropriateness to the developing world. This is a tall order for a short chapter, but 'the proposition that the new paradigm is producing convergence in administrative states is a ... dramatic claim' (Lynn, 1996); and this is a claim worth exploring.

The first problem is that NPM defies precise definition. Some attempts are normative (for example, Ferlie et al., 1996; Holmes and Shand,1995). Others, at best, locate NPM in theoretical frameworks based on management science and public choice theory (Aucoin,1990; Hood, 1991, 1995). The loose, and often contradictory nature of many NPM doctrines means that they appear to be applied in a haphazard fashion. Hood (1991) provided one of the first distillations of NPM as a set of identifiable components. Pollitt (1995, p. 133) saw NPM as a 'shopping basket' which countries choose from to improve their public sectors, with countries choosing different items for different reasons. On the other hand, Hoggett (1994) described NPM more broadly, as a collection of more flexible strategies in terms of service delivery and human resource management. Does the new management orthodoxy amount to little more than a collection of management techniques applied here and there?

This lack of coherence has not prevented NPM from being hailed as a new paradigm or 'gold standard' for the public sector. Are we talking about a paradigm shift? Fox and Miller (1995) argued that the traditional public administration paradigm, based on the Wilsonian dichotomy, Taylorist scientific management and Weberian hierarchical control, is dead. We are now living in an age of 'post-modern public administration'. The irony is that the separation of politics from administration, the removal of professional discretion over service delivery, and the enhancement of the measurement and monitoring capacity of government over public service delivery, actually lie at the core of NPM. No wonder NPM appears to be an international trend if it shares the same theoretical antecedents as public administration. However, a key distinguishing feature of NPM is the reliance on market-based mechanisms to deliver public services. Even in the absence of competitive marketplaces, both bureaucrats and politicians seem compelled to introduce NPM techniques, and it is this compulsion that appears to be the international phenomenon. As Peters (1996, p. 21) argued, whether administrative change is being considered in the most affluent country of Western Europe or the poorest country in Africa, the operative assumption appears to be that the best or even the only way to obtain better results from public sector organizations is to adopt some sort of market-based mechanism to replace the traditional bureaucracy.

Surveying NPM-type reforms is not a simple mapping exercise. This is partly because of the difficulty in defining terms and differentiating between substantial and cosmetic change, and also partly because of the close policy relationship with privatization (which is explored later). To move the discussion forward, I shall take NPM to be the reassertion of traditional public administration plus the introduction of managerial techniques and 'market values' (Lane, 1993, p. 147).

POLICY TRANSFER ANALYSIS AND INTERNATIONAL ORGANIZATIONS

The analysis of 'policy transfer' appears to offer an explanation for the seeming contagiousness of NPM by providing a method of inquiry to explain public policy transfer between countries. However, policy transfer is a generic concept that lacks a coherent theoretical and methodological base, mainly due to the lack of a unifying literature. This much it shares with NPM.

Dolowitz and Marsh's tentative policy transfer model (Chapter 3 in this book) locates international organizations as potential agents of policy transfer, alongside a range of actors such as politicians, bureaucrats and so forth. International organizations such as the United Nations, Organization for Economic Cooperation and Development (OECD), the European Union (EU), the World Bank, the International Monetary Fund (IMF) and the academic community (see also Wright,1994) have a role to play in the process of NPM policy transfer. Martin (1993) adds to this list other regional financial institutions such as the Inter-American Development Bank, and the European Bank for Reconstruction and Development, bilateral aid agencies, notably the US Agency for International Development (USAID), universities, think tanks, consultancies (for example, Coopers and Lybrand) and the General Agreement on Tariffs and Trade (GATT). Other additions to this list could include the UK Department for International Development (DFID) and the Commonwealth Secretariat.

The impact of international organizations on public administration in the developing world is unmistakable. However, this chapter focuses primarily on the World Bank, simply because of its considerable influence over policy making in the developing world. Also, Onimode (1989, pp. 25–6) treats the 'IMF and World Bank together' because of 'their joint location in Washington, systematic consultation about each other's activities, regular co-operation (even complementarity), their identical ideological perspectives, similarity of objectives and common programmes under structural adjustment'. These international organizations need to be understood both as facilitators of policy transfer and as a key source of pressure on governments to modernize their public sectors.

The explanatory power of Dolowitz and Marsh's framework (1996, and Chapter 3, this volume) derives from regarding *voluntary* and *coercive* policy transfer as two ends of a continuum. On one extreme, voluntary transfer assumes search activity by governments, or lesson drawing. International organizations can facilitate policy learning in a number of ways. For instance, the OECD does so among its members through its Public Management Committee, which produces a series of Public Management Studies. As Moran and Wood (1996, p. 129) note, 'such influence as it wields comes from the power of the analyses which it sponsors and from the influence of the individuals and institutions in the networks which it supports'. For example, the foreword to *Managing with Market-Type Mechanisms* is clear about one aim of the report, which is to draw 'some clear lessons in the immense field of public management practices which attempt to blend the advantages of market arrangements with the proven virtues of traditional public administration' (OECD, 1993, p. 3). Rose (1993, p. 105) argued that the EU 'promotes comparison' where members learn best practice from each other (see also

Moran and Wood, 1996). However, the OECD can only propose economic policies for Western states (Luard, 1990, p. 149); it cannot impose them. The key assumption here is that policy learning by any member state is voluntary, not enforced.

At the other extreme, many countries appear to be coerced into policy transfers. Sources of coercion may include the international organizations which have an interest in ensuring, rather than simply encouraging, best practice. Dolowitz and Marsh (1996, p. 348) argue that the EU can also act as a 'policy pusher'. However, looking for evidence of coercive policy transfer is not a straightforward task. Both bureaucratic and political élites may well support public sector reform for differing motives. Biersteker (1995, p. 186) argued that technocratic élites acted as a pressure for policy reversal within developing countries and were given 'crucial international backing from the IMF and the World Bank'. With respect to Turkey and Ghana, Mosley et al. (1991, p. 173) argued that the technocratic élite pushed 'through a liberalisation programme on terms more or less consistent with what the World Bank was asking for'. Garcia-Zamor (1994, p. 102) argued that

> bureaucrats of the developing countries were the most vocal supporters of the dependency approach. They questioned why capitalist development, such as occurred in the US and western Europe, had not taken place in the Third World. In their efforts to obtain more and more foreign aid, they deliberately presented an image of being unable to cope by themselves with the tasks of development.

Political élites may look to the international organizations in order to 'justify reform efforts in terms of what is being done elsewhere' (Suleiman and Waterbury, 1990, p. 17). However, as governments try to commit themselves to ambitious goals, pressure to reform within the political environment means that policy learning, according to Haas (1980, p. 377) 'may occur without a coherent intellectual understanding of causes and effects, and without a complete mastery of the means considered necessary and sufficient to attain the ends'. Haas adds that political ideologies will then act as 'simplifying mechanisms' to justify reform goals. 'Civil service curbing' then acquires political symbolism and the methods used take the appearance of classic scientific management. In this scenario, civil servants are reduced to 'managers' in the most technically limited meaning of the term. Although any policy transfer appears coercive, such reforms meet élite goals.

However, Kamensky (1996, p. 248) observes that 'the political value of reinvention ... is unclear' and he continues that 'the politics of reinvention are seen as less attractive because reinvention entails the distribution of authority' and 'it takes more than one term in office'. Kamensky (1996, p. 248) also argues that because the political value of reinvention is so vague, it should be differentiated from earlier attempts at structural public sector reforms. The basis of Kamensky's claim is the length of time taken to effect administrative change and, 'if it improves government too much', politicians lose capital for future campaigns. Also, as Pollitt (1995) pointed out, NPM is hard to evaluate, and so politicians are likely to distort the benefits of NPM implementation. If policy transfer has occurred, political élites 'for the most part are condemned to success or failure in terms of their impact within an individual state' (Wallace, 1996, p. 16). For policy transfer to occur, the aspirations of the recipient country have to match those of the donor. However, for élites faced with a pressing need for administrative reform, searching for ready-made solutions may appear akin to voluntary policy transfer.

Policy transfer may also occur by *diffusion*, where an enthusiastic management élite controls and spreads knowledge within an international policy culture. In the case of administrative reform, diffusion may be the result of proactive proponents of a particular administrative doctrine. International institutions have political agendas that are difficult to ignore and, as Held and McGrew (1993, p. 272) argue, 'these organisations are at the centre of a continual conflict over the control and direction of global policy', and have acquired entrenched authority over the years. Friedman (1995, pp. 79–80) argues that a global class structure has emerged, 'an international élite made up of top diplomats, government ministers, aid officials and representatives of international organisations such as the UN ... forming a kind of cultural cohort'. Academia can be added to this list: for instance, *The Economist* (1995) reported how Michael Porter of the Harvard Business School 'has been asked by governments from Portugal to Colombia to do for them what he and his kind have done for private enterprise'. Policy diffusion is difficult to test empirically simply because there is 'easy access to information about what other governments are doing' (Rose, 1993, p. 3).

Is policy transfer simply a process of policy *convergence*? Convergence theory is 'the idea that whatever their political economies, whatever their unique cultures and histories, the "affluent" societies become more alike in both social structure and ideology' (Wilensky, 1975). Kamensky (1996, p. 248) argued that 'the reinventing government movement originated simultaneously in the early 1980s in foreign countries, as part of their attempts to reposition their economies to cope with increasing global competition'. The convergence thesis assumes an end to ideology in explaining the crucial differences in public policy between countries; as Castles (1982, p. 27) argues, the convergence thesis postulates 'an increasing similarity in society, state and politics'. Thus, policy convergence may occur independently of policy transfer activity. However, in the case of NPM, Hood (1991, p. 8) argued that part of NPM's appeal was its apparent ideological neutrality – 'an apolitical framework', or an applicable and neutral tool-kit that appears attractive as governments engage in searches for policy solutions.

Globalization – Again?

Evans and Davies (1996) critically examined Dolowitz and Marsh's (1996) attempt to distil the policy transfer literature and question whether policy transfer activity is on the increase. If so, is it due to globalization processes or a long-term modernization process in the West? Farazmand (1994, p. 78) argues that an *invisible* (my emphasis) 'global bureaucracy' already exists consisting of international institutions such as the World Bank, IMF and USAID. The *visible* (my emphasis) global bureaucracy consists of the UN and its affiliated organizations. The role of the international organizations raises some theoretical issues about the relationships between globalizing processes, modernization and democratization.

In terms of public management, a key rationale for reform is 'modernization'. As Giddens (1990) observed, modernization is 'inherently globalising' and, arguably, modernization itself is a process of globalization. Modernity is open to interpretation; Walker (1996, p. 128) provides a prevailing view of modernization when he notes that 'the highest stage of development was defined in terms of political structures in industrial economy, and an associational/pluralist social structure – all characteristics of modernisation/ Westernisation', facilitated by social change. King (1995, p. 115), cited in Black (1966, p. 7) regards modernization as the 'political and social changes accompanying industrialization', or the idea that economic development breeds institutional convergence. Modernization can simply refer to improving the functions performed by the public sector.

Pressure to modernize their public sectors appears to force national governments into policy transfer activity, and international institutions offer exemplars and best practice to policy makers eager to learn. However, the looseness of the term 'modern' still causes analytical problems. As Friedman (1995, p. 80) argues, 'the World Bank can shift from all-out developmentalism to a serious support for tribal alternatives and ecosystem maintenance. It is not the Bank itself that is the source of either of these positions, which must be traced back ... to the specific identity space of "modernity" and its historical vacillations.' However, Heady (1996, p. 116) warns of the 'tendency to equate modernization with emulation of a few existing nation-states' and argues that it is often unnecessary to regard the West as a desirable exemplar. Riggs (1994, p. 38) argues that the American constitutional system is often regarded as an exemplar which, by institutionalizing a separation of powers, generates 'cross-pressures that severely hamper the capacity of any ... regime to control its bureaucracy', citing South Vietnam and South Korea as previous 'disasters'. The relationship between Westernization and modernization leads us to another facilitator of the transfer of NPM, democratization.

Democracy and New Public Management

NPM is a product of Western liberal democratic states. Linking NPM-type reforms to the consolidation of democratic structures appears a natural consequence of the deterministic link between economic development and political liberalization. Helgesen and Xing (1996, p. 96) argue that this theory holds in Eastern Europe, but a similar argument can be applied to Third World economic development. According to Przeworski and Limongi (1997, p. 157), the idea that 'modernization' equates with 'democracy' has, as a basic assumption, the theory that democratization is the final stage of modernization. As Przeworski and Limongi (ibid.) explain, 'modernization consists of a gradual differentiation and specialization of social structures from other structures and makes democracy possible'. The international organizations appear to be instrumental in establishing a link between modernization and democratization. For instance, Williams and Young (1994, p. 86) commented on a World Bank (1989) report that stressed the importance of political renewal in the Sub-Saharan region. The report traced the growing concern with the management of the public sector in developing countries to the late 1980s and connected it with the apparent need for wider political change (World Bank, 1989, p. 5). 'Political renewal' means the creation of pluralistic institutional structures, including civil service reform, modelled on Western liberal democracies. Such requirements for reform were presented as being ideologically free, and as being essential for a modern state. These themes continue to be addressed by the World Bank (1997) in its latest prescriptions.

Alternatively, it is possible to argue that authoritarianism may have to come first as a stage in development which contradicts assertions that democratization is necessary in order to assist development. Helgesen and Xing (1996, p. 110) argue that East Asian élites see authoritarian government as a useful expedient for effective policy making while maintaining political stability. From their point of view, what a country needs at its initial developmental stage is 'discipline more than democracy', a view they apparently shared with a former director of the World Bank's Africa department. Although Cammack (1996, p. 47) regards political development theory as a 'project for the establishment of *liberal* capitalism in the developing world', he argues that 'the *postponement* of the introduction of democracy' was necessary until 'liberal *capitalism* was firmly established'. Heald (1992, p. 69) also argues that 'the international agencies are vulnerable to being portrayed as facilitators of a new colonialism based upon foreign capital rather than foreign administration'.

Are we aggrandizing the motives of the international organizations? The reform measures promoted in the 1980s appear to mirror the effects and efforts of some governments in the West in terms of merely reducing the size of the public sector and weakening its power over policy making rather than consciously reforming or modernizing it. The headquarters of the international organizations, based in the USA, were unlikely to remain immune in the 1980s from a local political climate charged by the New Right, armed with public choice theory. Biersteker (1995, p. 186) remarked that 'there was a pronounced interest in the willingness, especially on the part of the US government, to use the Fund and the Bank to force changes in developing-country economic policy during the early 1980s'. Othman and Maganya (1989a, p. 90) argue that the World Bank and IMF have managed to hide political ideology behind 'technocratic solutions'. For instance, Mosley et al.'s (1991, p. 65) remark that conditionality, 'the vehicle which the Bank chose as a means of changing the economic policies of LDC governments', is 'designed to ensure the execution of a *contract*' smacks of public choice theory. Also, the World Bank has framed the nature of the problem of the public sector in public choice terms (World Bank, 1992, p. 6; 1997, p. 10), undermining any suggestion that NPM-type reforms are neutral policy transfers. As Shamsul Haque (1996a, pp. 206–7) notes, 'among international agencies, the World Bank, IMF, the US Agency for International Development, and the British Overseas Development Agency have influenced Third World countries to adopt pro-market policies'.

FROM PRIVATIZATION TO NPM – WHAT IS BEING TRANSFERRED?

Privatization

A key problem with analysing the spread of NPM is its close relationship with privatization. Rationales for public sector reform, and hence privatization, are different in the developing world. Aylen (1987) argues that it is pragmatism and expediency, rather than politics, that are the main motives of privatization in developing countries, and that outside pressures and force of circumstance are more important than domestic pressures and ideologies. As Heald (1992, p. 63) points out, 'the international dissemination of privatisation is sometimes characterized by a combination of aggressive ideology and of naive managerialism'. Yet it is the pro-privatization stance of the international organizations that provided the impetus to wider managerial reforms in the 1990s. Indeed, as Heald (1992, p. 68) remarks, 'privatization should not be seen as a free-standing policy, but rather as one set of instruments within a package of policy reform'. The anticipation of privatization requires public organizations to acquire the functional ingredients of a business to survive in a competitive environment. The appearance of NPM techniques may simply be the organizational prelude to eventual privatization. For example, in the UK, executive agencies all face the possibility of privatization at the review of their framework documents and thus are required to possess the functional ingredients of a business.

Ikenberry (1990, p. 89) examined the internationalization of privatization and argued that analysis 'simply in terms of national governments responding to the interests and power of domestic groups' failed to explain privatization. Rather, privatization can only be understood by taking into account the international environments that influence policy, including the economic, the technological and the political. Similar conclusions can be drawn for the spread of NPM. Although one cannot simply assume that where one finds privatization, one finds NPM, these observations can be applied to the spread of NPM, especially when public sector organizations prepare for privatization. In Britain, the first appearance of NPM was explained initially as the product of domestic pressure for the control of public spending, but later strains of NPM have antecedents abroad including quality management (Japan, the USA) and agencification (Sweden).

Privatization may appear more attractive to developing countries than managerial reforms because the equity costs are relatively small compared to those of the broader structural adjustment process, or large-scale administrative reform (Bienen and Waterbury, 1989, p. 617). As Mosley et al. (1991, p. 144) argue, 'changes in prices are administratively easy whereas changes in the organisation and operation of institutions are administratively very difficult'. McGowan (1994, p. 34) argued that the World Bank has only ever been interested in competition and efficiency, yet 'nonetheless the image of the World Bank's role in fostering privatisation persists'. Farazmand (1994, p. 76) noted that the general thrust of reform proposals was geared towards 'changes in the organisational structure and behaviour .... directed more toward serving the private market sector than toward serving the general public'. The consumerist emphasis of later NPM reform in the West remains largely absent in the developing world. If the message of the 1980s was privatization, then the message of the 1990s is 'good governance'.

'Good Governance' and the Role of International Organizations

Governance is a word that has become increasingly popular in the field of public administration, but a fuller discussion of its meaning is beyond the scope of this chapter. However, its use by the international organizations indicates a shift in emphasis from economic to political management in affecting policy outcomes. The shift towards issues of governance and a gradual reassessment of the usefulness of privatization as an economic policy in developing countries began in the late 1980s. In the words of World Bank staff, 'governance is a common theme now partly because public organizations in many countries seem to be ineffective and too expensive' (World Bank, 1991, p. 3). Stallings (1995, p. 13) noted that 'some cracks were beginning to appear in the consensus' of 'a reduced government role in the economy (deregulation and privatization)' and that policy recommendations started to appear unsophisticated. The World Bank (1991, p. x) had emphasized cost-containment in the 1980s, which was reflected in loan conditions. In one extreme example, a redundancy exercise in Ghana helped to shed nearly 40 per cent of civil servants by May 1987 (Jonah,1989, p. 144).

The watershed was arguably the publication of a report in 1989 (World Bank, 1989) entitled *A Framework for Capacity Building in Policy Analysis and Economic Management in sub-Saharan Africa* and, in particular, the introduction of adjustment lending that led the Bank to focus on 'improvements in overall public sector management, and the improvement of sectorwide institutions and service delivery' (World Bank, 1992, p. 12). Such a reassessment clearly meant that the international institutions were starting to doubt the efficacy of their earlier recommendations (Stallings, 1995, p. 13). The World Bank reinforced this view by arguing that 'the typical developing country has tried to do too much through the public sector' (World Bank, 1991, p. ix). Now the Bank saw its role as encouraging the state 'to manage less, but manage better' (World Bank, 1991, p. ix) but without clear exhortations to privatize. The latest World Development report (World Bank, 1997) simply calls for more competition.

Another key theme running through World Bank prescriptions is to improve the policy making capacity of governments. While commenting on the globalizing nature of the World Bank, Walker (1996, p. 124) argues that the main ingredients of the World Bank's structural adjustment project were financial management, accountability and efficiency reforms, prompted 'by the poor compliance record of developing countries implementing Structural Adjustment programmes'. Also, administrative capacity was deemed essential for economic growth. In particular, 'civil service reform consists of two complementary efforts: short-term measures to contain costs and medium-term programs to strengthen personnel management and improve the efficiency and effectiveness of public agencies' (World Bank, 1991, p. x). The Bank has achieved these aims through the use of 'technical assistance, supplied by specially recruited personnel or by Bank staff themselves, training, and studies and policy dialogue through the Bank's analytical and sector work' (World Bank, 1991, p. xi).

NPM: AN INAPPROPRIATE POLICY TRANSFER?

Although World Bank prescriptions appear to be changing, does this mean that policy transfers are becoming more appropriate to their administrative contexts? We need to consider that 'policy transfer is also dependent upon the transferring political system possessing the political, bureaucratic and economic resources to implement the policy' (Dolowitz and Marsh, 1996, p. 354). Furthermore, Hood's fourth 'acceptance factor' for NPM (Hood, 1991, pp. 7–8) was a 'set of special social conditions ... in the developed countries', yet these conditions remain largely absent in the developing world. Therefore, the surprise is that NPM policy transfer occurs at all until there is 'a shift to a more white-collar, socially heterogeneous population less tolerant of "statist" and uniform approaches in public policy'(Hood, 1991, p. 8).

Where policy transfer is coercive, the effects are inevitably negative. For developing countries, it may result in 'inappropriate administration' based on an 'expatriate model which has been developed in the context of big business, industrial society and metropolitan government' (Smith, 1992, p. 17). Also, Heald (1992, p. 72) acknowledges the dangers of coercive transfer when he comments: 'it should be a question of learning rather than of direct transplanting: differences in political culture, levels of economic development, country size and bureaucratic capabilities will determine which reforms are feasible'. A supporter of this view is Anyaoku (1989, p. 18), who remarks that 'experience has shown that there is validity in questioning the extent to which all the "policy conditions" set out in stabilisation and adjustment programmes should be instigated by external agencies and thrust upon reluctant governments'.

Is it too simplistic to regard the relationship between the international organizations and developing countries as damaging? Heald (1992, p. 69) claims their role can be positive as they are in a position to pool experience and knowledge (voluntary policy transfer), although he points out that it is difficult to find exemplars among the developing nations. To simply emulate 'the actions of an exemplar' (Bennett, 1991, p. 36) is problematic in that it may lead to inappropriate policy transfers, irrespective of the economic status of the recipient country. Onimode (1989, p. 30) points out that 'the Fund and Bank claim that they do not impose anything – countries run to them and invite them to become involved in their economies'. Harris (1989, p. 23) argues that the power of the IMF and World Bank is derived from operating on a 'country-by-country basis. Therefore, assisting individual countries appears as if it were the principal objective.' The problem remains that the involvement of these organizations raises the question of the ability of individual national governments to improve public management in ways suited to their own political and institutional contexts.

In a discussion of the influence of American public administration overseas, Riggs (1994, p. 21) argues that concepts of 'limited bureaucratic power'
and the 'role of professionals' are 'irrelevant' to the needs of other countries
since they reinforce the myth of the politics–administration dichotomy. This
myth continues to taint the advice of public management specialists overseas.
Farazmand (1994, p. 76) adds that 'the administrative reforms that have taken
place or will take place around the globe have mainly corresponded with
objectives of marketization, privatization and democratization'. Furthermore,
Farazmand (ibid., p. 77) adds that 'these reforms will be dominated by US
values and norms. Consequently, the dependency of developing countries on
the West will be likely to be perpetuated, leading to a "neo-colonization" of
the developing nations .... ' If we accept the claims of Farazmand and Riggs,
then the type of NPM that is being transferred is much more narrowly based
on American public administration than a broader market model.

Transferring NPM also presumes recipient Western-style bureaucracies. As
Helgesen and Xing (1996, p. 107) argue, 'contrary to the Western political
heritage East Asian political traditions encourage people to trust the moral
example and good-will of public officials ... focusing on relationship rather
than the individual (western thinking) makes hierarchy and authority inescapable basic phenomena in political thinking'. If we consider East Asia, it has
managed to reach 'a high level of economic development and status in the
global community' and consequently 'the magnetism of the Western/Ameri-
can model is gradually losing power' (Helgesen and Xing, 1996, p. 115). As
Shamsul Haque (1996b, p. 315) notes, 'most Third World regimes introduced
administrative changes based on western knowledge and experience rather
than indigenous contexts and thus, such changes reinforced rather than sup-
planted the colonial legacy' (see also Subramaniam, 1990). The World Bank
(1992, p. 11) blames the colonial legacy for poor development management,
but, as Shamsul Haque goes on to argue,

> the modern administrative framework adopted by Third World nations is hardly
> compatible with various dimensions of their political context. Foremost, the po-
> litico-ideological tradition of western liberal democracy, within which modern
> bureaucracy has evolved, hardly exists in Third World nations. Such a liberal
> democratic context, which assumes the neutrality, anonymity and impartiality of
> the administrative apparatus and its accountability to elected politicians, is either
> absent or fragile in most Asian, African and Latin American countries. (1996b,
> p. 319)

A further consideration put forward by Ansari (1996, p. 67) is the distinction between public administration and 'development administration', which
is that 'public administration tasks are static and highly bureaucratic, whereas
those of development administration are constantly increasing and varying'.

Moreover, Cammack (1996, p. 53) also comments that in the developing world, bureaucracies 'tended to be over-developed in relation to other parts of the political system'. Farazmand (1994, p. 76) appears to concur by predicting that

> more bureaucratization will likely characterize the organisational structure of developing countries. Their administrators and the bureaucratic cultures will have to internalize the exogenous, imported values and norms of administration and culture. Conversely, they will have to externalise their indigenous cultural and institutional values of their administrative systems. One manifestation of this externalisation tendency is, and will be, the internalisation of Western organizational values of rationality ... values associated with the Weberian ideal-type bureaucracy.

If we consider more bureaucratization to be an unintended consequence of policy transfer, then reforms based on American public administration, when grafted on to non-Western bureaucratic cultures, result in inappropriate policy transfer. In turn, inappropriate policy transfer becomes a major cause of policy failure.

CONCLUSIONS

Public sector managers now have to think internationally, but policy transfer analysis only goes some of the way in explaining the spread or internationalization of NPM. Cooper (1995, p. 187) argues that 'few of the reforms do anything to relieve developing countries from the pressures of international debt challenges', and that 'many systems remain more or less the same as before with slight modifications'. The internal dynamics of an individual nation's political system are capable of modifying transferred policies and programmes. If policy transfer occurs, its impacts are slight and the role of the international organizations is difficult to quantify. A key problem in assessing their influence is to isolate them from other variables that influence administrative reform. As Kamensky (1996, p. 249) argued, 're-inventing government is only one piece of a larger re-examination of governance in response to changing demographics, technologies, global competition, and public expectations'.

Where the notion of policy transfer is useful is in the importance it ascribes to an international policy culture which diffuses knowledge and information to both political and administrative élites. The international organizations act as mechanisms that increase the flow of knowledge in given policy areas, and thus the international arena has the potential to become 'an extension of or an alternative to the state arena' (Kapteyn, 1995, cited in Wallace, 1996). This takes us to the grand claims of those proclaiming the end of the nation-state, yet it is only individual governments that can in practice reform their administrations.

Further research may consider the incentives on offer to élites that encourage policy transfers. For political leaders, transferring NPM may help to bolster wider political support, but the symbolic impact may be of greater value, even if expressed in crude terms such as bureaucrat bashing. Also, bureaucratic élites may enjoy more tangible benefits as a result of NPM implementation if they are presented with the opportunity to 'bureau shape' (Dunleavy, 1991). To thoroughly understand why NPM is accepted in unpromising or inappropriate political contexts, we need to account for the incentives, both perceived and real, offered to policy makers that go beyond the conditions and prescriptions suggested or imposed by international organizations.

REFERENCES

Ansari, S.J. (1996), 'Development administration and bureaucracy in the contemporary Arab Gulf', *Indian Journal of Public Administration*, **42** (1), 66–76.

Anyaoku, E. (1989), 'Keynote address: the impact of IMF–World Bank policies on the people of Africa', in Onimode (1989).

Aucoin, P. (1990), 'Administrative reform in public management: paradigms, principles, paradoxes, and pendulums', *Governance*, **3** (2), 115–37.

Aylen, J. (1987), 'Privatization in developing countries', *Lloyds Bank Review*, No. 163, pp. 15–30.

Bennett, C. (1991), 'How states utilize foreign evidence', *Journal of Public Policy*, **11** (1), 31–54.

Bienen, H. and Waterbury, J. (1989), 'The political economy of privatization in developing countries', *World Development*, **17** (5), 617–32.

Biersteker, T. (1995), '"The Triumph" of liberal economic ideas', in B. Stallings (ed.), *Global Change, Regional Response,* Cambridge: Cambridge University Press.

Black, C.E. (1966), *The Dynamics of Modernization. A Study in Comparative History*, London: Harper & Row, p. 7.

Cammack, P. (1996), 'Domestic and international regimes for the developing world: the doctrine for political development' in P. Gummett (ed.), *Globalization and Public Policy*, Cheltenham: Edward Elgar.

Castles, F. (ed.) (1982), *The Impact of Parties: Politics and Policies in Democratic Capitalist States*, London: Sage.

Cooper, P. (1995), 'Toward the hybrid state: the rise of environmental management in a deregulated and re-engineered state', *International Review of Administrative Sciences*, **61** (2), 185–200.

Dolowitz, D. and Marsh, D. (1996), 'Who learns what from whom: a review of the policy transfer literature', *Political Studies*, **44** (2), 343–57.

Dunleavy, P. (1991), *Democracy, Bureaucracy and Public Choice*, London: Harvester Wheatsheaf.

The Economist (1995), 'Gurus in government', *The Economist*, 20 May.

Evans, M. and Davies, J. (1996), 'Beyond description: legitimating policy transfer analysis in political science', paper presented to the Conference on Policy Transfer, University of Birmingham (October).

Farazmand, A. (1994), 'The New World Order and global public administration', in J.-C. Garcia-Zamor and R. Khator (eds), *Public Administration in the Global Village,* Westport, CT: Praeger.

Ferlie, E. et al. (1996), *The New Public Management in Action*, Oxford: Oxford University Press.

Fox, C. and Miller, H. (1995), *Postmodern Public Administration*, London: Sage.

Friedman, J. (1995), 'Global system, globalization and the parameters of modernity', in M. Featherstone, S. Lash and R. Robertson (eds), *Global Modernities*, London: Sage, pp. 69–90.

Garcia-Zamor, J.-C. (1994), 'Neoteric theories for development administration in the New World Order' in J.-C. Garcia-Zamor and R. Khator (eds), *Public Administration in the Global Village*, Westport, CT: Praeger, pp. 101–20.

Giddens, A. (1990), *The Consequences of Modernity*, Cambridge: Polity Press.

Haas, E. (1980), 'Why collaborate? Issue-linkage and international regimes', *World Politics*, **32** (3), 357–406.

Harris, L. (1989), 'The Bretton Woods system and Africa', in B. Onimode (ed.), *The IMF, the World Bank and the African Debt, Volume 1: the Economic Impact,* London: Zed Books.

Heady, F. (1996), *Public Administration: A Comparative Perspective* (5th edn), New York: Marcel Dekker.

Heald, D. (1992), 'The relevance of privatization to developing economies', in B. Smith (ed.), *Progress in Development Administration,* Chichester: John Wiley & Sons, pp. 59–74.

Held, D. and McGrew, A. (1993), 'Globalization and the liberal democratic state', *Government and Opposition*, **28** (2), 261–88.

Helgesen, G. and Xing, L. (1996), 'Democracy or *minzhu,* the challenge of Western versus East Asian notions of good government', *Asian Perspective*, **20** (1), 95–124.

Hoggett, P. (1994), 'A new management in the public sector', in R. Smith and J. Raistrick (eds), *Policy and Change*, Bristol: SAUS, pp. 15–38.

Holmes, M. and Shand, D. (1995), 'Management reform: some practitioner perspectives on the past ten years', *Governance*, **8** (4), 551–78.

Hood, C. (1991), 'A public management for all seasons?', *Public Administration*, **69** (1), 3–19.

Hood, C. (1995), 'Contemporary public management: a new global paradigm', *Public Policy and Administration*, **10** (2), 104–17.

Ikenberry, G. (1990), 'The international spread of privatization policies: inducements, learning and policy "bandwagoning"', in E. Suleiman and J. Waterbury (eds), *The Political Economy of Public Sector Reform and Privatization*, Oxford: Westview, pp. 88–110.

Jonah, K. (1989), 'The social impact of Ghana's adjustment programme', in B. Onimode (ed.), *The IMF, the World Bank and the African Debt, Volume 2*, London: Zed Books.

Kamensky, J. (1996), 'Role of the "reinventing government" movement in federal management reform', *Public Administration Review*, **56** (3), 247–55.

King, A. (1995), 'The times and spaces of modernity (or who needs postmodernism?)', in M. Featherstone, S. Lash and R. Robertson (eds), *Global Modernities*, London: Sage, pp. 108–23.

Lane, J.-E. (1993), *The Public Sector*, London: Sage.

Luard, E. (1990), *The Globalization of Politics,* New York: New York University Press.

Lynn, L. (1996), 'The new public management as an international phenomenon: a skeptical view', paper prepared for presentation at the New Public Management in International Perspective conference, St Gallen, Switzerland (July).

McGowan, F. (1994), 'The internationalisation of privatisation' in T. Clarke (ed.), *International Privatisation: Strategies and Practices*, Berlin: Walter de Gruyter.

Martin, B. (1993), *In the Public Interest?*, London: Zed Books.

Metcalfe, L. (1994), 'International policy co-ordination and public management reform', *International Review of Administrative Sciences*, **60** (2), 271–90.

Moran, M. and Wood, B. (1996), 'The globalization of health care policy?', in P. Gummett (ed.), *Globalization and Public Policy*, Cheltenham: Edward Elgar, pp. 125–42.

Mosley, P., Harrigan, J. and Toye, J. (1991), *Aid and Power: the World Bank and Policy-based Lending,* London: Routledge.

OECD (1993), *Managing with Market-Type Mechanisms*, Paris: OECD.

Onimode, B. (1989), 'IMF and World Bank programmes in Africa', in B. Onimode (ed.), *The IMF, the World Bank and the African Debt, Volume 1: the Economic Impact,* London: Zed Books.

Othman, H. and Maganya, E. (1989), 'Tanzania: the pitfalls of the structural adjustment programme', in Onimode (1989).

Peters, B. (1996), *The Future of Governing: Four Emerging Models,* Lawrence, KA: University Press of Kansas.

Pollitt, C. (1995), 'Justification by works or by faith: evaluating the new public management', *Evaluation*, **1** (2), 133–54.

Przeworski, A. and Limongi, F. (1997), 'Modernization: theories and facts', *World Politics*, **49** (2), 155–83.

Riggs, F. (1994), 'Global forces and the discipline of public administration', in J.-C. Garcia-Zamor and R. Khator (eds), *Public Administration in the Global Village*, Westport, CT: Praeger, pp. 17–44.

Rose, R. (1993), *Lesson Drawing in Public Policy*, New Jersey: Chatham House.

Shamsul Haque, M. (1996a), 'Public service under challenge in the age of privatization', *Governance*, **9** (2), 186–216.

Shamsul Haque, M. (1996b), 'The contextless nature of public administration in Third World countries', *International Review of Administrative Sciences*, **62** (3), 315–29.

Smith, B. (1992), 'Introduction' in B. Smith (ed.), *Progress in Development Administration,* Chichester: John Wiley & Sons, pp. 1–21.

Stallings, B. (1995), 'Introduction: global change, regional response', in B. Stallings (ed.), *Global Change, Regional Response*, Cambridge: Cambridge University Press, pp. 1–30.

Subramaniam, V. (1990), 'Conclusion', in V. Subramaniam (ed.), *Public Administration in the Third World*, Westport, CT: Greenwood Press, pp. 385–402.

Suleiman, E. and Waterbury, J. (1990), 'Introduction: analyzing privatization in industrial and developing countries', in E. Suleiman and J. Waterbury (eds), *The Political Economy of Public Sector Reform and Privatization*, Boulder, CO: Westview Press, pp. 1–21.

Walker, J.-A. (1996), 'From Riggs to World Bank: recurring themes in development administration', *Indian Journal of Public Administration*, **42** (2), 119–31.

Wallace, H. (1996), 'Politics and policy in the EU: the challenge of governance', in H. Wallace and W. Wallace (eds), *Policy-Making in the European Union*, Oxford: Oxford University Press, pp. 3–36.

Wilensky, H. (1975), *The Welfare State and Equality*, London: University of California Press.

Williams, D. and Young, T. (1994), 'Governance, the World Bank and liberal theory', *Political Studies*, **42** (1), 84–100.

World Bank (1989), *A Framework for Capacity Building in Policy Analysis and Economic Management in sub-Saharan Africa*, Washington, DC: World Bank.

World Bank (1991), *The Reform of Public Sector Management: Lessons from Experience*, Washington, DC: World Bank Country Economics Dept, World Bank.

World Bank (1992), *Governance and Development,* Washington, DC: World Bank.

World Bank (1997), *World Development Report (Summary)*, Washington, DC: World Bank.

Wright, V. (1994), 'Reshaping the state: the implications for public administration', *West European Politics*, **17** (3), 102–37.

5. Public management for social inclusion

Maureen Mackintosh

SOCIAL EXCLUSION AND THE ROLE OF GOVERNMENT

'Social exclusion', a concept with a strong Western cultural bias in its early usage, is increasingly being employed and reworked by researchers in low- and middle-income countries. In industrialized countries, research has particularly focused on the exclusion brought by long-term unemployment from access to the goods and services associated with citizenship. A secondary theme in the literature on social exclusion in Europe has been the actual and potential impact of a widely signalled shift from universalist to targeted welfare provision (Brown and Crompton, 1994).

Despite this culturally specific origin of the concept of social exclusion, researchers from very different economic and cultural contexts, which lack the history of high average incomes and welfare states, have found the concept useful. Kaijage and Tibaijuka (1996), for example, in a Tanzanian study, find the concept attractive because it combines an emphasis on understanding individuals' experience of marginalization through social isolation and economic deprivation with an investigation of the context of that marginalization: the fragmentation of social relations, breakdown of social cohesion and emergence of new social and economic divisions.

Since, as Kaijage and Tibaijuka note, any analysis of this kind presupposes underlying concepts of social order and disorder, an analysis of social exclusion must be context-specific. The Tanzanian researchers stress (p. 183) the strong relationship between acute deprivation and a lack of access to the 'economic and cultural resources', notably land, education, and family, kinship and community support systems, that allow people to obtain and employ cash. They emphasize particularly the crisis of the extended family support systems and the failure of government social provision to replace them.

In the very different economic context of Thailand, Phongpaichit and fellow researchers (Phongpaichit et al., 1996) also found that the concept of social exclusion could be reinterpreted in relevant ways. They argue that a historically exclusionary culture and power structure (male-biased, Thai-national and centred on Bangkok) has interacted with severe competition for resources to create new patterns of exclusion. Their examples are small farmers losing land rights in forests; low-paid women workers made redundant without access to retraining; and slum dwellers excluded from land and homes. They trace the role of government departments and business organizations in reinforcing exclusion, and study the organized resistance of excluded groups.

Both studies consider the extent to which changing roles of government influence the identified patterns of social exclusion, and both argue for the need to redress and reorganize the relation between the state and its citizens into a format more appropriate to the reduction of social exclusion. The Thai researchers see the historic and actual role of government as a monopolistic one, in which resources are monopolized by the few. Arguing that a general lack of resources is not the key constraint in the fast-growing Thai economy, they propose that a mix of direct action by the excluded, and decentralization of administration and powers of taxation, is key to greater social inclusion. They argue that, despite the scope for voluntary action, 'most countries will have to rely on some form of action by government to secure the inclusion of disadvantaged groups' (Phongpaichit et al., 1996, p. 115).

The Tanzanian researchers, in a very poor and aid-dependent state, but one with a history of attempts at widespread social provision, stress the importance of much wider access to education, skills and capital resources, alongside more effective social safety nets and support for families and communities in acute distress. The authors recognize the failings of Tanzanian would-be universalist provision of public services well before the economic crisis of the 1980s, and argue for a 'partnership between government, the donor community, non-governmental organisations and the families themselves' (Kaijage and Tibaijuka, 1996, p. 193) as key to a move towards inclusion of the severely disadvantaged.

The Tanzanian and Thai researchers therefore analyse public services and government policy as both a reflection of inequality and a sphere for change. This perspective is found in the European literature, not so much in the work on social exclusion[1] as in the concept of a 'social settlement' developed by social policy researchers with a focus on social division (Williams, 1992; Lewis, 1996; see also Mackintosh, 1996a). In this perspective, the state builds its behaviour on the social structure of society, reproducing within public services, for example, many of the inequalities of the private sector. It also builds in assumptions about 'proper' private social relations. For example, European welfare states were constructed upon assumptions about how families should be composed, and the unpaid services that women, especially, should provide within them. And they are all built on concepts of nationality and citizenship, concepts that are invariably exclusionary along 'racial' lines. In that sense, the working relationships in public services are the bearers of the class, gender and ethnic divisions of the society of which they are a part.[2]

However, public services and the activities of the state are also a terrain for challenging division, and this too forms part of the social settlement notion. The enormous redistribution resulting from the universalizing of health and education services in Europe tends sometimes to be forgotten beside the evidence of the (considerable) limits on equality of access.[3] And the universalist notions underlying the generalization of welfare provision also provide a language in which to protest. Excluded groups can and do invoke the principles of the system to claim inclusion.

From this perspective, government and public services must play a key role in addressing social exclusion, not least because they are part of the problem. Public policy and provision do not form a 'box' separate from the rest of society; they both reflect society's divisions and provide a stage for challenging them. That kind of challenge has to come from 'the public' in another sense: the excluded themselves, and those who campaign for or represent them, a broader public opposed to a fissured society. Hence, addressing social exclusion can only happen through a (partly conflictual) process on the public stage, involving the government and those governed; the public services providers and their users; those in power and the excluded.

This is where public management comes in. In this chapter, I mean by 'public management' the process by which activity is organized and directed in the public sector of direct service provision and in the wider public interest sphere,[4] whether by people called managers or not, including the accountability and legitimacy of those doing the directing. My objective is to consider how the 'new public management' (NPM) may fit into, or conflict with, efforts to overcome social exclusion. In doing so, I hope to learn from the contextual and cultural sensitivity of the Tanzanian and Thai researchers. This chapter presents a highly context-specific analysis of some ways in which the new public management can reinforce social exclusion. It then argues that there are reasons to suppose, from this case study, that the new public management is not, in other contexts too, simply a way of doing public administration better, but may impede the design of a more inclusive public sphere.

REPRESENTATIONS OF PUBLIC MANAGEMENT

Every now and again there is a burst of political activity around our basic understandings, or representations, of the role of government and the state. One such burst happened in many European countries after 1945, in the consolidation of inclusive, social insurance-based concepts of what became known as welfare states. Another happened in Britain (with parallels elsewhere, including the USA) in the 1980s and 1990s, with the transformation of public administration into 'public management', and what has become known as the rise of 'managerialism' in the public sphere (Pollitt, 1993; Clarke and Newman, 1997). These key representations become part of popular understanding: the health service manager, for example, has become a subject of soap opera TV in Britain (Clarke, 1996).

A third burst of reinterpretation has been associated with the proposals by multilateral and bilateral agencies for reform of public administration and governance in less industrialized countries since the mid-1980s. This effort has drawn heavily on the NPM framework of efficiency targets, contracting and competition among service providers, while laying a specific emphasis on managing a fiscal squeeze and reduction in state services, and the development of targeting and safety nets to mitigate the social effects of structural adjustment (Mackintosh, 1995; Vivian, 1995).

The rise of the new public management ideas in the West has been associated with sharp increases in inequality and exclusion. A similar historical association exists with sharply worsening deprivation in low-income countries. The driving forces of social exclusion in both cases have been economic crisis: the collapse of near full employment in the West; debt and economic and fiscal crisis in low-income countries. The new public management framework is proposed in both contexts as an appropriate response, aimed at lowering expectations of governmental response, legitimating a rising reliance on voluntarism, and organizing a move to more targeted benefits.

Within the new public management model, however, there is an equivocation around the notion of management agency, with implications for managers' experience and hence their behaviour. The core distinction in the model between policy making and operational management, plus the political themes of relative social passivity and a few well-targeted interventions, imply that public management is an instrumental activity. Managers' aims are thus technocratic: efficiency and effectiveness in meeting restricted objectives.

However, there are also other discourses of new public management. In Britain and the USA, writers promote the reformed system in terms of enterprise, local responsiveness and diversity (an extreme is Osborne and Gaebler, 1992). The idea of managerial 'enterprise' lies behind the creation of opted-out providers and autonomous profit centres within public services (Pollitt et al., 1997), and is associated with promotion of choice by clients and providers, and acceptance of the associated inequality. In the low-income country context, multilateral policy documents have long argued for reform in a language of decentralization and local participation (World Bank, 1989), and have now added a stronger emphasis on client surveys and participation (World Bank, 1997).

These competing discourses can create profound confusion. On the one hand, managers are 'agents', in the sense of working on behalf of political 'principals', and their tendencies to work for themselves instead need to be sharply constrained by performance indicators. On the other hand, managers are 'change agents', principals in their own right, running autonomous organizations and responsible for addressing local needs.

How do these changed structures and the associated confusions influence social inclusion or exclusion? I go on to argue that, in the very specific social and cultural context of English social care provision, the new public management has tended to reinforce social exclusion, despite a rhetoric of decentralization and responsiveness. The arguments put forward are in good part about *representation*: about what people think is right, and who they think they are, and how they understand their world. They also focus on the link between social division within the public sector and division outside it.

PUBLIC MANAGEMENT REFORM IN SOCIAL CARE

The next four sections draw on the author's fieldwork on social care and home nursing provision in urban areas in Southern England and the English Midlands during 1993–6.[5] 'Social care' is a catch-all phrase for services such as bathing, basic physical care and domestic help, largely for elderly people. This is a service context where there has been time to see the effects of the new public management model working themselves out in practice.

The reforms to the National Health Service and the shift in funding of social care to local authorities in the early 1990s in England and Wales were billed as aiming for a seamless service that helped people to stay at home when they became frail. The resultant organization of 'community care' (a much contested representation of the reformed system) was along NPM lines: capped cash budgets managed by managers, and a separation of purchasers (those who decided how the cash was spent) from providers (those who spent it). There was a major exception to that separation (primary doctors could spend their budgets on their own activities as well as those of others) but other professionals were supposed either to assess needs and set priorities or to provide services.

Each argument that follows is illustrated with brief narratives. Some are my accounts of outcomes of a piece of research; some are the accounts of others. The narrative form is chosen to emphasize that these are my and others' interpretations of what is happening. Much of the research was done with a nurse and a sociologist, and reflects interdisciplinary views on what is occurring.

CLASS DIVISIONS IN SOCIAL CARE

The research in all the areas studied identified a social distancing effect of the new managerial structures. The purchaser/provider divide appeared to be reinforcing class division within the care services, by undervaluing the professionalism of lower-level professional staff and undermining their legitimacy in representing the needs of clients. As an example, Narratives 1 and 2 are drawn from a study of how seamless (or fragmented) the care service was for clients in one area, and of ways to improve integration of different types of care. Confidentiality excludes detail about context.

Narrative 1

The clients in this study were vulnerable elderly people, and their carers often also elderly and vulnerable. They included, for example, an elderly couple, one of whom had just had a stroke. They needed a mix of nursing, rehabilitation and domestic help. Another was an elderly lady living alone with multiple health problems, needing nursing care, bathing, physical and domestic care. All three wanted to stay in their own homes. We visited clients, shadowed staff and talked to carers.

Several conclusions emerged. First, there was no effective integration of different types of care. Nursing and social care were managed by different authorities. Only in a severe crisis for an individual client (the collapse of a carer, say) did the different agencies' managers get (expensively) together. Second, there was a declining level of skill (and rising level of perceived risk) in the care provision. Basic nursing tasks were increasingly performed by untrained people, and there were a number of instances where these were done poorly, and health deterioration occurred that could have been prevented. Third, care was increasingly provided (as the government then required) by private agencies, and coordination with them was poor.

The system on the ground felt overstretched, unintegrated and risky, constantly in crisis response mode. The district nurses (nurses who visit people at home) and the social care workers had created in some localities a pragmatic informal collaboration, including some training and support by nurses of their social care colleagues, and the informal sharing of information. None of that informal collaboration was recognized higher up the various hierarchies, and the managers tended to know little of what other agencies did.

Narrative 2

The second narrative is about what we, the researchers, suggested to improve integration, and what happened next. We came with up three broad options.

The first two – more effective joint purchasing between health and social services and hiring link workers to pull different professionals together[6] – were both impeded by budgetary and legal constraints and professional divisions.

So our proposed option was: start at the bottom. Instead of trying to get doctors, social workers and managers to collaborate (an expensive proposition), try to build on the links between the people doing most of the care. Attach social carers to primary health care teams. Get the social care workers (who often see problems first) to be the link workers. Institute mutual training and information, designed at field level. Set up systems that support information exchange. Blur the boundaries. Let the nurses train and advise, and the social carers coordinate.

We took these ideas to a meeting of the managers of the two main authorities involved. And the point of this story is the hostility with which the ideas were initially viewed (though there has been some softening since). There appeared to be two main reasons for that hostility. First, the proposal did not fit the contracting structure. In that structure it is the budget holders who decide who is to have what. To delegate the integration down the line meant a loss of control, the wrong person doing a job, specifically a 'provider' rather than a 'purchaser' making allocation decisions.

The second reason created the tone of the meeting: the managers did not have sufficient respect for the social care staff to see them in the proposed role. Social care is a low-status job, and the proposal that links between two services could be built by these social care workers and their supervisors (often ex-social care workers themselves) was seen as improbable and inappropriate. Indeed, the head of social care in the local authority was not even invited to the meeting, despite the crucial role of the service in improving integration.

All this posed something of a paradox. The community care reforms should surely have raised the status of social care, since it is the service on which turns the whole objective of allowing frail people to stay at home. Yet the service felt fragmented, stressed and (worst of all) denigrated. The staff who had to make the new system work seemed even further than before from having leverage.

The interviews suggest that the reasons for the paradox lie in the complex interaction created by the reforms between contracting behaviour and the role and presumptions of those with managerial authority. Contracting has created a layer of managers employing a language of responsibility for need and responsiveness, but having no day-to-day responsibility for service delivery, and no contact either with clients or with those who actually care for clients. The structure in principle (but *not* of course in practice) excludes the lower-level caring staff from the day-to-day management of need. A proposal to create a stronger role for those care staff in integrating service provision was a threat to that managerial prerogative.

The new contracting hierarchy, by detaching some managers further from provision, has thereby reinforced deep class divisions within the working process. England has a discreditable tradition of treating lower-paid professional staff as *non*-professionals – as people doing a job, whose opinion is not asked. The contracting reforms have reinforced this by allying a rhetoric of response to need to a deliberate downgrading of the proper role of lower-tier professionals in responding to need in both health and social care.

This interpretation is supported by other research. For example, we observed that the active role of experienced district nurses working in a poor housing estate in identifying (and managing) need through local knowledge and networking was explicitly denigrated by managers who saw managing as something only *they* did. Managers were simultaneously demanding more of staff and excluding them further from decision making. The effect has been to cut off the care services from information, and to disempower field-level staff. This created two inter-related impacts on social exclusion: many of the care staff were themselves in insecure work and poorly paid; and they had decreasing scope to respond effectively to clients who were often poor and lacking in confidence.

EXPERTISE AND ADVOCACY

This distancing of public sector field staff from managing response to need is part of a more general loss of public sector expertise resulting from the purchaser/provider split and the move away from direct public provision. This is a less remarked-upon aspect of the privatization of public assets: many of those assets are in the form of human knowledge and expertise. And some of that human capital is ethical in content: commitment to outcomes, and the capacity to act as advocates for others. The result is a loss of public sector capacity and commitment to resist exclusionary processes.

The next two narratives[7] illustrate this point, drawing on the effects of the reforms in social care on social workers working with the elderly. Social workers had been given budgets, or their team leaders had, from which to buy care for people at home or to pay for places in nursing homes. They allocate limited resources according to need, while others do the providing.

Narrative 3

Officially the prescribed division of labour between social workers ('assessors') and care providers is quite clear (Audit Commission, 1992). Social workers assess potential clients; providers provide services for individuals to purchasers' specifications. Social workers, however, rely heavily in practice on the expertise of their public sector provider colleagues, and those in the voluntary sector too. Here are some interviewees talking.

> ... my guesswork on housework and things like that can be pretty off mark! ... Home Care [the in-house care service] will ... come back to us and say, you've under-estimated or you've over-estimated, can we change it? I would always say yes, because they're very experienced at doing that and I trust them. (A social worker)

> Social workers ... over-allocate. They say Mrs Bloggs needs an hour, we find we can perhaps do it in three quarters ... that is quarter of an hour to us, we will give it to another client. ... they have no review system ... they are relying on us to say someone doesn't really need it. (A voluntary sector provider manager)

Social workers knew their behaviour contradicted the purchaser/provider divide:

> 'You're partly treating your own provider as a purchaser, that is, the supervisors are wearing two hats?'
> 'Well, that's right.'

The more closely we looked at the logic of the supposed separation of purchasing and providing, the more it looked like an expensive fiction. 'Assessment' did not divide buyers from sellers. Assessors had no time to monitor the care in detail. The neat institutional division between buyers and sellers was an illusion, because it omitted relations with clients, and disguised the control of the provider over quality of provision. Worse, it denied (delegitimized) the relations of professional trust which are the only basis for sustaining the quality of care.

Social workers themselves saw their jobs as much as fighting for resources and services on behalf of clients as assessing clients. They saw less of their clients than before, however (because of the time spent on assessment), and their advocacy role could conflict with their budget management role.

Narrative 4

This is a story told by a social work director coping with the new system. He had a financial management problem: he had a ceiling on financial commitments to any particular external provider; therefore he needed to spread his 'buying' of services around a number of agencies. So his instructions to his staff had been: 'if you find you have a lot of contracts with one agency, find another agency to use. But don't pull back from normal professional practice.' So, as he put it, 'I thought we had that agreement.'

The same man also helped to care for a neighbour 'in the middle stages of Alzheimer's', and recently widowed. The neighbour received a mix of public sector social care, private sector home nursing care, and health service district nursing. Shortly after the departmental agreement referred to above, the director learned that a social worker had walked into his neighbour's house and said, 'Because of financial constraints we're going to have to change, we can't use [the current agency] any more.' The manager had then said to the director, 'We've arranged for another care agency to come in.'

> Now [the director went on], this is a lady with Alzheimer's; she already has three different carers. So why is she being destabilized in this way? The reason for the anecdote is to show, (a) how sensitive the financial management is, how scared people get, how they fail to understand fairly basic issues; and (b) how even social workers, these very caring individuals, are still so threatened by what is happening that they're prepared to do things that 6, well, 12 to 18 months ago, they would have challenged as a professional issue. They would have thought nothing of phoning me up and saying, are you really suggesting that we change the carers for this Alzheimer's client for some sort of financial contracting reason? You must be crazy; I will complain to the social workers' association, or whatever. But the thinking has changed a lot. I think people feel, er, a bit bullied ... somehow the new language and the new thinking is pushing out commitments to professional practice.

This narrative is one among many examples of the conflict between the professional as advocate and as allocator of resources, a conflict much sharpened by the reforms. The difficulty is that the clients in these situations are often not capable of being their own advocates, and there is therefore a risk of worsening exclusion. Professional care staff may often be poor advocates for the excluded and vulnerable; but managers are, emphatically, not better. Furthermore, the public management reforms also seek to delegitimize advocacy for individuals by local politicians, on the grounds that this is improper meddling in professional decisions.

TARGETING AND EXCLUSION

Most of the methods of implementation of the new public management ideas in the social sector involve target setting for the 'outputs' of individuals and agencies. Primary doctors, schools, hospitals, colleges – are all given targets and paid accordingly. These target setting processes have potentially exclusionary effects. In primary health care, doctors in England have increasingly been given targets in two ways. Doctors may be paid per patient (capitation fees), with targets to meet on patient care, for example, percentage of young children inoculated. Or they may be given budgets (as 'fundholders') to buy patient care from hospitals, or in some cases from themselves. Narrative 5[8] is about the resultant incentives.

Narrative 5

This is a non-fundholding GP (primary doctor) talking. He works in an inner city practice, in an area of very severe deprivation.

> Capitation fees are supposed to vary according to social circumstances, based on Jarman indicators of deprivation [a set of indicators such as poor housing combined into an overall deprivation score for an area]. But this is not enough to compensate for the much greater use of services in poor areas. My consultation time per patient is twice that of a GP in a richer area, and I have less time to do other things which bring in income. The census also greatly underestimates deprivation in some wards [because of unwillingness among the most deprived to fill in the census in 1991 for fear of the poll tax].

We went on to discuss the problems created if GPs are fundholders. A GP with a budget to spend has a strong incentive to refuse to take on people likely to have (or who already have) expensive illnesses. Since it is the poor, the disabled and the elderly who are the most expensive to treat, this sort of selection is exclusionary. Called 'cream skimming', there is much anecdotal evidence for its existence, though many GPs also resist these incentives for professional and ethical reasons. Nevertheless, the incentive structure helps to explain why most fundholders are in the better-off areas of the country, while doctors such as the inner city GP (for whom cream skimming is not an option) have resisted taking on budgets.

This exclusionary incentive effect of performance indicators is not limited to health care. In education, competition among schools for pupils based on exam results provides incentives for exclusion from school and discouragement of difficult or slow pupils. The tighter the monitoring of performance, the greater the exclusionary incentive. And some researchers identify a trend to tighter monitoring of increasingly specific targets: a recentralization of the reformed structures leaving lower-level, supposedly autonomous managers with little real freedom of action (Rouse, 1997).

INDIVIDUALIZATION AND VULNERABILITY

Finally, a representational shift to individualizing the relation of the individual to the public services in the new public management model can increase exclusion. In the new model, the public sector relates to people in two ways.

First, it treats them as a population, whose levels of need are predicted on the basis of consultation with people and organizations who seek to represent interest groups, and uses statistical indicators of need. Second, it then relates to people as individuals whose particular needs are assessed and may be provided for.

The final narrative is about one elderly man's puzzlement at his experience of the individualized relations between those who need services, and the providers.

Narrative 6

Mr J was in his seventies. He had recently suffered a stroke, and lost the use of his right arm. He walked with difficulty. Before the stroke he was working part time and had active hobbies. Now he needed both some nursing, and practical help such as shopping and cleaning. He had received a leaflet from the social services department of his local authority that explained how much he had to pay for care at home, since he was not poor. He filled in detailed forms about his income, and agreed to pay around £6 an hour for care.

Mr J wanted his care to be provided by the local authority services. He was puzzled because, instead of a public sector care worker arriving, he was given a list of private providers and told to phone one of them and arrange his own care. He was upset about this. As he saw it, 'I can pay but I still can't get the services.' He thought local authority care 'safer' and, above all, he would not have had to arrange the care himself. He saw the private providers as 'unknown' and felt very awkward and unsure about ringing them up, and about what sort of person would come. He was still uncertain, when we met him, what help he would actually manage to arrange.

As this narrative suggests, the individualization of the relationship between clients and providers can be hard on the most vulnerable, including those who are not poor. Individualization is a key tenet of the public management reforms: people should be treated by the public sector as *consumers*, not as clients or citizens or voters. Many public services staff have resisted the implied shift from a support role for those with needs towards a direct exchange relation between users and providers. But it is, as the narrative shows, built into the new managerial forms: no one had offered to make Mr J's phone call for him or to monitor the result.

The story points to the general problem that vulnerable people find it hard to deal with choice in the market for care. Researchers call these encounters 'unscripted' (Baldock and Ungerson, 1994): in times of vulnerability people simply do not know what they can or are supposed to do. Choice can be disempowering where information, confidence and consent are lacking (Barnes and Prior, 1996).

PUBLIC MANAGEMENT FOR SOCIAL INCLUSION

I have suggested four ways in which the internal organization of the public sector under a new public management regime may reinforce social exclusion. These were:

- a widening of class division within the public sector, excluding lower-level professionals from the management of need, to the potential detriment of vulnerable clients;
- a decline in public sector expertise, including professional resistance to exclusion, and a delegitimization of advocacy, that can also work to the detriment of the most vulnerable;
- an increase in centralized control through the use of performance indicators that provide an incentive to exclude the expensive, which frequently means the most deprived; and
- an individualization of the relation of users to public services, that can disempower the more vulnerable users who lack advocates.

I have illustrated each of these with narratives from fieldwork on community care in England. Despite the acute economic and social differences between country contexts and experiences of public management, I suggest that the arguments have wider purchase outside the British context for two reasons. First, each of the four trends draws on a core aspect of the new public management model: they are culturally specific forms of general processes, not cultural add-ons. The purchaser/provider divide that separates professional providers from the assessors of needs, 'the target setting', and the individualization of the service relations are core processes that will take different forms in other places, but are not likely to be absent. And second, the processes draw heavily on representations (of professionals as self-interested providers, of budget holders as managers assessing need, and of users as consumers) that are part of the 'package' as it is exported between contexts.

Indeed, the advocacy of new public management has centred on reframing public service activity in individualist economic language, with the explicit aim of cultural and organizational change. Hence the rather odd way in which public management reform has often been evaluated: in terms of success in achieving structural reform rather than policy outcomes (Clarke and Newman, 1997, p. 21). A recent evaluation of decentralization and the introduction of competition into education provision in Chile (Parry, 1997) provides an example, labelling the reform a success although it had 'not had the expected positive impact on education quality while it had a negative effect on equity in education' (p. 223). Gordon (1996), in a widely cited essay on governmental reform, similarly concentrates on structural change.

To develop a public management with social inclusion at its heart requires, I suggest, three key shifts in focus. First, we need to start from desired socioeconomic consequences, rather than structural change and immediate output targets. A comparative study of public provision and social exclusion in Europe (Deakin et al., 1995) similarly argues that the objective of social inclusion implies monitoring of welfare provision in terms of its impact on economic and social cohesion; it requires cost-effectiveness calculations to be long term, not short term; and requires democratic accountability for all provision.

The second shift in perspective is from the framework of targets, cost-effectiveness and retrenchment to the other pole of the new public management discourse: decentralization, participation and enterprise. The burgeoning literatures on social capital and co-production offer ways to think about more locally accountable and inclusive processes of social provision (Putnam, 1993; Ostrom, 1996; Brown and Ashman, 1996). The attraction of these concepts is that they focus on increasing production through local collaborative networks between patient and nurse, learner and teacher, user and engineer, rather than simply on resource allocation.

However, many of our interviewees emphasized that such collaboration is not compatible with a new public management structure which stresses competition for contracts on price, arms-length working relations, and output-based performance indicators. A collaborative approach to social provision needs to build up long-term working relationships between parts of the public sector and other organizations. To have the collaborative capacity to achieve this, the public sector needs professional confidence, distinctive expertise and an ability to think long term, all of which can be undermined by the competitive framework. It also needs local accountability, rather than the focus on top–down monitoring characteristic of the new public management in practice. (Geoff Wood, 1997, makes some similar points in his critique of the 'franchise state'.)

Local networks, however, can also be exclusionary. The third shift in perspective is to recognize the inequality at the heart of the public sector, and to treat this as part of the problem. This was the point of the social settlement idea introduced above: it offers a conceptual framework for government and public action that has inequality and negotiation at its core. If the public sphere is treated as a terrain for developing, fighting over, negotiating and rethinking social settlements, then the core elements of a public management for social inclusion seem to me to be the following.

Such a system must begin by accepting that inequality is reflected in government, and that exclusion is always therefore partly deliberated. The public sphere, especially under economic stress, deliberately marginalizes vulnerable groups. Government must therefore propagate inclusive notions of citizenship and access that can be appealed to by the excluded as evidence of injustice. Public management must rest on some universalist principles.

Second, the concept of 'capabilities' seems a good building block for inclusive public management. The Tanzanian and Thai studies of social exclusion both focus on enabling economic and social participation, through improved access to assets (including human capital) and also support for the excluded to develop 'voice', through participation and collective action. Redistributing assets and encouraging organized voice should be core themes in an inclusive public management. They contrast sharply with the core ideas of the new public management.

Third, if the argument of the chapter is accepted – that the new public management tends to reinforce exclusion because its *internal* structures are divisive – then this suggests the converse argument. Inclusive public management should seek to design socially inclusive institutions: not perfect, just more rather than less inclusive. This implies the encouragement of institutional and local cross-subsidy (as opposed to a sole emphasis on individual targeted support), such as cross-subsidy within local health care institutions in a form that limits the stigma attached to receiving support (Huff-Rouselle, 1993; Frenk, 1993; Kutzin and Barnum, 1992). This sort of semi-inclusive institution, in the form of voluntary hospitals and mutual societies, was one of the building blocks of European health systems, but has been downplayed in the new public management context.

If the social divisions are not narrower within public institutions than in the wider society, then the state's capacity to promote social inclusion is likely to be small. A fourth principle of inclusive public management follows from this: a public management organization that does not value, build on and develop the capacities of its lower-level professional staff who deal with the services' clients, cannot be inclusive. The importance of valuing front-line staff is much rehearsed in the management literature; I have added the observation that new public management methods can, despite the rhetoric, have quite the opposite effect.

One reason for the empowerment of lower-level staff concerns collaboration. Inclusive collaboration requires (this is my fifth point) advocates for that social inclusiveness within the public institutions. Collaboration between institutions needs to mix engagement (treating each other as 'insiders') with openness to scrutiny, and this involves a fight against class exclusiveness. Creating accountable insiders in acutely class-divided societies is difficult, and needs conscious institutional design (Hutton et al., 1996).

Sixth, an inclusive public management has to identify and support good public interest institutions where it finds them. The worst failings of the new public management have occurred where it has undermined existing social commitment and probity. The converse is also true. Institutional breaks from poor provision may be essential to establish more inclusive institutions. The new public management is far too prescriptive about institutional form. Inclusive institutional forms will vary enormously between contexts, though polarization of provision for rich and poor is unlikely to figure.

Finally, let me return to my early point about public management structures as necessarily bearers of the divisions of class, gender and 'race'. That the public sphere reflects these divisions is a sign of *inclusion*, not its opposite. We should *expect* an inclusive public sphere to be fairly messy and conflict-ridden, a focus for discontents. That is one of its most important functions. Access to public debate and a valuing of plurality and dispute are core elements of a socially inclusive process. Inclusive public management has to be prepared to make rods for its back.[9]

Kaijage and Tibaijuka, in the study with which I began, refer to the concept of the developmental state. This is an inclusive concept with similar resonance in the South to the welfare state in industrialized countries. Inclusive public management could be understood as a more explicit incorporation of social inclusiveness into the developmental state: the 'socially developmental state'? Kaijage and Tibaijuka also note that analysing social exclusion and inclusion is necessarily an interpretative exercise. There are no 'right' answers; the aim is the development of a *local* political discourse on social exclusion and the scope for inclusive institutional change.

I have tried to follow that lead in this discussion. I have applied my interpretations to my own society, and tried to extract more general, if tentative, lessons for understanding the role of the new public management in social exclusion, and for imagining a more inclusive discourse of public management reform. The central lesson is that institutions of public management themselves need to be designed for mutual solidarity and inclusiveness, not least so that they may be criticized for failing to live up to their principles. Only public institutions that aspire to inclusiveness can hope to redress exclusion.

NOTES

1. The frameworks of thought in the Western social exclusion literature, such as Silver (1995), concentrate rather on broad principles of social order in Western societies.
2. The concept of social relations as 'bearers' of gender is taken from the work of Elson (1993).

3. See Besley and Gouveia (1994). The argument in this sentence is developed in Mackintosh (1996b).
4. That is, including 'voluntary', non-profit and other organizations with public interest objectives.
5. Much of the research cited here was undertaken with Pam Smith and Bridget Towers, to whom I owe many of the insights, but who are not responsible for the use I make of them here.
6. Poxton (1996) discusses these options.
7. This section draws on research undertaken jointly with Madeleine Wahlberg; she is not responsible for my interpretations here; see Mackintosh (1997) for further detail.
8. Mackintosh and Smith (1996) discusses incentives; on fundholding incentives see Matsaganis and Glennerster (1994).
9. This point is argued for the context of British local government in Mackintosh (1993).

REFERENCES

Audit Commission (1992), *Community Care: Managing the Cascade of Change*, London: HMSO.
Baldock, J. and Ungerson, C. (1994), *Becoming Consumers of Community Care*, York: Joseph Rowntree Foundation.
Barnes, M. and Prior, P. (1996), 'From private choice to public trust: a new basis for social welfare', *Public Money and Management*, October – December, pp. 51–7.
Besley, T. and Gouveia, M. (1994), 'Health care', *Economic Policy*, No. 19, pp. 200–258.
Brown, L. and Ashman, D. (1996), 'Participation, social capital and intersectoral problem solving: African and Asian cases', *World Development*, 24 (9), 1467–79.
Brown, P. and Crompton, R. (eds) (1994), *Economic Restructuring and Social Exclusion*, London: UCL Press.
Clarke, J. (1996), 'Grey suits, no hearts: aliens in the National Health Service', *Soundings*, No. 4, pp. 153–7.
Clarke, J. and Newman, J. (1997), *The Managerial State*, London: Sage.
Deakin, N., Davis, A. and Thomas, N. (1995), *Public Welfare Services and Social Exclusion*, European Foundation for the Improvement of Living and Working Conditions, Dublin.
Elson, D. (ed.) (1993), *Male Bias in the Development Process*, Manchester: Manchester University Press.
Frenk, J. (1993), 'The public/private mix and human resources for health', *Health Policy and Planning*, 8 (4), 315–26.
Gordon, D. (1996), 'Sustaining economic reform under political liberalisation in Africa: issues and implications', *World Development*, 24 (9), 1527–37.
Huff-Rouselle, M. (1993), 'Private sector initiatives in the public sector: the health sector in Bhutan', *International Journal of Health Planning and Management*, 8, 71–8.
Hutton, W., King, C. and Simpson, A. (1996), 'Accountable insiders? Reforming the pension funds', *Soundings*, No. 4, pp. 168–78.
Kaijage, F. and Tibaijuka, A. (1996), *Poverty and Social Exclusion in Tanzania*, Geneva: ILO Institute for Labour Studies, Research Series No. 109.
Kutzin, J. and Barnum, H. (1992), 'Institutional features of health insurance programs and their effects on developing country health systems', *International Journal of Health Planning and Management*, 7, 51–72.

Lewis, G. (1996), 'Welfare settlements and racialising practices', *Soundings*, No. 4, pp. 109–19.

Mackintosh, M. (1993), 'Creating a developmental state: reflections on policy as process', in G. Albo, D. Languille and L. Panitch (eds), *A Different Kind of State? Popular Power and Democratic Administration*, Toronto: Oxford University Press, pp. 36–50.

Mackintosh, M. (ed.) (1996a), 'The Public Good', theme section, *Soundings*, No. 4, pp. 104–223.

Mackintosh, M. (1996b), 'Redistribution' in M. Mackintosh et al. (eds), *Economics and Changing Economies*, London: International Thompson Business Press, pp. 778–814.

Mackintosh, M. (1997), 'Economic culture and quasi-markets in local government: the case of contracting for social care', *Local Government Studies*, 23 (2), 80–102.

Mackintosh, M. and Smith, P. (1996), 'Perverse incentives: an NHS notebook', *Soundings*, No. 4, pp. 135–48.

Matsaganis, M. and Glennerster, H. (1994), 'The threat of "cream skimming" in the post-reform NHS', *Journal of Health Economics*, 13 (1), 31–60.

Osborne, D. and Gaebler, T. (1992), *Reinventing Government: How the Entrepreneurial Spirit is Transforming the Public Sector*, Reading, MA: Addison-Wesley.

Ostrom, E. (1996), 'Crossing the great divide: coproduction, synergy and development', *World Development*, 24 (6), 1073–88.

Parry, T.R. (1997), 'Achieving balance in decentralization: a case study of education decentralization in Chile', *World Development*, 25 (2), 211–25.

Phongpaichit, P. et al. (1996), *Challenging Social Exclusion: Rights and Livelihoods in Thailand*, Geneva: ILO Institute for Labour Studies, Research Series No. 107.

Pollitt, C., Birchall, J. and Putnam, K. (1997), 'Opting out and the experience of self management in education, health and social care', ESRC Local Governance Programme Working Paper, No. 2, Strathclyde.

Pollitt, C. (1993), *Managerialism and the Public Services,* Oxford: Blackwell.

Poxton, R. (1996), *Joint Approaches for a Better Old Age*, London: King's Fund.

Putnam, R. (1993), *Making Democracy Work: Civic Traditions in Modern Italy*, Princeton: Princeton University Press.

Rouse, J. (1997), 'Performance inside the quangos: tensions and contradictions', *Local Government Studies*, 23 (1), 59–75.

Silver, H. (1995), 'Reconceptualising social disadvantage: three paradigms of social exclusion', in G. Rodgers et al. (eds), *Social Exclusion: Rhetoric, Reality and Responses*, Geneva: International Institute for Labour Studies, pp. 57–80.

Vivian, J. (1995) (ed.), *Adjustment and Social Sector Restructuring,* London: Frank Cass.

Wood, G. (1997), 'States without citizens: the problems of the franchise state', in D. Hulme and M. Edwards (eds), *NGOs, States and Donors: Too Close for Comfort?*, Basingstoke: Macmillan.

Williams, F. (1992), 'Somewhere over the rainbow: diversity and universality in social policy', *Social Policy Review*, No. 4, pp. 200–219.

World Bank (1989), *Sub-Saharan Africa: from Crisis to Sustainable Growth*, Washington, DC: World Bank.

World Bank (1997), *World Development Report*, Oxford: Oxford University Press.

6. Towards synergy in social provision: civic organizations and the state

Gordon White and Mark Robinson[1]

INTRODUCTION

The case for some form of complementarity between the state and civic organizations in the provision of social services is now widely accepted. The potential for developing closer and more enduring forms of inter-institutional collaboration is founded on the creation of mutually reinforcing relationships between governments and local citizens in the form of 'synergy'. A schematic framework is developed in this chapter for analysing the possible range of synergistic relationships that emerge in the determination, financing and production of social goods and services. It is argued that the efficacy of public–civic collaboration in any given society depends on the extent of structural inequality, the nature of the political regime and the legal framework governing the voluntary sector on the one hand, and the institutional character and capacity of the civic and public realms on the other. In Part II of this book (Chapter 13), we use the empirical literature to demonstrate the types of civic organizations involved in service provisioning (with particular reference to the health and education sectors), and variations across countries and regions; and to identify the conditions underlying success and failure of non-state provisioning.

THE IDEA OF 'SYNERGY'

In our analysis in this volume of the role of civic organizations in social provision in poor societies, we conclude that, while they are potentially important in certain areas of service provision, they have certain characteristic defects as well as advantages.[2] These include problems of inadequate or unstable funding, uneven or unequal coverage, lack of accountability and quality control, internal organizational inefficiencies, duplication, divisiveness or exclusion, and sustainability. Any assessment of the service provision role of civic organizations must consider ways in which these problems can be ameliorated. However, the performance of civic organizations and efforts to improve it in turn depend on a large number of conditioning factors of a structural nature in their social, cultural, economic and political environments. We intend to focus here on the specific set of issues surrounding relationships between civic organizations and the state.

The state is a crucial environmental factor which can influence civil welfare provision for good or ill, either directly through the effect of state institutions on particular civic organizations, or indirectly through the impact of state policies and regulations on other environmental factors such as internal and external markets or distributional patterns.[3] The state is also the sole agency capable of providing welfare services on an across-the-board, universalist basis founded on some principle of citizen's rights. Given that the social goods provided by specific civic organizations may be mutually exclusive or conflicting, and may reflect a variety of motives apart from altruism, the state offers a potential integrating framework to reinforce, regularize and rationalize civic provision, reflecting some broader notion of 'public' welfare which transcends specific embodiments of 'social' welfare.

Since there is a strong argument to the effect that both state and civil forms of provision have intrinsic, albeit different, strengths and weaknesses, the question arises as to the extent to which some kind of complementarity can be organized in the provision of services between state agencies on the one side and civic organizations of various kinds on the other. This dyadic relationship is one element in conventional thinking about 'pluralist' welfare systems which also include the market and the family. There is a growing body of literature on issues of 'synergy', 'partnership' and 'co-production' which originally developed in discussions of welfare reform in industrialized societies, but has more recently been extended to apply to developing societies.

The call for cooperation between the public and civic sectors is not new, either in regard to industrialized or developing societies. It has been an element of development discourse since at least the mid-1970s, but it has been given increasing impetus by welfare reforms in the industrialized countries over the past two decades, notably the USA and UK, and the dual movement in many developing societies in the direction of declining state intervention and growing NGO influence in the development process. Given movement towards the pluralization of provision, it is not surprising that increasing attention has been devoted to exploring the complex issues of inter-institutional coordination to which new systems of provision give rise.

While the notions of cooperation and complementarity would appear to be good sense by definition, there are particular reasons for stressing notions of 'synergy' at present. First, there is a tendency for advocates of developmental solutions based on civic and state institutions respectively to be organized in separate and often warring camps, often sharing derogatory images of each other and the sector each represents. This fosters a zero-sum approach to public and civic action, the former being castigated as élitist, bureaucratic and top–down, and the latter as naïve, anarchic and peripheral. Second, this intellectual and ideological divide has been paralleled in a variety of ways by the tensions and hostilities which have characterized relationships between government and civic organizations in many real-world situations where the two sectors have gone their separate and often conflicting ways in providing public goods and services.[4]

Complementarity, seen in terms of the state providing an enabling environment, is a common feature of current thinking about inter-institutional relations in the development field, operating not only through regulation, but also subsidies and various forms of contracting. However, these forms of complementarity involve 'at-a-distance' relationships, whereas current thinking about co-production, partnership or synergy goes beyond this to consider closer, more intense and enduring forms of inter-institutional complementarity. In the context of the USA, for example, the notion of co-production expanded from an earlier stress on the voluntary participation of individual citizens in the production of public goods by local governments to an increasingly broad conception involving a greater range of actors (including civic organizations and private sector firms) and a wider range of collaboration, including common decision making and funding (Warren, 1987).[5]

In contrast, Peter Evans's notion of synergy goes beyond mere complementarity to include 'embeddedness'. Thus synergy, defined as 'mutually reinforcing relations between governments and groups of engaged citizens' (Evans, 1996, p. 1119), rests on the following relational basis: '[An] intimate interconnection and intermingling among public and private actors is combined with a well-defined complementary division of labor between the bureaucracy and local citizens, mutually recognized and accepted by both sides.'

Consequently, Evans's notion of 'social capital', which is an essential underpinning of successful synergy, inheres 'not just in civil society, but in an enduring set of relationships that spans the public–private divide'.

Current conceptions of partnership also include the possibility that public and civic agencies and individuals may be tightly linked together through intermediary institutions. For example, Mitchell-Weaver and Manning (1991–92) describe an 'elite committee model' of partnership working through 'boards' or 'conferences' involving representatives from different institutional sectors, arrangements which characterize various forms of corporatist regime in Western Europe, Latin America and East Asia. There are also the 'government organised NGOs' (GONGOs), to be found, for example, in East Asian societies including China, whereby elements of state control and social participation coexist in various degrees of tension within putatively independent social organizations (White, Howell and Shang, 1996).

To clarify matters, it is perhaps useful to identify three basic processes which underlie various versions of synergy or partnership in the provision of social goods and services, namely *determination, financing* and *production.* If we relate these to the possible forms of collaboration between state agencies on the one side and civic organizations on the other, the resulting combinations are as depicted in Table 6.1.

Table 6.1   Forms of co-provision between state and community organizations (COs)

COs	Determination	Financing	Production
Determination	Co-determination	Enforced provision	Delegation
Financing	Devolution	Co-financing	Contracting/ granting
Production	Pressured provision	Fee for service	Co-production

The key elements of co-provision usually identified in the literature run diagonally across the table in cells (1,1), (2,2) and (3,3), each cell identified by row and column. *Co-determination* (1,1) is a process whereby both parties jointly determine what social service is to be produced and how. This collaborative process can be systematically organized, as in the case of various forms of corporatism which work through consultation in institutionalized forums; it can also be more *ad hoc* and one-off, as in the case of meetings organized to discuss and decide on the use of resources in a given project or locality. *Co-financing* (2,2) involves both parties in paying for the cost of supplying the service in cash or kind. For example, local communities may raise extra resources for a clinic or local school in addition to state funding. *Co-production* (3,3) involves both parties in actually supplying the service, involving a commitment of resources and labour time. For example, this could involve NGOs/community organizations and state agencies in providing services to vulnerable groups, such as women, people with disabilities and older people.

While most descriptions of co-provision refer to these three collaborative functions, there are other forms of interaction between state and civic organizations identified in other cells in Table 6.1. *Devolution* (2,1) refers to an arrangement whereby the state provides financing for a given activity, but a civic organization determines how the money is to be spent and the services are to be provided. This could happen in cases where particular areas of service are highly complex, sensitive or hard to target and when civic organizations may be best placed to make the necessary decisions and carry them out. Aid to certain types of vulnerable group could fall into this category. *Pressured provision* (3,1) is a less common phenomenon, referring as it does to cases where a civic organization determines what service needs to be provided and the state *has* to provide it. This arrangement would usually reflect the political influence of powerful groups in civil society, such as business and professional associations, but it is also conceivable that less advantaged groups could achieve it through actual or threatened direct action. *Enforced provision* (1,2), by contrast, implies that the state determines that a given service should be supplied and obliges civic organizations to pay for it, by political pressure or legal sanction. An example would be in cases where community organizations are required by law to contribute financially to the construction and upkeep of local welfare infrastructure. *Fee for service* (3,2) is a collective form of user fees whereby the state requires fees for a social service and these are paid by civic organizations as well as or instead of individuals. This arrangement could exist, for example, in the case of primary health care services, where there are community arrangements to supplement or subsidize individual payments. *Delegation* (1,3) refers to cases where the state determines what service is to be provided but delegates the entire responsibility of providing it to civic organizations. This could involve, for example, the creation and maintenance of small-scale sanitation infrastructure. *Contracting/granting* (2,3) is a more familiar process whereby the state provides financing for a given service and civic organizations are engaged to run it. These types of arrangements have become increasingly common in the UK, for example, where personal services have been contracted out to civic organizations on a competitive tendering basis.

Each of the processes identified in the nine cells is an ideal type, and specific instances of interaction between public and civic organizations may involve a mixture of various elements. The literature on co-provision tends to focus on co-determination, co-financing and co-production, but it is of course easy to conceive of forms of co-provision in which there is no co-determination (the state decides what is to be done and how), or no co-financing (the state pays for everything), or no co-production (civic organizations take on the entire responsibility for production). However, when Ostrom (1996) refers to 'coproduction' in service provision in developing societies, for example, she has in mind all three forms of cooperation. In her case study of sewerage infrastructures in Brazil, co-production involves all three processes: co-determination in the sense of 'the activation of local citizens to participate from the very start in the planning of their own condominial systems' (1996, p. 1074); co-financing in that citizens bear part of the costs of provision; and co-provision in that local residents are responsible for constructing and maintaining sanitation facilities.

Each of the three elements of co-provision promises benefits both for the parties involved and the clients they serve. Co-determination can enhance a feeling of ownership and participation on the part of social groups, influence policy to reflect specific needs thereby improving programme design, and exert pressures for accountability on public officials. Co-financing can mobilize extra resources and create incentives for economy on the part of both officials and clients. Co-production can mobilize extra inputs with low direct and opportunity costs and bring efficiency gains through a carefully specified division of labour and choice of appropriate technologies. Ostrom's study of schools and health clinics in Nigeria illustrates some of the opportunities lost in situations where the involvement of citizens and groups is discouraged. This and other experiences lead her to conclude (1996, p. 1083): '[Coproduction] of many goods and services normally considered to be public goods by government agencies and citizens organized into polycentric systems is crucial for achieving higher levels of welfare in developing countries, particularly for those who are poor.' She calls for a bridging of the intellectual and practical gulf between analysts and advocates of civic and state solutions to developmental problems.

There is no shortage of similar calls for greater cooperation between the public and civic sectors. Drèze and Sen enter this territory when they define 'public action' as including 'not merely what is done *for* the public by the State, but also what is done *by* the public for itself', and argue that 'the problem of integration of governmental and non-governmental activities is an important one in a programme of public action for social security' (Drèze and Sen, 1991, pp. 28–9). However, while they stress the need for a 'plurality of levers and a heterogeneous set of mechanisms' (ibid., p. 29), they do not focus precisely on the specific problems of inter-institutional coordination involved. John Clark (1995) makes a similar plea for 'a more strategic relationship between NGOs and governments'.[6]

All these conceptions of complementarity or synergy imply some degree of institutional collaboration between public and civic organizations to achieve some common set of social objectives. But it is also possible to conceive of 'synergy' in purely political terms as a process of political interaction between state and civil society more broadly, which does not imply institutional collaboration, but rather involves pressures exerted by social organizations to stimulate government provision of public goods and enforce government accountability to popular demands for them. Gita Sen describes this in her study of social provision in Kerala, noting that social services are better there than in the rest of India in large part because of 'the willingness of people to join together to demand accountability from the systems and their employees' (1992, p. 275). This phenomenon could be called 'political synergy' and is a crucial background condition for the success or otherwise of efforts at inter-institutional cooperation. This distinction coincides with the familiar distinction between the supply-side approach to civic organizations, whereby they are seen mainly in terms of their capacity to provide services or run projects, and the demand-side approach, whereby, in Clark's words (1995, p. 593), 'communities articulate their preferences and concerns so as to become active participants in the development process' through empowerment. Although we shall be concentrating on the former in this chapter, the latter should be kept in mind since successful synergy depends upon a virtuous interplay between institutional and political factors. We shall return to this question in our concluding remarks.

THE EXPERIENCE OF GOVERNMENT–CIVIC COLLABORATION: SOME COMMON PROBLEMS

There is also no shortage of successful cases of public–civic cooperation adduced to buttress general arguments for synergy.[7] Certain cases, such as the Philippine National Irrigation Administration's Communal Irrigation Programme, recur in the literature as models of successful collaboration (for example, in Korten, 1980, pp. 492–4).

To take the case of health care, even in countries where non-state providers account for a significant share of health facilities and services, it is uncommon for them to be insulated from national policy priorities or state provisioning. This is evident from the common practice of state financing of non-state health services in a number of countries in Asia and Africa. The Indian government, for example, supports NGOs with grants for treatment of indigents, covering the costs of post-partum beds under the national family planning programme, and subsidies for primary health care services (Berman and Dave, 1996, p. 36). In several African countries, the state has financed health services provided by missions through grants, subsidies and tax exemptions. For example, the Tanzanian government has designated certain voluntary agency hospitals as district hospitals, with a contractual relationship for providing some public services in exchange for grants and personnel. The Zambian government supports mission health facilities in rural areas through bed grants and staff secondment (Mogedal et al., 1995). In Ghana and Uganda the government pays the salaries of all health staff, and in Uganda government staff are seconded to church health facilities. Church organizations in Malawi can purchase drugs at subsidized rates and in Ghana missions are exempted from paying import duties on drugs, dressings and equipment. In these various ways state funding accounts for 33–45 per cent of civic health care financing in Ghana, Malawi and Tanzania. However, government financial support is not without problems: there are delays and uncertainties in the disbursement of funds, grants do not cover costs of provision, there is a lack of flexibility in the use of funds, or unacceptable conditions attached (DeJong, 1991; Gilson et al., 1994; Berman and Rose, 1996).

Some African governments have designated mission hospitals as primary referral centres and receive grants and subsidies in return. For example, in Malawi mission hospitals will become responsible for all services within their areas, whether owned by government or members of the Church Association of Malawi, following the creation of special health delivery areas (Gilson et al., 1994, p. 20). Governments and non-state health providers also collaborate in other ways. A good example is in the supply of drugs and medicines. In Cameroon, for instance, the Ministry of Health has created the legal framework enabling non-profit associations to hold funds and purchase drugs from a non-profit bulk supplier or on the international market (Sauerborn et al., 1995). But the roles of civic organizations and government are not always well demarcated, which can lead to inefficiencies in health provision. In Sierra Leone and Uganda, for example, there was a tendency for NGOs to provide the funds and materials for constructing health buildings, but without making provision for repairs and maintenance, which was assumed to be the responsibility of government, which did not have adequate resources. Consequently the buildings fell into disrepair and became unusable (Mitchell, 1995). Such problems of poor coordination underline the need for more effective working arrangements as a basis for a more comprehensive and integrated system of health provisioning in Africa.[8]

Experiences such as these show that, while a listing of successful cases of state–civic cooperation is instructive in identifying some of the factors affecting collaborative performance, it can also be misleading since the broader pattern of collaboration is much more problematic. There may be contingent reasons for clear successes, and the number of successful cases is probably a very small proportion of the potentially available universe of cases. Though each specific example of attempted collaboration may involve a wide range of contingent elements, moreover, some of the difficulties involved are structural, reflecting basic contradictions in the process of achieving synergetic co-provision: between types of institutions which operate in characteristically different ways; between social groups with different resource endowments and perspectives; and between political forces with different interests and values.

These tensions cause commonly observed problems, such as the following:

● The problem of *politicization*, resulting from conflict between civic organizations and the state or among civic organizations themselves, from the influence of wider patterns of local and national politics, or from distributional issues surrounding uneven or unequal service provision.

- Dangers of *corruption and croneyism* which may attend more intensive and long-term inter-institutional relationships.
- Organizational problems arising from the complexities of *inter-institutional coordination*, particularly given the divergent organizational cultures of the two sides. In addition to problems of public–civic coordination, there are also those involved in relations between different types of civic organization, such as national and international NGOs, or NGOs and grass-roots organizations (Brown and Ashman, 1996; Howes, 1997).
- Organizational problems involved in *adapting state institutions* and operatives to the requirements of external collaboration.
- The potential for conflict on the grounds of *ideology and values*. A well-known example is the refusal of Catholic Church missions to provide contraceptives in family health clinics in several African countries despite a national policy commitment to population control.
- Organizational problems concerning the *transformation of civic organizations* from coping or emergency service providers to more routinized agencies capable of maintaining high operational standards. Since this may involve their becoming more businesslike and professionalized, they may lose some of their distinctively voluntary character. Indeed, some may begin to act like commercial companies competing for market share or brand reputation. This is the organizational Catch 22 identified in studies of the voluntary sector in the industrialized countries: as the civic sector becomes more institutionalized, it comes to resemble the other sectors to which it is supposed to be an alternative.
- The problem of *dependence*, which is a potential feature of any inter-institutional relationship that is asymmetrical in terms of power and resources and a particularly severe problem in poor, dislocated societies where both states and civic organizations are financially dependent on different segments of the external donor system.

In the light of these basic problems, effective complementarity may be only a narrow sliver of the range of actual relationships between states and civic organizations, particularly in those developing societies ravaged by intense social hostilities, political instability, widespread poverty, repressive states, fiscal indigence and international dependence. The following types of public–civic relationship are common:

- An *adversarial* relationship in which mutual hostility reigns and civic organizations exist at least in part to protect their clientele from state repression or interference and provide benefits which the state is either unwilling to provide or finds positively threatening (for example, civic organizations in authoritarian polities such as Pinochet's Chile or South Korea under military rule).

- A *displacing* relationship whereby states act to replace the service role of civic organizations. Conversely, civic providers may displace ailing or threatened states by establishing 'independent kingdoms', areas of autonomy in which basic services are provided in lieu of state agencies (as in guerrilla bases). This can also happen in societies where states have collapsed (for example, the role played by religious organizations in Mogadishu).

- A *competitive* relationship in which civic organizations and state agencies compete to provide services. While this is a common feature of relationships between state agencies and commercial entities (for example, in areas such as pensions and personal service provision), it may also occur in the case of non-profit organizations: for example, religious organizations may seek to establish their own educational institutions in competition with a secular state.

- A *substitutive* or *subsidiary* relationship based on a mutually acceptable division of labour whereby civic organizations take over responsibility for the provision of certain services which the state cannot or does not want to provide. In the case of agreed subsidiarity, the state is likely to play an enabling role by providing a favourable policy or regulatory environment to institutionalize the division of labour and render it effective.

CONDITIONS FOR FAILURE AND SUCCESS IN EFFORTS TO ACHIEVE SYNERGY

In explaining patterns of failure and success in achieving productive complementarity, there is a current tendency to rely on abstract concepts such as 'social capital' or 'trust'. But these can take protean forms and have themselves to be explained in the first place. The analytical difficulty is finding ways to steer between the Scylla of complexity and the Charybdis of abstraction by developing some middle-range propositions about the experience of public–civic collaboration which might provide practical benchmarks for assessing performance and designing policy. Headway can be made by specifying certain central variables which influence the nature and efficacy of public–civic collaboration.

The first of these involves variations in *sociopolitical structural conditions* between and within individual societies which affect the feasibility of effective collaboration. The key structural variables here would appear to be the following:

- A society's degree of social cohesion, which depends on the amount of structural inequality and the intensity of social conflicts, both horizontal and vertical. Where gaps between social groups are wide and political power is consequently highly skewed, and where social relationships are fragmented and conflictual, systematic efforts at organizing the kinds of complementarity which can produce public goods and distribute them throughout the population are likely to be wasted.[9] The same will probably apply to societies which are highly disarticulated in the sense of glaring gaps between state and society, urban and rural populations, regional segments, and modern and traditional sectors.
- The nature of the political regime and, in particular, the legal framework governing the activities of the voluntary sector, respect for civil and political rights, and the overall accountability of governmental and political institutions. Authoritarian regimes are more likely either to discourage the activity of civic organizations or to seek to manipulate them. By contrast, democratization (even of a relatively superficial procedural kind) can open up more space for civic organizations and increase their influence by providing more channels of access to the policy process.

A second set of enabling or constraining conditions lies in the *institutional character and capacity* of a particular society. The institutional requirements of successful complementarity are formidable since they cover three terrains: the civic, the public and the realm of interaction. So far, efforts to identify the institutional conditions for complementarity have stressed the civic realm, in particular through the notion of social capital. In his analysis of 13 cases of public–civic cooperation, for example, Clark (1995) concludes that social capital, in the sense of 'relationships that are grounded in structures of voluntary association, norms of reciprocity and cooperation and attitudes of social trust and respect', is positively associated with the success of cooperative programmes. However, the relationship was not a clear one: as Clark observes (1995, p. 1471), '[there] were cases of clear and mixed success characterized by medium or even low levels of social capital ...'.[10]

The weakness of this relationship reflects the protean character of specific civic embodiments of the social capital ideal type. Unless social capital is defined in terms which make it a good thing by definition, and therefore analytically unhelpful (and some uses of Putnam's concept (Putnam, 1993) tend in this direction), the term is highly ambiguous: it can be a force for antisocial conspiracy as much as socially oriented cooperation; it can exclude as well as include and intensify as well as ameliorate conflict; and it can operate hierarchically as well as horizontally. In regard to organizing synergy, it may impede as well as facilitate cooperation among civic groups or between them and public agencies. In spite of these qualifications, however, one could accept a more limited proposition, to the effect that the existence of a stock of organizational capacity and relations of mutual solidarity, reciprocity and trust in the civic realm can often be a facilitating condition for organizing complementarity.

Two problems follow from this. First, what can be done if these stocks of social capital do not exist? Second, to the extent that they do exist, how can they be mobilized in the pursuit of synergy? These are questions which require us to look at two more institutional realms, the public and the public–civic intersection. The first of these questions relates to what might be called the 'Putnam paradox'. Since stocks of social capital accumulate over centuries and cannot be built up overnight, if you haven't got it you're not likely to get it. Moreover, since the amount of social capital is associated with actual and potential developmental performance, the localities which are the most needy in developmental terms are also likely to be the least endowed with social capital. Lack of social capital then operates as a kind of social debt, the burden of which debilitates groups and communities and intensifies the gaps between them and their counterparts with greater social assets. It might be said, however, that neither of these relationships hold decisively: there are many examples of effective community and group organizations forming speedily in response to emergency or dire need; moreover, poor and excluded communities in the most need may also have substantial organizational reserves to draw on.

But what can be done if stocks of social capital are weak and/or dwindling? It is clear from many studies of both industrialized and developing societies not only that stocks of social capital vary considerably between dissimilar types of communities and among similar types, but also that the kinds of structural problems that one would like community organizations to address (such as cutbacks in government funding or economic disruptions) may weaken existing associational ties.[11] Moser's study of four poor urban communities under stress documents (1996, p. 65) the extent to which 'economic crisis has ... eroded trust and co-operation in a number of important respects', notably by increasing crime and insecurity and reducing the time available for women to collaborate in community activities. Government cutbacks also contribute to this decline, for example a withdrawal of support for community child care centres reduced employment opportunities for women because of the increased burden of child care and shortened the time available for other activities, including community participation. At a deeper level, it led to a loss of trust between local people and the government, 'the rupture of a social contract carefully negotiated over the years' (ibid., p. 64).

This case not only demonstrates the difficulties in maintaining productive relations between government and community, but also highlights the fundamental problems involved in trying to organize collaboration in times of fiscal stress and economic crisis. It is in circumstances such as these, where both governments and communities are under stress, that the role of NGOs with external links is important. They can act in a substitutive capacity to restore local associational capacities when these would otherwise be weak or collapsing. In relation to the possibilities for complementarity, this finding has two significant implications: first, there are often significant differences between community or grass-roots organizations (GROs) and NGOs, and they should not be conflated when assessing the associational capacity of a particular locality; and, second, the process of organizing synergy is often triadic (government, NGO, GRO) rather than dyadic, and in many cases involves four or five parties when international NGOs and foreign donor agencies also play a role.[12]

The task of identifying the institutional underpinnings of government–civic complementarity should also be extended in ways suggested by Evans (1996), Ostrom (1996) and Tendler (1995) to cover two institutional terrains beyond the civic: within the state and between state and citizenry/civil society. The first would refer to the creation of efficient and accountable public institutions populated by people motivated at least partly by considerations of public service (for the importance of the latter, see Tendler and Freedheim, 1994): the realm of 'public capital'. The second would refer to relations of mutual trust, respect and cooperation across the state/society divide which are the fundamental underpinnings of any effort to organize synergy.

While the importance of the efficiency and effectiveness of public institutions would seem self-evident, current thinking about the role of the state in the process of organizing complementarity is inadequate in several ways. There is a good deal of normative discussion about the need for the state to establish an enabling environment for civic action, but there is insufficient attention to the severity of the problems experienced by many states in poor countries, particularly those facing economic crises or grappling with structural adjustment programmes. Indeed, the currently dominant intellectual paradigm for state behaviour (the 'new political economy' and the theories of 'public choice') tend to disparage the state as a realm of self-interest and rent seeking by definition, which makes thinking about issues such as 'public service', 'professional commitment' and 'public virtue' difficult, if not impossible. In practice, this can lead to a paralysing negativity about the possibilities for state action which may not only curtail such action where it is manifestly effective and desirable, but also undermine the motivation and effectiveness of state officials and employees, thereby producing a self-fulfilling prophecy. Drawing on their study of a public health programme in Brazil, for example, Tendler and Freedheim conclude that members of a state institution can be motivated by public service, that notions of self-interest and public

calling can be combined, and that these motives can be created and reinforced by a judicious combination of pressures from above and below. Thus
any inquiry into the feasibility of public–civic synergy would need to delve
systematically into the theory and practice of 'good governance'.[13]

The realm of government–civic interaction is yet another area of institutional inquiry of central importance for understanding synergy. On the basis
of a study of 16 countries in Asia, for example, Uphoff (1993, p. 613) concludes that 'countries which had the best linkage between central government
and rural communities through a network of local institutions had the best
performance in agriculture and in social indicators'. The problem with this
kind of finding, as Evans (1996) points out in his discussion of prospects for
synergy, is that these linkages are usually embedded in broader institutional
systems with a long history and depend upon basic structural factors such as
the capacity of the state machine, the cohesion of local communities and a
relatively egalitarian social structure. The key problem for synergy in less
well-endowed contexts is one of building institutional bridges in situations
where the relationship between state institutions and society has been distant
or antagonistic. While a problem for specific policy areas and projects, this
need for bridge building is often symptomatic of a society-wide process of
integrating or reintegrating state and society and establishing relations of
trust between citizens and officials.

AVENUES TO 'CONSTRUCTABILITY'

Discussions of the above sort, which emphasize the complexity of the problem and the structural constraints which obstruct positive action, are frustrating.
Poverty needs to be tackled in the here and now, and life-sustaining and
-enhancing welfare services need to be delivered soon, not in some distant
future. If synergistic public–civic cooperation is a potentially powerful way
of tackling problems, then we need to confront the problem of what Evans
(1996, p. 1129) calls 'constructability'. What are the areas of positive action
which are feasible in the short term? Let us begin by defining certain areas of
action.

Creating an Enabling Policy Environment

This is a familiar theme in discussions of complementarity and we need not
spend much time on it here. The basic message, assuming some minimal
level of state capacity, is that a balance should be struck between non-
intervention, promotion and regulation. In situations in which governments
have in the past imposed overly restrictive controls on civic organizations (as,

for example, in Tanzania), these should be relaxed, particularly in contexts where relaxation can reasonably be expected to result in a net increment of social provision. For example, in the context of the health sector in Africa, most observers are agreed that strict control is likely to prove counterproductive, and that the role of government is to provide the broad strategic and policy framework and a clear operating environment for civic organizations and NGOs to fit into (DeJong, 1991; Green and Matthias, 1995). Moreover, governments should actively encourage civic organizations by helping to open up opportunities for civic action and providing incentives for civic organizations to become involved in the welfare field. These might include tax concessions, simplified administrative procedures, additional sources of funding in the form of contracts or grants, and opportunities for closer consultation with government in determining national policy objectives. At the same time, there is a concomitant need for regulatory action to institutionalize the status of civic organizations, screen them to prevent malpractice and establish socially beneficial standards of performance. Overall, this approach implies a combination of measures to provide space for civic organizations, consolidate their social position, provide positive incentives for socially productive action and enforce certain standards of accountability.

Institutional Innovations in the Public Sphere

Governments can take steps to encourage the involvement of civic organizations in one or more of the three elements of co-provision indicated earlier: for example, by setting up intermediary institutions such as consultative bodies to solicit the views of social groups and involve them in defining priorities and programmes; or by actively seeking collaborative arrangements for co-financing and co-production. To the extent that localities are the natural context for such efforts, the balance between central control and local responsibility needs to be reassessed with a view to encouraging the kind of organic embedded type of relationship which many analysts and practitioners regard as an essential element of successful public–civic provision, but maintaining the controls necessary to uphold standards and enforce accountability. Achieving a desirable balance between centralization and decentralization, whether administrative, financial or political, varies between policy sectors and involves an incremental process of institutional learning to achieve synergy. Any reform plan of the blueprint variety would be wrong by definition, even if it were pointing in the right direction (Korten, 1980). Such reforms would also involve new incentive systems and forms of training for public employees to equip them for the new roles which collaboration with civic organizations would require. One of the major constraints on government–civic cooperation is the attitude of government officials and professionals: the former because the kind of action necessary to sustain collaboration is outside their professional ken, carries no career incentives with it and is perceived as troublesome and time wasting; the latter because sharing activities with civic organizations may offend their sense of professional identity and threaten to dilute standards which they consider inviolate. This is a common reaction on the part of professional groups involved in providing social services, such as doctors, teachers and social workers.

The 'Soft Technologies' of Organizational Design

Evans (1996) uses the term 'soft technologies' to refer to certain organizational features in the design of complementarity exercises which may influence their success. Tendler and Freedheim emphasize their importance in a municipality-based preventive health programme in Ceara, Northeast Brazil. Particularly important were two features: first, the careful combination of centralization and decentralization in the administration of the programme; and, second, the recruitment of local citizens who failed to be recruited formally into the programme as 'informed public monitors of the programme' (Tendler and Freedheim, 1994, p. 1778), which improved the efficiency and accountability of programme officers. Effective soft technology such as this is very context-specific and in the Ceara case depended on the successive arrival in power of two reformist state governors from the Brazilian Social Democratic Party which sought to break away from the previous pattern of corrupt clientelist politics. But this, and other successful cases of synergy, such as the urban infrastructure projects in Brazil described by Ostrom (1996), do provide ideas about the kind of organizational features which can ameliorate some of the commonly observed problems involved in achieving effective collaboration: for example, administrative arrangements designed to reduce corruption and neutralize political opposition; procedures to involve community groups in the design and implementation of the programme; ways to involve low-skilled community workers in projects while minimizing the resistance of professional staff; and intensive efforts to give the public servants involved a sense of mission. The central message of these successful cases is the need for a combination of multidirectional pressures: from above (higher levels of government); from the side (from local politicians and interest groups); from below (from organized community interests or activated individuals); and in some cases from outside (international agencies and other donors).

Particular Areas of Provision and Types of Collaborative Arrangement

Different problems tend to occur in areas of social provision where the contribution of civic organizations can be described as 'additive' and 'integral'. *Additive* implies an area of provision, often of a very focused kind, which can be tacked on to ongoing government activities with minimal institutional interaction required, such as small-scale, low-technology, community-organized facilities such as crèches, youth centres, victim support centres, family planning centres, women's refuges and the like. These can be disaggregated and linked only loosely with broader government programmes and institutions. *Integral* involves areas of provision in which civic provision is part of a broader, more integrated and hierarchical system of societal provision organized by government, with the following characteristics: highly stratified levels of technical knowledge and professional expertise, as in the areas of urban water services, health and education; large and complex physical infrastructures such as hospitals and urban water systems; organizational complexity in that coordination across sectoral institutional systems or geographical areas is required, as in the case of urban sanitation which involves a variety of local government agencies; and a commitment to standardized provision, for example through school curricula or public health regulations. In such systemic contexts, governments play a crucial role in marshalling and maintaining expertise, in designing and constructing infrastructure, in coordinating across institutional sectors and localities, and in defining and enforcing standards.

The role of civic organizations will vary within these integrated systems, depending on the particular character of the organization and the activity. In the case of community involvement, one would expect it to be locally specific, requiring relatively low-technology and low-expertise activities, participating less in the construction of infrastructure and more in its operation and maintenance, and in non-standardized, non-formalized forms of provision, such as informal education and self-help groups for care of children, aged and disabled people. The case of NGOs is often different since, particularly where they are large and have international connections, they can deliver higher levels of expertise, coordinate across institutional sectors and localities, and manage more complex physical and institutional concentrations: examples include religious bodies running hospitals and secondary/higher educational institutions, and specialized NGOs handling areas of public health, such as disease eradication programmes.

The key element of synergy in these integral systems of provision would seem to lie in the ability of the implementing agents to design ways in which different levels and sectors within a given system of provision can be assigned to different agents according to their institutional comparative advantage. This entails two parallel, and mutually reinforcing, processes of design and coordination: the technical and the political. In the case of the urban sewerage system in Brazil described by Watson (1995), for example, on the technical side, the urban water supply system was designed to be decomposible into two physical systems, one of which could be constructed and maintained by local residents. On the political side, local citizens were involved from the outset by means of neighbourhood meetings to discuss technical and financial issues, and planners were induced to incorporate certain design features which might not otherwise have entered their calculations. Complementary action in other areas of the social provision, such as health and education, comprises similar processes of technical decomposition, on the one hand, and an institutional division of labour arrived at through micro-political processes of consultation and mutual accommodation, on the other.

Facilitating Factors

Given the frustrating complexities of organizing synergy, it is perhaps rational to expect most efforts to end in failure or at least only partial success. But there are certain facilitating factors, some susceptible to design and some beyond the control of programme actors. The *political context* is very important. The nature of the political regime is crucial in that it opens up space for civic action and increases room for institutional experimentation. The quality of political leadership and of the political process more generally at regional and local levels is a key element of success: if local politicians or the leaders of civic organizations take against a project or are divided on the issue, the endeavour is imperilled from the outset.

Given the demanding range of skills necessary to broker complementarity, the *quality of individual leaders* (whether administrative, professional, political or civic) is a potentially decisive factor in smoothing the path towards synergy. On the public side, the adaptive capacity of public officials is a crucial factor, as Sundeen (1985) has demonstrated in the US context, identifying three roles for local administrators which can facilitate the co-provision of social services: broker, facilitator and community developer. On the civic side, the drive and skills of community and NGO leaders provide another positive impetus, and some analysts of the civic sector, particularly in the industrialized countries, are heralding the emergence of a new social stratum (the 'social entrepreneurs') who can combine the entrepreneurial flair of the commercial sector with the socially minded commitment of the voluntary sector.[14]

External agencies can also provide a positive impetus, given adequate leadership, knowledge and sensitivity. The operational performance of the external donor community is itself a variable, however, and can produce or intensify some of the problems found in the host country. External interventions to assist synergy can concentrate the minds of local actors through a combination of carrot, stick and persuasion, but these interventions need to be informed by an increasing grasp of international best practice (political and institutional as well as technical) and be able to use this knowledge flexibly.

To summarize, all the above factors influence specific processes of attempted complementarity in complex ways which make each particular instance highly 'path-dependent'. While we have suggested that certain maps and signposts do exist, their accuracy sometimes approaches that of their medieval equivalents. It is not surprising, therefore, that long-term observers have emphasized the organic nature of the complementarity process. Watson, for example, in her study of urban sanitation projects in Brazil, concludes as follows (1995, p. 23): 'The lesson is that there is no "right" way to approach projects, but that each project's design, implementation strategy, and management arrangements evolve during the course of give-and-take negotiations between the project team and residents.'

Similarly, Korten stresses the need for a 'learning process approach' when assessing the reasons for successful cases of both community and collaborative development in Asia (1980, p. 497):

> These five programs were not designed and implemented – rather they emerged out of a learning process in which villagers and program personnel shared their knowledge and resources to create a program which achieved a fit between needs and capacities of the beneficiaries and those of the outsiders who were providing the assistance. Leadership and teamwork, rather than blueprints, were the key elements.

There is in effect a three-dimensional process of learning, simultaneously technical, institutional and political. While the technical knowledge needed for service provision programmes is more likely to be forthcoming, knowledge of similar quality in relation to institutions and to micro-politics is in far less ample supply. Understanding the second and third dimensions of all forms of service provision, whether involving collaboration or not, requires the strengthening of applied organizational analysis (formerly confined largely to the public sector in the form of the much maligned field of public administration) and of political (in particular, micro-political) analysis.

SOME PRELIMINARY CONCLUSIONS

While civic organizations have undoubtedly made an important contribution to service provision, there are numerous examples of failure in such efforts and a determined bid to replace state by voluntary provision raises problems of quality control, sustainability, amateurism and poor coordination. For these reasons the state has to ensure that services are of high quality and delivered efficiently. But in view of the manifest problems of bureaucratic failure and fiscal constraints, the call to seek solutions through synergistic partnerships between state and civic providers appears to make eminently good sense. At the same time, however, there is something truistic about abstract notions of the alleged benefits of synergy or collaboration, as in similar paeans to the alleged virtues of community, participation and civil society. As we have seen, not only is the potential complementarity between state and civic organizations dependent on a complex array of enabling conditions, but even where these are present the process of organizing synergy is delicate and often tortuous.

Given these problems, if one regards efforts at organizing synergy to be a strategic, long-term priority for improving service provision in developing societies, how can developmental thought and action be reoriented to facilitate the task? First, it would suggest an intellectual approach which recognizes the separate importance of both public and civic institutional sectors. This would contrast with dualistic paradigms which disparage the state or belittle civic action. Over the long term the state is likely to be of crucial importance in organizing and financing social services. Moreover, no comprehensive system of social provision, whether civic or commercial, is likely to work satisfactorily without properly constituted state authority and institutions. Second, this new paradigm would also extend to include systematic consideration of the institutional character and effectiveness of external agencies engaged in development interventions. Since external agencies, whether civic, state or international, are often central actors in efforts to organize synergy, there is a need for greater reflexivity on their part, a willingness to apply the same rigorous forms of analysis to themselves that they apply to their domestic collaborators and clients.

Third, a more balanced and inclusive institutional perspective would require a rethinking of some of the concepts currently influential in the field. Notably, the notion of social capital could be extended beyond civil society to cover the public realm and the public–civic interface. Relationships of trust and reciprocity are not qualities confined to the civic realm. Concern with the public realm would relate to the creation of efficient and accountable public institutions populated by people whose motivations extend beyond crude self-interest or rent seeking. Concern with the interface would seek to identify relations of mutual trust, respect and cooperation across the state/society divide which are the fundamental underpinnings of any effort to organize synergy.

At the practical level, the detailed experience of action to organize various forms of synergy, co-production and partnership can be drawn together in the search for potential lessons and best practice, and new models of project/

programme design which can be successful in achieving effective complementarity between state and voluntary agencies. The results of this kind of work would be valuable in bringing about a cumulatively clearer specification of the precise factors, both favourable and unfavourable, which condition the success of efforts to organize synergy, the precise measures which may prove effective in remedying the inherent difficulties involved, the alternative ways in which inter-institutional collaboration can be organized and the specific areas of service provision where this collaboration may be particularly appropriate.

NOTES

1. This chapter is drawn from a larger piece published in the UNU/WIDER Research For Action series (Robinson and White, 1997). Some of the issues dealt with relatively briefly here are pursued in more detail there.
2. By 'civic organizations' we mean voluntary or membership organizations across a wide range, including NGOs, community organizations, business and professional associations, trade unions, and the like. (For a fuller discussion, see Chapter 13 in this volume.) By 'social provision' we mean health, education, housing and assistance to vulnerable groups.
3. The centrality of this relationship is stressed, for example, by Semboja and Therkildsen (1995, pp. 28–9) in their review of the recent experience of non-state service provision in East Africa.
4. Riker (1995) discusses these tensions in the context of Asia, and Clark (1995) more generally.
5. By contrast, the UK literature on public–civic cooperation in the provision of social services has not used the concept of co-production explicitly and has focused sharply on the institutional and managerial consequences of the mixed economy of care in the personal social services, particularly since the NHS and Community Care Act in 1993, involving a managerial mode of coordination in a multi-provider system regulated by contractual arrangements (Charlesworth, Clarke and Cochrane, 1996).
6. For arguments along similar lines, see Riker (1995), Taal (1993), and MacPherson (1989).
7. For example, Taal (1993) cites ten case studies from Asia, Africa and Latin America of which he regards eight as relatively successful; Clark (1995) covers 13 case studies and seeks to identify and explain degrees of success.
8. For analyses of needed reforms, see Mogedal et al. (1995, p. 359) on Zambia and Tanzania; and Walley et al. (1991) on the Wollo region of Ethiopia.
9. Controlled experiments by Aquino et al. (1992) on the relationship between inequality and support for public goods suggest that, because of the differential impact of the free-rider and sucker effects, 'inequality in the distribution of resources leads to less co-operation and reduced support for a public good'.
10. Similarly, Brown and Ashman (1996) argue that dense networks of social capital are not the only ingredients of success, and that organizational capacity is critical to effective performance.
11. Sundeen (1985) has investigated the relationships between co-production and community in the context of the USA, concluding that communities vary greatly in the extent and character of their capacity for organized group action and that this has important implications for the feasibility of co-production. The USA has numerous cases of functioning communities which are decimated by a particular market occurrence, such as the sudden withdrawal of a large employer which leads to a downward escalator of fiscal decline and community disintegration.

12. For a valuable analysis of the differences between NGOs and GROs, see Uphoff (1993).
13. For a critical discussion of the 'good government' agenda, see the special issue of the *IDS Bulletin* edited by Mick Moore (1993).
14. In the UK, for example, the country's most noted social entrepreneur, Michael Young, has established a School for Social Entrepreneurs, a 'businesslike non-business school' designed to train managers for the growing non-profit sector (*The Guardian*, 12 March 1997).

REFERENCES

Aquino, K. et al. (1992), 'The effects of resource distribution, voice and decision framing on the provision of public goods', *Journal of Conflict Resolution*, **36** (4), 665–87.

Berman, P. and. Dave, P. (1996), 'Experiences in paying for health care in India's voluntary sector', *International Journal of Health Planning and Management*, **11** (1), pp. 33–51.

Berman, P. and. Rose, L. (1996), 'The role of private providers in maternal and child health and family planning services in developing countries', *Health Policy and Planning*, **11** (2), 142–55.

Brown, L.D. and Ashman, D. (1996), 'Participation, social capital, and intersectoral problem solving: African and Asian cases', *World Development*, **24** (9), 1467–79.

Charlesworth, J., Clark, J. and Cochrane, A. (1996), 'Tangled webs? Managing local mixed economies of care', *Public Administration*, **74** (1), 67–88.

Clark, J. (1995), 'The state, popular participation, and the voluntary sector', *World Development*, **23** (4), 593–601.

DeJong, J. (1991), 'Nongovernmental organizations and health delivery in Sub-Saharan Africa', Policy, Research and External Affairs Working Paper No. 708, Washington, DC: World Bank.

Drèze, J. and Sen, A. (1991), 'Public action for social security: foundations and strategy', in E. Ahmed, J. Drèze, J. Hills and A. Sen (eds), *Social Security in Developing Countries*, Oxford: Clarendon Press, pp. 1–40.

Evans, P. (1996), 'Government action, social capital and development: reviewing the evidence on synergy', *World Development*, **24** (6), 1119–32.

Gilson, L., Sen, P.D., Mohammed, S. and Mujinja, P. (1994), 'The potential of health sector nongovernmental organizations – policy options', *Health Policy and Planning*, **9** (1), 14–24.

Green, A. and Matthias, A. (1995), 'Where do NGOs fit in? Developing a policy framework for the health sector', *Development in Practice*, **5** (4), 313–23.

Howes, M. (1997), 'NGOs and the institutional development of membership organisations: the evidence from six cases', *Journal of International Development*, **9** (4), 597–604.

Korten, D.C. (1980), 'Community organization and rural development: a learning process approach', *Public Administration Review*, **40** (5), 480–511.

Mitchell, M. (1995), 'Community involvement in constructing village health buildings in Uganda and Sierra Leone', *Development in Practice*, **5** (4), 324–33.

Mitchell-Weaver, C. and Manning, B. (1991–92), 'Public–private partnerships in Third World development: an overview', *Studies in Comparative International Development*, **26** (4), 45–67.

Mogedal, S., Steen, H. and Mpelumbe, G. (1995), 'Health sector reform and organizational issues at the local level: lessons from selected African countries', *Journal of International Development*, **7** (3), 349–67.

Moore, M. (ed.) (1993), 'Good government?', *IDS Bulletin*, **24** (1).

Moser, C.O.N. (1996), *Confronting Crisis: A Comparative Study of Household Responses to Poverty and Vulnerability in Four Poor Urban Communities*, Washington, DC: World Bank.

Ostrom, E. (1996), 'Crossing the great divide: coproduction, synergy and development', *World Development*, **24** (6), 1073–87.

Putnam, R. (1993), *Making Democracy Work: Civic Traditions in Modern Italy*, Princeton: Princeton University Press.

Riker, J. (1995), 'From co-optation to co-operation in government', in N. Heyzer and J.V. Riker (eds), *Government–NGO Relations in Asia: Prospects and Challenges for People-Centred Development*, London: Macmillan, pp. 91–129.

Robinson, M. and White, G. (1997), *The Role of Civic Organisations in the Provision of Social Services: Towards Synergy*, Research for Action 37, Helsinki, UNU/ WIDER.

Sauerborn, R., Bodart, C. and Essomba, R.O. (1995), 'Recovery of recurrent health service costs through provincial health funds in Cameroon', *Social Science & Medicine*, **40** (12), 1731–39.

Semboja, J. and Therkildsen, O. (eds) (1995), *Service Provision Under Stress in East Africa*, London: James Currey.

Sen, G. (1992), 'Social needs and public accountability: the case of Kerala', in M. Wuyts et al., *Development Policy and Public Action*, Oxford: Oxford University Press.

Sundeen, R.A. (1985), 'Coproduction and communities: implications for local administrators', *Administration and Society*, **16** (4), 387–402.

Taal, H. (1993), 'Decentralization and Community Participation for Improving Access to Basic Services: An Empirical Approach', Innocenti Occasional Papers, Economic Policy Series, No. 35.

Tendler, J. (1995), 'Social capital and the public sector: the blurred boundaries between public and private', paper presented at the conference of the Economic Development Working Group, Social Capital and Public Affairs Project, American Academy of Arts and Sciences, Cambridge MA (May).

Tendler, J. and Freedheim, S. (1994), 'Trust in a rent-seeking world: health and government transformed in Northeast Brazil', *World Development*, **22** (12), 1771–92.

Uphoff, N. (1993), 'Grassroots organizations and NGOs in rural development: opportunities with diminishing states and expanding markets', *World Development*, **21** (4), 607–22.

Walley, J., Tefera, B. and McDonald, M.A. (1991), 'Integrating health services – the experience of NGOs in Ethiopia', *Health Policy and Planning*, **6** (4), 327–35.

Warren, R. (1987), 'Coproduction, volunteerism, privatization and the public interest', *Journal of Voluntary Action Research*, **16** (3), 5–10.

Watson, G. (1995), *Good Sewers Cheap? Agency–Customer Interactions in Low-Cost Urban Sanitation in Brazil*, Washington, DC: World Bank.

White, G., Howell, J. and Shang, X. (1996), *In Search of Civil Society: Social Change in Contemporary China*, Oxford: Oxford University Press.

7. Public management: towards a radical agenda

Robert Chambers

It is not that we should simply seek new and better ways for managing society, the economy and the world. The point is that we should fundamentally change how we behave.

Vaclav Havel, 1992

A VISION

This chapter seeks a basis for a radical pro-poor agenda for public management. A radical agenda needs first a vision. One starting point is responsible well-being.[1] In the experience of facilitators of PRA (participatory rural appraisal),[2] it has again and again been something close to 'well-being' rather than wealth that local people have expressed as their aspiration. For its part, 'responsible' brings in considerations of equity and sustainability, and of relations with others. In relation to responsible well-being, the role of the state can be seen to differ between the poor and the wealthy, between the weak and the powerful. For the poor and weak, the role of the state is more to ensure conditions and controls permitting well-being. For the rich and powerful, it is more to provide conditions and controls for behaviour which is responsible. The ideal to which society should strive is, then, an environment in which both 'well-being' and 'responsible' are continually defined and redefined, both individually and collectively, and in which the role of the state is to enhance opportunities for responsible well-being for all its citizens.[3]

For national domestic policies, these roles can be seen to entail the three Ds: decentralization, democracy and diversity. These reinforce each other. Enabling conditions for responsible well-being need local control through decentralization, an equity orientation and responsiveness through democratic norms and institutions, and scope for diversity to accommodate and encourage different expressions of responsibility, initiative and creativity on the part of individuals, groups and communities. For public sector management (taken here to refer mainly to the maintenance of an equitable rule of law, the provision of basic services, the management of public finances, and the management of government bureaucracies) the implications are radical.

REVERSALS IN THREE DOMAINS

To achieve the vision and the three Ds requires reversals of what is normal. Normal bureaucracy, professionalism and behaviour have to be stood on their heads. 'Normal' here indicates what could be called the default mode: it is the condition which tends to prevail unless a special effort is made. The vision is of public sector management and public servants affirming and expressing reversals in three domains: procedural, professional and personal, the three Ps. These reversals imply institutions with procedures and rewards with more downward accountability; a professionalism which values and respects people and the individual; and personal commitments which seek to serve those who are weaker and more deprived, accepting and celebrating diversity.

Let us explore these three domains in more detail.

Procedural

Normal bureaucracy can be seen to have tendencies towards centralization, standardization and control. The challenge is to reverse these: to decentralize, to allow and encourage diversity, and to empower through minimizing controls. This inverts normal top–down control-oriented bureaucracy in favour of minimum rules for self-organizing local systems 'on the edge of chaos', and replaces targets with trust.

Top–down attempts to manage complex inter-relations rarely work.[4] The Integrated Rural Development Projects of the 1970s[5] are a case in point. Centralized top–down planning for local conditions generates dependency, high costs, low morale, misinformation, and actions which cannot be sustained. It is a problem, not a solution.

The computer-based science of complexity has reached the same conclusion (see, for example, Resnick, 1994). In one view 'top down systems are forever running into combinations of events they don't know how to handle. They tend to be touchy and fragile, and they all too often grind to a halt in a dither of indecision' (Waldrop, 1994, p. 279, citing Langton). To achieve life-like behaviour the key has been to start with a few simple rules, to use local control instead of global control, and to 'Let the behaviour emerge from the bottom up, instead of being specified from the top down' (ibid., p. 280).

A spectacular example is the computer simulation 'boids', devised by Craig Reynolds (Waldrop, 1994, pp. 241–3). Bird-like agents (boids) on a screen are given three rules of behaviour: to maintain a minimum distance from other boids and other objects; to try to match the velocities of nearby boids; and to try to move towards the centre of mass of boids in their neighbourhood. These three rules invariably lead to boids flocking about the screen like birds. A top–down rule, 'form a flock', would have been impossibly complex. The rules that worked were simple, local, bottom–up, and the system emergent and self-organizing. In computer simulation, thus, simple rules can generate behaviour which is complex, diverse and, for practical purposes, unpredictable in its detail.

Computers are one thing; social systems another. How transferable principles and experience are from one to the other is hard to judge. The parallels are, though, intriguing. Development projects can be paralysed by overload at their centres of control. They deal with varied environments and with idiosyncratic people as independent agents. By analogy, they should have simple rules which allow and enable people to manage in many ways in their local conditions, facilitating the diverse behaviour of individuals.

This runs counter to the administrative reflex to control. Bureaucratic caution calls for care to guard against all imaginable error or deviation, and for uniform and universal regulations to prevent these. In March 1992, I asked a group of Indian administrators what would be the basic minimum to standardize and regulate in setting up village-level savings and credit societies. Their list included rates of saving, application forms, eligibility, purposes of loans, rates of interest, repayments, penalties for default and credit ratios.

In contrast, the programme of some 2500 savings and credit societies initiated and supported by MYRADA, a non-governmental organization (NGO) in South India, allows diversity in practice, entrusting rule making to individual societies. Each society is free to meet its needs and its members' needs in its own way. Each makes its own rules for how much each member should save and at what intervals, what loans can be for, interest rates, conditions for repayment, penalties for default and so on. MYRADA insists on only two operating requirements. The first is transparent, accurate and honest accounting. The second is that those with special responsibility are regularly rotated through democratic election, and are not called presidents or secretaries, but 'representatives' (personal communication, Aloysius Fernandez, 1996).

These minimal rules or controls permit behaviour which is complex and locally diverse. The striking resonance by analogy with the few simple rules of non-hierarchical self-organizing systems in computer simulations poses the question whether we have here a deep paradigmatic insight, an interesting parallel, or an insignificant coincidence. Whatever the answer, it would seem, provisionally, that with both computers and people the key is to minimize central controls, and to pick just those few rules which promote or permit complex, diverse and locally fitting behaviour. The practical conclusion is to decentralize, with minimum rules of control, to enable local people to appraise, analyse, plan and adapt for local fit in their necessarily different ways.

However, a repeated experience is that decentralization transfers powers to local élites who then abuse their position for personal gain, or to local managers who are authoritarian and do not themselves behave in a participatory, decentralizing and trusting manner. The challenge is to identify just what minimum controls can offset this tendency. The experience with the savings groups may be defining here: their minimum controls concern transparency (through access to the financial records) and accountability through a democratic process of changing leadership and responsibility. A further control, in bureaucratic organizations which seek to become participatory, may need to be sanctions against those locally in power who act in an authoritarian manner and endanger participatory and democratic approaches 'below' them.

With these minimum controls in place, trust can then replace targets. The centralizing, standardizing and controlling mindset has many manifestations, some of them even disguised in participatory clothing. The 'logical framework' is arguably an example (for various points of view see Forster, 1996; Gasper, 1997). Top–down targeting is so deeply ingrained in the official mind in some countries that senior civil servants find it inconceivable that there could be an alternative. Yet targets have a tendency to demoralize, disable and distort: they demoralize because they are rarely negotiated, but rather handed down, often without regard for local conditions; they disable because they diminish flexibility (as situations evolve, it often makes sense to achieve something other than the original objectives); and they distort because of the tendency for prudent or threatened juniors to mislead in reporting achievements.

Professional

Normal professionalism (the concepts, values, methods and behaviours dominant in professions) tends to be related to things (or people-as-things) more than to people-as-people, and to value precise reductionist measurement in controlled conditions. The challenge is to reverse these: to place more value on qualitative and holistic judgements about complex realities. 'Things-and-numbers' professions and disciplines value and use measurement and precision often with extraordinary effect, usually in tightly controlled environments and conditions (for example in laboratories, operating theatres and with computers). They also tend to have the highest rewards and the highest status. Compare computer sciences with counselling, micro-surgery with physiotherapy; genetic engineering with agricultural extension; or macroeconomics with social work. Not surprisingly, the reductionist and controlling values and methods of the high-status professions and disciplines dominate and tend to set the norms for those of lower status. But where they are dealing directly with personal and local realities such as people and farming systems, which are complex, diverse, dynamic and unpredictable, those dominant values and methods often make little sense.

What is required here is an upending of professional values to give more recognition and reward to judgement, to approximations and comparisons without measurements, to flexible adaptation, and to complex and diverse realities which are local, social and individual. This is already occurring. An example is the transition and extension in agricultural research from the top–down transfer of technology to approaches which start more with farmers' own analysis of their realities and priorities. Another is the shift from poverty defined as income poverty, as used for poverty lines in many countries, to a multidimensional view of human deprivation[6] which can include lack of assets and vulnerability, physical weakness, social exclusion, powerlessness and humiliation. The professionalism that fits the local, complex, diverse, dynamic, uncontrollable and unpredictable realities of poor and marginalized people has its own paradigm.

Personal

On a personal level, the central issue is knowledge, power and interpersonal behaviour. Normal behaviour, especially in teaching institutions and bureaucracies, has tendencies towards dominance and subordination. In teaching institutions these are expressed in teacher–student relationships, in which teachers are assumed to know and students not to know. In government bureaucracies both are manifested internally, and in relationships between officials and the public. These tendencies are found pervasively in social relations between many forms of 'uppers' and 'lowers'.[7] The challenge is to change the relationships so that uppers respect and empower lowers without destroying the necessary minimum hierarchy and safeguards, to shift the balance of behaviour from teaching towards facilitating, and from controlling towards enabling.

The experience with PRA (participatory rural appraisal)[8] has pointed forcefully towards the prime importance of personal behaviour and attitudes on the part of uppers if lowers are to be empowered and enabled to learn for themselves (see, for example, Kumar, 1996). The various injunctions to uppers to 'unlearn', 'sit down, listen and learn', 'don't interrupt', 'hand over the stick', 'ask them' and 'believe they can do it' (having confidence in the lowers' capabilities) mean a shift from normal domination to facilitation. This often requires personal change. It is striking how frequently those who have been facilitating PRA for a matter of years report that they have themselves changed in how they relate to others, in their families as well as in their work.

THE THREE DS, AND THE QUESTION: WHOSE REALITY COUNTS?

Decentralization and democratic values combine in the recognition of personal realities which are local, individual and diverse. The conditions, values, preferences, criteria and priorities of poor people and of professionals often differ.[9] Again and again the realities of those who are poor and marginalized are ignored or misread. The challenge is how to give voice to those who are left out and to make their reality count.

This means that if public sector management is to serve the poor, measures have to be taken to enable poor people themselves to analyse and articulate their priorities. Until recently, this was a rare activity. But recently participatory poverty assessments (PPAs), initiated first by the World Bank through bilateral support, and now (1997) promoted and implemented on an increasing scale by the Bank, the United Nations Development Programme (UNDP) and bilaterals, and governments alike, have begun to provide a means for poor people to express themselves. Participatory methodologies, perhaps most notably PRA, have shown both power and popularity in enabling those who are subordinate to articulate and analyse their realities.[10]

Insights about the priorities of poor people in countries of the South have included, for example, the importance of all-weather roads for access to medical treatment and markets during the rains, the need to reschedule the timing of school fees away from the most difficult time of year, and training health staff to be friendly and respectful to poor people seeking treatment. In Bangladesh, where the focus of analysis by poor people was on 'doables', differences in priorities between women and men, and between urban and rural, were highlighted (UNDP, 1996). The first doable priority of urban women was drinking water, and the second private places for washing. A widespread desire of poor people was enforcement of the anti-dowry laws. Elsewhere, a better understanding of sectoral priorities, for example between health and education, and between services and infrastructure, has also resulted.

The PPAs are, however, no part of the analysis or recommendations of the *World Development Report 1997* (World Bank, 1997) on *The State in a Changing World*. In its 13 pages of references, none refers to any of the PPAs, even though there is an extensive literature and many PPAs have been carried out under the auspices of the World Bank. Nor does chapter 7 of the report, on 'Bringing the state closer to people', mention PPAs, nor does it consider how the realities of poor and marginalized people can be expressed. The words are there – 'participation' and 'decentralization' – but not the recognition of the other realities of the poor. The mindset remains centre–outwards, 'protecting the poor' (p. 27) rather than empowering them. The implicit answer of the report to the question 'Whose reality counts?' is that it is the reality of the poor as assumed and projected by the centrally placed, highly qualified and intelligent authors of the report, not that expressed and analysed by the poor themselves.

THE PRIMACY OF THE PERSONAL

The neglect of the personal dimension in development seems at first sight bizarre. Development professionals struggle with research, planning, policies, programming, implementation, monitoring, evaluation, procedures, negotiations, reports, reforms and much else, usually without reflecting on what sort of people we are who are engaging in and determining these activities. To be sure, there are programmes of training, human resource development, and the like, but these rarely touch our behaviour, attitudes, values, beliefs and commitments. Yet it is embarrassingly evident that most of what happens in development follows and flows from personal factors: what we do and do not do. Whether change is good or bad is largely determined by personal actions, whether of political leaders, officials, professionals or local people, by international currency speculators, executives of transnational corporations, NGO workers or researchers, by mothers, fathers or children, by soldiers, secret agents, journalists, lawyers, police, protesters, or other sorts of people. What these people do determines what happens, more perhaps than normally recognized: chaos theory (Gleick, 1988) and reflection on common experience tell us that big differences can result from small changes in starting conditions. And most people can affect a host of starting conditions with multiplying chain effects.

That said, what happens depends especially on those who have most power and wealth. What they do and do not do can make a phenomenal difference to the well-being of others. The *World Development Report 1997* quotes Napoleon's remark that 'Men are powerless to secure the future; institutions alone fix the destinies of nations' (World Bank, 1997, p. 29). The paradox is that Napoleon himself is an extreme example of the extraordinary ability of a single individual to shape history and in a sense secure the future through the institutions which he was responsible for creating.

One might have supposed, then, that trying to understand and change the perceptions, motivations and behaviours of those with power and wealth would have been at the centre of development and development studies, and a

major focus of concern for the International Monetary Fund (IMF), the World
Bank, other donor agencies, governments and NGOs. But studies of greed
and generosity are few.[11] There are dozens of institutes devoted to development studies but there is, to my knowledge, no institute devoted primarily to
the study of personal power, greed and altruism.

Part of the neglect may stem from academic culture with its hatred of
moralizing and evangelism, the value it attaches to supposed objectivity, and
its search for general rather than individual explanations. Potently, too, the
neglect is a defence against examining one's own actions and inactions. It is
disturbing to reflect on what one does and does not do. It is embarrassing to
be confronted by deprivation and suffering when one's own condition is
neither deprived nor suffering. When a poor farmer in India asked me about
my income I could not reply. To put the personal to the fore is to expose my
own hypocrisy. But hypocrisy is no excuse for silence about the centrality of
the personal dimension.

The enormity of this missing link is shown by the most recent *Human
Development* and *World Development Reports* (UNDP, 1997; World Bank,
1997). The *Human Development Report 1997* is concerned with poverty. It
recommends six essential actions: empowering individuals, households and
communities; strengthening gender equality; accelerating pro-poor growth; improving the management of globalization; ensuring an active state; and taking
special actions for special situations. All of these require action by those who
are powerful and relatively wealthy. For its part, the *World Development Report
1997* presents many recommendations for action. In recognizing the importance of leadership and vision (for example, pp. 14, 123, 154–5, 166), in noting
political constraints and vested interests, and in lamenting the 'unbridled pursuit of riches or power' (p. 159), it does indeed get closer to the personal. But it
does not go the whole way. It does not confront the need for personal change.
Where the moving force is to come from is not clear. Incentives are recom-
mended, but the question remains who determines and pushes through the
incentives. Neither report comes to grips with the personal dimension.

Nor does it appear prominently in academic analysis. There have been few
studies of individual officials as leaders.[12] Not surprisingly, given the sensitivity of the subject, studies of corruption (IDS, 1996; Harriss-White and
White, 1996), contrasting the 'old corruption' of economic *dirigisme* and
political authoritarianism and a 'new corruption' associated with economic
and political liberalization, do not deal in detail with the personal level.

Nor is the issue tackled by calling for political will. For political will arises
only from the commitment of people, usually in powerful positions, which
takes us back again to the personal.

Adopting the concept of responsible well-being is one way of putting the
personal in the centre. Responsible well-being is an individual condition. In a

recent statement the UK Secretary of State for International Development, Clare Short, said of the new pro-poor agenda 'the selfish and the greedy have to favour it too' (DFID, 1997). One might add, so too must all those who enjoy the exercise of power, almost all managers, and all who are out of touch with poor people. The major issue is how to encourage and enable the powerful and wealthy to accept the implications of responsible well-being, or something close to it, as an ideal, defining it for themselves in ways which make things better for those who are weak and poor.

TOWARDS A RADICAL PRO-POOR AGENDA

Any radical agenda should be permanently provisional, and always evolving and changing. It can have many elements. Each of us at any time would have our own list. The list which follows is simply a personal view, presented as a groping attempt to identify some of the implications of the analysis and assertions above.

For *procedural and institutional change*, the challenge is to transform public bureaucracies into responsive organizations which are friendly to the poor and weak (Blackburn and Holland, 1998). For this, they have to become participatory learning organizations (Senge, 1990). Some promising elements for this are:

- recruitment of staff with a participatory and pro-poor orientation;
- gender and other social balance and sensitivity;
- social audits;
- selective abolition of top–down target setting in rural and urban development;
- minimizing controls to enable 'edge of chaos' diversity, creativity and ownership;
- PRA-type activities at community and group levels;
- participatory monitoring and evaluation, in which local people monitor and evaluate their own projects and the actions of government and NGOs;
- downward accountability, for example through citizen empowerment (see, for example, the Bangalore report cards (World Bank, 1997, p. 118));
- transformative learning experiences for officials and especially managers (see *personal change* below).

For *professional change*, the challenge is changes in professional concepts, values, methods and behaviours. Professional roles change from control to empowering, from supervision to service, and from teaching and transferring knowledge to facilitating learning and analysis. Other professional changes include shifts of balance and degree from reductionism to holism, from measurement to judgement, and from product to process. Economists and accountants have their place but their modes of thinking would cease to dominate so much, with management more by trust than numbers. The equivalents of participatory poverty assessments would be an accepted practice for upper–lower relationships, to enable lowers freely to express their realities.

It is, though, *personal change* which is crucial. Changes which are procedural, institutional and professional, and what is called 'political will', all depend on personal commitment and action. This is, then, the key to all else. Those with power and wealth have to behave differently. For them we need a pedagogy for the non-oppressed,[13] with the aim of responsible well-being through awareness, commitment and action.

Pessimists will argue that it is improbable that the powerful will disempower themselves, or the wealthy willingly make do with less. Faced with the enormities of corruption, violence and mindless greed, it can indeed appear naïve to stress the positive side of human nature which is altruistic and generous. But it can be at least as naïve and unbalanced to stress the negative. In the context of both power and wealth, the underlying assumptions of pessimists are open to challenge.

Concerning power, we are trapped by syntax into treating it like a commodity: power is gained or lost. In the military idiom, it is seized and surrendered. This makes it sound like a zero-sum good, in which one person's gain is another's loss. Getting more power is then good, and having less is bad. This leads to the supposition that the exercise of power and control enhances personal well-being. The issues here are not simple. There is a place for good leadership, and the exercise and trappings of power bring satisfactions to many. But there is another, offsetting side. Power can be an addiction. A World Bank staff member remarked that he was a 'recovering controllaholic'; and personal disempowerment ('handing over the stick') can bring on withdrawal symptoms. Yet there can be many rewards from exercising less power and control: enhanced effectiveness, as with decentralization to permit self-organizing diversity; liberation, with the reduction of the controllaholic's stress; the opening of space for relationships which are friendly and collegial; and fulfilment, fun and satisfaction in the achievements of others, as many teachers know from their students, and many facilitators of PRA have found through the appraisals, analyses and actions of local people. To create the conditions for self-organizing systems and watch them emerge can be profoundly exciting and rewarding.

The common assumption is that more income and wealth leads to greater personal well-being. For the very poor and deprived this may indeed often be so, though it is striking how often they value other things more.[14] For the wealthy, it is empirically questionable, to say the least. The global neo-liberal monomania has reinforced and spread a vulgar economists' model of human-kind as rational maximizers. But people are more complex, as recognized even in the *World Development Report 1997*. This repeatedly stresses the importance of 'incentives' which are less reductionist and less based on the material than might have been expected. A defect of institutional reforms, it concludes, is that they have 'not focused on incentives, which come from *competitive pressures, partnership*, and *transparency*, and from *rule-based systems*' (World Bank, 1997, p. 167, my emphases). While these go beyond the directly material, the report does not consider the incentives of altruism and generosity (for which see Uphoff, 1992), nor dimensions of well-being which are social, ethical or spiritual. There is a social and materially unselfish side to human motivation which is left out of the analysis.

A problem node or knot is where power, wealth and corruption interlock. In the long term, the question is how far, as incentives, the satisfactions of right behaviour, disempowerment and generosity can outweigh losses in au-thority and rents. If sensitive action research could identify ways forward here, the payoffs could be huge. In the meantime, the radical agenda can be pursued by developing a pedagogy for the non-oppressed. Initially, this has been taking the form of transformative experiences. Many modes for these are needed. Three stand out, each at an early stage of methodological devel-opment:

Immersion learning   Under James Wolfensohn's leadership, senior World Bank staff are being encouraged to spend a week in a village or slum. The early feedback suggests that, for some at least, this is a normative experience, with potential for long-term personal significance.

Direct and democratic interaction   Policy makers can, through PRA, have direct experience of local conditions with unconstrained learning from poor people. Participatory poverty assessments have enabled those who are poor and marginalized to analyse their realities and express their priorities in ways which are credible to policy makers. Officials and managers can take part in these or other participatory activities which bring them into direct and non-dominating contact with poor people. Health service managers have done this in the UK. Poor people have presented their PRA outputs to policy makers and others in several countries in the South. As PPAs using PRA methods are increasingly carried out at sub-national levels (for example in India, Tanzania and Uganda), the potentials here will multiply.

Behaviour and attitudes training   With the rapid spread of PRA in govern-ment organizations as well as NGOs, behaviour and attitudes have often been relatively neglected, leading to strong concerns (Absalom et al., 1995; Mallik et al., 1996). A robust package of relatively straightforward behaviour and attitudes exercises and facilitated experiences is being sought for use by trainers (Kumar, 1996).

CONCLUSION

For contemporary public management and its future, three assertions can summarize and conclude:

1. *A pro-poor agenda demands radical changes*   These are procedural and institutional, professional, and personal.
2. *Personal change is the key*   The personal dimension of awareness, commitment and action remains a blind spot in development research, policy and practice. Those (policy makers, officials, and members of civil society including academics) who are serious about pro-poor public management have now to put the personal dimension at centre stage.
3. *The greatest methodological challenge we face as humankind is how to tackle this personal dimension*, how to enable those who dominate to become more democratic, and those with more power and wealth to experience being better off with less.

NOTES

1. The concept of responsible well-being is explored in *Whose Reality Counts?* (Chambers, 1997, pp. 9–12). The point is, though, not that it should be defined for everyone, but that anyone who wishes should define and redefine it for herself or himself, sharing ideas with others.
2. PRA as participatory rural appraisal has become an inappropriate acronym, since many applications are in urban and other non-rural contexts, and activities extend far beyond appraisal to include planning, action, monitoring and evaluation, and behaviour and attitudes. One suggestion is that PRA could now more accurately stand for participatory reflection and action. For a detailed review of PRA methods and applications see *Whose Reality Counts?* chapter 6. A major source for PRA materials is *PLA Notes*, published by the International Institute for Environment and Development, 3 Endsleigh Street, London WC1H 0DD. PLA stands for Participatory Learning and Action.
3. This need not imply a narrow nationalism. Responsible can and in my view should be defined to include international relations with other institutions and countries, and actions affecting poor and deprived people in other countries.
4. This and the following paragraphs are from *Whose Reality Counts?*, pp. 199–200.
5. For a devastating review of the experience with Integrated Rural Development Projects, see World Bank (1988).
6. See, for example, the *Human Development Report 1997* (UNDP, 1997) which firmly establishes income-poor and income poverty as terms to be used for that subset of deprivation which is measured for poverty lines.

7.   I apologize for referring again to *Whose Reality Counts?*, but 'uppers' and 'lowers' are elaborated and explored on pp. 58–62, and also in chapter 5, 'all power deceives'.
8.   For an early source on PRA see Mascarenhas et al. (1991). For reflective critiques, see *PLA Notes* 26 (published by IIED, 3 Endsleigh Street, London WC1H 0DD).
9.   For evidence supporting this assertion see *Whose Reality Counts?* especially chapter 8.
10.   PPAs using PRA approaches and methods have been pioneered in many countries starting in Ghana (Norton et al., 1995; Dogbe, 1996), Zambia (Norton et al., 1994), and South Africa (Attwood, 1996; May, 1996; Murphy, 1995; Teixeira and Chambers, 1995), and spreading from Africa to Asia (for example, Bangladesh; UNDP, 1996), using a variety of processes. For reviews see Robb (1997); Holland and Blackburn in press; Chambers and Blackburn (1996); Norton and Stephens (1995).
11.   One study (Frank et al., 1993) showed alarmingly that economists were more likely than non-economists to act in a non-trusting, non-cooperative, self-interested manner. The median gift to big charities by economists among 1245 randomly selected college professors was substantially lower than for non-economists; and about 9 per cent of economists gave nothing, as against a range of 1 to 4 per cent for other disciplines. In a prisoners' dilemma game economics students defected 60 per cent of the time compared with 39 per cent for non-economists.
12.   David Leonard's *African Successes: Four Public Managers in Kenyan Rural Development* (1991) and Emery Roe's study (1993) of James Leach are notable exceptions.
13.   Peter Reason (personal communication) has proposed, at the time of going to press, with apologies to Paulo Freire (1970), a 'pedagogy for the privileged' which may prove a better and more enduring title.
14.   Some of the evidence concerning the surprisingly low priority accorded directly to income by poor people, compared with qualities like health, self-respect, good social relations, and spending time at home, is presented in *Whose Reality Counts?* (1997), pp. 176–9.

REFERENCES

Absalom, Elkanah et al. (1995), 'Participatory methods and approaches: sharing our concerns and looking to the future', *PLA Notes*, No. 22, pp. 5–10.

Attwood, Heidi (1996), 'South African Participatory Poverty Assessment process: were the voices of the poor heard?', paper for the PRA and Policy Workshop, IDS, Sussex, 13–14 May.

Blackburn, James and Holland, Jeremy (eds) (1998), *Who Changes? Institutionalising Participation in Development*, London: Intermediate Technology Publications.

Chambers, Robert (1997), *Whose Reality Counts? Putting the First Last*, London: Intermediate Technology Publications.

Chambers, Robert and Blackburn, James (1996), 'The Power of Participation: PRA and Policy', Briefing Paper, IDS, University of Sussex, Brighton, UK.

DFID (1997), 'Democracy, Rights, and Governance', Address by Clare Short, UK Secretary of State for International Development, to the international conference on Public Sector Management for the Next Century, Manchester University, 29 June–2 July.

Dogbe, Tony (1996), 'The one who rides the donkey does not know the ground is hot', Paper for the PRA and Policy Workshop, IDS, Sussex, 13–14 May.

Forster, Reiner (ed.) (1996), *ZOPP marries PRA?*, Deutsche Gesellschaft für Technische Zusammenarbeit (GTZ), Germany: GmbH, Eschborn.

Frank, Robert, Gilovich, Thomas and Regan, Dennis (1993), 'Does studying economics inhibit cooperation?', *Journal of Economic Perspectives* (Spring), as reviewed in *The Economist*, 29 May 1993.

Freire, Paulo (1970), *Pedagogy of the Oppressed*, New York: The Seabury·Press.

Gasper, Des (1997), 'Logical frameworks in perspective: managerial theory, turbulent realities, pluralistic practice', paper to the international conference on Public Sector Management for the Next Century, Manchester University, 29 June–2 July.

Gleick, James (1988), *Chaos: Making a New Science*, London: Penguin.

Harriss-White, Barbara and White, Gordon (1996), 'Editorial introduction: corruption, liberalization and democracy', in *Liberalization and the New Corruption, IDS Bulletin*, **27** (2), April, 1–5.

Havel, Vaclav (1992), 'Report of a speech to the Davos Development Conference', *New York Times*, 1 March.

IDS (1996), *Liberalization and the New Corruption*, IDS Bulletin, **27** (2), April.

Kumar, Somesh (ed.) (1996), *ABC of PRA: Attitude Behaviour Change*, South–South Workshop on PRA: Attitudes and Behaviour, 1–10 July 1996, organized by ACTIONAID India and SPEECH, Bangalore: ActionAid.

Leonard, David K. (1991), *African Successes: Four Public Managers in Kenyan Rural Development*, Berkeley, Los Angeles and Oxford: University of California Press.

Mallik, Abu Hena et al. (1996), 'Sharing our experiences: an appeal to donors and governments', *PLA Notes*, No. 27, October, 74–6.

Mascarenhas, James et al. (1991), *Proceedings of the February 1991 Bangalore PRA Workshop*, *RRA Notes*, No. 13, August.

May, Julian (1996), 'Kicking down doors and lighting fires: participating in policy: the SA–PPA experience', paper for the PRA and Policy Workshop, IDS, Sussex, 13–14 May.

Murphy, Carol (1995), *Implications of Poverty for Black Rural Women in Kwazulu/ Natal*, Report for the South African Participatory Poverty Assessment, Institute of Natural Resources, Scottsville, South Africa.

Norton, Andy, Owen, Dan and Milimo, John (1994), *Zambia Participatory Poverty Assessment:Volume 5: Participatory Poverty Assessment*, Report 12985–ZA, Southern Africa Department, Washington, DC: World Bank.

Norton, Andy, Kroboe, David, Bortei-Dorku, Ellen and Dogbe, Tony (1995), *Ghana Participatory Poverty Assessment. Consolidated Report on Poverty Assessment in Ghana Using Qualitative and Participatory Research Methods: Draft Report*, AFTHR, World Bank.

Norton, Andrew and Stephens, Thomas (1995), *Participation in Poverty Assessments*, Environment Department Papers Participation Series, Social Policy and Resettlement Division, the World Bank, Washington, June.

Resnick, Mitchell (1994), *Turtles, Termites and Traffic Jams: Explorations in Massively Parallel Microworlds*, Cambridge, MA and London: MIT Press.

Robb, Caroline (1997), 'Is Local Knowledge Legitimate? Influencing Policy Through Participatory Poverty Assessments', draft paper, World Bank, 28 August.

Roe, Emery (1993), 'Public service, rural development and careers in public management: a case study of expatriate advisers and African land reform', *World Development*, **21** (3), 349–65.

Senge, Peter (1990), *The Fifth Discipline: the Art and Practice of the Learning Organization*, New York: Doubleday.

Teixeira, Lynne and Chambers, Fiona (1995), *Child Support in Small Towns in the Eastern Cape*, Black Sash Advice Office, Port Elizabeth, South Africa.

UNDP (1996), *Report on Human Development in Bangladesh: A Pro-Poor Agenda, Volume 3: Poor People's Perspectives*, UNDP, Dhaka, Bangladesh.

UNDP (1997), *Human Development Report 1997*, Oxford: Oxford University Press.

Uphoff, Norman (1992), *Learning from Gal Oya: Possibilities for Participatory Development and Post-Newtonian Social Science*, Ithaca and London: Cornell University Press (paperback 1996 with new introduction, London: Intermediate Technology Publications).

Waldrop, M. Mitchell (1994), *Complexity: the Emerging Science at the Edge of Order and Chaos*, Harmondsworth: Penguin.

World Bank (1988), *Rural Development: the World Bank Experience 1965–86*, Operations Evaluation Department, World Bank, Washington.

World Bank (1997), *World Development Report 1997: The State in a Changing World,* Oxford: Oxford University Press.

8. Professionalism, participation and the public good: issues of arbitration in development management and the critique of the neo-populist approach

David Brown

INTRODUCTION

Three aspects of recent trends in rural development policy are especially worthy of note. The first is a dramatic *change of scale* in the level of perceived authority in decision making. In place of a presumption that policy decisions must be made at the highest levels of policy analysis and be informed by information only available at those levels, has been a growing belief that the proper locus of decision making is at the lowest levels, indeed within the very rural communities which are the ultimate target of international aid.

The second (and related) change has been in the conception of the relevant *policy community*. Here the trend has been to undermine the legitimacy of the development professional, in favour of a growing faith in the power of the rural poor themselves both to identify the broad character of the initiatives which best serve their interests and to manage them in a way which will most effectively respond to their needs. In short, there has been a change in the locus of authority from 'professionalism' to 'participation'.

The third trend concerns the policy implications of the *'groundswell of democratic pluralism'* which pervades present aid management (Farrington, 1996), and which implies a belief that the rationality of the market can be recreated by a widening of public participation through the growth of civil society and the weakening of the state. Interestingly, the vehicle for this democratization is held to be provided mainly by the activities of a category of non-governmental organizations (NGOs) which are not themselves democratically constituted, and whose identities derive from their claimed independence from political processes (Farrington and Bebbington, 1993).

These trends are not, of course, unique to development management. They form part of a broader movement which has set the tone for political debate in the wealthiest of nations as well as the poorest of the poor. What is unexpected, however, is the extent to which an agenda that, in the context of democratic politics has been laid out by those on the right of the political spectrum (and often the far right, at that), has, in relation to equity-oriented international aid, been captured by those who claim quite the opposite political sympathies. An unexpected aspect of the evolution in rural development thinking has been a coming together of two seemingly irreconcilable positions. The views of the Right concerning the need to break down the power of powerful interest groups (Flynn, 1990) have found their counterpart not in the traditional anti-aid lobby, but in the softer more socially responsive traditions associated with the championing of poverty-focused international aid. Calls on the Right for the voice of the people to be heard have their resonances not just among the free marketers, but also among those committed to the empowerment of the poor.

These are strange bedfellows. How is it possible, one wonders, to reconcile the interests of those who espouse the primacy of the marketplace, whatever its social consequences, with those who argue that, left to itself, the market has little to offer the poor, and that an equity-oriented perspective must draw on wider structures of responsibility than those of the market alone, in the interests of a fundamental change in the patterns of wealth and influence?

This chapter will address this paradox, and consider the extent to which the participatory movement is likely, in the event, to be able to deliver on its radical promises. It should be made clear at the outset that the aim is not to question the Third World public's right to participation, still less to challenge the principle of democracy, but merely to assess the ability of the current trends to hold fast to these laudable aims.

PROFESSIONS AND PARADIGMS

A number of interconnected themes have converged in support of the new agenda in development management: the attack on 'normal professionalism' and the need for a 'new professionalism' to take its place; the recognition of indigenous technical knowledge; the promotion of participatory, farmer-led research methodologies; and the championing of the participatory rural appraisal (PRA) movement both as a research tool and a development philosophy. Increasingly, these themes are being developed into a challenge to what is seen as the dominant paradigm of development: the need to substitute the Western paradigm of scientific rationalism or positivism by a more value-laden approach, which seeks to place human perceptions and interests at the centre of the analysis, in place of a search for objective standards of reality. The interweaving of these themes is most evident in the works of writers such as Chambers (1983; 1993; Chapter 7 in this book) and Pretty (1995). Their influence on the wider practices of development management has been quite pervasive, however, and their views have increasingly set the agenda not only for non-governmental organizations but also for all forms of aid intervention. This movement will be referred to in this chapter as, for want of a better term, 'neo-populism'.

The chapter examines the central tenet of this movement: the challenge to the normal professions.

THE CRITIQUE OF NORMAL PROFESSIONALISM

The view that the normal professions which have hitherto dominated aid management are themselves a major contributory factor to failures in development, and that, in consequence, new standards of professionalism must be sought to take their place, is a key element in the neo-populist thinking on development. At the same time, the promise of a new order of development practice, which the critique holds out, accounts for much of the optimism that pervades the neo-populist literature, and is its major contribution at the level of policy.

The central issue is the perceptions of the normal professionals, and the complaint is that by the very acts of specialization and refinement, the interests of the poor and marginal become obscured to the professional practitioner. Chambers's views on the need for an alternative professionalism (the new professionalism), based on a series of role reversals and the premise of new forms of truly participatory development, stem from this critique (1993, p. 83).

Such ideas are seemingly as radical as they are ambitious, and the fact that they disclaim the need for an intervening revolutionary movement or political intervention of any substantive kind clearly sets them apart from much of the sociological theorizing which has hitherto been the stock in trade of studies of rural development. It also, no doubt, increases their attractiveness to the non-governmental sector, to which, for a variety of reasons, formal types of 'political' activity are denied.

At the same time, the boldness of the approach should not conceal the ambiguity of the underlying argument. Indeed, much of the attractiveness of this argument, and also its resilience, derives from the interweaving of a number of (arguably conflicting) elements held together not by any managerial or intellectual rigour but by their enclosure within a powerful normative boundary.

THE ELEMENTS OF THE CRITIQUE

Though articulated in terms of the critique of professionalism, a concern with the professions as a form of status group is in fact only part of the argument. The analysis also addresses a number of other themes, most notably a preoccupation with personal values and attitudes and the functioning of bureaucracies. These three elements of the critique can be labelled as, respectively, the professional, the normative and the administrative. We shall consider each in turn; in each case, what is omitted from the analysis proves to be quite as important as what is held to be central to it.

The Normative Critique: Values and Attitudes

At one level, the central concern of the neo-populist mission is a personal, almost proselytizing one, in which questions of power and authority are treated as largely subordinate to individual values and attitudes. A significant dose of moral rearmament underpins the approach, and accounts for at least some of its appeal to a movement dominated by organizations whose boundaries are primarily normative (see, for example, Chambers, 1983; 1993; Chapter 7 in this book; Pretty, 1995). On the one hand are the values and attitudes of normal professionals: 'it is not they who have been wrong, but us. The first step, then is humbling. It is to recognise our ignorance and error. ... It is with ourselves that we have to start' (Chambers, 1997, p. 32).

On the other hand are the new professionals: 'The key is personal choice. ... People can choose how to behave and what to do. ... Altruism is a fact in human behaviour and can be chosen. ... No one is fully determined; No one is immune from altruism' (Chambers, 1997, pp. 12–13).

It is interesting that despite its preoccupation with the injustices experienced in the societies of the South, this normative orientation draws only peripherally on the literature of political sociology and the sociology of development, and concerns itself surprisingly little with the political origins of the values which are questioned. While the historical origins of many of these values in colonialism and neo-colonialism are occasionally acknowledged, their structural dimensions (and the fact that they can be viewed as variables dependent on class relationships rooted in neo-colonial economy) do not seriously detain the analysis. Again, this restraint considerably widens the appeal in a context in which the institutional dimensions of the new thinking are rooted in the non-governmental sector, itself an essentially middle-class movement in both the North and South, and one whose attendant class relations have been remarkably little explored.

The Administrative Critique: Normal Professionals and Normal Bureaucrats

To the extent that the neo-populist critique is one concerned primarily with the values and attitudes associated with particular processes of governance, its primary points of reference (in so far as they are not merely individual) could be said to be more administrative than professional. Where a more focused institutional dimension is brought to the analysis, this is arguably concerned as much with the workings of bureaucracies as with professions as such. The concepts of normal professionalism and normal bureaucracy appear in the critique more or less as synonyms (see, for example, Chambers, 1997, pp. 63–5).

The implied critique of the Third World bureaucracy is not, however, that familiar in development management. Traditionally, in the literature on Third World bureaucracies, the tendency has been to regret the (alleged) failure of public administration to conform to the bureaucratic ideal because of its subversion by relations of patronage and dependence and by the ascriptive and particularistic values associated with the 'traditional state' (Brown, 1989). In the neo-populist critique, by contrast, Third World bureaucracies tend to be accepted at their face value; their limitations are seen as lying not in their abuse of the ideal but in its proper functioning. This is an unexpected position in so far as it is associated with an analysis imbued with a strong value orientation. Its origins may be found in the depoliticization of the approach. Here, as elsewhere in the writings of the neo-populists, the political and institutional dimensions of the situation are consistently discounted, and the argument is diverted from structural relationships to individual responsibilities (Brown, 1995, p. 14).

The Professional Critique: Professional Loyalties

While part of the problem is thus an attitudinal one, normal professionalism also stands condemned by the neo-populists on the grounds of its loyalties. Normal professionalism, it is argued, feeds the centralization of control, the standardization and conservatism inherent in normal bureaucracies, and thus reinforces the barriers to the true empowerment of the mass. This critique provides the intellectual underpinnings for a desire to weaken professional involvement in public decision making and to shift the locus of legitimacy towards the grass roots, both strong points of sympathy with neo-liberal politics.

To the extent that this critique is accepted, important questions are thus raised both as to the decision making roles which have hitherto been played by normal professionals and also (of equal importance) as to the alternatives the neo-populists would seek to establish in their place. A brief digression into the sociology of the professions allows us to place this debate in its wider theoretical context.

THE SOCIOLOGY OF THE PROFESSIONS

Sociological interpretations of the professions have tended to adopt one of two approaches. The conventional approach is to treat the characterization of the professions primarily as a question of definition. On this interpretation, the central concern is with the traits which define the professions, justify their high status and remuneration, and separate them from other occupational groups lacking such attributes. Typical examples of these traits include the possession of a body of theoretical knowledge linked to high educational achievement; competence standards and other ways of licensing the profession; and considerable occupational autonomy (Laffin, 1986).

The alternative view focuses on the negotiation of professional status as a political phenomenon, and emphasizes the ways in which occupations which are accepted as professions relate to other power centres in the society. On this view, the emergence of internal attributes would be primarily interpreted as the means by which a profession can seek support for its own elevated status and actively maintain its social boundary, rather than as performance standards *per se* (Laffin, 1986, p. 196). This view of the professions suggests a definition of professionalism as a 'peculiar type of occupational control, rather than an expression of the inherent nature of particular occupations' (Johnson, 1974, p. 57), and emphasizes the crucial element of self-determination, 'the right to control its own work' (Friedson, 1970, p. 71), which a profession claims for itself.

On the face of it, this is a potentially more interesting perspective from the sociological point of view. On the one hand, it avoids the functionalist trap (the view that privilege exists because of society's need for valued services, not because of the exercise of power). On the other, it can also accommodate change and evolution in the relationships of professions to the societies in which they are embedded. It is evident, for example, that occupations can both lose and gain professional identity, and also that occupations which share with professions many of their defining characteristics may not gain public recognition as professions themselves, because they lack the power to establish the independence of managerial action integral to that identity.

It is, however, possible to overplay the issue of self-determination, for absolute autonomy is not necessarily the sole influence over the public perception of a profession. Even those occupations which are clearly viewed by the public as professions are subject to some degree of external influence, so that the issue at stake may be less a case of the presence or absence of mechanisms of external control than of politically induced changes in the locus and extent of existing patterns of influence. Changes in professional status may be more the result of a change in the areas of influence over occupational decision making than of the imposition of a hierarchical relationship.

Thus, it is arguable that the defining characteristic of professions is not absolute independence but maximization of autonomy. There is an important element of subjectivity in the propensity of society to recognize an occupational grouping as meriting professional identity, and there is also a subjective component relating to the manner in which any challenges to the *status quo* are accompanied by a successful challenge to such professional legitimacy.

A number of issues must be examined in relation to the claims of the new professionalism to represent a radical departure from the standards of normal professionalism.

Standards of Arbitration in Professional Decision Making

In the first instance, the recognition that changes in professional status are a negotiated process in which other interest groups attempt to establish an influence over the performance of professional roles raises important issues as to the standards of arbitration which are to be applied when changes in processes of decision making come about. In the ideal-typical instance of professional autonomy, such decisions are left to the occupational groups themselves, who will apply their own procedural standards, and (at least in theory) be held fully accountable for them. At the other extreme is a situation of maximum external influence, in which the lack of any independent decision making power leads to the imposition of rules on the group (which effectively ceases, therefore, to conform to the standard of professional autonomy). In between these two extremes is a range of interesting alternatives in which claims to legitimacy by those seeking to influence professional standards by appeal to a wider consensus must be carefully judged for their representativeness.

Professional Boundary Maintenance

A second area of interest concerns the ways in which groups that claim professional status attempt to legitimize those claims, in part at least by creating and sustaining social and occupational boundaries. This involves consideration of the entry qualifications which the members of the association use to control movement across the boundary, the regulatory mechanisms applied to validate those qualifications, and the procedures which ensure that the accepted practices of the profession are properly upheld. We can represent the possible alternatives along a continuum with, at one pole, the ideal-typical professional body, in which skills and competences are validated by the internal rules of an association, and, at the other, standards of validation which are set entirely by external entities. In between is a range of alternatives in which a balance is sought between self-definition and external control.

Licensing Professionals

A third area of interest is the identities and influence of external entities in providing licence to groups to practise particular occupations and to identify themselves thereby as of professional status. These entities may include various levels of government, though they may also involve other actors with power in society.

STANDARDS OF ARBITRATION IN THE NEW PROFESSIONALISM

The next stage in the argument is to consider these three areas in relation to the agenda of the new professionalism. The first question concerns the standards of arbitration which are to be applied in a situation where normal criteria of professionalism are no longer regarded as valid. What alternative standards, it must be asked, do the neo-populists seek to put in their place?

In terms of the overall thrust of the argument, the clear implication is that there is need for a radical change in the locus of authority. The neo-populists are, it would seem, unequivocally in favour of a transfer from the outsider to the community, particularly its poorer members, and the role of the new professionalism is seen primarily as putting in place the means for the achievement of this by a series of 'reversals' of normal practices.

Indications of what this might mean in terms of decision making in the field are rather few and far between, for the analysis tends to be higher on rhetoric than it is on concrete instances. There are two particular areas of difficulty. The first concerns the ways in which missionary zeal is balanced by populist accommodation and compromise, leading to a reluctance to identify too clearly any prescriptions for practice which might alienate the public from the cause.The second difficulty relates to the proselytizing vision, which presents the new professionalism less as a coherent orientation than as a voyage of discovery. 'Our' mission is to apply whatever means are at our disposal to come closer to 'their' values and interests, and over-precision of aims would contradict the participatory philosophy.

But in those rather limited instances in which the precise nature of 'their' values and understandings are addressed in other than rhetorical terms, the radicalism proves to be unexpectedly circumscribed. An interesting note of caution enters the analysis, putting in doubt the extent to which real changes in the locus of authority are actually implied. For example, writing of the central preoccupation of the new professional (the incorporation of indigenous knowledge into public decision making), what Chambers (1983) actually proposes is rather less than a full transfer of authority across the class boundary. That populist action has limits of tolerance is clear; what these limits are is less certain:

> In seeking a balanced view of rural people's knowledge, it is as well to note that it can be overvalued as well as despised. ... Nor is rural people's knowledge always valid or useful. A further danger is that some observers may be tempted to revive the Noble Savage. ...
> But these positive biases may be no bad thing. ... To balance the [outsider's negative presuppositions] requires positive discrimination. (Chambers, 1983, pp. 84–5)

This conflation of 'overvaluation' and 'positive discrimination' is an interesting one, though it is by no means a necessary consequence of Chambers's argument, and its implications at the level of policy are obscure.

The French anthropologist, Olivier de Sardan, has explored this tension in a particularly illuminating way (1992; 1995). While noting the strong and positive anthropological leanings in Chambers's writings, Olivier de Sardan notes also the tendency to project on to the poor simple stereotypes, almost to the point of caricature. For example: 'Case studies show that poor rural people are usually tough, hard-working, ingenious and resilient' (Chambers, 1983, p. 103). Similarly: 'Rural people's knowledge can be underpinned and enhanced by a richness of discrimination not easily available to outsiders' science. This derives from an ability to use a wider range of experience and more of the human senses than a scientist' (Chambers, 1983, p. 90). To which might be added: 'The learning of scientists tends to be stepwise, that of local people incremental. Local people are continuously observing and experiencing. ... Scientists often rely on averages, which slows learning about change; the knowledge of local people is more dynamic and up-to-date' (Chambers, 1997, p. 173).

The difficulty with such caricatures, Olivier de Sardan argues, is that they are very readily inverted into negative stereotypes. The support which might appear to be given for a particular value orientation at one moment is liable to turn into a denunciation of that orientation at the next. Thus, the claimed positive predispositions in peasant culture (solidarity, self-reliance, consensus and tradition, the very bases of an alternative development) can easily be reconstructed as a set of cultural obstacles (cf. Hyden, 1983). Olivier de Sardan construes this as an ambivalence between 'populisme' and 'misérabilisme'. While the former overvalues the poor and idealizes them, the latter devalues their capacities, and sees their salvation as lying not in their own behaviour, but in the interventions of outsiders on their behalf. This tension and oscillation between populism and domino-centrism is seen by Grignon and Passeron (1989) as typical of populist writings in the social sciences. Its effect in the present instance is to draw into serious question the consistency of the standards of arbitration which the new professional is expected to apply.[1] If the quest for a new professionalism serves to undermine the established standards of arbitration in decision making inherent in normal professionalism, it should thus not be assumed that the new professionalism offers any superior standard of its own. There is an apparent inconsistency on the issue of the question of alternative standards, with an oscillation between an acceptance of the authority of the peasantry to claim control over their own sphere of action, and a rejection of such a position in favour of the retention of authority by a corps of (non-peasant) activists.

THE BOUNDARIES OF THE NEW PROFESSIONALISM

The next stage in the critique must be to explore this identity further, and to consider the two remaining issues of professional performance: how are the boundaries of the new professionalism to be defined, and by whose authority are these boundaries to be accepted as legitimate?

The neo-populist position would appear to be that commitment creates its own criteria for action. This has obvious appeal to young activists at the start of their careers, to whom long periods of apprenticeship and demanding and restrictive methodologies are understandably rather unenthusiastically received:

> We can all think for ourselves, use our personal best judgement, and help others to do the same. We can all define responsible well-being in our own ways for ourselves. ...
> Good changes flows from personal decision and action. There is no need to wait. There is a vanguard to join and new high ground to explore. (Chambers, 1997, p. 237)

The new professionals are advised: 'use your own best judgement at all times'; 'rely on personal judgement, not manuals or rules' (Chambers, 1997, p. 216). They are, in this sense, subject to a form of self-election within a religious community, bound not by any identifiable professional standards but by a shared faith in their own destiny and a desire to achieve a change in personality through a form of emanation.

At one level, of course, such exhortation is difficult to challenge. Responsible behaviour, involving respect for the values and practices of others, and reliance on one's judgements, are all sound precepts for action, with which few would be likely to disagree. But there are inherent problems with the elevation of such ideas to the status of sole guiding principles, particularly in the contexts in which they are most likely to be applied: management across national boundaries, in a situation of aid-funded development. In the first instance, there is the obvious paradox that, if there are no guarantees as to valid standards other than on the basis of personal judgement, how can one ensure that decisions will not merely exhibit normal professional prejudice? There is also the problem of cultural relativity. Whose personal judgements are to be applied where there is a conflict in cultural values between two or more actors, and no way to reconcile the different views? A third set of problems relates to the institutional dimensions of accountability.

PROFESSIONAL LICENCE AND THE INTERNATIONALIZATION OF AUTHORITY

The institutional settings of normal professionalism are largely unexplored in the critique of the new professionals, but they are, by the nature of the context, largely ones in which the basic structures of accountability are defined by what has been, hitherto, the dominant power of the Third World state. It would be difficult to argue, in many situations, that the Third World public services have been either fully accountable to their citizens (transparently this has not been the case under many regimes), or have acted in support of the public interest. The critique of the 'typical' Third World state is a fairly damning one, and the arguments in favour of the international community either intervening to limit its powers, or at least ceasing to use its aid to support its worst excesses, are powerful ones. To the extent that these views are accepted, then so must the critique of normal professionals (that is, bureaucrats) be regarded as justified. The fact that the functioning of Third World bureaucracies has often been misunderstood (particularly their role in providing a form of political stability through largely incorporative means) does not, of itself, rationalize the use of international aid to support the *status quo* (cf. Brown, 1989, *passim*).

However, this critique of the state should not be allowed to obscure the fact that in most of their manifestations in the developing world, normal professionals have at least had some degree of public accountability. Even if the bureaucracies have functioned in support of an élitist agenda which has marginalized and oppressed the peasant mass, and even if the relevant publics have not been empowered to oppose the abuses of power which have resulted thereby, then at least the boundaries of responsibility have often been identifiable to those publics, sooner or later – a fact to which the chronic instability of many Third World governments arguably attests. Again, this does not legitimize these (low) levels of public accountability, but it does at least provide a standard of comparison against which new forms of public action can be judged.

When we come to the new professionals, the boundaries of responsibility are arguably even less clear. One group of those who are likely to answer the call may be mainstream public servants working within a national funding frame. Where the institutional framework is one which rewards downward accountability, they may be able to influence the arenas of decision making. But the vast majority of the new professionals are likely to be working for development agencies, often in the non-governmental sector, where the dominant actors do not come from the (declining) state, but from the (increasingly powerful) donor agencies. These individuals are subject to little by way of public licence to validate their right to practise in their chosen fields; they are not even, in many cases, nationals of the society in which their influence will be felt, nor (unlike aid-funded consultants to Southern governments) are they at all accountable to national boundaries. The new professionals certainly include such nationals, but the terms of their employment and their career prospects often tie them very strongly not to their own societies but to organizations and donors outside their national boundaries (Hulme, 1994), in situations in which their ability to be true to themselves, and to use their own best judgement, is very far from guaranteed.

The institutional frameworks of the new professionalism are not, therefore, ones in which real accountability is likely to thrive. The language of self-questioning (the references to the challenge to 'our' values and assumptions) now takes on a different level of meaning, reflecting this external orientation, and distancing the intervention from the constraints which tie down both peasant and bureaucrat. When applied to the new professionals, this language is redolent not so much of the empowerment of the populations of the Third World, but of the globalization of the authority of the First. The growing influence of the new professionalism is arguably more a reflection of this shift in power than any growth in public accountability.

Nevertheless, it could be argued that accountability might still result in such situations, provided that two additional conditions are met: first, that the occupational practices which are associated with the new professionalism are themselves subject to public control and scrutiny, and are open to regulation according to established criteria of validity; and second, that the frameworks of inquiry within which those practices are discharged are themselves ones which are rigorous, consistent and predictable. The reality here is hardly any more reassuring, however, for the methodologies associated with the new professionalism, while in many ways innovative and revealing, are arguably a retrogressive step in terms of transparency.

QUESTIONS OF METHODOLOGY

If the oscillation between the two poles of populism and miserabilism is clearly a contentious feature of the new professionalism, casting doubt upon the extent to which new standards of arbitration are intended to be applied, its methodological pretensions are even more problematical. For the neo-populists have nailed their standard very clearly to a research methodology, rapid rural appraisal/participatory rural appraisal (RRA/PRA), which is inherently negotiable, and have done so in a way which has stigmatized methods with claims to independence, rigour and objectivity.

Critical studies of RRA/PRA, like other aspects of participatory theory, are not common in the literature, a reflection of the strongly value-laden tone of the championing of the theme, and of the strong sense of taboo which has thus come to surround it (though see Pelkey, 1996). In familiar fashion, the promotion of PRA has been imbued with claims that the methodology is not only an innovative one, but a harbinger, indeed, of a totally new set of values in the practices of development. Those works which have chosen to question the approach have, therefore, run the risk of appearing to challenge not only its assumptions but also its humanitarian values. More often researchers have contented themselves with questioning certain elements of its application (the privileging of the visual and the 'public', for example), leaving the premises of the overall approach intact.

A central and defining feature of the PRA movement has been its resistance to any institutionalization of its methods or precision as to the qualifications and qualities required of its practitioners. Again, the onus is on personal judgement and responsibility:

> PRA is experiential, not metaphysical. It springs from actions in the field, not analyses in academe. Theory has been induced from practice, not deduced from propositions. ... Guidance has come not from written rules, regulations and procedures, but from personal self-critical reflection and judgement. In this mode, each PRA experience has been unique. ... 'Use your own best judgement at all times' has been a sort of meta-manual. (Chambers, 1997, p. 208)

Such arguments suffer from the same limitations earlier discussed, namely a lack of clarity as to the standards of judgement which are acceptable as best judgements (particularly in the socially complex situations in which aid projects are typically active); a lack of certainty as to the identities of those who are intended to use their own best judgement and self-critical reflection; and an underplaying of the influence of the institutional contexts in which the experience of PRA is likely to take place. These institutional contexts are ones in which relationships tend to be multiple, and heavily conditioned by resource flows and material benefits. The quality of the interaction is thus liable to fundamental distortions, such that neither the local participants nor the facilitator can guarantee that they are operating in terms of what might be regarded as the independent interests of the community. In such situations, the absence of standardized methodologies, dependent on rules and procedures, is arguably much more of a vice than a virtue, and personal responsibility an insufficient safeguard against manipulation and distortion.

THE NEED FOR A NEW PARADIGM?

The challenge to normal professionalism inherent in the neo-populist approach is thus questionable on grounds of both accountability and methodology. The final element in the critique of the new professionalism concerns the most elevated of its claims, to represent an incipient new paradigm of development practice. The view that the new professionalism represents an emergent paradigm of participatory development has been asserted, with growing conviction, over the last decade, initially in relation to the 'farmer-first' movement, more recently as part of a broader challenge relating to sustainable agriculture (Pretty, 1995; Röling, 1996), rural development administration (Chambers, 1993) and, latterly, biodiversity conservation and sustainable forest management (Pretty and Pimbert, 1995).

The theoretical challenge to the existing scientific paradigm, in relation to the goal of sustainable natural resource management, is partly seen to lie in the broad range of interests which determine the behaviour of the peasant farming community (Pretty, 1995, p. 14). It is partly also an acknowledgement of the unique nature of the social sciences which, alone among the sciences, are significantly affected by the motivations and intentions of the subjects of inquiry. Surprisingly, however, the way to address this challenge is not seen by the neo-populists as a refinement of existing research methodologies to take more fully into account the multivariant nature of the decision making involved, or to accommodate the role of values as contentious (but not necessarily independent) variables. Instead there is a call for an abandonment of the principles of positivist science in favour of an alternative paradigm or paradigms which place the value-laden nature of any process of understanding of human communities squarely at the centre of the analysis. Such a change of vision is presented as an essential element in the search for a truly participatory approach to development, and as part of a broader movement in which participation is viewed as intimately concerned with a moral agenda of values and attitudes.

Now, whatever the limitations of the approaches in the social sciences which the neo-populists label as 'positivist' (and this group is hardly the first to point to the need to bring the notion of social intention into the analysis of human affairs), there is one quality which is central to the claims of positivism to scientific method: a sceptical attitude to the place of values in explanatory models, and a reluctance to accord values, *a priori*, a status superior to any other constraints. This principle of disengagement from the values of the subjects of the social inquiry (whatever status these subjects may have) is an important aspect of positivist claims to analytical discipline and legitimacy. By contrast, the paradigm of the new professionalism (in so far as it is defined at all) is marked out by an approach to values which treats them not only as the defining influences in the reality of the practitioners, but as qualities which must be actively engaged by those who intervene on their behalf. The challenges to the new paradigm which Pretty acknowledges rhetorically (but fails to address) are fundamental, and ones to which the neo-populists need adequately to respond, namely: 'If information is changeable, locally valid, value-laden and entirely open to interpretation, how can it be trusted? Whose illusion are we going to believe today? Where is the order? Does this not suggest that ... "anything goes"?' (Pretty, 1995, p. 17). These questions would be pertinent in any situation of social analysis. In a context in which the principal actors are individuals whose professionalism is subject to no independent assessment and who are exhorted to abide by their own standards of arbitration as to those interests which they should promote (or alternatively, one supposes, oppose) they are surely critical.

PROFESSIONAL REVERSALS IN THE CONTEXTS OF INTERNATIONAL AID

In this section, we return to the broader dimensions of the debate, the parallels between the neo-populist agenda in development management, and the free market ideology which now pervades Western political thought and development policy.

The present context of development management is a particularly constraining one. The neo-liberal view that markets are the most efficient means to allocate goods and services has found ready support among international donors in an era of structural adjustment, even in relation to those societies where market mechanisms operate very imperfectly, if at all. In many societies of the developing world, the neo-liberal notion that the individual should be the central actor in the analysis, and that individual freedoms are superior to any perceived social needs or societal values, jars with the extreme polarization of wealth and influence, and the very uneven levels of access to both public and private services. For the poor, access to such services is already very limited, and becoming ever more of a lottery as provision passes from statutory public agencies to non-governmental and other private sector providers. For the wealthy, public services are already of marginal importance. For the middle grouping, the capture of both public and private services represents an important (and often still attainable) way to improve their life-chances, in a situation of overall decline.

If this is the prevailing scenario in much of the developing world, there is need also to reflect upon aid management's present aims. Aid is increasingly concerned with the management of the transition from public to private goods, and the progressive withdrawal from services by which all might benefit. And it is also increasingly preoccupied with the provision of alternative services very largely on the basis of voluntarism, through the voluntary sector (NGOs) and by other means. This is a sector which is traditionally high on commitment but low on obligation, and often effectively unregulated by public authorities (Bratton, 1989).

Into this arena is introduced a philosophy which offers the promise of a new professionalism with radical pretensions, apparently (and miraculously) able to transcend the conditions of poverty. This philosophy is also, however, of an essentially voluntaristic kind. The language of the new professionalism is, with few exceptions, short on political analysis, and puts its emphasis rather on personal commitments and calls to public-spiritedness. Though couched outwardly in the language of certainties, it offers no standards of arbitration between competing interests other than that its practitioners should abide by judgements of their own. Those judgements are subject to little by way of external regulation or moderation. The same licence is given to the methods of inquiry (and even the paradigms) through which the judgements are to be formed. The participation of the poor is presented largely as a matter of the values and attitudes of the new professionals.

The central methodology of the new professionalism has been presented by its foremost advocate as promising not only unexpected findings but values of an essentially political kind: 'Paradigmatically, [PRA] validates and justifies decentralization, democracy and trust' (Chambers, 1997, p. 208).

This is surely very wide of the mark. The growth of interest in participatory methods may reflect decentralization, among other influences. It may or may not justify trust. But it can make no legitimate claims to validate democracy in any meaningful sense.

In such a scenario it is necessary to consider the contrary case: to pose questions as to what would happen if, in a particular instance, the new professionalism turned out not to support the interests of the have-nots against the interests of the haves. In the language of the new institutional economics, this implies a concern with the mechanisms of 'voice' and 'exit' available to the poor (Hirschman, 1970).

It might well be the case that, in this situation, the poor would not gain an increased influence, but suffer a diminished one. Their voice is now largely dependent on their ability to establish rapport with the new professionals. The philosophy favours this, but gives little indication of how it is to be achieved. On past evidence it would seem less likely than an alliance between the professionals and the local élites (cf. Leonard, 1977; Tendler, 1982). One reason for this is the essentially public nature of most participatory research techniques which tends to privilege certain types of interest (Mosse, 1993). Another is the relatively high opportunity costs to the poor of participatory methodologies (see Johnson and Clark, 1982). And third, the encompassing institutional frameworks may exert their own influence over the extent to which particular interests are taken into account (Leonard, 1977; Mosse, 1995); in the worst-case scenario, participatory methods might well be used to legitimize the established interests of the élite (Wood, 1981).

Should voice thus fail the poor, then the option left to them (exit) is one which would almost certainly also act to their personal disadvantage. For the essentially voluntaristic character of the contexts at issue poses few questions as to whose interests should be addressed; the decisions as to how and when to accommodate particular interests are left largely to the perceptions of the new professionals. It is questionable, indeed, whether the methodologies of intervention need even register the withdrawal. Even were they to do so, the emphasis on participation in terms of values and attitudes makes it difficult for the system to take those defaulting interests adequately into account.

Thus, the paradoxical conclusion is that the new professionalism might well, despite its best intentions, end up marginalizing the very interests it is intended to enhance. This may not happen in the high-profile and very public initial phase, where significant resources are committed to the enterprise, but is increasingly likely as it becomes routinized within development services.

CONCLUSION: THE DOMESTICATION OF DISSENT?

Much of the neo-populist literature is of high moral tone, and there will be few who would question its main aim to reorient development bureaucracies and attitudes towards the interests of the poor. The problem with the new professionalism is not its critique of the *status quo* but its failure to transcend it. This failure derives in part from the constant prioritization of personal values and attitudes, to the detriment of political analysis. At the end of the day, public participation (and the participation of the poor) are not normative questions but democratic rights. These rights need to be enforceable regardless of the values and attitudes of either the public or those who seek to champion them. To argue otherwise is to risk a situation in which the right of participation becomes *contingent* on certain values and attitudes. Where populism gives way to *misérabilisme* then the conditions are created for the right of participation no longer to liberate but to oppress.

The critique of normal professionalism has much to do with the lack of public accountability of development bureaucrats. Such accountability will not be brought about, however, by substituting one form of self-regulation by another, nor by handing power to a new category of aid workers whose loyalties are even more obscure than those of their predecessors. This shift does not represent a realization of public responsibility, but rather its conversion to a form of voluntarism in which authority lies firmly with an increasingly globalized middle class. If it is to have any meaning beyond the rhetorical, the right of participation must involve the subordination of all the fractions of the middle class to the interests of the mass. In other words, the new professionalism, whenever this comes about, will be defined primarily by the structures of democratic control upon it, and only secondarily by its values and attitudes.

NOTE

1. I have elsewhere considered a second consequence of this tension – the ability to claim alliances with others holding seemingly divergent views (Brown, 1995, *passim*). The critique focuses particularly on the claims that Chambers makes of a direct lineage between his own position and that of the icon of the neo-populist movement, Paulo Freire.

REFERENCES

Booth, D. (ed.) (1994), *Rethinking Social Development: Theory, Research and Practice*, Harlow: Longman.

Bratton, M. (1989), 'The politics of NGO–government relations in Africa', *World Development*, **17** (4), pp. 569–87.

Brown, D. (1989), 'Bureaucracy as an issue in Third World management: an African case study', *Public Administration and Development*, **9**, 369–80 (reprinted in P. Blunt et al., *Managing Organizations in Africa,* Walter de Gruyter, Berlin, 1993).

Brown, D. (1990),'Rhetoric or reality? NGOs as agencies of grassroots development', *AERDD Bulletin*, No. 28, pp. 3–10.

Brown, D. (1994), 'Strategies of social development: non-governmental organizations and the limitations of the Freirean approach', *The New Bulmershe Papers*, Faculty of Education & Community Studies, University of Reading.

Brown, D. (1995), 'Seeking the consensus: populist tendencies at the interface between research and consultancy', Working Paper No. 5, AERDD, University of Reading.

Cernea, M. (ed.) (1991), *Putting People First: Sociological Variables in Rural Development* (2nd edn), Oxford: Oxford University Press.

Chambers, R. (1983), *Rural Development: Putting the Last First*, Harlow: Longman.

Chambers, R. (1991), 'Shortcut and participatory methods for gaining social information for projects' in Cernea (1991), pp. 515–37.

Chambers, R. (1993), *Challenging the Professions: Frontiers for Rural Development*, London: Intermediate Technology Publications.

Chambers, R. (1997), *Whose Reality Counts? Putting the First Last*, London: Intermediate Technology Publications.

Farrington, J. (1996), 'Anglo-French initiative: background paper on farmer participatory research', mimeo, London: Overseas Development Institute.

Farrington, J. and Bebbington, A. with D. Lewis (1993), *Reluctant Partners: Non-Governmental Organisations, the State and Sustainable Agricultural Development*, London: Routledge.

Flynn, N. (1990), *Public Sector Management*, London: Harvester Wheatsheaf.

Freire, P. (1972), *Pedagogy of the Oppressed*, Harmondsworth: Penguin.

Freire, P. (1976), *Education: The Practice of Freedom*, New York: Writers' and Readers' Cooperative.

Friedson, E. (1970), 'Professions and the occupational principle', in E. Friedson (ed.), *Professions and their prospects*, New York: Sage.

Grignon, C. and Passeron, J.-C. (1989), *Le Savant et Le Populaire: Misérabilisme et populisme en sociologie et en littérature*, Paris: Gallimard – Editions Le Seuil.

Hirschman, A.E. (1970), *Exit, Voice and Loyalty*, Cambridge, MA: Harvard University Press.

Hulme, D. (1994), 'Social development research and the third sector: NGOs as users and subjects of social enquiry', in Booth (1994), pp. 251–75.

Hyden, H. (1983), *No Shortcuts to Progress*, London: Heinemann.

Johnson, T. (1974), *Professions and Power*, London: Macmillan.

Johnson, B. and Clark, W. (1982), *Redesigning Rural Development: A Strategic Perspective*, Baltimore, MD: Johns Hopkins University Press.

Laffin, M. (1986), *Professionalism and Policy: The Role of the Professions in the Central–Local Government Relationship*, London: Gower.

Leonard, D. (1977), *Reaching the peasant farmer: Organisation theory and practice in Kenya*, Chicago, IL: University of Chicago Press.

Mosse, D. (1993), 'Authority, gender and knowledge: theoretical reflections on the practice of participatory rural appraisal', AGREN Network Paper No. 44, ODI, London.

Mosse, D. with KRIBP Project Team (1995), 'People's knowledge in project planning: the limits and social conditions of participation in planning agricultural development', AGREN Network Paper No. 58, ODI, London.

Olivier de Sardan, J.-P. (1990), 'Populisme développementiste et populisme en sciences sociales: idéologie, action, connaissance', *Cahiers d'Etudes Africaines*, **120** (4), 475–92.

Olivier de Sardan, J.-P. (1995), *Anthropologie et développement: Essai en socio-anthropologie du changement social*, Marseille and Paris: APAD–Karthala.

Pelkey, N. (1996), 'Please stop the PRA RRA Rah', *Out of the Shell*, **5** (1), 17–24.

Pretty, J. (1995), *Regenerating Agriculture: Policies and Practice for Sustainability and Self-reliance*, London: Earthscan.

Pretty, J. and Pimbert, M. (1995), 'Parks, people and professionals: putting 'participation' into protected area management', UNRISD Discussion Paper No. 57, Geneva.

Röling, N. (1996), 'Towards an interactive agricultural science', *European Journal of Agricultural Education and Extension*, **2** (4), 35–47.

Tendler, J. (1982), 'Turning private voluntary organisations into development agencies: questions for evaluation', USAID Program Evaluation Discussion Paper No. 12, Washington, DC.

Wood, G. (1981), 'The social and scientific context of Rapid Rural Appraisal', *IDS Bulletin*, **12** (4), 3–7.

PART II

Changing institutions and practices in public
management and governance

9. Civil service reforms: limping into the twenty-first century

Moses N. Kiggundu

INTRODUCTION

From Albania to Zimbabwe, governments and their citizens the world over are engaged in various forms of civil service reform (CSR). These reforms promise to have far-reaching implications for a wide range of global, national, and micro-issues including global markets, regional peace, national economic management and governance systems, competencies and capacities, service delivery, minority and human rights, and individual human quality of life (de Haan and van Hees, 1996; ICPOL, 1996; Ingraham, 1996; Klitgaard, 1996; Kiggundu, 1996a; Nunberg, 1996). Therefore, the success or failure and the lessons we learn from current CSR initiatives may well set the agenda for the first quarter of the twenty-first century.

The purpose of this chapter is threefold. First, it briefly discusses the genesis, motives and driving forces for CSR in developing countries and transition economies. Why are so many countries of different economic, social, political, cultural and historical attributes all currently engaged in the same common enterprise called CSR? To what extent have these initiatives been locally initiated and internalized? Second, the chapter discusses some aspects of CSR progress made to date, especially as regards approaches and results. Results will be discussed in terms of inputs, process, outcomes, impact, lessons of experience and lessons learnt. Third, based on CSR achievements to date, the chapter looks ahead and projects CSR, its prospects and implications, into the twenty-first century. Recognizing that most CSR initiatives in most of these countries are lacking in strength, vigour and firmness, it is observed that this collective 'limping' behaviour will only get worse unless fundamental changes are made in the way CSR is conceptualized, designed and implemented. In the future, CSR must be strategic, integrative, experimental, knowledge-based, transformational, service- and results-oriented, and participatively citizen-driven (Dia, 1996; Jeding and Gustafsson, 1995; Kiggundu, 1996b; Morgan, 1992; Steedman and Howes, 1996). Reform initiatives must also be locally grounded and contextualized, emphasizing the development of broad-based politically, technically and managerially sustainable core competencies and capacities supported by democratic institutional arrangements. The civil service must reflect and be reflected by the society in which it exists and functions (Palmer et al., 1993). Services must be provided through a wide range of alternative service delivery institutional arrangements (Ford and Zussman, 1997).

THE ORIGINS OF CIVIL SERVICE REFORM PROGRAMMES

The reasons, motives and expectations for CSR vary from country to country. Over the years, however, some general trends have become obvious. In the industrialized northern countries, CSR was driven by ideology in response to citizen and taxpayer demands for improved public services (Epstein, 1990), a smaller role for governments at all levels, private sector participation, and reduced tax burdens (Gore, 1993). For transition economies, the goal was to break down authoritarian institutional structures and expedite democratic development and economic market reforms (Chaudhry et al., 1994; Schiavo-Campo, 1996). Developing countries, especially in Africa and South America, undertook reform as a direct consequence of the early experiences of structural adjustment programmes (Chaudhry et al., 1994; Kiggundu, 1996c).

In addition to ideology and economic reform, other reasons for the vigorous push for CSR include globalization, democratization, aid conditionality, the advent of the computer and information technology, the private provision of public services (Roth, 1987), state collapse and institutional decay, capacity development and managerialism. For most cases where CSR has been essentially driven by the need for improved efficiency in service delivery and reduced costs, the emphasis tends to be on applications of computer and information technology, capacity development and managerialism, leading to what others have called a new paradigm in public administration (Borins, 1994) and management (Common, 1997).

The resumed fiftieth general assembly session of the United Nations (April 1996) focused almost exclusively on public administration and development and drew on expert reports from the various regions of the world. The Secretary General's report observed that 'efficiency in government is a sine-qua-non for sustainable economic growth' and called on donors and governments to promote CSR, especially in finance and administration (Bertucci, 1996). The leading role of the specialized agencies such as the World Bank, the UNDP and, to a lesser degree, the ILO in promoting CSR is very well known (Nunberg and Nellis, 1995; UNDP, 1997). Although bilateral European donors and other multilateral agencies such as the Commonwealth Secretariat (Kaul, 1996) have been active in supporting CSR, the main driving force has come from the increasingly interventionist role of the United Nations and its specialized agencies, especially in the area of economic management and, more recently, good governance and democratic development of member states.

The evolution of CSR over the years bears interesting resemblances to restructuring in the private sector. At the beginning, private sector restructuring was characterized by 'slash and burn' down-sizing, threatening the core and integrity of the organization. More recently, the pendulum has swung back to a more balanced right-sizing as private sector firms, especially those operating in competitive markets, realize the need to protect and preserve their core values, competencies and corporate memory. Likewise, while at the beginning CSR was focused on reducing the size and cost of the state, more recent thinking calls for a more capable state (World Bank, 1997). It is reasonable to assume, however, that the debate about the proper role of the state in a changing world will continue well into the next century.

PROGRESS AND RESULTS TO DATE

CSR programmes have been subjected to various forms of review and assessment, especially by the multilateral and bilateral donors who have been financing these initiatives. The calls for CSR assessments and evaluations are promoted by several considerations. First, there is the general belief that the results of CSR initiatives range from mixed, circumscribed, to disappointing (Nunberg and Nellis, 1995; Nunberg, 1996). Second, within the broader framework of overseas development assistance (ODA) and technical cooperation, donors are being challenged, especially by their domestic constituencies, to be accountable and demonstrate positive results for their development programmes, including CSR. For example, several studies have documented serious problems, failures and negative consequences with technical cooperation (Morgan and Baser, 1993). Critics argue that CSR shares many common attributes with technical cooperation and is therefore likely to have similar results. Lack of prior experience with CSR means that donors and reforming governments are constantly looking for lessons of experience from which they can learn to improve their CSR programming and management. Recently, donors have even produced guiding principles on civil service reform (de Haan and van Hees, 1996).

Apart from Eastern and Central Europe, which is under-represented, other regions of the world seem to be represented within this body of studies more or less in the same proportions as their involvement with CSR. For example, using data from the World Bank, Nunberg (1996, p. 2) found that, for the period 1987–96, Africa accounted for 64 per cent of all CSR operations. The figures for other regions were: Latin America and the Caribbean 18 per cent, East Asia–Pacific 7 per cent, Middle East/North Africa 5 per cent, Europe and Central Asia and South Asia each 3 per cent. There is a predominance of African countries among CSR assessment studies.

Almost all the assessment studies reviewed for this chapter gave CSR programmes less than a pass grade. Most of them provided documentation of disappointing results. For example, consistent with her earlier findings (Nunberg and Nellis, 1995), Nunberg recently observed:

> evaluation ratings suggest that unsatisfactory performance of CSR-related projects are due to a very broad set of deficiencies: overall political and economic crisis, poor donor coordination, inadequate Bank–Country dialogue, use of unsuitable lending instruments, lack of continuity in project teams, inadequate supervision, lack of administrative and financial capacity, flawed project design, lack of reform consensus among domestic groups, and, most prominently, lack of government commitment to and/or ownership of the reforms. (1996, p. 3)

Impediments to Effective CSR

Several studies have identified common impediments to CSR, especially in transition and developing countries (Kiggundu, 1996b; Pinto and Mrope, 1994; Barlow, 1997). Among these is a lack of strategic visioning linking CSR to the broader aspects of the country's political economy, including governance, macroeconomic management and social development. Instead, CSR has tended to be seen as discrete projects, often funded by external donors pursuing different and sometimes conflicting agendas unrelated to the needs or realities on the ground.

Second, in most countries CSR lacks sustaining political and community support, resulting in the entire reform effort being perceived as externally driven with limited local understanding, commitment and ownership. CSR depends too much on external resources, conditionalities, and intellectual and professional leadership. CSR lacks an effective domestic constituency or champion by way of voice, input, resource mobilization or political pressure.

Third, CSR carries with it a greater burden of expectations than most governments have the capacity to deliver on a sustained basis. For example, most countries do not have the institutional capacity to manage and coordinate the entire reform effort, communicate with the various domestic and international stakeholders, improve customer service, contain corruption, reduce cost and size, democratize and protect human rights and alleviate poverty, while at the same time creating an enabling environment for globalization and private sector investment and development.

Finally, some of the reasons why CSR is needed in the first place can become impediments at least in the short run. For example, the lack of equipment, supplies, computers and vehicles, poor physical plant, inadequate pay, and a general lack of positive work values, motivation and attitudes which characterize the civil services of most reforming countries impede the effective and sustainable implementation of reform.

CSR Results: Is It All Bad?

Reading through the recent evaluation and stocktaking reports of the results of CSR, one gets the distinct impression that it is all doom and gloom. Yet, most of the conference preceedings (Borins, 1994; EDI, 1995; Common-wealth Secretariat, 1992), consultants' reports (Langseth, 1995; Kasumba, 1996), and government publications (Government of Uganda, 1993) give a much more promising and even rosy picture of the results of CSR. Who is right? Although one can expect biases resulting from self-evaluations by consultants and government officials, we have attempted to explain these variations by looking at different types and levels of CSR results. Specifically, we have attempted to look at the differences by distinguishing between CSR results based on inputs, process, outputs, outcomes, and impact on selected desirable goals.

Table 9.1 provides ratings of CSR results in terms of different dimensions and time perspectives. For example, the results of CSR as they relate to mobilization of inputs such as funding, equipment and technical assistance have been quite impressive. This is mainly because of current donor support and the conditionalities associated with CSR (Husain and Forugee, 1994). Equally successful are the various processes which are undertaken in prepa-ration for the active implementation of CSR. These processes, which are essentially diagnostic and preparatory in nature, include dialogues, especially between donors and senior government officials, consultations, training and political pronouncements (Pinto and Mrope, 1994; Dia, 1996; Kiggundu, 1997). Stories of successful CSR initiatives told by consultants and govern-ment officials have tended to concentrate on inputs and processes. In a recent World Bank report, for example, the consultant, who was working with government officials on Uganda's civil service reform programme, wrote:

> The achievements of the CSRP have been impressive. The decentralization proc-ess ... led by the Decentralization Secretariat ... [is] carrying out the objectives of the reform program ... the size of the civil service and the military has been reduced dramatically ... Efficiency reviews of all government ministries have been carried out in the 39 districts, and pay levels have been raised roughly 50 percent a year from 1990–94. (Langseth, 1995, pp. 14–15)

*Table 9.1   Ratings of civil service reform results according to different
dimensions*

Dimension	Examples	Rating	Time perspective
1. Inputs	Funding, office equipment, vehicles, office space, computers	High	Short term
2. Processes	Dialogues, consultancies, studies, workshops, seminars, training, political pronouncements, study tours, head-counts	High	Short term
3. Outputs	Revenue generation, staff and cost containment, pay increases, incentives, compression, legislative changes, size and scope of government	Medium	Medium term
4. Outcomes	Service delivery, customer/ citizen satisfaction, core competencies and capacities, equity, strategic planning, local ownership, accountability, transparency	Medium Low Unknown	Long term
5. Impact	Democratic development, restructuring and renewal, good governance, citizen participation, voice, self-sustaining responsive institutions, social and economic development, improved quality of life	Unknown	Long term

The results of CSR outputs, on the other hand, have not been as impressive. Although initial results for several countries such as Ghana, Uganda, Senegal and Tanzania show significant improvements in revenue collection, reductions in employment due mainly to 'deghosting' and retrenchment, and nominal pay increases, many of these improvements have been hard to sustain. In Africa, where most governments do not pay a minimum living wage to their employees, remuneration and benefits are so low as to lead to 'institutionalized corruption', laxity and general lack of discipline (Klitgaard, 1996). In the Caribbean (Kitchen, 1994) and Latin America (Naim, 1994), a combination of inadequate incentive pay, resistance to reform from political, civil service and union leadership, and a relatively weak state combine to create serious impediments to the successful implementation of CSR.

The weakest CSR results are those associated with actual impact on specific goals and objectives (see Table 9.1). There is hardly any objective evidence to show that CSR in most of these countries has had a significant positive and sustaining impact on service delivery, citizen (customer) satisfaction, enhancement of civil service institutional core competencies and capacities, transparency and accountability. Nor is there evidence to support CSR contributions to macro-objectives such as better economic management, poverty alleviation and good government. For example, the authors of a recent UNDP comprehensive review of Ghana's civil service reform programme observed that 'There was so much concentration on the means towards this end in the CSRP that we think that the end itself – the ultimate target of improved delivery of services and outputs to 15 million citizens – became distant and diffused' (UNDP, 1995, para. 6.12).

Other reviews seem to suggest that the net impact of CSR may be negative and possibly counterproductive. For example, a recent UNDP-sponsored review of ten years of CSR in the Central African Republic (Rambourg, LeGay and Bay, 1995) conceded some minimal progress in terms of paying more attention to the search for productivity improvements and better human resources management, but concluded that the overall impact was negative. It described the results of the CSR programme as stagnant or going backwards (one step forward, two steps back) and said there was too much emphasis on logomachy (battle for words) rather than substance. The review concluded that no positive system-wide changes in attitudes or behaviour occurred in support of the CSR objectives.

The review was equally critical of the CSR training efforts. Training, especially abroad, was not linked to the trainees' job specifications. Instead, civil servants were more interested in hunting for paper qualifications, leading to various perversities of the civil service, especially in the areas of compensation and staffing. In one training programme, turnover rates were higher than 80 per cent of the trainees in spite of careful screening of trainee applicants.

Another area where CSR seems to have had a noticeable negative impact is on total employment and labour markets. Historically, the public sector has always been the major employer for most developing countries and countries in transition. Not only does CSR require governments to retrench staff, but it also calls for blanket or at least selective hiring freezes. Budget restrictions also limit the government's freedom to hire professionals and technical staff at competitive market rates.

It is true that the expected CSR impact on these indicators is long term. Therefore, it has been argued that it is unrealistic to expect significant impact in a relatively short period of time (10–15 years). However, lack of baseline data and proper field experimentation mean that the actual impact may never be known. Moreover, several researchers, including those close to the World Bank (Nunberg, 1996; Klitgaard, 1996; de Merode, 1991) are beginning to question the internal logic of CSR programme design and implementation. They are calling for a fresh start: rethinking, cleaning up and invigorating the civil service. Other donors (for example, DFID, SIDA, Special Programme of Assistance for Africa Working Group on Civil Service Reform) are engaged in ongoing dialogues in search of better approaches to CSR. At the same time, some of the reforming countries are beginning to question the assumptions, design principles, conditionalities and implementing strategies associated with CSR (African Governors of the World Bank, 1996).

Lessons of Experience

Various CSR stakeholders are engaged in producing long lists of lessons of experience in the hope of learning something useful and usable. Donors are particularly active in this area (Corkery, 1995; de Vos, 1996; Langseth, 1996; Nunberg and Nellis, 1995; Wescott, 1996), partly because of the record of mixed results, and partly because of the importance attached to CSR as a prerequisite for achieving sustainable improvements in service delivery, economic management and good governance. There is yet little evidence that CSR lessons of experience have been translated into lessons learnt.

In addition to pointing out the need to develop a strategic framework and to generate local ownership through a participative process approach to capacity development, the lessons also point to the importance of developing a sustainable national political capacity for CSR implementation. Donors are learning the hard way that political commitment is not an event secured and sustained only after one or a few meetings and handshakes with top political leadership. Rather, it is a process which must be nurtured and reinforced throughout the various stages and levels of CSR conceptualization, design and implementation.

Experience also shows that political commitment may be necessary but not sufficient if there is a lack of political capacity for CSR. Political capacity assessment requires an understanding of the strengths and weaknesses of the reforming country's political institutional infrastructure: its capacity for political risk assessment and management, for policy formulation and management, and for dealing with the opposition. This includes assessment of the quality of political leadership, the organization of the major political parties, indigenous institutions such as the chieftaincy systems in several African countries, opposition and interest groups including trade unions, the media, underground movements, and civil society in general. In essence, it calls for an assessment of the structure and capacity of the country's governance institutional infrastructure, including its national integrity systems and the capability for sustaining reforms.

The two most active bilateral donors have recently documented lessons of CSR experiences from a wide range of countries. Although the countries differ in their commitment and experience with CSR, the results show several cross-cutting lessons of experience: for example, the need which I have already emphasized for a national policy or strategic framework. Indeed, some donors have stressed this approach in their programming. For example, USAID, through its Implementing Policy Change project (IPC) 'provided capacity-building assistance and undertook studies that concentrated on the implementation and management side of policy reform in over 30 developing countries' (Brinkerhoff, 1996, p. 1393). Yet the constraints and challenges of sustaining a strategic management-enabling environment for most institutions in developing countries are also well known (Kiggundu, 1989; 1996d).

A second cross-cutting issue is local commitment and ownership achieved through broadly participative process consultations. Again donors are promoting these methods with instruments such as the World Bank's *Participation Source Book* (1996) and the governance approach to civil service reform using the Institutional Environment Assessment tools (Dia, 1996; Pinto and Mrope, 1994) as well as UNDP's 'Process consultation' manual for public sector management improvements. The overall objective is to ensure that the whole of CSR strategy and programming – design, content, process, tone, leadership – reflects the needs and public interests of the citizens of the reforming countries rather than the realities of the donors and their agents (Chambers, 1997).

Yet participation is not a panacea. It must take into account local realities. For example, a recent ODA and DANIDA (Danish International Development Agency) review of the Uganda CSR programme concluded that, at the beginning, a participative approach could not have worked because of strong resistance to change from senior civil servants. The report therefore concluded:

> The evidence from Uganda, therefore, suggests that both directive and participative approaches to change can be effective, depending on the situation. Directive change works best when the changes are 'macro' or civil service wide and the implementing agency, the MPS [Ministry for Public Service], has the necessary power and resources to make it happen. On the other hand, participative change works best when the changes are of the micro variety requiring behavioural

change and user support, provided those enlisted have the necessary ability. The clear lesson for donors is not to view change approaches as either solely directive or exclusively participative. There is a range of possibilities which may be adopted depending on the situation. (Brown, Kiragu and Villadsen, 1995, p. 53)

Where Do We Go From Here? From Reform to Transformation

CSR is at a crossroads. The actions and decisions of its champions in the next two to three years will determine whether it will go down in history as another passing fad in international development, or an important spring-board for transforming public administration and management for much needed improvements in governance and human development in developing countries and transitional economies. On the basis of the lessons of experience to date, it is obvious that we need to rethink, reconceptualize, and restrategize all aspects of CSR, and we need to do this collaboratively and through consultation, taking past lessons to heart. CSR is too important to be left to the experts – political leaders, senior civil servants, consultants and donors. Citizens must take centre stage.

Calls for fundamental changes are not new. For example, Nunberg (1996) calls for deprojectizing CSR, while Klitgaard and Baser (1997) call for more strategic use of incentives and partnership with the private sector to fight corruption. To add to this small but growing voice, this chapter calls for transformation. Figure 9.1 provides a framework for rethinking CSR from reform to transformation. Transformation, as opposed to transaction, is strategic, system-wide, long term, interactive, process-oriented, and aims at bringing about fundamental changes in values, principles, beliefs, attitudes, systems, structures, behaviours, and performance of the entire public sector of which the civil service is one part.

Figure 9.1 identifies four inter-related component parts of transformational CSR. These are:

1. Stabilization
2. Developing a national consensus on the essence of the state
3. Promoting good governance and democratic development
4. Developing civil society and indigenous institutions.

Stabilization covers three areas: public security, economic management, and public administration and management. The concept of stabilization has been used for structural adjustment programmes (SAPs). It is being extended here to include public security, especially for countries in transition from war to peace (Colletta, Kostner and Wiederhofer, 1996). Stabilization is necessary for transition economies, countries emerging out of war or conflict, and those with a history of prolonged institutional decay and human rights abuses.

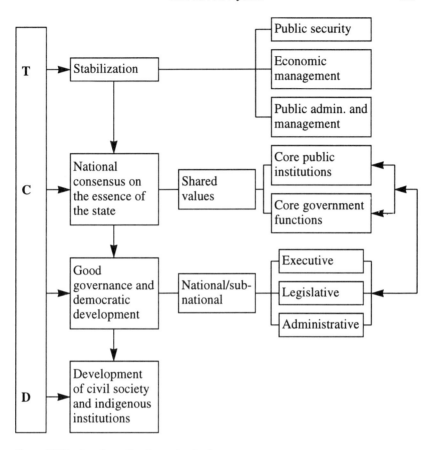

Note: TCD = transformational capacity development

Figure 9.1 Framework for rethinking civil service reform

The second component calls for a national dialogue to develop consensus, or a shared understanding of the essence of the state. Out of this consensus should emerge a set of national shared values which in turn help define the country's core institutions and core functions. There is no point in strengthening institutions or analysing core functions if there is no consensus on their relevance for good governance and human development. In the twenty-first century, countries will be held together not by military force but by shared values and common vision and purpose. Those countries which fail to be bound together by virtue of strongly shared values may not hold together, and CSR would then become academic. Examples may include Canada (the best country to live in, according to the UNDP's Human Development Index),

Congo and Cambodia. When national governments from Afghanistan to Zaire are either collapsing or being taken over by bandits, the need for reaffirmation of the essence of the state and the core values that hold it together becomes even more compelling.

The third component in Figure 9.1 is good governance and democratic development at both the national and sub-national levels, focusing on the executive (political), legislative and administrative (technical) branches and their inter-relationships. This is an area where CSR is already quite active, unlike the first two components discussed above.

The fourth and final component is the development of civil society and indigenous institutions. Again, while work has already started in this area, current CSR efforts have not fully exploited the potential contributions which indigenous institutions could make to good governance, poverty alleviation and social development for many of the reforming countries. Finally, Figure 9.1 adds another dimension by subjecting each of the four components to transformational capacity development.

Transformational capacity development relates to the overall capacity to create, communicate and implement a new vision for the civil service and its relationships with other branches of government, the private sector, civil society and individual citizens. The vision should be widely shared and crystallize the long-range image of what CSR should accomplish. The words 'civil' and 'service' must be taken seriously in civil service reform. The vision should stretch stakeholders beyond contemporary thinking and capabilities and should be a source of inspiration for achieving higher levels of commitment and performance. It should result in a different kind of relationship between the civil service and its publics. Drawing upon shared values and beliefs, and carefully crafting indigenous knowledge systems, modern management and technology, the new vision should bring about fundamental changes in the structuring, management, leadership and performance of the civil service and associated public agencies. An important aspect of rethinking and restrategizing CSR will be the assessment and development of transformational capacity in reforming countries.

Transformational capacity development calls for charismatic or strategic leadership (Kiggundu, 1989). This requires the political, administrative and civic leaders to have the sagacity to identify with and articulate national sentiments, ideology, cultural norms and practices, and development goals, and translate them into a coherent mission, or set of goals, plans and objectives for CSR. They must also have the capacity to mobilize, organize and utilize resources, technical and political support for the successful and sustaining accomplishment of CSR objectives. In addition, they must have the ability, motivation and perseverance to remain focused in the face of adversity. Finally, they must have the knowledge, skills, respect and emotional appeal to develop and maintain social capital, unity, identity and integrity of the civil service by protecting its values and core competencies from undue outside interference.

To date, CSR has emphasized transactional rather than transformational change and capacity development. Most initiatives have been aimed at cranking up the bureaucratic machine to provide more and faster services at the lowest possible cost. In future, only those countries with sustaining capacity for transformational change can expect long-term positive results from CSR.

LIMPING INTO THE TWENTY-FIRST CENTURY: WINNERS AND LOSERS

The Websters New Collegiate Dictionary defines limping as to fall short, to walk lamely, to go unsteadily favouring one leg, to proceed slowly with difficulty, toward a standstill, lacking or seeming to lack firmness and body, drooping or shapeless, not stiff or rigid, lacking in strength, vigour or firmness, spiritless, floppy, flaccid, flabby, flimsy or sleazy. Is this a fair characterization of CSR in developing countries and transition economies? I like to think so, but I also invite readers to reflect on the question, drawing on their personal and professional experiences.

Regardless of personal views on current CSR initiatives, the twenty-first century is likely to see a much more differentiated picture of CSR among the reforming countries, with winners and losers becoming more distinct. In this last section, the chapter briefly identifies the characteristics which will separate the winners from the losers. If today most of them are limping, the next century is very likely to see some (perhaps most) completely stuck in the mud and unable to move, and others moving ahead in high-speed trains.

Table 9.2 lists the attributes which will separate those countries that succeed in transforming their public sectors for sustainable good governance and human development from those that fail. This list is partly based on current lessons of CSR experiences from those countries doing relatively well, and those experiencing most difficulties. It is based on personal beliefs and predictions of the values most likely to dominate public policy for at least the first decade of the twenty-first century. These 15 distinguishing characteristics are not preconditions for successful CSR, but the outcomes of successful or unsuccessful reform efforts.

The characteristics in Table 9.2 can be used as a guidepost for assessing progress during CSR implementation, monitoring and evaluation. Over time, they can be used to demonstrate the extent to which the reform's impact is temporary or sustaining. For countries yet to embark on CSR, they can form part of the diagnostic framework and the establishment of baseline data. As

Table 9.2   *Civil service reform into the twenty-first century: distinguishing characteristics of winners and losers*

Winners	Losers
• Stable, free, democratic	• Authoritarian, dictatorial, totalitarian
• Strategic, sagacious, innovative	• Tactical, opportunistic
• Economically sound	• Economically weak
• Driven by shared values and principles	• Driven by force, militaristic
• People-centred, investing in social capital	• Power-centred, investing in forces of coercion
• Transformational	• Transactional
• Socially responsible and equitable	• Inequalities, social discord
• Selectively interdependent, open and networked	• Dependent, parochial, closed
• Service- and results-oriented	• Rules- and process-oriented
• Knowledge-based	• Authority-based
• Technologically adept	• Technophobic
• Respectful of rule of law, human rights	• Weak in law enforcement, protection of human and minority rights
• Institutionally strong, rooted	• Institutionally weak, disconnected
• Right-sized, agile	• Bloated, bureaucratic, resistant to change
• Relatively clean, with an effective national integrity system	• Corrupt, ineffective or non-existent national integrity system

they begin the formidable task of preparing their respective civil services for the challenges of the twenty-first century, senior CSR managers, donors and other stakeholders can use this list to reflect on their experiences and achievements to date, determine the extent to which they are walking or limping, and develop long-term strategies for building winning capacities and competencies.

REFERENCES

African Governors of the World Bank (1996), 'Partnership for capacity building in Africa: strategy and program of action', report of the African Governors of the World Bank to Mr James D. Wolfensohn, President of the World Bank Group, 28 September.

Barlow, John (1997), 'Policy transfer: the management of change in a Hungarian authority', paper presented at the international conference on Public Sector Management for the Next Century, University of Manchester, 29 June–2 July.

Bertucci, G. (1996), 'Professional developments: public administration and development: resumed 50th session of the United Nations General Assembly', *Public Administration and Development*, **16** (5), 513–16.

Borins, Sandford (1994), 'Government in transition: a new paradigm in public administration', Toronto: CAPAM.

Brinkerhoff, Derick W. (1996), 'Implementing policy change: editor's preface', *World Development*, **24** (9), 1393–4.

Brown, Kevin, Kiragu Kithinji and Villadsen, Soren (1995), 'Uganda civil service reform case study: final report', Special Programme for Africa.

Chambers, Robert (1997), *Whose Reality Counts? Putting the First Last*, London: Intermediate Technology Publications.

Chaudhry, Shahid Amjad, Reid, Gary James and Malik, Waleed Haider (eds) (1994), 'Civil service reform in Latin America and the Caribbean: proceedings of a conference', Technical Paper No. 259, Washington, DC: World Bank.

Colletta, Nat J., Kostner, Markus and Wiederhofer, Ingo (1996), *The Transition from War to Peace in Sub-Saharan Africa*, Washington, DC: World Bank.

Common, Richard (1997), 'The new public management and policy transfer: the role of international institutions', paper presented at the international conference on Public Sector Management for the Next Century, University of Manchester, 29 June–2 July.

Commonwealth Secretariat (1992), 'The changing role of government: administrative structures and reforms', proceedings of a Commonwealth roundtable held in Sydney, Australia, 24–28 February.

Corkery, Jean (1995), 'Civil service reform: hurdles and helps', *Development Policy Management Forum Bulletin*, **III** (1), 9–11.

Cupido, M.F. (1996), 'Civil service reform priorities in a new nation: focus on Namibia', *African Journal of Public Administration and Management*, **V–VII** (2), 36–45.

de Haan, Peter, and van Hees, Yvonne (1996), *Civil Service Reform in Sub-Saharan Africa*, The Hague: Government of the Netherlands.

de Merode, L. (1991), 'Civil service pay and implementation experiences', Institutional Development and Management Division, Washington, DC: World Bank.

de Vos, Robert (1996), 'Civil service reform in Mali: experiences and prospects', in de Haan and van Hees (1996).

Dia, Mamadou (1996), *Africa's Management in the 1990's and Beyond: Reconciling Indigenous and Transplanted Institutions*, Washington, DC: World Bank.

EDI (1995), 'Civil service reform in Anglophone Africa', Pretoria: Economic Development Institute, Overseas Development Administration/Government of South Africa.

Epstein, Joyce (1990), 'Public services: working for the consumer', Dublin: European Foundation for the Improvement of Living and Working Conditions.

Ford, Robin and Zussman, David (eds) (1997), 'Alternative service delivery: sharing governance in Canada', Toronto: KPMG Centre for Government Foundation and Institute of Public Administration of Canada.

Gore, Al (1993), *Creating a Government that Works Better and Costs Less: The Gore Report on Reinventing Government*, New York: Random House.

Government of Uganda (1993), 'Management of change: report on the proceedings of the seminar of ministers and permanent secretaries', Kampala.

Husain, I., and Forugee, R. (eds) (1994), *Adjustment in Africa: Lessons from Country Case Studies*, Washington, DC: World Bank.

Ingraham, Patricia W. (1996), 'The reform agenda for national civil service systems: external stress and internal strains', in Hans A.G.M. Bekke, James L. Perry and Theo. A.J. Toonen (eds), *Civil Service Systems In Comparative Perspective*, Bloomington: Indiana University Press, pp. 247–67.

International Commission on Population and Quality of Life (ICPOL) (1996), *Caring for the Future: A Radical Agenda for Positive Change*, Oxford: Oxford University Press.

Jeding, Lars and Gustafsson, Lennant (1995), 'Draft synthesis paper on lessons of SPA country studies on civil service reform', Stockholm.

Kasumba, D.G. Williams (1996), 'Decentralization of donor cooperation: experiences and challenges for institutional capacity development', Paris: DAC Workshop on Technical Cooperation and Capacity Development.

Kaul, Mohan (1996), 'Civil service reform: learning from Commonwealth experiences', *Public Administration and Development*, **16** (2), 131–50.

Kiggundu, Moses N. (1989), *Managing Organizations in Developing Countries: An Operational and Strategic Approach*, West Hartford, CT: Kumarian Press.

Kiggundu, Moses N. (1996a), 'The African public administration and development: from firefighting to prevention', background paper prepared for the United Nations Regional Meeting on Public Administration and Development, Windhoek.

Kiggundu, Moses N. (1996b), 'Civil service reform in Africa: lessons of experience', discussion paper presented to Policy Branch, Canadian International Development Agency, Hull, Quebec.

Kiggundu, Moses N. (1996c), 'A longitudinal study of the size, cost and administrative reform of the African civil service', *Journal of African Finance and Economic Development*, **2** (1), 77–107.

Kiggundu, Moses N. (1996d), 'Integrating strategic management tasks into implementing agencies: from firefighting to prevention', *World Development*, **24** (9), 1417–29.

Kiggundu, Moses N. (1997), 'Retrenchment programs in Sub-Saharan Africa: lessons for demobilization', Discussion Paper No. 10, Bonn: Bonn International Centre for Conversion.

Kitchen, Richard (1994), 'Compensation upgrading in Caribbean public services: comparative needs and experience', in Chaudhry et al. (1994).

Klitgäard, Robert (1996), 'Cleaning up and invigorating the civil service', background paper prepared for the Civil Service Reform Study Operations Evaluations Department, Washington, DC: World Bank.

Klitgaard, Robert and Baser, Heather (1997), 'Working together to fight corruption: state, society and the private sector in partnership', in Suzanne Taschereau and Jose Edgardo L. Campos (eds), *Building Government–Citizen–Business Partnerships*, Ottawa: Institute on Governance.

Langseth, Petter (1995), 'Civil service reform in Uganda: lessons learned', Washington, DC: World Bank.

Langseth, Petter (1996), 'Governance and civil service reform', in de Haan and van Hees (1996).

Morgan, Peter, and Baser, Heather (1993), *Making Technical Co-operation More Effective: New Approaches By the International Development Community*, Hull, Quebec: Technical Cooperation Directorate, CIDA.

Morgan, Philip E. (1992), 'Civil service systems configuration in developing countries: synthesizing the normative and the positive', unpublished draft.

Naim, Moses (1994), 'Public bureaucracies in developing countries: ten paradoxes', in Chaudhry et al. (1994).

Nunberg, Barbara (1996), 'Re-thinking civil service reform: an agenda for smart government', draft paper, Washington, DC: Poverty and Social Policy Department, World Bank.

Nunberg, Barbara and Nellis, John (1995), 'Civil service reform and the World Bank', Discussion Paper No. 161, Washington, DC: World Bank.

ODA/SIDA (1994), 'Report from a joint ODA/SIDA seminar on civil service reform', Stockholm: Akeshofs Slotts.

Palmer, Monte, Kondowe, Moses and Palmer, Princess (1993), 'Indigenous institutions and management in Zambia', paper presented at the 36th annual meeting of the African Studies Association, 4–7 December, Boston, MA.

Pinto, R.F. and Mrope, A.J. (1994), 'Projectizing the governance approach to civil service reform: institutional environment assessment for preparing a sectoral adjustment loan in the Gambia', Discussion Paper No. 252, Washington, DC: World Bank.

Rambourg, Michel, LeGay, Jean-Claude and Bay, Mohamen Ould (1995), *Administrative Reform in Central African Republic, African civil service observatory*, Cotonou, Benin: UNDP.

Roth, G. (1987), *The Private Provision of Public Services in Developing Countries*, New York: Oxford University Press.

Schiavo-Campo, Salvatore (1996), 'Reforming the civil service', *Finance and Development*, September, pp. 10–13.

Steedman, David W. and Howes, Stephen (1996), 'Civil service reform in the Philippines', Asia Technical Department Paper Series No. 12, Washington DC: World Bank.

UNDP (undated), 'Process consultation: systematic improvement of public sector management', New York: UNDP.

UNDP (1995), 'Review of the civil service reform programme in Ghana: a case study', report on a mission to Ghana, 19 February–10 March.

UNDP (1997), 'Reconceptualizing governance', Discussion Paper No. 2, New York: UNDP.

Wescott, Clay (1996), 'Civil service reform: lessons from Africa', in de Haan and van Hees (1996).

World Bank (1996), *The World Bank Participation Sourcebook*, Washington, DC: World Bank.

World Bank (1997), *World Development Report 1997: The State in a Changing World*, New York: Oxford University Press.

10. Civil service reform equals retrenchment? The experience of 'right-sizing' and retrenchment in Ghana, Uganda and the UK

Willy McCourt

INTRODUCTION

The policy interventions which go under the heading of 'civil service reform' have done much to change public management. Attempts to improve the structure of public administration are of course a perennial feature of public administration, but from roughly 1980 onwards they have had programmes of job reduction as an integral feature, whether labelled 'right-sizing' or 'down-sizing' or 'retrenchment'. Civil service reform in developing countries has in fact often been synonymous with job reduction or, more narrowly still, with the sacking of civil servants. That was certainly true in the 1980s and early 1990s: as Holland's minister for development cooperation, Jan Pronk, said in 1996, 'At first Civil Service Reform simply meant retrenchment of civil servants, with a view to bringing down the wage bill' (Pronk, 1996, p. 7). But the two are still frequently equated, for instance by Lienert (1998). In any case, job reduction still looms large in developing, transitional and industrialized countries alike. Retrenchment programmes were carried out between 1987 and 1992 in the public sectors of 22 of the 27 member countries of the OECD. No other human resource initiative was taken by so many of them.

And in some developing countries the impact has been enormous. Figure 10.1 shows the scale of reduction in one African country, Uganda.

In this chapter I shall review the experience of job reductions, drawing on relevant literature, but also on some recent field research carried out in Ghana, Uganda and the UK. Job reduction has been, as we have seen, a major plank in public service reform. Failure to do it effectively jeopardizes reform, and may also cause gratuitous hardship to the public servants who are often its victims. I shall say something about the research project on which the

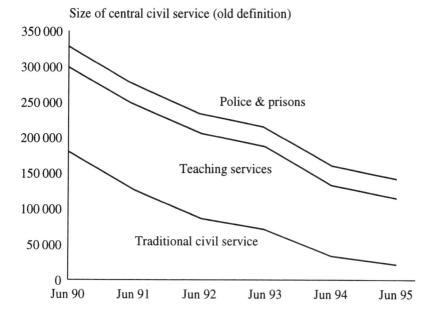

Size of central civil service (old definition)

Source: Ministry of Public Service, Kampala, Uganda.

Figure 10.1   Staffing change in Uganda

chapter is based, review some relevant literature and provide a commentary on some aspects of job reduction in the light of that review.

THE RESEARCH PROJECT

Between March and May 1997 the Institute for Development Policy and Management (IDPM) at the University of Manchester carried out a comparative study of the experience of job reduction in two African countries and one industrialized country. We hoped that comparing the experiences of developing and industrialized countries might inform the conduct of civil service reform, especially in developing countries (and might also challenge the assumption that there is a dichotomy between reform processes in developing and industrialized countries). Ghana, Uganda and the UK were chosen because all three have been reported as examples of right-sizing 'success' (see for instance Langseth and Mugaju, 1994), and in all three the experience is of sufficiently long standing (beginning as long ago as 1982 in Ghana and 1979 in the UK) for a literature to have begun to appear.

THE LITERATURE ON JOB REDUCTION

Despite its prominence among reform activities, job reduction has not been studied very much. There are some agency reports which are not easily accessible and not generalizable. But there is little in the public domain. That is equally true of the private sector in industrialized countries, where job reductions are also commonplace: for instance, Cameron (1994) sees downsizing as one of the least studied aspects of business in the USA.

In view of the scarcity of published material, it is necessary to cast the net wide. There are at least five bodies of literature which shed light on job reductions: the development literature on pay and employment reform; the human resource management (HRM) literature which focuses on the management of redundancy; the private sector literature which focuses on corporate recovery; the public management literature which focuses on the 'new public management' model; and the literature on the social cost of structural adjustment. We shall review them briefly in turn.

Pay and Employment Reform: Steps to Cost Containment

A model which distils the World Bank's experience is a good place to start, since the Bank has been in the forefront of programmes of job reductions. Between 1981 and 1991 no fewer than 26 developing countries received World Bank programmes of assistance which had job reduction as a component, 20 of them taking the form of structural adjustment loans. Surveying that experience, Nunberg (1994) lists steps which governments have taken, placing them, interestingly, in ascending order of political difficulty:

- Remove ghost workers
- Delete empty posts
- Retrench temporary or seasonal workers
- Enforce retirement ages
- Freeze recruitment
- End guaranteed entry to the civil service from the education system
- Suspend automatic advancement
- Introduce voluntary redundancy
- Freeze salaries
- Introduce compulsory redundancy.

Nunberg's list goes beyond the dramatic popular image of job reduction: many of the steps – removal of ghost workers, voluntary redundancy and so on – do not entail the forcible redundancy of anyone. Second, it has a strongly mechanical and prescriptive aspect: it offers the attractive prospect of a simple, relatively painless route to employment reform.

Nunberg's is an inductive model which aims to systematize the World Bank's experience. However, it may be coloured by its origins, since Bank involvement in job reduction is usually in the context of a structural adjustment or other similar loan. It is therefore useful to complement this model with a review of some other literatures which have different origins.

The HRM Literature on Redundancy

Treatment of job reduction in the HRM literature is generally confined to the management of redundancy, with an emphasis on legal provisions which limits its applicability outside the country in which it is written. It presumes that the job of the HRM specialist is to minimize redundancy. Thus Fowler (1993), in his practical handbook, advocates the use of human resource planning to anticipate staffing reductions and curtail recruitment, thus limiting the need to make reductions later on. He also stresses the importance of increasing job flexibility by removing unnecessary demarcation barriers between jobs (such as arbitrary qualification requirements) which prevent the redeployment of redundant staff; the importance of retraining for staff whose skills are no longer in demand; and also the role of natural wastage in achieving job reductions without redundancy. Finally, he argues that orderly job reduction is facilitated by drawing up redundancy procedures before job reduction begins; these include provision for redeployment of redundant staff to other jobs.

The Private Sector Literature on 'Turnaround'

When a British magazine, aimed at practising managers, reported on the British civil service's experience of job reductions, the article was headed 'Civil servants join the real world' (Johnston, 1996). The 'real world' which civil servants were joining was, naturally, the world of the private sector. One argument used to support the case for retrenchments in the public sector of Western countries is that the private sector has already gone through a similar process; private practice is held up for public emulation. For instance, when 1200 jobs were cut from the British prison service between 1995 and 1997, following a 13 per cent overall budget reduction which was much larger than the reduction imposed on other parts of the public sector in the same period, government ministers justified the cuts by referring to the significantly lower staffing levels in comparable private prisons. A review of private sector experience is therefore instructive.

In Western private companies, job reduction often takes place in the context of what the management literature calls 'turnaround', the dramatic, almost miraculous reversal in the fortunes of a previously sickly firm which goes from near-bankruptcy to prosperity in the space of a couple of financial years. It is a phenomenon that appears to fascinate the Western corporate mind in the same way that stories of overnight conversion from a life of vice to a life of piety and religious sobriety fascinate the religious mind, both having in common a tendency to exaggerate past problems, the better to dramatize present achievements.

Job reductions are a pervasive feature of turnaround. To take a typical example, when the new managing director of Ireland's ailing Waterford Glass Group set about reducing costs in 1987, he removed 750 jobs – exactly 25 per cent of the company's workforce (Nelson and Clutterbuck, 1988). A number of writers have argued that recovery without cost (and therefore job) cutting is simply not possible. For instance, Pearce and Robbins (1994) found that firms emerging from decline in the American textile industry which pursued a 'retrenchment strategy' (abandoning unprofitable businesses and the staff that went with them) were generally more successful than firms which pursued an 'entrepreneurial strategy' (trying to generate new business while preserving their existing business intact and retaining their existing staff).

But it has been argued that such reductions have often had a negative impact on organizational effectiveness, inducing 'organizational anorexia', and on staff morale (Gordon, 1996; Heller, 1996). Not all the turnaround literature focuses exclusively on retrenchment. One widely quoted model (Slatter, 1994) includes product-market reorientation, investment and organizational change and decentralization among its elements alongside asset and cost reduction. In consequence, support has been growing recently for a two-stage model of corporate recovery, where emergency actions to cut costs led on to strategic planning for the future, generating stakeholder support and strategic development of the organization's staff and so on (Arogyaswamy et al., 1995).

The 'New Public Management' (NPM) Model

The similarities between reforms in the civil services of the English-speaking industrialized countries have led some writers (such as Dunleavy and Hood, 1994) to identify the emergence of a new model of public management which they have called the new public management. Two of its features are relevant to us here: the presumption that the good state is a small state (hence the title of the relevant chapter in the 1996 *World Development Report*, 'Towards better and slimmer government' (World Bank, 1996)) and the preference for agency models of public management where heads of department or even middle managers are given considerable budgetary autonomy. This leads to the belief that staffing is best managed through budgets rather than through headcounts: in other words, where job reductions are concerned, that local managers should be allowed to decide how to make financial savings rather than having a target for a reduction in the number of staff imposed on them from the centre. However, while decentralized management of staff in line with the NPM model has been widely advocated, it has also been opposed where non-industrialized countries are concerned by those who argue that it places too great a strain on the supposedly weak capacity and integrity of public administration (Nunberg, 1995; Minogue, Chapter 2, this volume).

Structural Adjustment

One aspect of the extensive literature on the experience of structural adjustment is relevant to us here, namely the concern with the social cost of adjustment. It has been argued that structural adjustment has had a negative impact on the poor, and that efforts to alleviate it have been 'too little, too late' (Stewart, 1992). That concern has led to a number of studies of the impact of job reductions on the welfare of retrenched civil servants, notably two conducted in Ghana and Guinea (respectively, Younger, 1996; Mills and Sahn, 1996). These studies concluded that the impact had been less dramatic than anticipated, though more severe in Guinea than in Ghana because the previous government's policies militated against the entrepreneurialism which would have allowed civil servants to start their own businesses. They saw payment of redundancy benefits in a lump sum rather than instalments as crucial, and they were sceptical about the value of other assistance measures such as retraining and counselling.

IMPLEMENTING JOB REDUCTION IN GHANA, UGANDA AND THE UNITED KINGDOM

Actions in Compliance with the Prescriptive Literature

It was reassuring to discover that some at least of the actions taken in the three countries that we studied comply with prescriptions that we have listed. In keeping with Nunberg's model, Ghana discovered 10 000 ghost workers in the system, enabling them to reduce their initial annual job reduction target from 15 000 to 12 000. Uganda's initial target of reducing the number of civil servants by 34 000 was placed in perspective by the discovery of no fewer than 40 000 ghost workers. Similarly, Uganda was able to identify 3000 jobs for reduction merely by enforcing the standard retirement age.

In keeping with Fowler's model, one large UK local authority attributed the success of their job reduction programme partly to having a redundancy procedure in place as far back as 1977. This enabled them to use a combination of natural wastage, redeployment and voluntary redundancy, with the result that less than 1 per cent of job reductions came from compulsory redundancy. Similarly, use of natural wastage and voluntary redundancy in the UK civil service contributed to a reduction in the number of civil servants from a peak of 732 000 in 1979 to just under 500 000 in 1996; again, an official in the UK Cabinet Office estimated that fewer than 1000 in any given year were compulsory redundancies.

However, there were three respects in which the countries we studied did not comply with the prescriptions: cases where the prescriptions were not followed but arguably should have been; cases where countries added ingredients of their own to the standard recipe; and cases where there were other factors which had a bearing on the success of reform. We shall deal with each of them in turn.

Actions that were not taken but arguably should have been
We found little evidence in Ghana and Uganda of familiarity with HRM practice, so it is perhaps not surprising that some of the measures for avoiding redundancy were not taken. Neither country had pre-existing procedures for redundancy, redeployment or retraining, and there was no evidence that natural wastage was taken into account in setting targets (possibly because no reliable data for wastage were available). It is likely that the absence of such procedures added to the disruption and hardship which job reduction caused.

More generally, actions to address the social cost of job reduction were patchy. Performance in financial compensation appeared relatively good. Although the early retrenchees in Uganda, who were deemed to be inadequate performers, received no pension at all, later retrenchees fared better, receiving a standard 'safety net' figure of US$1000 plus three months' salary for each year of service up to a maximum of 20 years. In addition, those over 45 who had served at least ten years received their pensions immediately. Ghanaian civil servants received a severance payment of four months' salary and an end-of-service payment of two months' salary for each year of uninterrupted service; in addition, their pension entitlement was frozen until their normal retirement date.

The financial fortunes of the retrenchees following retrenchment varied. A year after retrenchment in Ghana, 3 per cent of them were unemployed, with a further 8 per cent under-employed (farming their fields for want of a salaried job); overall, 50 per cent had regained their former level of income. Levels of both unemployment and income were in line with the general population (Younger, 1996).

Research on unemployment in industrialized countries shows that its impact is psychological as well as economic (Argyle, 1989). This was corroborated by the civil service trade union representative whom we interviewed in Uganda, who said that anecdotes abound of retrenchees losing status in their villages, marriages breaking up and so on. Despite the scepticism of the economists who carried out the Ghana and Guinea studies which we reported earlier, it is not difficult to argue that information, counselling, advice and training are necessary to offset the psychological impact of retrenchment, just as financial compensation is necessary to offset the economic impact. But performance in these areas was generally poor. Uganda had elaborate plans for counselling, retraining and loans which it failed completely to implement. It was assumed that the Ministry of Labour and the banks would help with retraining and loans respectively, but their support was not obtained. A hospital trust in the UK overlooked the need to provide assistance, so caught up was it in negotiations over redundancies with the trade unions. Even in Ghana, with its elaborate 'Programme to Mitigate the Social Costs of Adjustment' (PAMSCAD), provision started late, as much as one year after retrenchment, and take-up was consequently low. Although Ghana imaginatively used the mass media to inform potential retrenchees about what was going on, partly a reaction to problems experienced in an earlier round of retrenchment, where many retrenchees mistakenly believed that their severance was only temporary, this was exceptional. The cynical suggestion that all these aborted plans were mainly cosmetic would not be wholly unfounded.

Additional actions not specified in the literature

Privatization and contracting out In all three countries, but notably in the UK, these two measures accounted for some reduction, though much more in the public enterprises than in the traditional civil service. Privatization was introduced as part of a macroeconomic strategy unconnected to right-sizing, though it has the fringe benefit of reducing public sector numbers. Contracting out is likely to have a greater impact on the traditional public service: in the UK, 40 per cent of job reductions over the last five years have been attributed to it. Its influence is increasing, partly because of the potential it offers for reducing the number of civil servants: Zimbabwe has recently embarked on it, and Malawi was about to at the time of writing.

'Book transfers' A significant proportion of the reduction in numbers in Uganda was achieved through divestment, for instance through the setting up of the Uganda Revenue Authority which took a large number of staff off the books of the traditional public service. Although there was no net reduction in the number of public employees, government was able to include it when presenting evidence to donors and others of the effectiveness of their reforms.

The UK has done the same thing, for instance with the transfer of responsibility for housing benefits payments from the Department of Health and Social Security to local authorities. Although most staff responsible transferred too, government officials informed us that they were instructed by ministers to present the transfer as a reduction in the size of the civil service.

Additional factors bearing on the success of reform

In our research we found evidence of other factors which influenced the success of reform: political commitment and the political process; process issues; coordination between government agencies and establishment control; and the choice between a focus on the number of civil servants and the cost of the wage bill. Again we shall deal with them in turn.

Political commitment and the political process   We saw earlier that Nunberg's list of steps was presented in ascending order of political difficulty: governments should find the earlier items in the list easier to carry through than the later ones. Given the popular image of retrenchment – of established civil servants being the victims of compulsory redundancy – it is understandable (and perhaps laudable!) that governments hesitate before embarking on job reductions.

As Nunberg's list implies, political commitment is crucial. Commitment in the three countries was signalled by symbolic actions. The Ugandan government took a decision to reduce the number of ministries from 35 to 21 in 1992. The Conservative government in the UK set tough job reduction targets shortly after its election in 1979. Though these were substantive actions, they also symbolized the governments' commitment to making serious job reductions, and probably blunted the resistance which otherwise would have occurred. Moreover, all three governments were politically strong: Ghana's and Uganda's had a military character which reflected the circumstances of their seizing power; the Conservative government enjoyed an unusually firm grip on political power in the UK throughout the 1980s.

Reducing the size of the civil service can be politically costly, but need not always be; the early actions in Nunberg's list are not. Indeed, action against ghost workers may be politically advantageous as it demonstrates to the public the government's commitment to eliminating corruption in staffing.

A second political aspect of job reduction is the impact of the political process. It is inevitable that there will be a staffing response to new issues coming on to the political agenda. In 1997 the Ugandan government introduced a policy of universal primary education which entailed the recruitment of many more primary teachers; they also recruited extra police officers in response to security problems in the north and the west of the country. In the UK, similarly, staffing in the area of law and order increased in the early

1990s, even while the government was bearing down on staffing elsewhere. These actions, part of the normal political process, were not built into job reduction calculations.

A learning process   Job reduction programmes are often slow to start. In both Ghana and Uganda there was an initial period of about two years between agreement in principle to reduce and the process of reduction actually getting under way. This may partly reflect uncertain political commitment, but partly also technical uncertainty about how to proceed, especially in circumstances where the workforce data on which job reduction must be based were unreliable. Gathering reliable data takes time, of course, but it is almost inevitable that mistakes will be made early on, given the complexity of reform. Uganda's first round of job reductions targeted civil servants who were 'incompetent'. Unfortunately the assessment of competence derived from the annual confidential reports written by their superiors, which were sometimes biased or harsh, so that it is likely that some competent employees were unjustly dismissed. The UK had the paradoxical experience of seeing the number of civil servants decrease in the early 1980s while spending on staffing increased (we shall look at this in more detail in the next section).

In all three countries, therefore, reform has been an iterative process, where original targets have been modified and new targets introduced to supersede them. Ghana was still bearing down on staffing in 1997 after 15 years of activity; the UK was doing likewise after 18 years.

Coordination and establishment control   Coordinating right-sizing has left some governments with egg on their faces. At the same time that the retrenchment team in the Ministry of Public Service in Uganda was working towards job reductions, their colleagues on the other side of the building were carrying out a rolling programme of restructuring reviews in the ministries whose net result was to recommend a staff increase!

The problem of coordination, so simple to state, does seem extraordinarily difficult to overcome. Right-sizing mechanisms seem to be crucial. The key steering committee in Ghana, the Redeployment Management Committee, had cross-departmental membership, with Finance closely involved. In Uganda there were three levels of committees: the Public Service Review and Reorganization Commission, the Civil Service Reform Coordination Committee, a committee of directors general of departments, and the Implementation and Monitoring Board, which took operational decisions about right-sizing.

The problem of coordination is compounded by the almost universal mistrust between ministries of finance and public service. In some African countries the latter is seen by Finance as a 'trojan horse' inside government, acting as a kind of informal trade union, especially on behalf of senior civil servants (Corkery and Land, 1996). Staff in the Ministry of Finance in Ghana whom we interviewed in the course of our research saw their Public Service counterparts as the biggest single threat to the success of job reduction!

Establishment control is an important aspect of coordination. Some countries like Tanzania made sizeable reductions in the number of civil servants only to find that they had as many people as before, because recruitment had been carrying on in the meantime. In the unwieldy structure of government, there can be hundreds of points of recruitment, with the rigidity of central recruitment mechanisms – operated by a public service commission or the like and introduced, ironically, in an effort to control recruitment – being offset by local flexibility, with local managers having discretion to make temporary appointments outside the establishment. Sustainable job reduction entails integration with establishment control.

Numbers or costs?   All the countries which we studied started by setting a target for a reduction in the number of posts. Britain aimed to reduce from 732 000 to 630 000 between 1979 and 1984; Uganda's initial target was to reduce from 320 000 to 286 000. Both countries were successful, and both went on to set further targets which again they managed to meet. This was certainly a kind of success, especially given that targets in other countries have not by any means always been met. And yet in the case of Britain senior government officials concerned with staffing in the early 1980s see it as a period of failure masquerading as success, where, as Figure 10.2 shows, the number of staff decreased but overall government spending increased.

Of course wages and salaries represent only a portion of government expenditure (17.1 per cent in the UK in 1983/4, though in many developing countries it is much higher). There could be a variety of reasons for the discrepancy; there is no hard information that enables us to explain it in a completely satisfactory way. But we can get a pointer from the anecdotal experience of officials who were involved in policy making in the period in question. A senior British government official whom we interviewed commented that trying to reduce staffing in isolation from other kinds of expenditure is like squeezing a balloon (hence the caption of Figure 10.2): you might succeed in achieving a reduction in one part, but only at the expense of a corresponding increase in some other part. What is occurring has been called 'manpower substitution': in financial terms, spending on staffing is simply being transferred from one budget to another. The UK's decrease in staff numbers was real, but was achieved partly at the expense of an increase in spending in another area.

In Ghana and Uganda, by contrast, most major staffing decisions are taken by the centre. In Uganda, for instance, the programme of job reduction in local authorities carried out in the mid-1990s was implemented exclusively

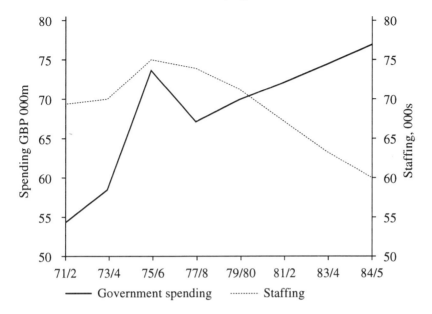

Source: Based on Dunsire and Hood (1989), p. 90.

Figure 10.2 The 'balloon problem'

by the Ministry of Public Service in Kampala – it was only at the stage where severance cheques were disbursed to individuals that the districts became involved.

Consistent with the new public management model, the UK government now manages staffing principally through budgets: the Treasury merely monitors spending on programme and non-programme budgets, but does not formally monitor staffing levels, so there is no longer an incentive for 'manpower substitution'. Ghana and Uganda, by contrast, continue to control numbers as well as budgets. The choice between controlling numbers and controlling costs was the most complex issue that we found in our research: moving from numbers to costs has important potential advantages, but important potential disadvantages too.

Three advantages were reported to us. The first is *administrative simplicity*: the UK government's move in this direction has enabled it to dismantle cumbersome central personnel controls, solving the problem of mistrust, discussed earlier, between the Treasury and the Cabinet Office, the UK agencies responsible for finance and staffing. The second advantage is *flexibility*: individual departments now have freedom to spend budgets as they choose (a micro-example quoted to us was of a school in Lancashire, an area with a wet climate, which chose to reduce their staffing establishment by half a teacher in order to find money to replace the rotten window frames!). The third advantage is *social progressiveness*. Targeting numbers tends to be socially regressive. The temptation is to meet a numerical target by focusing on lower-echelon staff, of whom there are many, even though the cash saving may be no greater than focusing on a much smaller number of higher-echelon staff. That has been the case in Uganda, where the government decided in 1997 to target junior support staff again, even though they had already been targeted more than once. It is striking that, for this very reason, a representative of the Uganda Civil Servants' Union whom I interviewed had a clear preference for a cost-based approach.

But moving from numbers to costs has potential disadvantages too. The first is a *lack of financial skills*. Budget management skills may not exist, and systems take time to be set up. It has been reported that this had a negative effect on the implementation of the financial management initiative (FMI), an initiative taken in the UK in the early 1980s to devolve financial responsibility. The second is *scope for nepotism and corruption*. There may be greater scope for corruption away from the centre, either because the centre is honest while the periphery is not, or simply because delegating responsibility allows more fingers to get in to the pie. While this problem was not reported to us in any of the three countries we studied, we found evidence of it in separate research in Nepal and Tanzania. The third disadvantage is the gap between *appearance and reality*. Central government may give up the appearance of power but retain the substance: a personnel specialist in an outlying agency in the UK claimed that the Treasury continues to take account of numbers, especially when there is an organizational review of the prior options or fundamental expenditure variety, partly because staff numbers are a currency which is understood by both politicians and the public. Nunberg (1995) suggests that in the short term delegation may lead to an increase, not a decrease, in the information which the centre demands from individual ministries. A related, final disadvantage is *economies of scale and transaction costs*. Delegation entails the loss of economies of scale and the introduction of transaction costs because of information transfer requirements.

The strategic choice between a focus on numbers and a focus on costs is therefore a complex one, perhaps best considered as an aspect of the new public management debate. As with the NPM model in general, it is mainly the English-speaking industrialized countries that have adopted this approach, though the recent decisions by the governments of Singapore and South Africa to adopt it may be straws in the wind.

CONCLUSION

In this chapter I have presented a review of five literature sources: the development literature on pay and employment reform; the HRM literature which focuses on the management of redundancy; the private sector literature which focuses on corporate recovery; the new public management literature; and the literature on the social cost of structural adjustment. I went on to present some results of our research in Ghana, Uganda and the UK in the light of that review. We saw that experience does reflect some of the prescriptions in terms of specific measures such as elimination of ghost workers, but that the three countries have adopted some additional measures such as the use of contracting out to reduce staff numbers. More importantly, we saw four additional factors which influenced the success of reform: political commitment and the political process; coordination between government agencies and establishment control; process issues; and the choice between a focus on the number of civil servants and the cost of the wage bill.

As I said at the beginning of this chapter, we chose to focus on Ghana, Uganda and the UK because they have been reported as examples of success. If we define success as a lasting reduction in the number of public servants, then the steady decrease since, respectively, 1982, 1980 and 1979 in the three countries is impressive evidence. But evidence elsewhere is less impressive. At the time of writing, IMF officials have informed me that the IMF is about to publish a report which concludes that job reduction programmes have largely been a failure, in contrast with relative success in other areas of government reform. And of course it is possible to question the definition of success. All too often job reduction has been exclusively finance-driven, with no thought given to prioritizing the tasks which governments need to carry out. As a representative of the South African trade union movement said in giving evidence to the Presidential Review Commission on the Transformation of the Public Service,

> We believe that fundamentally, fundamentally wrong in this approach is in the rightsizing program [sic]. It is an approach that looks at your budget without looking at the needs at the same time ... and the recommendation that we want to make, Chairperson ... is that ... of ... looking at the needs of the people as superseding an arbitrary target. (COSATU, 1997, pp. 7–8)

My chapter may contribute to the search for a model of employment reform through providing a review of relevant literature and some empirical data. Evidence from my study suggests that it is not necessary to cause great hardship, that political difficulties can be avoided and that job reduction can act as the prelude to strategic development of the public service. All of that may be an encouragement to governments hesitating to embark on it.

Our consideration of factors such as political commitment and coordination suggests that sustainable employment reform is a more complex matter than simple 'recipe' approaches imply, and that is without taking into account deeper influences such as patrimonialism which are outside the scope of this chapter but which arguably exert a powerful upward pressure on staff numbers in many countries. The next step must be to address those deeper influences and, in general, to try to understand better the reasons for both success and failure so as to improve the likelihood of success in the future. Perhaps it is banal to discover that many employment reform efforts have 'failed' – according to one school of thought, development projects always do. But as one of the Irish writer Samuel Beckett's characters says, 'Ever tried. Ever failed. No matter. Fail again. Fail better.'

REFERENCES

Argyle, M. (1989), *The Psychology of Work*. Harmondsworth: Penguin.

Arogyaswamy, K., Barker, V. and Yasai-Ardekani, M. (1995), 'Firm turnarounds: An integrative two-stage model', *Journal of Management Studies*, **32**, 493–525.

Cameron, K. (1994), 'Investigating organisational downsizing: fundamental issues', *Human Resource Management*, **33** (2), 183–8.

Corkery, J. and Land, A. (1996), *Civil Service Reform in the Context of Structural Adjustment*, Maastricht: European Centre for Development Policy Management.

COSATU (Congress of South African Trade Unions) (1997), 'Presentation to the Presidential Review Commission', Pretoria, South Africa: Department of Public Service and Administration.

Dunleavy, P. and Hood, C. (1994), 'From old public administration to new public management', *Public Money and Management*, July–September.

Dunsire, A. and Hood, C. (1989), *Cutback Management in Public Bureaucracies*, Cambridge: Cambridge University Press.

Fowler, A. (1993), *Redundancy*, London: Institute of Personnel Management.

Gordon, D. (1996), *Fat and Mean: The Corporate Squeeze of Working Americans and the Myth of Managerial 'Downsizing'*, New York: Martin Kessler.

Heller, R. (1996), 'Downsizing's other down side', *Management Today,* March, p. 23.

Johnston, I. (1996), 'Civil servants join the real world', *Management Today*, March, p. 5.

Langseth, P. and Mugaju, J. (eds) (1994), *Post-Conflict Uganda: Towards an Effective Civil Service*, Kampala: Fountain.

Lienert, I. (1998), 'A decade of civil service reform in sub-Saharan Africa', working paper, Washington DC: International Monetary Fund.

Mills, B. and Sahn, D. (1996), 'Life after public sector job loss in Guinea', in D. Sahn (ed.), *Economic Reform and the Poor in Africa*, Oxford: Clarendon Press, pp. 203–30.

Nelson, R. and Clutterbuck, D. (eds) (1988), *Turnaround: How Twenty Well-known Companies Came Back from the Brink*, London: Mercury.

Nunberg, B. (1994), 'Experience with civil service pay and employment reform: An overview', in D. Lindauer and B. Nunberg (eds), *Rehabilitating Government: Pay and Employment Reform in Africa*, Washington, DC: World Bank, pp. 136–7.

Nunberg, B. (1995), *Managing the Civil Service: Reform Lessons from Advanced Industrialised Countries,* Washington, DC: World Bank.

Pearce, J.A. and Robbins, D.K. (1994), 'Entrepreneurial recovery strategies of small market share manufacturers', *Journal of Business Venturing*, **9** (2), 91–108.

Pronk, J. (1996), 'Preface', in P. de Haan and Y. van Hees (eds), *Civil Service Reform in sub-Saharan Africa*, The Hague, Netherlands: Ministry of Foreign Affairs, p. 7.

Slatter, S. (1984), *Corporate Recovery*, Harmondsworth: Penguin.

Stewart, F. (1992), 'Protecting the Poor during Adjustment in Latin America and the Caribbean in the 1980s: How Adequate Was the World Bank's Response?', International Development Centre, University of Oxford: Working Paper No. 44.

World Bank (1996), *World Development Report 1996: From Plan to Market,* New York: Oxford University Press.

Younger, S. (1996), 'Labour market consequences of retrenchment for civil servants in Ghana', in D. Sahn (ed.), *Economic Reform and the Poor in Africa*, Oxford: Clarendon Press, pp. 185–202.

11. Management decentralization in practice: a comparison of public health and water services in Ghana

George A. Larbi[1]

INTRODUCTION

Along with reforms in its economy under a structural adjustment programme adopted in 1983, Ghana has been making efforts to reform the management of its public services. Management decentralization is part of these reforms. Using the Ministry of Health (MOH) and the Ghana Water and Sewerage Corporation (GWSC) as case studies, this chapter examines how management decentralization, as a component of the new public management (NPM), is informing reforms and being applied in the public services in Ghana. The central argument is that in Ghana and other developing countries public sector management reforms tend to focus more on the design and policy content of reforms than on the process of implementation. Governments and donor agencies tend to put more emphasis on questions of *what* to implement, and less on the *process* of reforms, that is, on questions of *how* to implement (Brinkerhoff, 1996). Implementation is usually taken for granted as the assumption seems to be that the decision to reform will lead to actual implementation (Grindle and Thomas, 1991). In emphasizing content over process of reforms, governments and donors tend either to overlook or downplay contextual factors and capacity issues in implementation.

Capacity, in the context used here, means the ability to carry out a particular task or function, in this case the ability to introduce and implement decentralized management within the health and water sectors in Ghana. It has two dimensions: (a) internal organizational capacity, which is a function of human resources, management/leadership, financial resources, physical/ logistic resources, and information resources; and (b) external/institutional context within which the mobilization and use of organizational capacity occurs – factors emanating from the economic, social and political environment may either enable or constrain the capacity to introduce and implement reforms (Grindle and Hilderbrand, 1995; Cohen, 1995; Dia, 1993, 1996).

The research reported here is based on work carried out in Ghana in 1996. The methodology was essentially qualitative, based on in-depth, open and semi-structured interviews with relevant officials, document analysis and observation. The rest of the chapter is structured as follows. The next section examines the concept of management decentralization as a component of the new public management. An outline is then given of the background to reforms in Ghana's health and water sectors. Subsequently, management decentralization in practice in the two sectors is analysed, highlighting the institutional constraints and capacity issues. The final section draws conclusions and key lessons from the study.

WHAT IS MANAGEMENT DECENTRALIZATION?

Management decentralization is an aspect of decentralization (Devas, 1997) and a key component of the new public management (Ferlie et al., 1996). Decentralization itself has several overlapping connotations including devolution, deconcentration, delegation and privatization (see Rondinelli, 1981; Cheema and Rondinelli, 1983; Mills et al., 1990; Turner and Hulme, 1997). As a component of NPM, decentralization takes a more managerial dimension.

Management Decentralization as a Component of NPM

The new public management (NPM) captures the structural, organizational and managerial changes which have taken place in the public services of most Western countries since the late 1970s (Farnham and Horton, 1996; Ferlie et al., 1996; Hood, 1991; Dunleavy and Hood, 1994; Pollitt, 1993; Walsh, 1995). Management decentralization is a strand of NPM derived from increasing 'managerialism' in government (Mellon, 1993; Hood, 1991). Its introduction and application in the public domain is part of the efforts to 'debureaucratize' public services (Ingraham, 1996, p. 255) or 'delayer' the hierarchies within them. The key concern here is 'whether managers are free to manage their units in order to achieve the most efficient output' (Mellon, 1993, p. 26; see also Hood, 1991, pp. 5–6).

The key elements of management decentralization may be summarized as follows:

- Breaking up monolithic bureaucracies by disaggregating separable functions into semi-autonomous agencies, involving a split between a small strategic policy core and large operational units. Executive agencies are the best examples of this form of management decentralization.

These agencies then relate to the parent ministry *not* through the traditional hierarchy but by contractual agreements and on an arms-length basis.

- Organizational unbundling or delayering of vertically integrated organizations – replacing traditional 'tall hierarchies' with flatter, flexible and more responsive structures.
- A shift of power to senior management in public organizations, with a clear responsibility and accountability relationship.
- New forms of corporate governance and a move to a board of directors model.
- The emergence of separate purchaser and provider organizations.
- Devolving budgets and financial control to decentralized units, for example, creating separate budget centres or spending units in order to give managers greater control over resources.

The economic and administrative cases for decentralizing management rest on bringing service delivery closer to consumers, improving central government's responsiveness to public demands, improving efficiency and quality of public services, and empowering lower units by giving them more managerial involvement and control. As Mellon (1993, p. 26) points out, in the case of the executive agency concept, it 'seeks to decentralise the civil service to take authority away from the centre and delegate it more clearly to the service deliverers'.

The UK, New Zealand and Australia are often cited as countries that have gone furthest with NPM-type management decentralization. In recent years, however, there has been a noticeable trend towards the executive agency-type of management decentralization (along with other NPM components) not only in Western Europe but also in some developing countries, prompting some to suggest convergence in public management reforms (Kickert and Beck Jorgensen, 1995). The next section will examine the background and context for management decentralization in Ghana's health and water services.

BACKGROUND

Crisis and Adjustment

Reforms in the Ministry of Health (MOH) and in the Ghana Water and Sewerage Corporation (GWSC) have been closely linked to the broader socioeconomic reforms under structural adjustment. Like reforms in the main civil service (Larbi, 1995), initial reforms focused on short-term cost containment measures, notably retrenchments and removal of subsidies across a number of services in order to redress fiscal deficits, rather than on institutional issues.

From the late 1980s and early 1990s, as attention began to shift to capacity and good governance issues with impetus from the international donor community, decentralization and other institutional reforms became priorities on the reform agenda. The World Bank, which has been a prominent actor in Ghana's reforms, generally argued for the need 'to reduce the number of tasks performed by central government and to decentralise the provision of public services' (World Bank, 1989, p. 19). Decentralization appeared to be seen as the political and administrative correlate of economic liberalization and deregulation (Bienefeld, 1991). However, in Ghana the government gave more attention to political rather than administrative/management decentralization, as evidenced in the creation of 110 district councils in 1988 (Crook, 1994; Ayee, 1994).

Both MOH and GWSC have traditionally been very centralized and bureaucratic. In the health sector, the development of vertically organized public health programmes has influenced the organizational structure of the MOH over the years. As some keen observers on Ghana's health sector have rightly noted, 'Vertical organisational structures have, necessarily, resulted in the development of separate, vertically-organised management systems: for the transmission of information, for supervision, and for in-service training' (Cassels and Janovsky, 1992, p. 145). Besides, the central MOH was weak and fragmented, with roles and responsibilities between technical and administrative staff confused, as well as duplication and competition between centrally managed vertical programmes. With this background, the reorganization of the MOH was one of the key concerns of major donors; restructuring of the MOH was one of the conditions of the World Bank's second Health and Population Loan.

Unlike health, which has historically been part of the civil service, water has been operated as a public enterprise by the Ghana Water and Sewerage Corporation (GWSC) since 1966, under Act 310 of 1965. Inherent defects in Act 310 became evident over the years, including ministerial control and interference, especially in the determination of adequate and timely tariffs and in appointments. Previous reforms failed to rectify these defects as they were merely cosmetic. Under World Bank/IDA finance, a management improvement study was undertaken in 1984 which was to form the basis for restructuring GWSC as from 1986/87.

GWSC was among the initial core of 17 strategic state-owned enterprises (SOEs) which became the focus of renewed reforms. Of relevance here was the proposal to modify Act 310 to give the Corporation more authority and flexibility to act on matters of personnel, tariffs, policy and programmes.

Reforms also aimed at decentralizing and strengthening GWSC's management, including its regional and district offices.

In summary, there were pressures to restructure both the MOH and the
GWSC, with management decentralization as part of the process. What
progress has been made in practice? What are the institutional constraints and
capacity issues encountered? How have these affected implementation? The
next section will examine these questions.

MANAGEMENT DECENTRALIZATION IN PRACTICE

In the process of restructuring the MOH and GWSC there is some evidence
of a shift towards new forms of corporate governance or a board of directors
model in health, and attempts to break up the public health bureaucracy into a
strategic core and operational units along with agency-type relationships.
Some devolution of budgets and financial control is also evident. These
developments are examined in detail in what follows.

Towards Organizational Unbundling and Delayering of Hierarchies

Organizational restructuring and the delayering of hierarchies are key components of management decentralization. Both the MOH and the GWSC have
made efforts to move in this direction. Starting with the MOH, it has made
progress in unbundling its structure in three main ways. First, hierarchical
technical/programme structures, which encouraged the building of empires
and hampered decentralization, have been replaced by functional/manage-
ment directorates. There are seven such directorates covering various health
management functions. This has led to a more coherent management structure based on functional rather than technical divisions.

Second, a unitary command structure has been created by appointing a
Director General of Health Services. This was to minimize conflict between
the administration and operational divisions which, in the past, plagued the
MOH. It was also to enable administrative, financial, and technical matters
to be managed from a holistic perspective in order to improve the delivery
of services and to ensure that the allocation of resources was responsive to
needs. These changes were to give the functional divisions some control
over financial resources instead of concentrating all spending decisions at
one point. The above reorganizations at the centre were seen as a next step
to 'create a platform from which a separate [Ghana Health] Service can
take off in the future' (WHO/MOH, 1994, p. 1). Third, apart from the
management restructuring at the centre, there has been vertical decentralization to health management teams in the regions and districts. This is a

reflection of one of the declared strategies of the health sector in Ghana, which is to

> decentralise health management to lower levels and to restructure the regional and national levels of the Ministry to respond to the needs of the district and sub-district levels and to strengthen planning, monitoring and evaluation at all levels to promote integration and co-ordination of health services and programmes. (MOH, 1994, p. 5)

With its experience in delivering primary health care services, the MOH has played a leading role in decentralizing management functions to its regional and district health management teams.

In the case of the GWSC, the first serious attempt at management decentralization was in the 1970s when regional managers were appointed and some authority delegated to them from the head office. In the mid-1980s the position and role of regional managers were strengthened by upgrading them to regional directors and granting the regions more autonomy. Unfortunately, the move towards regional autonomy in GWSC was curtailed in 1990 when the head office reinstated controls over several management and operational functions, especially accounting and personnel functions. These counter-decentralization measures were to enable GWSC to streamline its financial affairs. It also gave the head office control over the surpluses generated by viable regions in order to account for liabilities in the non-viable regions, and to settle redundancy payments and end-of-service benefits for a large number of retrenched workers. Thus financial exigencies overshadowed the rationality and benefits of management decentralization. This move has, however, resulted in considerable friction between the regional directors and the head office, with the regions advocating more decentralization of authority to them, especially over financial and personnel matters.

Perhaps one of the most significant organizational changes in GWSC is the separation of the management of rural from urban water supply systems, with the encouragement of the World Bank. The Rural Water Department has been upgraded to a Community Water and Sanitation Division which is expected to be hived off from GWSC in the future, leaving the large and more complex urban systems to be managed as public utilities. This separation is apparently to prepare potentially profitable urban systems for possible private sector participation in production, distribution and management of water services.

Shift to Board of Directors and Agency Models

As public services become increasingly disaggregated and hived off into executive and semi-autonomous agencies, new forms of corporate governance and the role of boards of directors are becoming more important in the management of such organizations. For public enterprises like GWSC, boards of directors are not new, but the extent of operational autonomy granted to top management is crucial. The following paragraphs will describe these developments, starting with health. Three developments in the health sector suggest a shift to board of directors and agency-type models.

Institutionalizing autonomous hospital boards

The first example of a shift to the board of directors model in health is the institutionalization of autonomous hospital boards for the two teaching hospitals, that is, Korle Bu and Komfo Anokye Teaching Hospitals (KBTH and KATH respectively). The legal framework for this was provided by the Hospital Administration Law, 1988 (PNDC Law 209), and boards were appointed in 1989/90. In principle, the autonomous hospital concept is to 'empower' teaching hospital boards and to reduce the financial and managerial burden of big hospitals on the government. The perception here is that local hospital management boards are likely to improve hospital standards where the central bureaucracy had failed (Smithson, Asamoah-Baah and Mills, 1997).

In December 1996 Parliament enacted a new law – the Ghana Health Service and Teaching Hospitals Act (Act 525). The new law grants more independence to autonomous hospitals by separating them from the proposed Ghana Health Service (see below) and the civil service. Under these changes, a teaching hospital board is granted the 'freedom' to manage the hospital, including, *inter alia*: determining the policies of the teaching hospital within the broad framework of government health policies; ensuring sound financial management of the hospital's funds; and determining the scale of fees to be paid by patients subject to the approval of the minister. As in executive agencies, the relationship between the MOH and the teaching hospitals will be governed by a framework agreement under which funding for the teaching hospitals will increasingly be based on the number of patients requiring specialist treatment and referred to them by other hospitals (MOH, 1996a). This is expected to provide incentives for hospital managers to reduce the number of unnecessary referrals to teaching hospitals since such referrals will be paid for from their budget. This will help to decongest facilities at the teaching hospitals.

Strengthening health management teams

The second example of management decentralization in health is the strengthening of regional and district health management teams (RHMTs and DHMTs) by delegating more managerial powers and functions to them. The difference is that these management teams are not autonomous, but are, rather, vertically linked to the MOH. Unlike the concept of autonomous teaching hospitals, that of health management teams is not new in Ghana's health sector as they date back to the 1970s. What is new is the delegation of more managerial powers and functions to them.

Towards an executive agency in health

The third example, perhaps the clearest indication yet of NPM-type management decentralization in health, is seen in the current initiative to create a Ghana Health Service (GHS) as an executive agency under the Ministry of Health. Its conceptualization is along the lines of the UK's National Health Service. Though this is yet to be implemented, it is worth exploring the changes that are expected in the public health organization. The Ghana Health Service and Teaching Hospitals Act, 1996 (Act 525) provides the legal framework for the GHS. Section 3(1) of the law defines the objectives of the GHS as to: (a) implement approved national policies for health delivery in the country; (b) increase access to improved health services; and (c) manage prudently resources available for the provision of health services.

The law separates the GHS and teaching hospitals from the civil service. Consequently, these organizations will no longer be required to follow all civil service rules and procedures. The GHS, as an executive agency, is expected to reinforce management decentralization in the sense that 'Its independence, and the independence of the Teaching Hospitals, is designed to ensure that staff have a greater degree of managerial flexibility to carry out their responsibilities, than would be possible if they remained wholly within the civil service' (MOH, 1996a, p. 4).

According to the new arrangements the central MOH will remain part of the civil service and will, *inter alia*, be responsible for policy making, strategic planning, monitoring the performance of the GHS and the teaching hospital boards against agreed objectives, accounting for the use of public funds, and negotiating with external assistance agencies. Thus, there is a conscious attempt to make a clear distinction between policy making by the core central ministry and policy implementation by the operational arms of the health sector. It is expected that the GHS will eventually take on a 'purchaser role' in relation to the provision of referral services provided by the teaching hospitals.

Unreformed governance framework in GWSC

As a public enterprise, having a board of directors is not new to GWSC. However, the governance framework for GWSC and other state-owned enterprises (SOEs) has historically been characterized by: (a) centralized institutions; (b) intervention authorities reserved or assigned to government and sector ministries by an instrument of establishment and other legislation; and (c) agencies established to regulate and control SOE pricing, procurement and employment policies and actions (SEC, 1995). These characteristics of the SOE governance framework have been major constraints on the autonomy of the GWSC board and its senior management. As part of the reform of SOEs, the State Enterprises Commission (SEC) has initiated the reform of the legal frameworks for SOEs' governance, aimed at concentrating accountability for enterprise direction and performance on boards of directors and significantly increasing operational autonomy by reducing the extent of both authorized and *ad hoc* ministerial interventions in enterprise decision making (SEC, 1995). Although the legal framework for commercial SOEs has changed under the Statutory Corporations (Conversions to Company) Act, 1993, that of GWSC has not changed. GWSC is classified as a public service by the 1992 constitution and so the general framework for managing public services applies, with two principal features:

- the power to appoint is vested in the President, acting in accordance with the advice of the governing council of the service concerned, given in consultation with the Public Services Commission (PSC) (section 195);
- the PSC establishes terms and conditions of employment in the public services (section 196).

The result of the above legal provisions is that the current governance framework of GWSC limits its operational autonomy as an economic service. The position of the PSC is an obvious limitation on the autonomy of the public services in personnel management. Although it is expected to operate in such a way as to break even, the unchanged legal and governance framework makes this difficult. There is thus a mismatch between operational expectations and the institutional framework within which GWSC operates.

The discussion of management decentralization has, so far, focused on organizational restructuring. Organizational structures, however, need to be matched with the right processes and procedures if decentralized management is to function well. The degree of operational freedom given to boards and to senior management, and to lower-level units, is crucial to the proper functioning of decentralization within the public services. These aspects of management decentralization are discussed in what follows.

Devolving Budgets and Financial Control

Financial devolution in health

Despite its leading role in decentralizing management, the health sector has, until recently, been highly centralized in its financial management. To illustrate, before 1992 the acting chief director was the main spending officer at the head office. Also by 1992 the head office administered 66 per cent of the total non-wage recurrent expenditure, with districts and teaching hospitals controlling only 10 and 8 per cent respectively (Smithson, Asamoah-Baah and Mills, 1997). With the changes in organizational structure, there was an express need to put in place a system which allowed a coherent allocation and use of resources. Part of this was to decentralize financial control by appointing the new functional directors and the director general as spending officers, in addition to the acting chief director. This new arrangement was to allow the directors in the headquarters to play a more active role in monitoring the use of funds and ensuring that their divisions have control over the resources needed to fulfil their responsibilities in the new structure. Recent reforms have also decentralized controls to allow a relatively greater allocation of resources from the centre to the decentralized units and from the regions to districts. Based on the 1995 recurrent budget estimates, the MOH/head office's control over total (non-wage) recurrent budget has declined to 28 per cent and that of teaching hospitals and districts, which are at the cutting edge of service delivery, has increased to 17 and 23 per cent respectively. This shift has been facilitated by the restructuring of the budget to allocate a budget to each designated cost centre.

The teaching hospitals also have greater autonomy over the use of internally generated funds and over non-salary recurrent budget. Recently the KBTH secured approval from the Ministry of Finance (MOF) and the Comptroller and Accountant General (CAG) to operate on a subvented status, giving it much greater control over its recurrent budget. The current Five Year Programme of Work (1997–2001) of the MOH requires that managers at both institutional and district levels will have greater authority in the allocation and use of available resources as well as allowing some aspects of conditions of service and staff incentives to be decided locally, similar to trends in the UK (MOH, 1996b). The expectation is that this will help improve the efficiency of resource usage as well as targeting and management of resources.

Financial control in GWSC
Financial management in GWSC has been very centralized. Limited financial devolution was introduced only from March 1996. First, according to the 1996 Operating and Maintenance Budget, apart from training expenses, purchase of capital items, project claims and external audit fees which will be handled at the head office, all other expenditures are to be disbursed in the regional offices (GWSC, 1996). Second, some virement is allowed within the non-salary recurrent budget. The maximum amount that can be vired varies according to regional contributions to GWSC's total revenue, ranging from 15 million cedis (about $9000 in 1996) for the largest region to 5 million cedis (about $3000) for the smallest region. Third, from 1996 the central

purchasing system has been decentralized to allow regions and districts to purchase their own supplies, except for chemicals, which are still centrally procured. Stationery and claims/compensation, which were hitherto central-ized, have also been decentralized with effect from 1996 to enable regional offices to purchase directly from the market.

The above analysis suggests a trend towards decentralized management in both MOH and GWSC, though the health sector appears to be making more progress in decentralization than the water sector in this regard. Two major explanations may account for the differences in progress. First, water is by its nature organized as a state monopoly whilst health is more disintegrated, making it easier to decentralize operations to individual health institutions. Second, there is a small but influential team of reform-minded officials or change agents in the MOH who are driving reforms, with backing from the lobby of the medical profession. This is lacking in the GWSC which is dominated by engineers with little or no management background.

Despite the progress made in decentralizing management, critical con-straints and limitations remain in both public services. These constraints raise questions of capacity in the implementation of management decentralization. These issues are examined next.

Institutional Constraints

The constraints identified may be categorized into: (a) inertia/resistance to change; (b) lack of planning for implementation; (c) centralized control over operational resources partly arising from (a); and (d) defects in institutional frameworks. These constraining factors are not mutually exclusive but rein-force each other. The following paragraphs will elaborate on them.

Inertia and resistance to change

Despite the trend towards decentralization, there are forces within both GWSC and the MOH which reinforce a centralized organizational *status quo*. In health, Cassels and Janovsky (1992) observed that those controlling technical divisions were reluctant to relinquish power for fear of losing control over programmes and possibly losing programme coverage. Indeed, those involved have taken more time than originally anticipated to adjust to the restructuring carried out since 1992.

The fear of losing control over the teaching hospitals can also be partly blamed for delays in the full implementation of the autonomous hospital con-cept. In the view of some senior hospital managers, 'there are people at the top' in the MOH who are not willing to lose control over the teaching hospitals, especially KBTH, which is seen as the 'flagship' of the MOH. Similarly, the GWSC head office has demonstrated reluctance to devolve more management authority to the regions. The rhetoric of management devolution has not been matched with action. One explanation is that control over resources does not only confer prestige on central officials but also provides rent seeking opportunities (for example, in the award of contracts). To decentralize such powers would mean loss of an important source of organizational influence in a system where patronage and 'empire building' are still prevalent.

Lack of planning for implementation

Inertia and resistance to change are reinforced by the lack of preparation for implementation. This has contributed to long time lags between decision making and implementation. For example, although the law establishing the autonomous hospitals was passed in 1988 and boards appointed in 1990, it was not until 1994 that real implementation started, and the initiative is yet to be fully implemented. It was apparent that both the MOH and the teaching hospitals had under-estimated the full implications of autonomy and the demands this will make on their respective management capacities. In a similar vein, most recommendations on the restructuring of GWSC, especially those relating to management decentralization, have not been carried out since 1985. The delays are partly explained by resistance to change and partly by the fact that the implementation process was not given adequate attention during the policy design stage.

Centralized control over operational resources

Control here can be categorized into personnel management controls and financial controls. The lack of decentralization of personnel management has taken two main forms. The first is limitations on the power to hire and fire. In the Ministry of Health the power of the autonomous hospitals to hire and fire is limited to temporary workers paid from internally generated revenue. For the regional units of MOH and GWSC, though powers may be delegated to them, experience shows that in most cases such delegation has not gone beyond the lowest grades of staff. In the MOH, including the autonomous hospitals, the establishment of posts, recruitment, terms and conditions of service are determined by central government agencies like the Public Services Commission (PSC), the Office of the Head of Civil Service (OHCS), and the Ministry of Finance (MOF). In the GWSC the need to obtain head office approval for all new appointments has resulted in recruitment periods of up to 12 months, sometimes with negative effects on operational efficiency because of shortages of skills in the interim.

Second, devolved units have no control over pay and grading of staff since these are centrally determined and follow national policy. Indeed, decentralized units cannot tamper with personal emoluments, what is called 'item one' in the budget. The salary budget is fixed from the centre.

Apart from controls over personnel management, there is a paradox of financial centralization in the midst of the official policy and efforts to decentralize management in the two public services. In the case of the MOH, though there has been good progress in decentralizing financial control, the head office still administers about a third of the non-salary recurrent expenditure. Furthermore, almost all payroll expenditure is centralized in both the MOH and the GWSC, except for daily paid workers in the teaching hospitals. Powers to vire funds remain very limited even after the recent changes.

Three main explanations may be given for the persistence of central controls. First, there is unwillingness on the part of central control agencies – the MOF, the CAG, the OHCS, and the PSC – to liberalize control in order to give the management of public services greater autonomy. As noted earlier, this unwillingness is partly explained by the tendency for bureaucratic empire building.

Second, there is mistrust of officials in decentralized units and the fear of abuse of public resources. In exercising control there is some degree of shared authority among the above central agencies. The MOF and the CAG are financial control and monitoring organs which are expected to ensure that salary expenditure is within the budget; the PSC approves higher-level appointments and disciplinary actions and helps to ensure fair and meritorious practices; the OHCS sometimes overlaps with the PSC in developing personnel policy, but OHCS also sets manpower ceilings for civil service organizations in consultation with the Ministry of Finance. Whilst the sharing of authority may be necessary for checks and balances, the problem is that no clear lines of responsibility are drawn and coordination mechanisms are weak among these agencies; vertical and horizontal linkages and sharing of information are not effective. This sometimes leads to policy confusion and conflict of authority in exercising control.

Third, structural adjustment policies have contributed to centralized controls over personnel and finance. This is one of the interesting paradoxes associated with public sector reforms in the context of structural adjustment – the demand for strict fiscal control, especially over employment cost, and for decentralization at the same time. The need for tighter fiscal control has led to centralization of staffing and financial regulations. Though firm central controls over recruitment and redeployment have been instrumental in reducing staff numbers (Larbi, 1995) the downside of this has been to leave managers of decentralized units with little influence over the management of the personnel for whom they are responsible. Also, rigid financial controls have stifled initiative and creativity by the devolved units and, in the case of GWSC, this has left viable regions with no control over their surpluses.

Constraints in legal/governance frameworks

The operational autonomy of the GWSC and the teaching hospitals is also constrained by existing legal frameworks and institutionalized practice: autonomy in making business decisions in a number of areas such as pricing of services, appointment of external auditors, investment decisions, contracts for goods and services, and raising capital is restricted, especially for GWSC, which delivers an economic service. The need to refer to a number of external agencies for reviews and approvals of what should be normal and routine business decisions (for example, procurement) is a major source of operational inefficiency.

The GWSC is a statutory corporation whose instrument of incorporation makes a distinction between ministerial authority to issue directives in respect to general policy of the corporation on one hand, and board responsibility for day-to-day operations management on the other hand. A recent survey found 'the persistence of Ministerial interventions in the appointment and dismissal of managers at all levels, in the award of contracts for consultant services and procurement, as well as in corporate planning, borrowing and decision making' (SEC, 1995, p. 23). A recent illustration of this was the dismissal by the president of GWSC's managing director and his two deputies in August 1996 for 'poor performance' without recourse to the board.

Similarly, in the case of the teaching hospitals, the boards' ability to determine policies and plans has been undermined by formal and informal controls retained by the central MOH. The senior managers of the hospitals are inclined to have divided loyalties as they look to the centre and the board for direction at the same time. Ministerial and other political interventions continue to compromise the operational autonomy and accountability objectives of reform in GWSC and the teaching hospitals.

It is obvious from the above that there are many outstanding issues yet to be settled before the policy of management decentralization can fully be implemented in health and water services. There are difficult institutional constraints that need to be redressed – or rather, should have been tackled before the introduction of decentralized management reforms.

Capacity Issues in Decentralized Management

The constraints discussed above have implications for capacity since they limit the proper functioning of decentralized systems. However, implementing management decentralization has specific implications for management capacity at the level of both the centre and the decentralized units in both GWSC and the MOH. These are categorized and discussed in what follows.

Capacity issues at the centre

An MOH document captures the key concerns for capacity arising from management decentralization as follows:

> [The ministry has] limited capacity to develop and analyse macro policies at the national inter-sectoral level, and alongside the need to develop specific technical policies required to meet the ongoing decentralisation process and institutional changes. This concern is underscored by the limited training of staff, lack of policy information, advocacy, and poor dissemination and inadequate logistics. (MOH, 1996a, p. 29)

More specifically, in decentralizing management, the following capacities need to be assessed and developed:

Capacity to manage central support services, for example procurement and supplies, maintenance and personnel management. In health there have been problems such as delays and quality of procurement by the central medical stores, whilst central maintenance services and procurement of chemicals are also problematic in GWSC.

Capacity for resource allocation   The MOH, for example, needs to develop and implement a formula to guide resource allocation to districts and GHS hospitals and make clear decisions in relation to the range of services that will be financed from public resources.

Capacity to develop performance indicators and agreements with the devolved agencies such as teaching hospitals, and ability to monitor them. The GWSC has been able to do this with its regional offices based on its performance contracting with the government. In contrast, the MOH is yet to develop such relationships with its devolved units.

Capacity for policy formulation and development planning in health and water. It is acknowledged within MOH and GWSC that whilst operational and management authorities are being transferred to the regions, to autonomous agencies, and to other decentralized units, there is the need to strengthen the centre's capabilities in developing a broad policy framework, technical guidelines, policy implementation indicators, monitoring and evaluation mechanisms. At the moment such capacities are weak.

Capacity for managing and using information   In both public services there are weaknesses in financial information and control systems leading to gross embezzlement and misappropriation, instances of which have been exposed in recent reports of the auditor general. In health, the processes of planning, budgeting and monitoring expenditures have, admittedly, been disjointed and incoherent. Though financial management is currently being tackled as a priority there is still much to be done to improve capacity in this area.

Capacity issues at the level of decentralized units

As greater autonomy is granted to decentralized units, there is an apparent need to strengthen planning, budgeting, management and administrative systems within these units. The provision of adequate recurrent budget and logistic support (for example computers and vehicles), as well as the ability to attract and retain the right calibre of personnel, are as necessary for operational effectiveness and efficiency at the decentralized levels as they are at the centre.

In both GWSC and MOH, the devolution of management authority has to be matched by increased capacity for sound financial management and accountability systems. This type of capacity is currently weak in the decentralized units and partly explains the reluctance of central control agencies, such as the Ministry of Finance, to liberalize control. The ability of decentralized units to manage information and feed it back to the centre is crucial for monitoring and evaluation.

All the above responsibilities require those at both the centre and the devolved units to have expertise in relevant disciplines, analytic skills, technical knowledge and operational experience. There is currently a shortage of technical and managerial expertise at the centre, especially in the MOH.

CONCLUSIONS AND LESSONS

There is evidence of a trend towards decentralized management in Ghana's public health and water services, but this is more noticeable in MOH than in GWSC. Management decentralization has taken place in MOH in the sense of the transfer of operational responsibility and management functions to 'autonomous' hospitals, and delegated functions to health management teams. However, 'autonomous' hospitals are not really autonomous because of prevailing limitations on their operational freedom. Though the Ghana Health Service is yet to become a reality, its legal provisions indicate a move towards an NPM-type executive agency.

The analysis suggests, however, that there are serious institutional constraints on and capacity implications for the implementation of management decentralization and these need to be addressed if decentralized management systems are to function as expected and if their benefits are to accrue to the public services adopting them. Most of the constraints identified have to do with processes and procedures rather than structures, perhaps because there has been more emphasis on creating and reforming structures rather than reforming existing processes and procedures which do not enable the structures to function well.

It is apparent from this study that there are forces and counter-forces of centralization and decentralization, especially in the governance of GWSC and the teaching hospitals. Finding the right balance between central direction and control on one hand, and autonomy on the other, has apparently been difficult. Central agencies are reluctant to let go of control over finance and personnel management. Consequently, management decentralization in MOH and GWSC is taking place within a framework of central controls and within organizational frameworks that are still hierarchical.

One lesson that can be drawn from the study is that the centre has to be strong before it decentralizes functions, if it is to perform its integrative, coordinating, and monitoring role effectively. Here one may agree with Nunberg (1995) that reforming developing countries need to strengthen central management systems as a first priority before considering the issues of flexibility and responsiveness which underlie the argument for management decentralization. Another key lesson is that greater recognition needs to be given to the time and attention required for change, especially institutional change, to take effect. The lack of mature public services and the lack of the necessary preconditions call for realistic and gradual adaptation. For policy to be relevant it must be sensitive to operational reality and context; it must be implementable. Perhaps the key message from the study is that the process of implementing reforms cannot be taken for granted. Implementation needs to be planned and managed carefully.

NOTE

1. I would like to thank officials in the two public services for their cooperation and support during fieldwork for this study. They cannot be named for obvious reasons. The helpful comments and encouragement of Professor Richard Batley of the Development Administration Group, University of Birmingham, and of Charles Polidano of the Institute for Development Policy and Management, University of Manchester, are gratefully acknowledged.

REFERENCES

Ayee, J.R.A. (1994), *An Anatomy of Public Policy Implementation*, Aldershot: Avebury.
Bienefeld, M. (1991), 'The scope and limits of decentralisation in Africa', in CAFRAD (1991), *Seminar Proceedings on Decentralised Administration in Africa*, Tangier (Morocco), 22–26 April.
Brinkerhoff, D. (1996), 'Process perspectives on policy change: highlighting implementation', *World Development*, **24** (9), 1395–1401.

Cassels, A. and Janovsky, K. (1992), 'A time of change: health policy, planning and organization in Ghana', *Health Policy and Planning*, **7** (2), 144–54.

Cheema, G.S. and Rondinelli, D.A. (eds) (1983), *Decentralisation and Development: Policy Implementation in Developing Countries*, Beverly Hills: Sage.

Cohen, J.M. (1995), 'Capacity building in the public sector: a focused framework for analysis and action', *International Review of Administrative Sciences*, **61** (3), 407–22.

Crook, R.C. (1994), 'Four years of the Ghana District Assemblies in operation: decentralisation, democratisation and administrative performance', *Public Administration and Development*, **14** (4), 339–64.

Devas, N. (1997), 'Indonesia: what do we mean by decentralisation?', *Public Administration and Development*, **17** (3), 351–67.

Dia, M. (1993), 'A governance approach to civil service reform in Sub-Saharan Africa', World Bank Technical Paper No. 225, African Technical Department Series, Washington, DC: World Bank.

Dia, M. (1996), *Africa's Management in the 1990s and Beyond: Reconciling Indigenous and Transplanted Institutions*, Washington, DC: World Bank.

Dunleavy, P. and Hood, C. (1994), 'From old public administration to new public management', *Public Money and Management*, July–September.

Farnham, D. and Horton, S. (1996), 'Public service managerialism: a review and evaluation', in D. Farnham and S. Horton (eds), *Managing the New Public Services* (2nd edn), London: Macmillan, pp. 259–76.

Ferlie, E., Pettigrew, A., Ashburner, L. and Fitzgerald, L. (1996), *The New Public Management in Action*, Oxford: Oxford University Press.

Ghana, Republic of (1996), *Ghana Health Service and Teaching Hospitals Act, 1996 (Act 525)*, Tema: Ghana Publishing Corporation.

Ghana, Republic of (1992), *Constitution of the Republic of Ghana, 1992*, Tema: Ghana Publishing Corporation.

Ghana, Republic of (1988), *Health Administration Law, 1988 (P.N.D.C.L 209)*, Tema: Ghana Publishing Corporation.

Ghana Water and Sewerage Corporation (1996), *Operating and Maintenance Budget, 1996*, Accra: GWSC.

Ghana Water and Sewerage Corporation (1986), *Five Year Rehabilitation and Development Plan*, Accra: GWSC.

Grindle, M.S. and Hilderbrand, M.E. (1995), 'Building sustainable capacity in the public sector: what can be done?', *Public Administration and Development*, **15** (5), 441–63.

Grindle, M.S. and Thomas, J.W. (1991), *Public Policy and Policy Change: The Political Economy of Reform in Developing Countries*, Baltimore and London: Johns Hopkins University Press.

Halcrow, Sir William and Partners (1995), *Consultancy Services for the Restructuring of the Water Sector Final Report*, Accra, Ghana: Ministry of Works and Housing.

Hood, C. (1991), 'A public management for all seasons?', *Public Administration*, **69** (1), 3–19.

Ingraham, Patricia W. (1996), 'The reform agenda for national civil service systems: external stress and internal strains', in H.A.G.M. Bekke, J.L. Perry and T.A.J. Toonen (eds) (1996), *Civil Service Systems in Comparative Perspective*, Bloomington and Indianapolis: Indiana University Press.

Kickert, W.J.M. and Beck Jorgensen, T. (1995), 'Introduction: managerial reform trends in Western Europe', *International Review of Administrative Sciences*, **61** (4), 499–510.

Larbi, G.A. (1995), 'Implications and Impact of Structural Adjustment on the Civil Service: the Case of Ghana', Role of Government in Adjusting Economies Paper Series No. 2, Development Administration Group, School of Public Policy, University of Birmingham.

Mellon, E. (1993), 'Executive agencies: leading change from the outside', *Public Money and Management*, **13** (2), 25–31.

Mills, A., Vaughan, P., Smith, D.L. and Tabibzadeh, I. (eds) (1990), *Health System Decentralization: Concepts, Issues and Country Experience*, Geneva: World Health Organization.

Ministry of Health, Ghana (1996a), *Institutional Reform in the Health Sector*, Accra: Bel-Team Publications.

Ministry of Health, Ghana (1996b), *Health Sector 5 Year Programme of Work*, Accra: Ministry of Health.

Ministry of Health, Ghana (1994), *Policies and Priorities for the Health Sector 1994–1995*, Accra: Ministry of Health.

Nunberg, B. (1995), 'Managing the civil service: reform lessons from advanced industrialized countries', World Bank Discussion Paper No. 204, Washington, DC: World Bank.

Pollitt, C. (1993), *Managerialism and the Public Services* (2nd edn), Oxford: Blackwell.

Rondinelli, D. (1981), 'Government decentralization in comparative theory and practice in developing countries', *International Review of Administrative Sciences*, **47** (2), 133–45.

Smithson, P., Asamoah-Baah, A. and Mills, A. (1997), *The Role of Government in Adjusting Economies: The Case of the Health Sector in Ghana*, Development Administration Group, University of Birmingham.

State Enterprises Commission, Ghana (1995), *SOE Reform Program 1984–1994: Review and Recommendations for 1995–2000*, Accra: State Enterprises Commission.

Turner, M. and Hulme, D. (1997), *Governance, Administration and Development: Making the State Work*, Basingstoke: Macmillan.

Walsh, K. (1995), *Public Services and Market Mechanisms: Competition, Contracting and the New Public Management*, Basingstoke: Macmillan.

World Health Organization/Ministry of Health, Ghana (1994), *Restructuring the Ministry of Health: Review of Progress*, Geneva: WHO.

World Bank (1989), *Sub-Saharan Africa: From Crisis to Sustainable Growth*, Washington, DC: World Bank.

12. Private markets, public identities, management and tertiary education in contemporary Vietnam

Helen Chauncey

INTRODUCTION

This chapter examines the impact of market-driven education reform on Vietnam's civic expectations and the context in which those expectations are articulated. It will examine the changing character of state–societal relations by highlighting conceptual issues in the field of public management raised by the Vietnamese case. In so doing, the chapter suggests alternative approaches to interpreting the relationship between the state, public management, the public sphere, and civil society. Three possible constructs for the conceptualization of public management highlight this. From one perspective, public management is a product of deliberative or conflictive dialogue between two distinct, mutually wary spheres, those of the state and civil society. In this regard, the exercise of public management is the negotiated product of civil intent and state power. From another perspective public management is exercised in a disinterested, politically attenuated sphere, an extension of the state but insulated from its politics. The Vietnamese case suggests a third approach: a reconfiguration of the spherical template, positing an intermediate arena, the political public, between civil society (daily, associational life, conducted in public view) and the state. This third view examines distinctions between deliberative and collaborative state–societal relations which occur in this 'political public'. Public administration, conducted by the state, is understood as the projection of these deliberations.

In 1909, the Carnegie Foundation for the Advancement of Teaching commissioned a study to analyse tertiary education in the USA through the lens of Frederick W. Taylor's newly minted 'scientific management'. The result brought down upon American state schooling an efficiency and standardization campaign embraced by advocates of the intensely fashionable 'managerial revolution', and resisted by the professional academic community in almost equal measure (Merkle, 1980, pp. 72–4).

As a tool of efficiency, scientific management fared poorly in an educational setting. Of two common charges levied against it, one (the resulting pseudo-science of education administration) is largely unassailable. The second, the subordination of the learning process to business interests, however, calls into play fundamental questions about the meaning and social purpose of education (Callahan, 1966). Relevant to the post-industrial societies of Western Europe and North America, this interrogation is equally essential for countries such as Vietnam, the still battered Third World character of its economy notwithstanding. Beyond the country's economic needs, education's purpose and the challenge of reform highlight the slow development of citizen management in Vietnam and the accompanying emergence of a non-state public sphere.

In 1975, after two decades of war against the world's most powerful military force, the Democratic Republic of Vietnam, soon to be renamed the Socialist Republic of Vietnam (SRV), sank into a thoroughly understandable orgy of joy and domestic arrogance, filling the administrative space that accompanied peace with rigid, state-dominated formulae for economic production and political loyalty (see, for example, Fforde, 1989). Within four short years, the Socialist Republic wallowed in catastrophe. Twin invasions captured the imagination of the Western media, as Vietnamese forces swept the sanguinary Khmer Rouge from power in Cambodia and Chinese forces occupied northern Vietnam in an unsuccessful effort to retaliate for this perceived display of socialist insubordination (Chanda, 1986). By the summer of 1979, less visible to the foreign eye, hunger stalked the land (Vo Nham Tri, 1988). Any semblance of an economy (a recognizable system of production and exchange) broke down. In the shadow of that collapse, one of the Socialist Republic's more remarkable accomplishments, a coherent, socially equitable education system, plunged headlong into crisis.

By 1996, the world had turned again. Unleashed from punitive diplomatic and economic embargoes and welcomed into the dizzying currents of regional trade and investment, Vietnam had become, for however long its patrons would support their largess, a darling of the international aid and development community (Tombes, 1997). Vietnamese policy makers earned that status the hard way. Stunned by the shabbiness its postwar policies produced, Hanoi opened the doors to its own domestic creativity well before it opened its arms to the army of foreign advisers now loose in its halls of power. Ineluctably these came, however, bringing with them the discourse and dynamics of the late twentieth century. With stunning consistency, foreign advisers have advocated a model of open market investment, production and exchange, supported by fiscal responsibility, regulatory conservatism and government restraint (see Dapice et al., 1995).

Equally impressive has been the awkwardness and inconsistency of efforts to apply the globalized wisdom of policy reform to the social sector. In place of a coherent, serviceable vision, a diffuse catch-all of governance and management has emerged, accompanied by disparate tinkering and an ill-defined recognition that the weakened state apparatus Vietnam now has (the contradictory product of foreign development advice, a weak domestic economy, and poor political management) may not be in its society's best interest. For the extremists, the extent to which this shortcoming matters is obscured by near cult-level confidence in the market's own capacity to minister to social need. Beyond the margins, however, governance and management in the social sector highlight an agenda of contending theoretical issues. For Vietnam's educators, the agenda includes no less than an exploration of the ethos, parameters and purpose of the state, the public sector, education and management. This chapter seeks to contribute to a delineation of these issues.

THE ISSUES

Since the founding of the Vietnamese Communist Party in 1930, education has been intimately associated with the Party (which represented and assumed the right to speak for its people), rather than structurally articulated in an independent public sphere. Nor, for that matter, were the Party and the state theoretically distinguished. Sixty years later, as the Party moved to put its imprimatur on free-market reforms, the practices of the state in the international community were undergoing radical redefinition. Two late twentieth-century versions of the modern state (the communist state and the welfare state) were widely in retreat. Increasingly, in commonly accepted international parlance, the well-being of the state, now conflated with government, has come to be evaluated less in institutional terms than through the process of governance. That process, in turn, is increasingly commingled in international policy discourse with management.

There are few defenders of the costly and over-regulatory communist and welfare states. In the enthusiasm to re-engineer them, however, the theoretical underpinnings of the state have gone largely unexplored. The cost of that lacuna is more than academic: what one understands the state and its accompanying public sphere to be are critical to the implementation of management in the public sphere.

As both institution and process, the state has been definitional: through much of the industrial era, it has delineated the parameters within which regulatory and coercive power were considered legitimate (Badie and Birnbaum, 1979, esp. pp. 11–24). This legitimizing agency is regarded as essential; it is, of course, society's capacity to distinguish legitimate from illegitimate that limits the daily exercise of physical violence. The founding fathers of sociology, such as Weber and Durkheim, in particular concerned themselves with the state they saw in the early twentieth century: autonomous, impersonal, bureaucratic, necessarily centralized as a result of the particular complexity of industrial society. That state, however, was itself the product of a more formative one, relevant to contemporary policy implementation.

The ostensibly ahistorical bureaucratic state of the early twentieth century was the offspring of an intensely historical state making process that spanned some four hundred years (see Tilly, 1975). What early modern states won by force of arms they implemented through social mediation: John Locke's social contract can be found in the cultural practices of the nineteenth and early twentieth century. This, the second stage of modern state making, is critically relevant for three reasons. First, the liberal state resulted from unavoidable power sharing as the 'middle classes' encroached upon the absolutist state (Chauncey, 1992, pp. 8–11). That this process saw incursion into the state sphere, as distinct from the contemporary extrusion of power out of that sphere into the extra-state public, is of less consequence than the fact that the two processes are immutably linked in purpose. Understanding the latter, the challenge of our times, requires understanding the former. This is particularly true with regard to the service capacities of the state: assumed by many critics of the welfare state to be an intrusive burden on the capacities of the citizenry, historically these have been essential not only to the formation of the industrial economy but also to the social contract that accompanied it.

Second, a predominant strategy of the power-seeking middle classes was what might be called the associative phenomenon: the establishment and management of ostensibly apolitical cultural and social organizations, creating a dense structure to the non-state arena, acquiring the idiom of and access to the state (Anderson and Anderson, 1967; Grew, 1984). The evolution of the public sphere so popular in contemporary writing on and policy toward civil society, in other words, has been a long-standing exercise, with particular historical trappings, that closely associates social and political groupings: the organizations, parties, assemblies, gatherings and congregations to which public management is now being redistributed. Finally, one of the last inclusive stages of the modern state making process was an explicitly cultural one, as the modern state intruded upon local society as an agent of common terms of reference such as language, schooling, and familial habits and obligations (Weber, 1976). This modernist cultural commonality, closely linked with the rise of the state and now much battered by the post-modern embrace of cultural diversity, is paradoxically being lamented in its passing. Management of the contemporary public sphere will require careful consideration as to how to fill the resulting vacuum.

In understanding the policy message communicated to countries such as Vietnam, one needs to distinguish the state described above, both in process and outcome, from the welfare state. It is the latter (spendthrift, possibly although not indisputably inhibiting of economic initiative) that is now largely in remission everywhere. This matters because the down-sizing, if applied to a different state construct, produces different and not always welcome results. Down-sizing the welfare state has called for recasting an understanding of the state. No longer the institution or process determining the parameters of legitimacy, or a social arbiter, the welfare state has conceptually become a service bureau. This service state is not without its value, even to its critics, but its capacities are residual. It is the role of the service state to tend to the margins, to address poverty alleviation, for example, and to ensure minimal standards for human resource development (World Bank, 1997). Services of this sort develop resources for economic purposes rather than those of human community or social contract.

That is a choice. It may or may not be the right one; it must, in any event, be a conscious one. As we shall see, in the Vietnamese case the state the Communist Party supervises is not the service state of Western reformers. Not only are its economic models now drawn from their discourse, however, so too is much of the policy programming oriented toward the state itself. The result is fundamentally discordant.

The discordancy is compounded by three factors. First, even the residual duties of the service state incorporate powerful, often unacknowledged social values. It is widely accepted, for example, that successful human resource development and poverty alleviation are predicated upon gender equity and popular decision making (UNDP, 1977). Both are powerful, explicitly political ideals. Second, even governance widely dispersed within the non-state public sector depends upon rule of law, by definition dependent on the state. Finally, however differently rights may be defined (as individual or collective, material or political), the parameters in which rights are debated continue to be defined by the state and interaction between states. It may be that civil discourse no longer requires the state to ensure such parameters, but the legal enforcement of such rights cannot escape the state. Neither can the mediation that may be necessary to accommodate the growing inequities of wealth accompanying late twentieth-century global economics.

To the extent to which such challenges are met outside the formal state structure, the trend in contemporary policy programming is toward the enhancement of the non-state public sphere. With its origins theoretically enunciated since at least the Enlightenment, if not Greco-Roman times, the public sphere has been articulated by voices as politically diverse as de Tocqueville and Marx. It has enjoyed an intellectual revival of late, fuelled by the collapse of the socialist bloc and the financial retrenchment of the service state. The public sphere has correspondingly become the object of considerable public policy programming. As with the state, the public sphere is many things to many people. The implications of the diversity, especially for management programming, are considerable.

Recent articulations of the public sphere tend to create a stark binary division between the state and all other activities and institutions (see Gellner, 1994). This understanding of the public sphere, which might be called the associative approach, emphasizes the formation and sustenance of social groups with public intent, functioning outside formal state channels, performing functions previously conducted by the state. Such an approach assumes a contradiction between, rather than a mutual dependency of, the state and public and is particularly accommodating to the reductionist model of the state. A competing model of the public sphere understands it to contain an intersection of associations and dynamics, exercised in turn by a multifaceted convergence of state, non-profit, commercial, and cultural interests. In this model, discourse and political processes are paramount over the sustenance of specific organizations. In this public sphere, rights, obligations and social purposes are negotiated and administered (Habermas, 1994). The distinction between these two approaches affects a variety of policy decisions. In education, in particular, it affects the vital but often tense relationship between the dictates of the commercial economy and those of cultural learning. The former lend themselves comfortably to an associative, 'state-free' public sphere. Cultural learning, whatever its specific definition, is less apolitical and decidedly more oriented to public discourse.

Vietnamese education crawled out from under its Soviet shadow simultaneously with a general radical redefinition of the relationship between formal education and the economy, especially in Britain and North America, symbolized in the former by the 1988 Education Reform Act, for example (Flude and Hammer, 1990). In Britain and Canada, standardization and economic rationalization have had the paradoxical effect of opening schooling to private, for-profit arrangements while strengthening the hand of state regulation.

That is not the only paradox in this particular reform process. When the Carnegie Foundation introduced scientific management to state schooling in the USA, it was driven by the belief that particular assumptions about administrative organization would produce maximum efficiency. Beyond basic skills, however, how maximum efficiency was to be defined in the culturally and socially diffuse America of the early twentieth century was not at all clear. By the end of the century, the discourse of market competition has assumed a far more dominant position. Education's contribution to economic productivity has increasingly become its sole public measure. Although the management profession has been radically transformed since Frederick Taylor's day, Taylor would recognize the calls for efficiency, standardization, cost recovery and the like that now underpin educational re-engineering.

The process highlights a deep, definitional controversy over the public purpose of education itself. Of four prominent interpretative arguments, two contend here. The first distinguishes education from training and postulates a critical role for education in defining 'meaning', that is, cognizant participation in the broad culture of civil society (see Bruner, 1996). The second approach is instrumentalist. Culturally and socially indifferent, its purpose is defined in terms of its dispassionate capacity to refine economic input, human or otherwise (see, for example, World Bank, 1993, p. 52).

Each of these debates (the nature of the state, the public sphere, and education itself) is implicit in a welter of experimental domestic reforms visited on Vietnamese education, especially after the officially approved renovation period began in 1986. Less obvious, because it is represented by silence, is the fact that none of these debates has been consciously examined within Vietnam. The tone of the reform discourse has attempted as much distance from the politically explicit as possible. It has sought recourse, instead, in the politically neutral language of management.

Such an approach is understandable. Even in its infancy the approach sought an apolitical, technology-oriented means to organize and administer productive processes. The promises of scientific management were as fragile as they were potentially revolutionary. Taylor himself consciously dehumanized the division of labour, in the mistaken belief that such an approach could sustain increased productivity, which would more than compensate workers for their loss of skilled authority (Merkle, 1980, pp. 15, 30). If Taylor was mistaken in that regard, his approach had the advantage of being compellingly straightforward. By contrast, contemporary management theories, increasingly collective and democratic in orientation, navigate a thicket of options but profess the same capacity to intellectualize human organizational patterns to maximize efficiency and productivity (see O'Shea and Madigan, 1997). As with their progenitor, contemporary management theories are also seeking to jump their traces, looking for the same returns in the fields of government and education as in industry. At the end of the century, as with its beginning, that exercise is a gamble.

With the murmurings of privatization and management in the background, Vietnamese educators have stumbled through a decade of reform. On two notable occasions, the voice of the West weighed in, with commanding and comprehensive 'sector studies'. Both, one issued under United Nations auspices (MOET et al., 1992), the second conducted by the World Bank (World Bank, 1996), understood explicitly what government officials in Hanoi understood implicitly: in the ostensibly arcane minutiae of management processes lie great potential sources of power. The first of these exercises effectively privileged human resource management; the second, concerned over the prospects for this, turned to financial management. Neither sector study, important in encouraging official acceptance of a development mentality, openly seeks to enhance the role of a politically conscious non-state public.

As we shall see, after all of this, the Vietnamese have struck upon yet another approach, officially legalistic, which, if implemented properly, may provide the country with its first true opportunity to debate publicly the goals of education. Through such a debate, given the state's manifest inability financially to sustain state schooling, the potential for a true public sphere may begin to be exercised.

CRISIS AND EXPERIMENTATION IN VIETNAM

The nature of Vietnam's educational crisis has been detailed extensively in the secondary literature. Few measures of educational competence were unaffected by it. Poorly maintained teaching material disintegrated; classrooms fell into disrepair. Overworked staff cut back teaching hours as moonlighting supplemented their inadequate salaries. Classes were burdened with irrelevant, wartime curricula while rigid, Soviet-inspired organization made the cross-fertilization of teaching and research as well as intellectual specialisms all but impossible. When the government began to relax control at the top, growing numbers of graduates, especially at the tertiary level, faced unemployment. Predictably, enrolments declined throughout the system; ominously, literacy (the cultural highwater mark of wartime policies) declined as well (Interviews, Hanoi, 1993).

It is widely recognized that early efforts to reform the disaster-ridden wartime economy percolated upward from local initiative. Whether this was the product of paralysis at the centre or a conscious embrace of non-state ingenuity, the same dynamics were in evidence as tertiary education creaked slowly out from under its Soviet legacy. From 1979, in higher education the better part of a decade experienced a quiet, experimental free-for-all. In no obviously apparent order, Vietnam's universities explored new financial arrangements, core curricular requirements, the restructuring of research and teaching, the redistribution of administrative authority within the university itself, redesigned graduate and postgraduate degrees, and explored new approaches to the organization of professional knowledge. These were the efforts of distinct and often competing segments of the political and academic community.

Early in the exercise, the Vietnamese began to repackage, reorganizing a variety of ostensibly disparate items that cumulatively, through the formal management of knowledge, confer authority and intellectual status. One obvious move consolidated administrative authority at the ministerial level: by 1990 four agencies previously responsible for various aspects of education had effected a staged merger into one single ministry, the Ministry of Education and Training (MOET et al., 1992). Had the Ministry subsequently taken a proactive role, this reorganization would have concentrated state management in the field of education. In the absence of a competent, policy-oriented state capacity, however, public authority began to drift. The reorganization triggered a firestorm of competing proposals from tertiary-level institutions anxious to secure their own status and circumstances; the result blurred logical patterns of government control, as explicitly state-owned institutions gravitated toward a semi-state role, to become a more explicitly non-state public with the onset of privatization.

Even a simplified version of this proposal competition underscores the potential stakes involved. There was and is a conflict of authority between MOET and institutes outside its chain of command, including colleges and training institutes that answer to the line ministries. By the end of the 1980s, one study listed 105 tertiary institutions, exclusive of those managed by the Ministries of Defence and the Interior. Of those 105, only 39 were under direct MOET management (Vu Van Tao, 1991, p. 104). Among the competing proposals, MOET, for example, proposed an amalgamation of all research institutes and centres, together with all colleges and universities in the country, under its command. This would have transferred institutes from a wide variety of ministries to the MOET. It would also have transferred such bodies as the then National Centre for the Social Sciences and the then National Centre for the Natural Sciences to MOET. Not surprisingly, each of these centres (which currently answer directly to the Prime Minister's office) submitted reorganization proposals of their own. Each claimed a new, reform-related mandate. Each now has a new name. Both were successful in keeping their distance from the MOET (Interviews, Hanoi, 1993).

There was a similar conflict within the MOET's own chain of command. As the proposal frenzy mounted, with some logic MOET sought to address the problem of institutions that duplicated teaching functions. It called for the amalgamation of a variety of such competing institutions and the creation of one or more comprehensive universities. In attempting to enact this ambitious plan, however, MOET killed it. Its initial approach to reorganization was self-described as 'administrative'. In Hanoi, for example, MOET announced the intended combination of eight tertiary institutions into one. The purported 'winner' in this comprehensive take-over would have been the venerable University of Hanoi. Not surprisingly, the seven rectors who would have been out of a job resisted. The MOET then called for the combination of four schools, and met with the same result. The Ministry retreated to a proposed merger of three loosely associated schools, a project design that finally produced Vietnam's first officially designated national university.

In these early and uncertain years of reform, rectors across the country responded to MOET efforts with little enthusiasm. MOET, undeterred, shifted its efforts to what it called the 'financial' approach. The Ministry received permission from the Prime Minister's office in early summer 1993 to explore the feasibility of concentrating state funds on only two universities: the University of Hanoi and the University of Ho Chi Minh. At its extreme, this policy suggested that *all* other tertiary institutions would have been cut off from state funding (Interviews, Hanoi, 1993).

These institutions would then have been 'semi-public' institutions. By 1993, this phrase already applied to virtually all colleges and universities in the country in any event. The term came into use after 1987, when colleges and universities were given permission to accept fee-paying students. While visions of grand, privileged institutions danced at MOET, the defunding of all other institutions would have brought new political significance to an already sensitive phrase: semi-public institutions would have become those that did not receive any government funding, but which would not have to pay the government back for the buildings and equipment in their possession at the time of their financial disinheritance. This institutional exercise in the semi-public sphere echoed more far-reaching efforts at cost recovery and direct privatization under way throughout the system.

At the university level, not uncharacteristically, a compromise was struck. Initially, two proposed mega-universities were designated as national universities, structured out of the partial amalgamation of available teaching and research institutes in Hanoi and Ho Chi Minh City. The first, the National University of Vietnam/Hanoi, officially opened in September 1995 (USSH, 1996, p. 2). By February 1996, the board of directors for the National University of Vietnam/Ho Chi Minh City had also been constituted (Saigon Giai Phong, 1996a). In a significant move, considering the politics behind the proposal scramble, each was given direct access to the Prime Minister's office, thus quasi-ministerial independence, MOET notwithstanding. The national universities remained within the government's umbra, but at the cost of weakening logical channels of policy and control.

Restructuring in two other arenas, one to date considerably less coherent than the other, have more fundamental social and cultural ramifications. The period 1988–89 marked the beginning of experiments with a division, at the university level, between an initial core curriculum and specialized higher level training (Vu Van Tao, 1991, pp. 113–14). An obvious effort to break the grip of overspecialization, this move has also opened the door to debates, akin to liberal arts arguments, about what an appropriate core curriculum in Vietnam should be, that is, what appropriate common discourse should be for an educated Vietnamese citizen. In the meantime, the compelling need for the technical skills of a modern economy propelled forward courses in economics, business, information technology and English.

Twice, in 1982 and 1990, the Vietnamese government approved a new listing of academic programmes. The second inscription was intended to broaden existing specialisms, perceived to be too narrowly defined. In the main, however, it appears to have represented a political compromise between the government, represented by MOET and the General Department of Statistics on the one hand, and the universities on the other. The list included 34 specialized groups covering 127 disciplines. The specialized groups were selected by the government; the disciplines were allocated by the universities. In some cases, such as history, the specialized group and the discipline were the same. Some groups covered a wide variety of disciplines. The group Applied Economics, for example, included 13 areas of specialization, each designated as a discipline (Vu Van Tao, 1991, pp. 110–13). Practical skills, in other words, were intensely articulated if not over-articulated; cultural capacity was notably less so.

Not all educators lack an awareness of this. By the early 1990s, Vietnamese educators and intellectuals were beginning to worry about the cultural implications of all this, notably the potential loss of a distinctly Vietnamese identity so powerfully sustained by traditional education (Interviews, Hanoi, 1993). In the event, neither the country's understandable hunger for a market-based economy nor the development wisdom of the West have provided much guidance on how to address the problem.

Easily the most explicit challenge to prevailing values and practices has come with authorization for the opening of private schools and the levying of student fees. Particularly extreme by Vietnamese standards has been the approval of outright private schools, whose costs are entirely supported by tuition and voluntary donations. Early in the 1980s, reforms began to experiment with shifting the costs of education to the students themselves, beginning with the sale rather than free allocation of textbooks. By the mid-1980s officials began experimenting with the imposition of tuition fees as well (Rubin, 1988, p. 48; Interviews, Hanoi, 1986). By the end of the decade, tuition fees had become standard practice, producing the distinction that would play into the hands of those who wanted to reorganize authority through institutional restructuring: universities that accepted fee-paying students along with scholarship students were designated semi-public institutions; the linguistic exercise allowed these institutions briefly to be targeted for full financial divestment. Within a matter of a few years, it has become clear that the social costs are greater than the institutional ones. Evidence is mounting that cost recovery within the education system has begun radically shifting educational opportunities, favouring high-income families across the social and geographic spectrum (Interviews, Hanoi, 1986; World Bank, 1996, esp. ch. 5b). As a result, Vietnam is in the early stages of a fundamental shift in the character of society itself.

Quality may also be an issue. With the privatization of schooling, the absence of a coherent curricular vision (and therefore an over-riding cultural purpose) has become telling: in the first private college opened in Vietnam since 1975, the only courses available were for technical training. There was no value-specific training of any kind (no civics, history, literature or art, for example). Technically competent students graduated with no exposure to mores and ethics (Erlanger, 1989). The absence of civic direction, coupled with the economists' call for technical skills, has begun to produce similar problems even in government-managed institutes. Ho Chi Minh College of Economics, for example, then a state-run school, entered the 1990s with no classes in the traditionally value-specific fields of literature and history (Pho Ba Long, 1990).

In the main, the private education trend has not overwhelmed state education schooling in Vietnam. With small numbers (as of 1996 there were only five such institutions at the tertiary level, for example), they have engendered considerable ambivalence on the part of established powerholders. A few moved quickly to join the boards of the new private ventures, as if investing their names on the futures market of the non-state public sphere. This jostling for influence is, of course, a struggle for power; by its nature it will shape the balance between cooperation and competition and between state and private in the public sphere. In an interesting variation on this, élite patrons of private schools and scholarship funds have been known to view the 'open universities' (effectively private tracks within the public system) as unwelcome competition (Pham Luong Can, 1995).

THE VOICE OF THE WEST

By the late 1980s, with the inchoate exploration of educational reform under way, a near insatiable craze for management training struck. A trio of technical skills (management, computer training and English) became an illusory, widely sought-after panacea for the pains of the country's transition to a free market economy. Into this mindset reached the helping hand of development aid, in the form of a massive study of Vietnamese education. This ill-fated work was, at the time, a high point in the reform effort. On 26 September 1990, a national project document was signed by the Vietnamese Ministry of Education and Training and two influential United Nations development agencies, the United Nations Development Programme (UNDP) and the United Nations Educational, Scientific and Cultural Organization (UNESCO). The project document inaugurated a comprehensive review of Vietnamese education and the development of educational reform strategies. The scope of the analysis, the prestigious organizations that facilitated it, and the large financial outlays it called for (in excess of one billion US dollars) commanded public attention and a wave of optimism (World Bank, 1996).

The educational sector analysis also brought with it the anodyne of generic management theory. Throughout, the analysis called for improved management and control of data. There is no dispute whatsoever with the need for improved management of education, together with other social services. Statistical data and bureaucratic technicalities can be organized in numerous ways, however; how they are used is determined by a system's overall vision and purpose. The sector analysis cited undifferentiated poor management together with a weak economy as education's primary shortcomings, without recognition of an overall pedagogical or social vision as a foundation for the country's educational system (MOET et al., 1992, p. 32). After noting that primary school drop-out rates are relatively higher in the south than in the north, for example, the sector analysis provided no explanation for the phenomenon. It reverted instead to calling for better information systems to 'provide a clear picture of the situation' (MOET et al., 1992, p. 69). In a similar vein, after two years of data collection, one of the trends the analysis identified was declining enrolments in the country's secondary schools. The lack of information in this regard came despite a sector analysis task force, representing key government bodies, having been assigned to work on this very problem (MOET et al., 1992, p. 141). The fact that these shortcomings are not couched in the vocabulary of state authority or state–societal discourse, but rather in the language of poor management, weakens an articulation of state and civil society in the collective determination of public authority.

In the event, financially and in terms of management methodology, anticipation exceeded output. The sector analysis did create, at least temporarily, a broad collaborative venture, not the norm in the dynamics of reform at the time. While MOET was the dominant facilitating agency for the Vietnamese, the sector analysis was designed to be an inter-agency effort. The project was fashioned to draw on the activities of MOET, the then State Planning Committee, the State Committee for Science and Technology, the Ministry of Finance, the Vietnam Youth Union, the Vietnam Women's Union, the National Economics University, and the Education Management College (MOET et al., 1992, p. 6). For a political system in which inter-agency cooperation is not common, all of this in itself distinguished the study from other reform efforts. It also, inadvertently, underscored the many institutional claimants to education's social authority. Beyond that, however, the significance of sector analysis lay in its voice. Quintessentially rooted in the dynamics of traditional foreign assistance, the analysis none the less significantly legitimized a vocabulary now tied to the marketization of education, a vocabulary that has facilitated the particular package of values associated with globalization.

There is an additional concern that may be a product more of the structure of the study than the intent of the Vietnamese educators who worked on it.

This issue is public audience, and its implications in the determination of legitimacy. This concern is highlighted in particular by the overall structure of the study, which evolves from overview and general recommendations into a detailed list of concrete project proposals, the penultimate argument of the analysis. With few exceptions, the proposed projects are all dependent for their implementation on foreign support, most explicitly discussed in terms of foreign models, reliant upon foreign study tours for their full conceptualization. That is, by the time analysis has turned to action, the primary audience is foreign, not domestic. The result, if the sector analysis had indeed provided formative guidelines, was the risk that it would privilege foreign donors over domestic activists, even when the two shared common goals. The structure of the medium reinforced that message. In the event, the sector analysis did not have a seismic impact on formal education in Vietnam. So easily had it slid to the back of the shelf that when a copy of the analysis was showed to a senior UNDP official in 1997, he did not recognize it (Interviews, Hanoi, 1997).

Throughout the UNDP report echoes a distinct, ostensibly apolitical managerial voice, carefully refined in both management and education schools in the West. The study talks about the opportunity costs of education, measured in terms of internal efficiency rates; it refers to school drop-outs as wastage: human capital rather than citizens of a patriotic or socialist venture (see, for example, MOET et al., 1992, pp. 65, 67, 69). The nature of the discourse in the analysis may have facilitated a transition to the distinct, sharply focused *Sector Study* commissioned by the World Bank, and published just over three years after the UNDP sectoral analysis, and which represents, for understandable reasons, the near perfection of the marketized vocabulary integral to globalized discourse, but discordant at best with the non-market cultural projection key to any society's identity and survival.

With little indication of significant output to show for the UNDP reform agenda, the World Bank joined the fray and stumbled almost immediately over an ill-conceived proposal to finance the publication of Vietnamese primary textbooks (Interviews, Hanoi, 1995). The availability of primary-level teaching material is an indisputable problem in Vietnam; the central government, however, balked at the prospect of a sizeable loan burden for goods not currently on its budget or under its management in any event, since primary school costs are borne almost entirely by local government bodies. Eventually, the Bank recast its strategy, fixing on a fiscal approach to achieve market-appropriate school reforms. The result was a new sector study, completed in 1996, with an emphasis on financial authority in the management of education (World Bank, 1996).

The two sector studies are only some three years apart in publication and the World Bank study self-consciously presents itself as a supplement to its predecessor. The methodological approach and the cultural filter through which educational management is conceived could hardly be more different, however. Tightly organized and precisely focused on the quantification of education, in the World Bank study education metamorphosed into flow charts, bar graphs and exponential equations. The implications of the methodology transfer involved in the creation of such a study remain to be explored. The sector study's discourse is intensely marketized and, not surprisingly, its goals are closely tied to market performance. The study is cautious in its explicit policy recommendations; no random billion dollars in donor funding is called for, as was the case with the UNDP study. This wariness is certainly conditioned by the UNDP study's thin record; it is also shaped by the Vietnamese government's scepticism towards loans in a field such as education, where the state's own potential for direct profit is low.

Despite the caution, however, and to the Bank's considerable credit, its report highlights a fundamental conundrum in the use of quantified management methods. When the report's authors ran the numbers, abstracted from their social setting, Vietnam's performance, compared in particular with other 'Asian Miracle' case studies, ranges from respectable to excellent. The report's authors, however, recognized that numbers alone leave unaddressed at least two crucial questions: the quality of the education delivered to its 'clients' and the fit between the product and Vietnam's social as well as its economic goals. Unabashedly, along with the mathematics, the World Bank study includes a litany of such observations, with one concern (the growing social inequities in the reform period) glaring unavoidably out from much of the report. Neither foreign donors nor management methodologies have the authority or capacity to address the future of such an issue. For that the Vietnamese will need to turn to their own, publicly sanctioned social vision of the future.

EDUCATION AND PUBLIC DISCOURSE

There is understandable urgency and a notable lack of direction in this experimentation and proposal making, indisputably driven at least in part by economics: the collapse of government funding and the manifest misfit between the curriculum and hiring practices, inherited from the war period, on the one hand, and the needs of postwar economic development on the other. Some measure of concern, however, may be as fundamentally existential as it is economic: the nub of the issue may rest with the distinction between political orthodoxy (official policy, that is) and public orthodoxy, the latter determined by public discourse, which achieves a common, accepted parlance which society uses to understand and express itself (on public discourse, see Pocock, 1971). If the state does successfully come to share governance with the public sphere, such a common discourse will be essential. So too will be an understanding of the parameters and legitimacy of that sphere.

Education in Vietnam came out of the war mantled in a coherent, public argument, under the credible guardianship of the Communist Party. In Vietnam, at no time after the defeat of the French was the public idiom of educational policy subjected to the divisive political polemics imposed upon education in the People's Republic of China. The public rhetoric in use up to the eve of the current reform period embraced the twin mandates of cultural and civic identity on the one hand, and economic advance on the other.

After 1954, in the north, nominally primary education inherited the political vision of the communists' guerrilla years, which spoke of an educational revolution, a war campaign against illiteracy, which, in the absence of a formal school system, employed mass-oriented night classes and work/study sessions to propagate basic literacy as extensively as possible. After the defeat of the French, however, the Party openly rejected reliance on 'guerrilla education', adopting a formal school system befitting what it perceived to be the demands of economic development (Woodside, 1983, esp. pp. 408–11). At the post-secondary level, from early on, Party officials filtered their approach to education through a Soviet-style preference for technical expertise over radical egalitarianism. Primacy was given to the 'revolution in technology'. Le Duan, then secretary general of the Vietnamese Communist Party, argued publicly that increased production was the primary measure of the Party's political success. This commitment produced a conscious effort to style education in Vietnam after the Soviet model. Such a system sought to produce a highly qualified élite, with training in primary and secondary schooling emphasizing academic over practical skills (Elliott, 1982, pp. 37–8, 42, 47). This commitment was retained throughout the American war years, despite the need to disperse educational institutes during the air war. At the height of the bombing, for example, the then Prime Minister Pham Van Dong publicly praised the educational system's emphasis on specialization, hierarchical learning structures, and the advanced training they produced (Woodside, 1972, p. 659). Student preference embraced these values. Through the late 1960s, with the air war in full swing, while enrolments in academic colleges increased over 80 per cent, those in tertiary vocational institutes increased only 35 per cent (Elliott, 1982, p. 49, n. 58).

None of this is surprising. There is in these routines a synthesis of tradition and logic, given a Confucian legacy and the Soviet preference, however awkward its organization, for advanced academic training. While, in large measure, education's public purpose was encapsulated in practice, there was also a verbal idiom, a pastiche which, unlike Maoist rhetoric, sincerely sought to integrate (at least verbally) morality and economic competence.

The rhetoric remained unchanged, however, as the reforms moved forward, understandably riveted in practice on material gain, leaving behind in their wake any credible claim to civic purpose. In 1979, in the early stages of the then still unofficial free-for-all, education was publicly heralded as 'part of the ideological and cultural revolution, an important factor that boosts technical, scientific, cultural and economic development. Theory [should go] hand in hand with practise; education is [to be] combined with production work; school is [to be] linked with society' (Pham Minh Hac, 1991, pp. 31–3). These ringing claims were accompanied by stirring references to pre-colonial literary heroes, in an effort to use national pride as part of the language of public purpose (Woodside, 1983, pp. 417–18). In 1993, six years after the official reform period began, the Vietnamese Minister of Education comfortably used pre-reform language, describing the goal of Vietnam's educational system as 'nurturing talent, forming a pool of workers with knowledge and skills, ... revolutionary virtues, patriotism and love for socialism' (Tran Hong Quan, 1993, p. 1).

The problem here is not exactly the obvious: the worn rhetoric of socialism despite the pre-eminence of free market reform. The problem, rather, is that the compelling current of educational reform has failed to carry with it any stated form of civic purpose. It has also yet to develop a forum in which such a purpose can be publicly crafted and sanctioned. A newly minted domestic effort to channel the diverse currents of educational experimentation, however, may in fact begin to develop the habits of such a forum, an active public sphere in which state and civic interests meet for purposes of mediation and management.

By the time the World Bank *Sector Study* was completed, an exercise in authority of another sort was also under way. In the spring of 1997, a draft law on education, reviewed extensively by the same mixture of offices and voices familiar to all other reform efforts, made its way, tentatively, on to the spring session of the country's biannual sitting of the National Assembly, only to find its hearing postponed into at least the next legislative year, if not beyond. The draft law covers a wide variety of issues, including educational standards, administrative authority, financial responsibility, the rights and obligations of private institutions and the like. Almost without exception, there is no overwhelming enthusiasm for the draft law, which (possibly as a result of the amount of editorial input) is over-general and makes few provisions for implementing or oversight capacities (Interviews, Hanoi, 1997).

Despite this, the draft law is significant. In the country's slow but determined effort to transfer direct governance from individuals and institutional fiefdoms to the impersonal arbitration of law, bringing education into this catchment is important in the effort itself. More important, although all draft laws are technically available for public comment, in this case, the draft law will not be passed when it first comes to the Assembly floor. Instead, after reviewing it, the National Assembly will mandate a series of sessions, throughout the country, for public response. This unusual exercise in constituency dialogue will certainly further complicate the juridical content of the law; it may also contribute directly to the changing nature of the dialogue between state and public society in Vietnam.

CONCLUSION

One round of public debates on a single legal document will not create a sustained habit of public dialogue. Such an outcome will be a long time in coming. In the process, it may be to the advantage of the Vietnamese not to confuse a politically purposeful state, to which they now lay claim at least officially, with the more emaciated service states of the West. There is little evidence that a model of public management that posits mutually exclusive interests between the state and society, necessitating conflictive mediation, offers up much capacity to define meaningful social cohesion. Rather the public sphere may be best served by configuring its relations with the state in an intermediate arena, a 'political public', that represents the intersection of civil society (daily, associational life, conducted in public view) and the state.

Vietnam has entered the fray of governmental reform at a pivotal historical moment, when international recognition of the role of the state is being fundamentally recast, state and government have been largely conflated, government is increasingly understood as governance, and governance, in turn, is increasingly being articulated through the self-consciously apolitical voice of management. In one of the reform period's many ironies, Vietnam may yet prove a model to its teachers, if it can embrace this equation of state transformation while simultaneously not succumbing to the loss of a broadly defined political voice, answering to both state and society, that can revive a conscious, culturally coherent social contract.

NOTE

All interviews with Vietnamese were conducted as the result of formal requests, vetted through the relevant ministry or ministerial-level organization. Interviews were conducted in English and Vietnamese; in addition to notes taken from official interpretation, most interviews were taped to allow confirmation of content. The individuals interviewed were determined by a mix of my specific requests and alternatives suggested by the relevant office if the individual in question was not available.

Although all interviews were conducted 'on the record', they have not been attributed to particular individuals because of the politically sensitive nature of some of the materials discussed. In each case where findings in the text are cited to the interviews, the material is drawn from a minimum of two interviews in separate offices or departments.

As is always the case, official interviews can produce a degree of formality removed from the immediacy of the subject under discussion. On rare occasions, however, I was presented with unexamined official dogma; those interviews were of little use in this research. Individuals frequently disagreed with one another, but often in each other's presence. On more than one occasion, an official interview would elide into a constructive dialogue, a mutual inquiry as much as a formal interrogation. At no time, where interviews are cited in the text, are they used to express the author's own opinion.

Interviews, Hanoi, January 1986
Nguyen Thi Binh, Minister of Education.
Dao Van Tap, Deputy, National Assembly, Hanoi.
Nguyen Dinh Tu, Minister of Higher Education.

Interviews, Hanoi, July 1993
Vu Dinh Bach, Rector, National Economics University, Ha Noi, S.R.V.
Le Thac Can, Chairman, National Environmental Protection Research Program, National Research Institute for Higher Education, Hanoi.
Vu Cao Dam, Director, Institute for Science Management, Ministry of Science, Technology and the Environment.
Pham Minh Hac, First Vice Minister, Ministry of Education and Training.
Pham Gia Khiem, Vice Chairman, State Planning Committee.
Le Viet Khuyen, Deputy Director, Higher Education Department, Ministry of Education and Training.
Dang Ba Lam, Director, National Research Institute for Higher and Vocational Education, Hanoi.
Phan Huy Le, Director, Centre for Cooperation for Vietnamese Studies, Hanoi.
Vu Van Tao, Assistant to the Minister, Ministry of Education and Training, Hanoi.

Interviews, Hanoi, March 1995
Kathryn Johnston, Education Specialist, The World Bank.

Interviews, Hanoi, April 1997
Rosellini, Nicholas, Deputy Resident Representative, United Nations Development Programme, Hanoi.

Interviews, Hanoi, August 1997
Tran Trong Cao, Director, International Cooperation, Vietnam National University/Hanoi, University of the Social Sciences and Humanities, Hanoi.
Ngo Doan Dai, Deputy Director for Academic Affairs, Vietnam National University/Hanoi, Hanoi.
Dang Ba Lam, Director General, National Institute for Educational Development, Ministry of Education and Training, Hanoi.
Dang Duc Nga, Director, Academic Affairs, Vietnam National University/Hanoi, Hanoi.
Pham Sy Tien, Director, Department of Postgraduate Training, Ministry of Education and Training, Hanoi.
Mai Van Tinh, Expert, Higher Education Department, Ministry of Education and Training, Hanoi.

REFERENCES

Anderson, Eugene N. and Anderson, Pauline R. (1967), *Institutions and Social Change in Continental Europe in the 19th Century*, Berkeley: University of California Press.

Badie, Bertrand and Birnbaum, Pierre (1979), *The Sociology of the State*, Chicago: University of Chicago Press (translated by Arthur Goldhammer).

Bruner, Jerome (1996), *The Culture of Education*, Cambridge, MA: Harvard University Press.

Callahan, Raymond E. (1966), *Education and the Cult of Efficiency: A Study of the Social Forces that have Shaped the Administration of Public Schools*, Chicago: University of Chicago Press.

Chanda, Nayan (1986), *Brother Enemy: the War after the War*, New York: Harcourt Brace Jovanovich.

Chauncey, Helen R. (1992), *Schoolhouse Politicians: Locality and State During the Chinese Republic*, Honolulu: University of Hawaii Press.

Dapice, David, Haughton, Jonathan and Perkins, Dwight (eds) (1995), *In Search of the Dragon's Trail*, Cambridge, MA: Harvard Institute for International Development.

Elliott, David W.P. (1982), 'Training revolutionary successors in Vietnam and China, 1958–1976: the role of education, science and technology in development', *Studies in Comparative Communism*, **XV** (1–2) (spring/summer), 34–70.

Erlanger, Steven (1989), 'From ashes of ideology, a private college rises', *New York Times*, 25 April.

Fforde, Adam (1989), *The Agrarian Question in North Vietnam, 1974–1979*, Armonk, NY: M.E. Sharpe.

Flude, Michael and Hammer, Merril (1990), *The Education Reform Act, 1988: its Origins and Implications*, New York: Flamer Press.

Gellner, Ernest (1994), *Conditions of Liberty: Civil Society and its Rivals*, New York: Allen Lane/Penguin Press.

Grew, Raymond (1984), 'The nineteenth century European state', in Charles Bright and Susan Harding (eds), *State-Making and Social Movements*, Ann Arbor: University of Michigan Press, pp. 83–120.

Habermas, Jurgen (1994), *The Structural Transformation of the Public Sphere*, Cambridge, MA: MIT Press (translated by Thomas Burger).

Merkle, Judith M. (1980), *Management and Ideology: The Legacy of the International Scientific Management Movement*, Berkeley: University of California Press.

MOET et al. (1992), *Final Report: Vietnam Education and Human Resources Sector Analysis, Volume 1*, Hanoi: Ministry of Education and Training (MOET), United Nations Development Programme (UNDP), United Nations Educational, Scientific and Cultural Organisation (UNESCO).

O'Shea, James and Madigan, Charles (1997), *Dangerous Company: the Consulting Powerhouses and the Businesses they Save or Ruin*, New York: TimesBusiness/Harper.

Pham Luong Can (1995), 'Interview with Pham Luong Can', *Bangkok Post*, 14 February.

Pham Minh Hac (1991), 'Education Reforms', in Pham Minh Hac (ed.) *Education in Vietnam, 1945–1991*, Hanoi: Ministry of Education and Training, pp. 28–38.

Pho Ba Long (1990), Director, Small Business Management Program, Georgetown University, Briefing, 5 September.

Pocock, J.G.A. (1971), *Politics, Language, and Time: Essays on Political Thought and History*, New York: Atheneum.

Rubin, Suzanne (1988), 'Learning for life? Glimpses from a Vietnamese school', in David G. Marr and Christine P. White (eds), *Postwar Vietnam: Dilemmas in Socialist Development*, Ithaca: Cornell University, Southeast Asia Program, pp. 45–60.

Saigon Giai Phong (1996a), 'National University of Ho Chi Minh, plan and structure of organization', 6 August. *Online: Australia–Vietnam Science Technology Link* <AVSL-1@coombs.anu.edu.au> 11 October. Database access <http://coombs.anu.edu/~vern/avsl.html>

Tilly, Charles (ed.) (1975), *The Formation of National States in Western Europe*, Princeton: Princeton University Press.

Tombes, Jonathan (1997), 'The development game', *The Vietnam Business Journal*, February, 31–2.

Tran Hong Quan (1993), 'Data on SRV Education', unpublished paper, Hanoi, Ministry of Education and Training.

United Nations Development Programme (1997), *Human Development Report, 1997*, Oxford: Oxford University Press.

USSH (1996), University of Social Sciences and Humanities, Hanoi: University of Social Sciences and Humanities.

Vo Nham Tri (1988), 'Party policies and economic performance: the Second and Third Five-Year Plans examined', in David G. Marr and Christine P. White (eds), *Postwar Vietnam: Dilemmas in Socialist Development*, Ithaca: Cornell University, Southeast Asia Program, pp. 77–89.

Vu Van Tao (1991), 'Higher education', in Pham Minh Hac (ed.), *Education in Vietnam, 1945–1991*, Hanoi: Ministry of Education and Training, pp. 100–129.

Weber, Eugen (1976), *Peasants into Frenchmen: The Modernization of Rural France*, Stanford: Stanford University Press.

Woodside, Alexander Barton (1972), 'Problems of education in the Chinese and Vietnamese revolutions', *Pacific Affairs*, **49** (4), 648–66.

Woodside, Alexander Barton (1983), 'The triumphs and failures of mass education in Vietnam', *Pacific Affairs*, **56** (3), 401–27.

World Bank (1993), *East Asian Miracle: Economic Growth and Public Policy*, Oxford: Oxford University Press.

World Bank (1996), *Vietnam: Education Financing Sector Study*, Hanoi: World Bank.

World Bank (1997), *World Development Report 1997: The State in a Changing World*, Oxford: Oxford University Press.

13. Civil society and social provision: the role of civic organizations

Mark Robinson and Gordon White[1]

THE RISE OF 'CIVIL SOCIETY'

In recent years, civic organizations of various kinds (broadly labelled 'civil society') have been playing an increasing role in the provision of social services in response to fiscal stress, state weakness or inefficiency and an ideological environment favouring non-state action. In this chapter we examine the types of civic organizations involved in service provisioning, the forms of provisioning that characterize the health and education sectors, and variations in provisioning across countries and regions. From the empirical literature the chapter highlights the advantages and disadvantages of non-state provisioning and identifies the conditions underlying success and failure.

Over the past few decades there has been a rapid growth of associational activity across the globe, reflected in a growing number of private voluntary organizations outside the realm of the state pursuing public objectives on a non-profit basis. This expansion of civil society, which is characteristic of both developed and developing countries, has taken place in response to three sets of pressures. One is simply the spontaneous efforts of organized citizens to create an independent space outside the control of the state, as a means of escaping political oppression or improving their own living conditions. A second factor is external assistance provided by international agencies, private voluntary organizations and national aid donors, which has boosted the resources available to indigenous non-profit organizations. Third, governments have fostered the growth of the voluntary sector by contracting out public services and by increasing the involvement of churches and non-governmental organizations in official development programmes (Salamon, 1994).

Organizations of this nature, commonly referred to collectively as 'civil society', have also been playing an increasing role in the provision of social services, and this trend has received growing attention and encouragement from government and aid donors. The civil society argument for the importance of civic organizations in welfare provision is a central element of current development thinking and is a part of wider debates about the relative developmental contribution of three societal agencies: states, markets and social organizations. It reflects an extraordinary area of consensus among otherwise widely disparate political and ethical creeds, including populism, communitarianism, socialism and neo-liberalism. The central thesis is that elements of civil society, commonly understood as the realm of formal and informal associations notionally intermediate between state and individual, can and should function as key elements in social provision within a wider context of welfare pluralism which also involves state and market provision. The case for civil society is buttressed by both negative and positive arguments. In negative terms, states and markets have certain widely rehearsed defects as agencies of social provision which require institutional alternatives. Commercial organizations are primarily driven by the search for profit and are not interested in forms of provision that do not offer a guaranteed return. It follows that groups which lack the resources to pay for services, and remote areas where the costs of provision are high, will be poorly served by the market. Equally, state organizations have proved to be inefficient, to offer a poor quality of service and to be unresponsive to customer needs. In positive terms, the organizations of civil society are perceived to have certain inherent characteristics capable of providing better quality and more equitable service. It is argued that civil organizations are more participatory and less bureaucratic, more flexible and cost-effective, with a particular ability to reach poor and disadvantaged people, all of which appear to justify an enhanced role in service provisioning.

Unfortunately, the use of the term 'civil society' in development discourse tends to be confused and confusing, reflecting both the ambiguous theoretical heritage of the term itself and the competing uses to which its motley adherents try to put it.[2] Actual civil societies are complex associational universes encompassing a wide diversity of organizational forms and institutional motivations. They contain repression as well as democracy, conflict as well as cooperation, vice as well as virtue; they can be motivated by sectional greed as much as by social interest. Thus any attempt to compress the idea of civil society into a homogeneous and virtuous stereotype is doomed to failure. It is, moreover, intellectually harmful not only because it misrepresents the reality of civil societies, but also because it distorts development discourse more broadly by encouraging similarly simplified but overwhelmingly negative conceptions of other societal agencies, whether state or market. For the purposes of this chapter, therefore, we have decided to narrow our focus to that particular sub-sector of organizations which is the conventional focus of development discourse about the service delivery role of civil society. This includes those organizations (commonly called NGOs, voluntary associations or membership organizations) which are involved in developmental and service delivery work independently or in collaboration with international agencies and domestic states. We shall refer to these collectively as 'civic organizations'.[3]

Any analysis of non-state provisioning should begin with an assessment of the various types of civic organization engaged in such functions. A distinction is made between formal and informal organizations, in which the former adhere to codified rules and regulations governing organizational behaviour, and gain legal recognition as a legitimate actor from state authorities, whereas the latter refer to groups of individuals who cooperate in the financing and provisioning of goods and services for the benefit of their own communities, through reciprocal exchange. The former include intermediary service providers in the form of non-governmental and non-profit organizations (NGOs), churches and membership organizations such as labour unions, farmers' organizations, and business and professional associations for whom service provisioning is an ancillary activity. Informal civil society groupings include user groups of various sorts organized for collective action, focused on irrigation, thrift and credit and natural resource management, as well as parent–teacher committees, which have a more explicit service function. Forms of cooperation can be episodic or long term and intergenerational, framed by norms of exchange and reciprocity, mediated by rules and institutions which may not assume concrete organizational forms.[4] Seen in this light, reciprocal service agreements between neighbours, kinship groups, landlords and tenants all constitute informal mechanisms of service provisioning that form part of civil society. Community or grass-roots organizations in their various forms span the formal/informal divide. For the purpose of this analysis the focus is on formal, intermediary forms of voluntary provisioning, though examples will be drawn from informal mechanisms where appropriate.

The next section assesses the distinctive capacity and role of the civic sector in service provisioning in the light of actual experience. It examines the types of organization involved, the forms of provisioning that characterize the health and education sectors, and regional variations in provisioning, with a particular focus on Sub-Saharan Africa. From the empirical literature it highlights the advantages and disadvantages of non-state provisioning and identifies the conditions underlying success and failure. In the last section we draw together our findings on the strengths and limitations of civic provision.

CIVIC ORGANIZATIONS AND SERVICE PROVISION

The Nature and Scope of Non-State Provision in Health and Education

The involvement of civic organizations in the financing and provisioning of health and education services is an increasingly important feature of service provisioning, particularly in Sub-Saharan Africa and parts of South Asia. In India and much of Latin America the non-state sector is not a major actor in direct provision, but tends to play more of an advocacy role, mobilizing communities to demand services from the state.[5]

In the *health sector* there are considerable variations in the nature and scope of service provisioning by civic organizations. The main types of civic organizations involved in non-state health care provision are NGOs (southern and northern), religious organizations, self-help groups, trade unions, business and professional associations and non-profit health maintenance organizations. Civic organizations have four broad health sector functions: providing comprehensive services (health facilities and disease prevention); social welfare activities (care for vulnerable groups such as children, women, the disabled, and the elderly); support activities (such as training and the procurement of drugs); and research and advocacy (developing and promoting new approaches, such as primary health care and community financing, promoting health awareness and mobilizing demand for health services) (Gilson et al., 1994).

There are significant regional differences in the form and extent of health provisioning by non-state actors. Non-state provisioning of health services appears to be most prevalent in Sub-Saharan Africa where churches, NGOs and self-help groups have all made a significant contribution. In Latin America trade unions, business and professional organizations play some role in health care provision, in a context where state and private for-profit provision are dominant (Zuckerman and de Kadt, 1997). NGOs and medical foundations are more common in Asia, in a context where the level of private provision is relatively high, especially in curative services.[6]

In the *educational field* civic organizations are engaged in direct service provision by funding the construction and maintenance of primary and secondary schools, paying the salaries of teachers and covering the costs of training. Direct involvement in the formal sector is characteristic of NGOs and religious organizations in Sub-Saharan Africa, which also has many examples of self-help educational initiatives (Semboja and Therkildsen, 1995). In Asia and Latin America, the role of NGOs and intermediary organizations tends to be focused more on non-formal education and adult literacy work, rather than on direct provision, though religious institutions in India and Bangladesh also run schools. As in the health sector, NGOs in South Asia also mobilize poor people to demand better-quality educational provision from the state, rather than providing services directly. Latin American NGOs have tended to favour a more radical conscientization approach where functional literacy and adult education are designed to promote the empowerment of the popular sectors, notably landless peasants, workers and slum dwellers (Picon, 1991; Zuckerman and de Kadt, 1997). This approach has also proved influential among NGOs in India and the Philippines, where community organization focused on awareness creation and functional literacy forms an intrinsic element of social action in poor communities.

In Sub-Saharan Africa the non-state sector has played a significant role in the provision of health and education services since the colonial period. In no other region has the direct involvement of civic organizations in service provision achieved such prominence and for this reason it merits more detailed consideration. The form and extent of non-state provisioning in Africa has fluctuated over time in response to four sets of factors: (i) the extent of health problems or educational requirements which determine the demand for services and the respective roles of state and non-state actors in responding to demand; (ii) government attitudes towards voluntary organizations and state policies in the health and education sectors which have varied with political fashion and regime; (iii) economic factors which play a key role in determining the amount of resources available to the state sector for service provision and the scope for voluntary provisioning; and (iv) the involvement of foreign aid donors and northern NGOs in providing resources and shaping domestic social policy, which has become increasingly important in the context of economic crisis and structural adjustment from the 1980s on.

In the colonial period church missions were the dominant source of provision for health care and education in many African countries, especially in rural areas. After independence, nationalist regimes came to power in many African countries, which were committed to providing comprehensive services to the largely rural African majority. Some governments sought to introduce universal state provision of health and education, through nationalization and curbs on the voluntary sector.[7] Many of these efforts foundered in the 1970s and in the 1980s and 1990s a series of economic and political factors induced major changes in the role of government in health service provision which gave an impetus to the expansion of the voluntary sector in the region. A number of governments found that they did not have the fiscal capacity to maintain a good-quality system of state-provided services free of cost. In many countries the quality of government health facilities is often very poor, coverage is limited, technical capacity is inadequate, decision making is overcentralized, and service provision is plagued by inefficiencies and petty corruption (Mburu, 1994). There are also increasing demands placed on an already overstretched system with the appearance of new diseases such as AIDS and chloroquine-resistant strains of malaria and deteriorating health indicators. A major resource gap has appeared which, it is argued, can only be filled by the non-profit sector, and by private providers of health services (World Bank, 1993). The education sector is also plagued by poor educational standards, low enrolments (especially of girl children), and high drop-out rates.

The poor state of health and education services has forced a number of governments to reconsider their attitude towards NGOs and church organizations. In some countries democratically elected regimes have come to power which are better disposed towards the voluntary sector and perceive it to be a valuable partner in development. Controls on voluntary provisioning have been abolished and official encouragement is now given to churches and NGOs to gear up their involvement in the provision of health and educational services.

This change in government attitudes towards the non-state sector has been influenced to a significant degree by external considerations. Bilateral and multilateral aid agencies have come to play an increasingly important role in recent years, in influencing health policy and financing the provision of health services.[8] This has entailed a concerted emphasis on the privatization of government health facilities, and the simultaneous relaxation of controls and the creation of incentives to encourage private provision. With this shift of emphasis the influence of foreign NGOs has increased their presence, either in the form of direct involvement or by means of increased funding for their domestic counterparts which have grown rapidly in number in recent years.[9] As a result NGOs now constitute a major source of health provisioning in Africa, in many cases with the active support of official donors (Green and Matthias, 1995).

In some African countries church organizations have remained the dominant provider of health services to the present day, despite the imposition of controls by some governments.[10] The extent of non-state provisioning in selected African countries in the early 1990s is evident from Table 13.1, though these figures under-estimate the significance of non-state provision in rural areas and the role of the voluntary sector in offering specific types of services where government is weak.

There is a similar pattern in the education sector. The rapid increase in donor financing for the voluntary sector and a change in the domestic policy environment has resulted in a rapid growth in the number of schools run by NGOs and church organizations. For example, in Uganda, 12 districts were prioritized for community rehabilitation of primary schools as part of the Programme for the Alleviation of Poverty and the Social Costs of Adjustment, with the help of foreign NGOs which have been assigned a lead role in

Table 13.1   Extent of non-state provisioning of health services in Africa

Country (organization)	Percentage of total no. of hospitals/hospital beds	Percentage of total no. of services/contacts
Cameroon	40 (facilities)	
Ghana (church)	25 (beds)	40 (population)
		50 (outpatient care)
Kenya (NGOs)		35 (services)
Lesotho (non-profit)	50 (hospitals)	
	60 (clinics)	
Malawi (church)		40 (services)
Tanzania (church)	40 (hospitals)	
Uganda (church)	42 (hospitals)	
(NGOs)	14 (facilities)	31 (services)
Zambia (church)		35 (services)
Zimbabwe (church)	68 (beds/rural areas)	40 (contacts)

Sources: DeJong (1991); Gilson et al. (1994); Nabaguzi (1995).

each district (Passi, 1995). In other countries, such as Kenya, the state sector remains the dominant provider of education services, with a heavy reliance on voluntary contributions of labour and materials. Voluntary provisioning through self-help initiatives is an important manifestation of civic activity at the grass roots, and distinct from service provision through intermediary organizations such as NGOs and church-based organizations. As such, it merits separate attention.

Self-Help Initiatives: Civic Action and Service Provisioning from Below

In the African context, NGOs and churches are the dominant types of civic organization engaged in providing social services. But the construction, maintenance and financing of health, education and minor infrastructure facilities depend to a large extent on the mobilization of resources from local communities, and special groups are often formed for this purpose. These include parent–teacher associations, community health groups, water user groups, and a range of other local organizations variously referred to as people's organizations, grass-roots, or community-based organizations. Some emerge autonomously in response to local economic and political circumstances as a vehicle for collective action, while others are formed at the instigation of political leaders and intermediary organizations. Such groups also play an important role in mobilizing demand for services and pressing for micro-policy reforms, and for ensuring accountability on the part of intermediary service providers.

Self-help initiatives have been important in the production of health infrastructures in Kenya, and to a lesser extent in Tanzania and Uganda. Under the political patronage of the KANU regime Jomo Kenyatta instigated the *harambee* self-help movement which drew on voluntary contributions of labour, money and materials for the construction of health and educational facilities in rural Kenya. These self-help initiatives contributed to the creation of a wide network of health facilities and schools which are primarily under the control of the public sector, though grass-roots involvement in the construction of such facilities has declined under President Moi (Oyugi, 1995).[11] In Tanzania, people were encouraged to undertake self-help initiatives with the villagization campaign in the 1970s, but an underlying element of coercion limited the impact of such efforts.

Collective self-help initiatives are important when government authorities are unable or unwilling to provide services, due to civil unrest, resource constraints or conscious policy choice. The economic chaos and civil war which followed Idi Amin's military *coup* in Uganda resulted in the collapse of state services and the withdrawal of voluntary agencies, leaving people to finance locally based health and education initiatives with the support of the church (Nabaguzi, 1995). In Latin America, there are numerous examples of community self-help initiatives springing up in response to state inefficiency or cutbacks in public spending on social services (Zuckerman and de Kadt, 1997). For example, in the Peruvian squatter settlement of Villa el Salvador in Lima, community organizations set up health care committees and arranged loans for the provision of water and other amenities during the initial stage of illegal occupancy when the government desisted from providing services (Asthana, 1994; cf. Barrett, 1996 on Nicaragua). These experiences suggest that community initiatives have been important in sustaining social provision during times of political turbulence and government inaction. It should also be noted that local community groups (such as village health committees) can play an important role in mobilizing people to engage in mass campaigns, demand better services, and monitor actual provision (Picon, 1991; Sundar, 1994).

There are few documented examples of health care provision by trade unions, cooperatives or business associations.[12] This may reflect the fact that such organizations do not tend to engage directly in service provisioning, either because they lack the capacity and resources to do so, or do not consider health provision to be part of their remit.[13] One illuminating example of health provisioning by a trade union comes from South Africa, where the Food and Canning Workers' Association in rural Western Cape established a Medical Benefit Fund in 1951 to provide members with limited access to services provided by private practitioners. The Fund, which is self-financing and administered by a joint management–worker committee, was reasonably successful in providing a basic level of health care, but with relatively high administrative costs in relation to expenditure on benefits. Over time private practitioners were reluctant to accept the level of remuneration offered by the Fund, which forced it to look into the possibility of direct provision. As a result, the Fund established an independent clinic in 1981 which offers direct services to its members and to disadvantaged members of the community. Costs are lower than comparative services in the private sector and the quality and range of services are superior, reflected in shorter waiting times, improved treatment of chronic illnesses, intervention in work-related disease and initiation of alternative health programmes (London, 1993). While the scheme is a novel innovation in direct health provision by a civic organization, its potential for replication in other African countries is limited by weaker trade union structures and smaller memberships. Nevertheless, it does open up the possibility for a much wider range of non-state forms of health provision which may prove to be cheaper and potentially more sustainable than services provided by non-profit intermediaries.[14]

STRENGTHS AND LIMITATIONS OF CIVIC PROVISIONING

Proponents of an increased role for NGOs and civic organizations in the financing and provision of health services base their prescriptions on a series of assumptions about their ability to deliver high-quality services at low cost to the poorest and most disadvantaged people (World Bank, 1993, pp. 127–8). Sauerborn et al. (1995) suggest three main criteria for assessing the relative competence of various organizational actors engaged in health care provision: operational efficiency, equity of access and quality of care. However, it is difficult to arrive at well-founded conclusions, since much of the available evidence is anecdotal or only covers a limited number of particular organizations. Comprehensive assessments of the effectiveness, efficiency, relevance and sustainability of state versus non-state provisioning of health and education services are virtually non-existent.[15] Insights from various studies must therefore be treated with a high degree of caution.

The Quality of Non-State Health Provision

Gilson et al. (1994, p. 18) note that a major justification for civic provision of health services is that they are of higher quality than those of either government or private sector providers, but that 'available evidence is limited and variable'. Numerous studies have drawn attention to the deficiencies of state provision and indicate a higher level of preference for private health care, though there are few assessments of the quality of care in the non-profit sector (Aljunid, 1995). Studies from Zambia question the common assumption that NGO provisioning is of better quality than state services (Gilson et al., 1995, p. 18; Mogedal et al., 1995, p. 359; Kaiser, 1995, p. 191). Although one or two studies have found that NGO health staff have stronger technical skills as compared to their government counterparts, it is difficult to generalize. A number of NGO health projects depend heavily on expatriate staff, who may have the requisite skills but find it difficult to integrate with local government health services. Intensive programmes where an NGO concentrates its effort on a small area, with a high level of expatriate involvement and external resources, cannot be easily replicated or sustained by local health authorities (Walley et al., 1991).

The quality of non-state provision is often claimed to be a direct function of the participatory or consultative character of voluntary organizations which, unlike the situation in the state and the private sector, involves the intended beneficiaries in decisions about the nature and mode of provisioning. As a result, projects and programmes supported by civic organizations have more of a tailor-made character, in contrast to the blueprint approach characteristic of the state sector. However, not all activities of the voluntary sector are consultative and tailor-made, as various studies have shown, and nor do NGO approaches have to be participatory to be effective (Brown and Ashman, 1996). For example, a review in Zambia found that health sector activities supported by the voluntary sector were 'mainly oriented to curative services, without particular strengths in terms of community participation of activities' (Mogedal et al., 1995, p. 359).

There are few studies of the quality of educational provision by the non-state sector. Mission schools in Africa and Asia have acquired a reputation for high educational standards, reflected in their popularity and continued expansion. Religious schools in India continue to recruit students from families disillusioned with the quality of provision in the state sector, especially in rural areas, who are willing to pay for better education. But heavy reliance on parental contributions can have an adverse impact on the quality of teaching in a context where salaries are low, training is poor and incentives are weak. For example, in Uganda, where parental contributions account for between 65 and 90 per cent of the costs of primary education, the quality of education is low, especially in the more remote rural districts (Passi, 1995; Archer, 1994).

Local-level initiatives centred on non-formal education provision reveal a mixed picture of success. For example, NGO literacy programmes in Namentenga province of Burkina Faso were found to be of questionable long-term benefit for poor rural communities in that literacy skills were rarely practised and pedagogic methods were inappropriate to local needs (MacLure, 1995). A more successful initiative is the non-formal primary education programme pioneered in rural Bangladesh, which is targeted at drop-outs or children who have never attended school. By 1995 it was running an estimated 50 000 centres for 1.5 million children, with a drop-out rate of just 2 per cent (compared to a drop-out rate of 45 per cent in state primary schools), with 90 per cent of children entering formal primary schools (Archer, 1994). However, as in the health sector, the absence of comparative studies of state and non-state education provision makes it difficult to derive firm conclusions on the educational standards of the non-state sector.

Operational Efficiency

There are few data available on the operational efficiency of non-state health facilities. According to the World Bank (1993, p. 127), 'recent data from Africa suggests that NGOs are often more efficient than the public sector', citing studies from Uganda as supportive evidence. In Ghana, missions were found to have a lower cost per visit than government facilities and were more efficient in procuring pharmaceuticals (DeJong, 1991, p. 9). However, comparisons of cost have to take into account variations in staff salaries, the range of services offered, and the availability of drugs and equipment, before any conclusive assessment can be made. One of the few available comparisons of the costs of NGO and government health services from India reveals that NGO hospital services were found to be operating at a level comparable to the lower end of the range reported for government facilities, on a similar level to the private for-profit sector (Berman and Rose, 1996). For curative care and immunization, costs are comparable, that is, 'there is no evidence of systematic differences in efficiency between the government and the voluntary sector' (ibid., p. 47).

Other studies have highlighted a series of operational problems in NGO health provisioning, though it is difficult to make generalizations. One detailed study from Tanzania identified a number of inefficiencies which included: few outreach facilities; poor performance of health workers; low technical efficiency; and employment of untrained or poorly trained staff (Gilson et al., 1994). Management systems in NGO health facilities are often very weak. For example a review of non-state health care in Zambia found that 'Dependence upon external financing and expatriate leadership, poor continuity in staffing, and weak management systems' threatened financial and organizational sustainability (Mogedal et al., 1995, p. 359). Many NGOs have to maintain links to external funding agencies, parent organizations, local government bodies and local communities, which can give rise to weak and unstable organizational structures characterized by personality-based leadership, little formal accountability and limited participation by client groups (Gilson et al., 1994; Edwards and Hulme, 1995). This confirms similar findings from assessments of NGO poverty alleviation programmes in Africa and Asia (Riddell and Robinson, 1995). On the other hand, some health NGOs have developed innovative management techniques to monitor and improve efficiency. One NGO in India treats individual clinics as separate cost centres which are required to produce detailed monthly performance indicators, while another has introduced a village-level register system to track the preventive health needs of individual households (Berman and Dave, 1996, p. 48).

Operational efficiency is also affected by the source of financing. External donor support is often project-specific and is generally only available for limited periods. Financial dependence, combined with a tendency to rely on expatriate staff, means that many NGO health projects have poor prospects for long-term sustainability (DeJong, 1991).[16] This is a particular problem for many NGO health initiatives in Africa where there is limited scope for local cost recovery or securing additional resources from government. In India this is less of a problem since health NGOs raise the bulk of their funds from domestic sources, either from user fees or government grants, and staff are largely nationals (Berman and Rose, 1996).

Effective coordination between non-state providers and between non-state providers and government health organizations is a *sine qua non* of an efficient national health system, but there are problems in this area. These include duplication of services, heterogeneous (and sometimes incompatible) approaches, and competition for resources. In some countries national umbrella organizations have been formed to overcome such problems and have been found to work effectively in promoting exchanges and dialogue; these include the Voluntary Health Association of India, the Private Health Association of Malawi and the Christian Hospital Association in Ghana. Such umbrella organizations can facilitate cooperation between NGOs by providing technical support to members, promoting information sharing, encouraging cost-effective practices and facilitating participation in national policy making (Gilson et al., 1994).

Studies of five NGOs involved in health provisioning in Bangladesh highlight the difficulty of recruiting and retaining trained medical staff, especially at the field level, who were lured away by higher salaries in other organizations or the security of government employment. Difficult working conditions and minimal allowances also acted as disincentives. Drug supplies from the government were erratic, leading to frequent shortages. As a result clinical services faced disruption and a lack of continuity (VHSS, 1990). Similar problems of staff retention and rapid turnover were also found to be characteristic of the NGO health sector in India (Pachauri, 1994).

Equity of Access

The inability of the private for-profit sector to produce equity in health care provision through universal access to services is a well-established example of market failure in both developed and developing countries (Bennett and Tangcharoensathien, 1994). Even though universal access might be a stated policy objective, moreover, government services are uneven in their coverage and there is a tendency for resources to be concentrated in urban areas. The non-state sector, by virtue of philanthropic, political or religious motivations, is assumed to have innate advantages in delivering health services to low-income or socially disadvantaged people.

Numerous studies support the contention that non-state health facilities primarily cater to poor and disadvantaged sections of the population in rural areas. In Africa the proclivity of church missions to locate health facilities in remote rural areas is frequently cited as a comparative advantage and in a number of countries non-state organizations fill gaps in the spatial coverage of state health facilities. NGOs in India tend to work mainly with poor and disadvantaged communities living in urban slums or remote rural areas poorly served by government facilities (Pachauri, 1994).

Many NGO health projects rely on user fees as a means of recovering costs and it is commonly assumed that charges are levied in accordance with ability to pay so that no one is excluded. User fees are the single most important source of funding for NGO hospitals in India, though in most cases there is a progressive fee structure and the poorest are usually exempted from charges (Berman and Rose, 1996). However, the Indian case may not be typical. There is evidence from a health project in Uganda which suggests that user fees can act as a disincentive for poor people to use health facilities (De Coninck, 1992). Moreover, it has been observed that a downturn in financing has forced some NGOs to raise their fees to meet funding shortfalls. According to Gilson et al. (1994, p. 18), 'Such actions may not only have negative consequences for equity but may initiate NGOs into the vicious cycle of falling resources, rising prices, lower quality, lower utilisation, falling resources.'

In the education sector NGOs concentrate on providing services to poor and disadvantaged communities, though mission schools in Africa and Asia also cater to the educational needs of the élite. As in the health sector, there is also a close relationship between ability to pay and equity of access to educational facilities. In Kenya, the high degree of reliance on voluntary contributions of labour and materials for the construction of schools through *harambee* has resulted in regional disparities in educational provision, reflecting existing levels of socioeconomic inequality (Zamberia, 1996). The high costs of education in Uganda act as a disincentive for poorer parents who are unable to afford fees, and there is evidence that schools discriminate in favour of richer parents (Nabaguzi, 1995; Passi, 1995). As a result drop-out rates remain high. The ability of schools in wealthier districts to charge higher fees reinforces educational inequalities as these schools can attract better teachers, lured by higher salaries. Since civic organizations are now heavily involved in educational provision, especially in Sub-Saharan Africa and parts of South Asia, there is a need for effective coordination between various providers to ensure proper coverage and to enforce basic educational standards (Archer, 1994; Nabaguzi, 1995).

Not all attributes of non-state provisioning are captured by quality, equity and efficiency criteria. One important positive attribute of civic organizations is their capacity for innovation and disseminating good practice, either to other NGOs or to the state sector. Primary health care is perhaps the best example of an approach that was initially pioneered by NGOs and then taken up by government agencies (Cumper, 1986). Integrating traditional health practitioners into the formal system of health provision is another example of innovation. Another innovation is the emphasis that many civic organizations give to mobilizing people to demand better services from the state, and treating health as an integral component of socioeconomic development, rather than in isolation (Sundar, 1994).

From their review of NGO health sector provisioning, Gilson et al. (1994, p. 22) conclude that NGOs should only be promoted where: they have a long-term and sustained comparative advantage in provision (better performance relative to standards) and financing (long-term resources not available to government); they can meet a need not otherwise met and make a positive contribution to the health system (for example by improving coverage and enhancing managerial efficiency); and use an untapped potential (health mo-bilization or community mobilization). We would endorse this conclusion and would add that a similar rationale holds good for civic organizations involved in educational provision.

CONCLUSIONS

This review of the role of civic organizations involved in the provision of public services suggests that they play an important role when state provision is limited and the private sector primarily caters for better-off sections of the population. The comparative strength of civic organizations lies in their abil-ity to work with the poorest and most disadvantaged people. Unlike state organizations, which aspire to universal provision, civic organizations con-centrate resources on the most needy and underprivileged through targeted provision. They also work in poor and remote regions where government services are limited and where needs are often greatest.

At the same time, the scope and coverage of the voluntary sector is deficient in a number of key respects. Resources are inadequate to ensure comprehensive coverage and there is fragmentation of effort since a multitude of organizations are engaged in welfare provision using different approaches and operating procedures. Despite the ability of some organizations to work in remote areas, some regions and groups of people are poorly served or are beyond the reach of civic organizations, due to resource constraints and a tendency towards concentration in core areas and to working with more accessible and vocal groups. Gaps in coverage are a problem, and certain groups of poor people can be excluded by virtue of physical location and the apparent intractability of their situation.

While civic organizations have undoubtedly made an important contribution to service provision, whether in the form of direct health and education provision on a large scale in many parts of Africa, or by developing community-based approaches and mobilizing demand for services in India and Latin America, their contribution should not be overstated. There are numerous examples of voluntary failure and a determined bid to replace state by voluntary provision raises problems of quality control, limited prospects for sustainability, pervasive amateurism and inadequate coordination. For these reasons the state has to ensure that services are of high quality and delivered efficiently, but in view of manifest problems of bureaucratic failure and resource constraints, potential solutions lie in the creation of collaborative, synergistic partnerships between state and non-state providers. Such partnerships are premised on a scenario in which the state has overall responsibility for ensuring a coherent policy framework and the bulk of financing, while civic organizations perform an essentially catalytic role, fostering innovation and community initiative, while avoiding a wholesale transfer of responsibility for the financing and provisioning of services to the voluntary sector.

NOTES

1. This chapter is drawn from a larger piece published in the UNU/WIDER Research For Action series (Robinson and White, 1997). Some of the issues dealt with relatively briefly here are pursued in more detail there.
2. For a discussion of the terminological confusion surrounding the idea of civil society, see White (1996).
3. There is a good deal of discussion about the differences between types of organizations within this sector (for example Uphoff, 1993).
4. The concept of 'mediating institutions' is a useful way of conceiving the role of these organizations, which link 'individuals to larger institutional structures by groups and associations, the mediating structures that facilitate both individual influence upward and the downward transmission of institutional response' (Van Til, 1987, p. 53).
5. Venezuela is something of an exception in this regard, since community organizations and

private foundations have substantially increased their involvement in the direct provision of health services following the recession of the mid-1980s (Cartaya, 1997).

6. A large proportion of the hospitals and health facilities are in the hands of the private sector in Asia and Latin America, though preventive measures (for example vaccinations) are largely the responsibility of the public sector (Aljunid, 1995; Berman and Rose, 1996).

7. For Tanzania, see Ishumi (1995) and Munishi (1995); for Uganda, see Nabaguzi (1995).

8. For example, it is claimed that 'Tanzania demonstrates a situation where further reform efforts are now being rushed, to a large extent driven by the World Bank, as the severe under-financing of the system makes compliance with donors an overriding concern' (Mogedal et al., 1995, p. 353). Despite the increased prominence of official aid agencies in health and education policy, however, the social sectors account for less than 10 per cent of global aid flows.

9. The World Bank (1993, p. 166) estimates that resource flows from northern NGOs and foundations for investments in health services amounted to $1.16 billion in 1990, equivalent to a quarter of all external assistance for the health sector.

10. NGO health provision in Asia is more limited. In India and Indonesia NGOs supply 10 per cent of clinical services, while in Nepal the church runs 19 per cent of all hospitals in the country (World Bank, 1993, p. 127; Gilson et al., 1994, p. 15).

11. According to Zamberia (1996, p. 52), community efforts through *harambee* were mainly directed towards building secondary schools which resulted in a rapid growth of education provision up to the mid-1980s.

12. In Brazil a principal function of trade unions, until quite recently, was the provision of health and other social services to their members. Emmanuel de Kadt, personal communication.

13. Members of business and professional associations are likely to have private medical insurance and direct provision by such groups would generally not be favoured. Cooperatives have acted as an entry point for literacy work and adult education in numerous countries in the past but such endeavours have disappeared with the decline of cooperatives as development institutions (see, for example, Fiagbey, 1992).

14. In Israel, the large-scale provision of health services by the General Federation of Labour (Histradut) conflicted with its organizational role in defending the interest of workers, and the quality of provision suffered from its attempt to provide comprehensive services to all its members, regardless of their existing health status and level of contributions (Yanay, 1990).

15. Berman and Rose (1996) examine the comparative costs of government and NGO health services in India, but in the absence of data on quality and impact, are unable to arrive at firm judgements of cost-effectiveness. See Zuckerman and de Kadt (1997) for a discussion of this issue in the Latin American context.

16. For instance in the church facilities linked through the Private Health Association of Malawi, only 30 per cent of the senior staff are Malawi nationals (DeJong, 1991, p. 11).

REFERENCES

Aljunid, S. (1995), 'The roles of private medical practitioners and their interactions with public health services in Asian countries', *Health Policy and Planning*, **10** (4), 333–49.

Archer, D. (1994), 'The changing roles of nongovernmental organizations in the field of education (in the context of changing relationships with the state)', *International Journal of Educational Development*, **14** (3), 223–32.

Asthana, S. (1994), 'Primary health care and selective PHC: community participation in health and development', in D. Phillips and Y. Vershasselt (eds), *Health and Development*, London: Routledge, pp. 182–96.

Barrett, B. (1996), 'Integrated local health systems in Central America', *Social Science & Medicine*, **43** (1), 71–82.

Bennett, S. and Tangcharoensathien, V. (1994), 'A shrinking state – politics, economics and private health care in Thailand', *Public Administration and Development*, **14** (1), 1–17.

Berman, P. and Rose, L. (1996), 'The role of private providers in maternal and child health and family planning services in developing countries', *Health Policy and Planning*, **11** (2), 142–55.

Berman, P. and Dave, P. (1996), 'Experiences in paying for health care in India's voluntary sector', *International Journal of Health Planning and Management*, **11** (1), 33–51.

Brown, L.D. and Ashman, D. (1996), 'Participation, social capital, and intersectoral problem solving: African and Asian cases', *World Development*, **24** (9), 1467–79.

Cartaya, V. (1997), 'Venezuela: a private nonprofit approach', in Zuckerman and de Kadt (1997), pp. 89–125.

Cumper, G. (1986), 'The changing role of NGOs: no longer the eunuch in the harem?', *Health Policy and Planning*, **1** (4), 335–44.

De Coninck, J. (1992), 'Evaluating the impact of NGOs in rural poverty alleviation: Uganda country study', Working Paper No. 51, London: Overseas Development Institute.

DeJong, J. (1991), 'Nongovernmental organizations and health delivery in Sub-Saharan Africa', Policy, Research and External Affairs Working Paper No. 708, Washington: World Bank.

Edwards, M. and Hulme, D. (eds) (1995), *Non-Governmental Organisations – Performance and Accountability: Beyond the Magic Bullet*, London: Earthscan and Save the Children Fund.

Fiagbey, E.D.K. (1992), 'Community cooperatives and adult-education in Scotland and Ghana – some lessons from the developed and developing world', *International Review of Education*, **38** (3), 275–85.

Gilson, L., Sen, P.D., Mohammed, S. and Mujinja, P. (1994), 'The potential of health sector nongovernmental organizations – policy options', *Health Policy and Planning*, **9** (1), 14–24.

Green, A. and Matthias, A. (1995), 'Where do NGOs fit in? Developing a policy framework for the health sector', *Development in Practice*, **5** (4), 313–23.

Ishumi, A.G.M. (1995), 'Provision of secondary education in Tanzania: historical background and current trends', in Semboja and Therkildsen (1995), pp. 153–65.

Kaiser, P.J. (1995), 'State–society relations in an international context – the case of Aga Khan health care initiatives in Tanzania', *International Journal of Comparative Sociology*, **36** (3–4), 184–97.

London, L. (1993), 'The Ray Alexander Workers' Clinic – a model for worker-based health services in South Africa', *Social Science & Medicine*, **37** (12), 1521–7.

MacLure, R. (1995), 'Nongovernment organizations and the contradictions of animation rurale – questioning the ideal of community self-reliance in Burkina Faso', *Canadian Journal of Development Studies*, **16** (1), 31–53.

Mburu, F.M. (1994), 'Health delivery standards – vested interests in health planning', *Social Science & Medicine*, **39** (9), 1375–84.

Mogedal, S., Steen, H. and Mpelumbe, G. (1995), 'Health sector reform and organizational issues at the local level: lessons from selected African countries', *Journal of International Development*, **7** (3), 349–67.

Munishi, G.K. (1995), 'Social services provision in Tanzania: the relationship between political development strategies and NGO participation', in Semboja and Therkildsen (1995), pp. 141–52.

Nabaguzi, E. (1995), 'Popular initiatives in service provision in Uganda', in Semboja and Therkildsen (1995), pp. 192–208.

Oyugi, W.O. (1995), 'Social service provision in Kenya: who benefits?', in Semboja and Therkildsen (1995), pp. 121–40.

Pachauri, S. (1994), *Reaching India's Poor: Non-Governmental Approaches to Community Health*, New Delhi: Sage.

Passi, F.O. (1995), 'The rise of people's organizations in primary education in Uganda', in Semboja and Therkildsen (1995), pp. 209–22.

Picon, C. (1991), 'Adult education in the context of state and NGOs', *Convergence*, **24** (1–2), 80–90.

Riddell, R. and Robinson, M. (1995), *Non-Governmental Organisations and Rural Poverty Alleviation*, Oxford: Clarendon Press.

Robinson, M. and White, G. (1997), *The Role of Civic Organizations in the Provision of Social Services: Towards Synergy*, Research For Action 37, Helsinki: UNU/WIDER.

Salamon, L.M. (1994), 'The rise of the nonprofit sector', *Foreign Affairs,* July/August, 109–22.

Sauerborn, R., Bodart, C. and Essomba, R.O. (1995), 'Recovery of recurrent health service costs through provincial health funds in Cameroon', *Social Science & Medicine*, **40** (12), 1731–9.

Semboja, J. and Therkildsen, O. (eds) (1995), *Service Provision Under Stress in East Africa*, London: James Currey.

Sundar, P. (1994), 'NGO experience in health: an overview', in Pachauri (1994), pp. 309–33.

Uphoff, N. (1993), 'Grassroots organizations and NGOs in rural development: opportunities with diminishing states and expanding markets', *World Development*, **21** (4), 607–22.

Van Til, J. (1987), 'The three sectors: voluntarism in a changing political economy', *Journal of Voluntary Action Research*, **16** (1–2), 50–63.

Voluntary Health Services Society (1990), *5 NGOs in Health: A Summary of Past, Present and Future*, Dhaka: VHSS.

Walley, J., Tefera, B. and McDonald, M.A. (1991), 'Integrating health services – the experience of NGOs in Ethiopia', *Health Policy and Planning*, **6** (4), 327–35.

White, Gordon (1996), 'Civil society, democratization and development', in R. Luckham and G. White (eds), *Democratization in the South: The Jagged Wave*, Manchester: Manchester University Press, pp. 178–219.

World Bank (1993), 'Investing in Health', *World Development Report 1993*, Washington, DC: World Bank.

Yanay, U. (1990), 'Service delivery by a trade union – does it pay?', *Journal of Social Policy*, **29** (2), 221–34.

Zamberia, A.M. (1996), 'Self-help secondary education in Kenya', *International Journal of Comparative Sociology*, **37** (1–2), 48–71.

Zuckerman, E. and de Kadt, E. (eds) (1997), *The Public–Private Mix in Social Services: Health Care and Education in Chile, Costa Rica and Venezuela*, Social Policy Agenda Group, Washington: Inter American Development Bank.

14. Central–local relations in the Asia–Pacific: convergence or divergence?[1]

Mark Turner

INTRODUCTION

In the 1960s, modernization theory predicted that as countries developed they would become more alike. Among other things they would have increasingly similar politico-administrative systems modelled after Western democratic pluralism (for example Moore, 1963). In short, there would be convergence. Development administration concurred with this judgement and focused on the technical task of making bureaucracies work better. Experience proved such thinking to be wrong. In the Asia–Pacific region a variety of state configurations emerged, with similarities between some countries of the region contrasting with differences between them, and between themselves and others outside the region.

Convergence is again a theme of public sector and political reform in the 1990s, this time according to the conceptual dominance of new public management (NPM) and 'good governance' ideas. The impetus for public sector reform has been a permanent fixture in the Asia–Pacific region but has intensified in recent years. To be seen to be engaged in public sector reform, countries are now expected to devise programmes of great national significance. The imported ideas of good governance and NPM are championed by multilateral agencies and much discussed by politicians and public sector managers in regional forums, conferences and international visits. Easy communication makes the ideas instantly available from Pakistan to Papua New Guinea, and academics and practitioners concur that the NPM is not simply a management fad.

The leading proponents of the NPM (Osborne and Gaebler, 1992) believe that a 'global revolution' in public sector management has been taking place, leading to universal convergence on an agreed model. There is certainly evidence to support this view in similar prescriptions and common items on the menus for public sector reform that can be found in Asia–Pacific countries. The language of reform undoubtedly shows convergence. Whether those speaking it actually mean the same thing is highly doubtful. There is also some dispute over what NPM actually means in its own heartlands. One recent book on the UK identified four different types of NPM (Ferlie et al., 1996, and see the discussion by Common in Chapter 4, this volume).

This chapter looks at the question of convergence and divergence in public sector reform by examining the nature of central–local relations in a selection of Asia–Pacific countries. Three broad categories are utilized to give a loose classification to the countries under consideration and to alert the reader to the wide range of experiences and directions in central–local relations evident in the Asia–Pacific region.

CATEGORY 1: DECENTRALIZATION

One thread of the NPM sees decentralization as an integral feature of any public sector management system (Ferlie et al., 1996). Organizations should become more flexible and more loosely coupled at the local level. This stress on technical efficiency is complemented by views on good governance which invariably stress the importance of participation by citizens in government (ODA, 1993). What this adds up to is support for decentralizing government in order to ensure improved performance in service delivery and participation in local decision making. There is a leaning towards a devolutionary mode which can be seen in Papua New Guinea and the Philippines.

As Papua New Guinea prepared for independence in 1975 the integrity of the state was threatened by an outburst of micro-nationalism, not surprising in a country of under three million people but over 800 languages. The attempts of these local movements to disengage from the state were countered by decentralization. The Constitutional Planning Committee strongly urged decentralization but it was a secessionist movement on the mineral-rich island of Bougainville that finally persuaded parliamentarians, in 1977, to pass an Organic Law on Provincial Governments.

This was a popular piece of legislation as it appeared to give 'power to the people' and provide another avenue of opportunity to aspiring politicians (Turner, 1990). Nineteen provinces were established, each with an elected assembly and a premier, who in most cases was elected by the assembly. Responsibility for provincial administration was vested in the department of the province, with each province deciding the functional divisions into which its own department would be configured. The functions transferred by central government to the provinces were considerable and included most aspects of health, education, primary industry, public works and business development. All public servants assigned to the province remained national government employees, but while working for the department of the province they came under the control of the elected provincial government. Funding for provincial government came mainly from central government in the form of a number of grants and attempted to follow several basic allocative principles: derivation, equity and needs.

This radical decentralization did not work out quite as its architects imagined or desired (Turner, 1990). National politicians began blaming provincial government for seemingly all of the country's ills, although this may well have been a smokescreen for concern about the increasing power of provincial assemblies and their individual members. But popular support for provincial government also declined, as in many places the quantity and quality of service delivery deteriorated, some provincial assemblies experienced constant leadership changes, and suspensions of provincial governments for financial misdemeanours became more common. Also, in most provinces, the system of local government set up by the colonial power as a mode of political socialization into democratic ways suffered from severe neglect. Decentralization to the province was accompanied by centralization within the province.

Serious moves to reform the devolved system of provincial government began in 1992 and culminated in 1995 with a new Organic Law on Provincial Governments and Local-Level Governments (OLPGLLG) which is characterized by elements of both recentralization and reinvigorated decentralization. On the centralizing side, the new provincial governments are headed by a governor who is the national member of parliament representing the provincial electorate. The old ministerial system has been dropped and a committee system installed with the governor appointing committee chairpersons. Other national parliamentarians from the province also sit in the provincial assembly. The departments of the province have been abolished and their operations will come under the relevant national department through a provincial administrator, to be chosen by the National Executive Council from a list of persons nominated by the provincial executive council.

On the decentralization side, some members of the provincial assemblies are drawn from elected local-level bodies. Provinces will retain their primary powers while local-level governments have also been given significant law making powers. The latter have been identified as the cornerstones of the new system and have been promised full legal status and significant funding and manpower.

Confusion is also an element of the new arrangements. There is uncertainty about the roles, responsibilities and authority of national line departments, provincial administrators and district administrators. The Organic Law was pushed through parliament hastily and there is a pressing need to rectify confusion and omissions in what promises to be a huge programme of legislative amendment (May, 1997). A further issue is whether in the effort to shift power and responsibility to local-level government there has been a serious over-estimation of the political, administrative and technical capacities of these institutions to perform adequately. In this respect, the Provincial and Local Government Affairs Minister, Peter Barter, told a May 1997 seminar in Port Moresby that 'in the 22 months since the reforms commenced little improvement has been achieved in the operation of provincial administrations and almost nothing in most of their sub-units' (*The Independent*, 30 May 1997).

The Philippines is a more recent convert to formal decentralization. The impetus for the Philippine experiment derives from the 'people power'experience which contributed to the overthrow of President Marcos, and a deep-seated commitment to democratic politics. It can even be portrayed as a rediscovery of a decentralized past interrupted by more than three centuries of colonial centralization, belief in whose efficacy was initially absorbed into the psyche of the independent republic.

The Philippine experience is of particular interest because it demonstrates a new-found confidence in the strength of the state: that the state can cope with radical structural reform. It is also occurring at a time when the Philippines has apparently shrugged off the undesirable label of 'the sick man of ASEAN' (Association of South East Asian Nations). Several years of good economic growth, plus a consistent policy orientation compared to previous years, have given hope that developmental promises may at long last be realized.

The history of local governance in the Philippines is conventionally described as several centuries of centralization. While centripetal forces have certainly been dominant, there is also evidence of centrifugal tendencies, not surprising in an archipelagic country made up of more than 7000 islands and multiple language groups. Politicians and administrators in different regimes, even when appointed by central authorities, have been able to exercise considerable degrees of *de facto* autonomy in their own domains in pursuit of their own objectives. Thus the history of local-level governance may be better depicted as a story of tension between the forces of centralism and localism in which the former have always been dominant.

That domination has been neutralized by the passage of the Local Government Code in 1991. This legislation instituted four major changes in a system which already has elected assemblies at the levels of province and city, municipality, and *barangay* (local community). First, the Code decrees decentralization from national to local levels of responsibility for the delivery of certain basic services in health, agriculture, public works, social welfare, and environment and natural resources. Second, additional regulatory and licensing functions have been given to local government units. Third, the amount of funds allocated by central government to the local government units has been greatly increased. Finally, the Code provides for participation in local governance by non-governmental organizations (NGOs) and the private sector.

The process of decentralization has not been plain sailing. Even before the Code was passed in Congress it was watered down by national legislators. Many local officials habitually complain of insufficient funds while the World Bank (1995) has alleged that funding arrangements have been inequitable, creating both winners and losers among local government units. There has been a lack of innovation in revenue raising by local governments, ensuring their continued dependence on central funding and traditional taxes and fees. Regarding service delivery, it appears that the devolved tasks have been absorbed by local government units throughout the country, although there is considerable variation between units and functions. But absorbing the devolved services is no easy matter as it requires both structural and cultural reorientation away from top–down centralized service delivery to an area-based mode of operation. This necessary reorientation has been made more difficult by 'the resistance of central agencies to aggressively implement the code' (Associates in Rural Development Inc., 1996), although recent reports from most regions indicate improvement in national–local relations. Despite such problems, basic service delivery is becoming more integrated into the fabric of local government units and is regarded as such by officials and population. Whether there are improvements in services is difficult to ascertain, though this is one of the principal aims and expectations of the decentralization experiment.

Personnel matters have received considerable publicity during the process of decentralization, as approximately 70 000 staff have been transferred to local government control. Mass rallies by health workers in opposition to the Code were the most obvious manifestation of public servants' worries about decentralization. Their concerns focused on career security and advancement within local government units, which pay lower salaries than national departments and which often have very limited opportunities for promotion. The local government units themselves have also expressed misgivings about having to absorb officers who were perceived to be inept, incompetent or who were duplicating functions.

A final issue has been that of participation, a leading objective of decentralization and an integral component of the move to increased autonomy. There are two ways in which this participation is secured: through the election of persons to political office and through representation on newly established local advisory bodies. Critics of the electoral system argue that the post-Marcos period has seen the re-emergence of political clans which are able to dominate political representation in municipalities, cities and provinces either through direct officeholding or by establishing strong ties with other political leaders (Gutierrez et al., 1992; Panganiban, 1995). NGO representation on local advisory bodies has been an important development which can curb the excesses of local political élites and ensure that diverse voices in the community are heard. While the most recent 'rapid field appraisal' (Associates in Rural Development Inc., 1996) reports a positive trend, with more NGOs being accredited and more special bodies being constituted with at least the minimum number of NGO/private sector representatives, whether they have been activated is another matter. Potentially the most important of the local advisory bodies, the local development councils, have been criticized by both NGOs and local government officials as inappropriate organizations for the planning and coordination of development.

Overall the decentralization of governance set out in the Local Government Code of 1991 has met with widespread approval in the Philippines. It has also enjoyed the full backing of the chief executive, an essential requirement of major government reform. The decentralization programme has proceeded steadily if not always smoothly, and there are certainly indications that real gains have been made in promoting local autonomy and enabling local governments to run much more of their own affairs in cooperation with NGOs and the private sector.

CATEGORY 2: CENTRALIZED

A second type of central–local relations regularly encountered in the Asia–Pacific region is characterized by strong central control. Although the language of autonomy and decentralization may be employed and governmental arrangements ostensibly introduced in pursuit of these ideals, the real picture is one in which the central state maintains firm control of local governance. In this chapter, Bangladesh and Indonesia will be utilized to illustrate this model.

Since the emergence of the stabilizing New Order government in 1966 from political turmoil and a national bloodbath, Indonesian leaders have been preoccupied with national integration and maintaining the unity of their state, which sprawls across a massive archipelago and now has a population approaching 200 million. This is complemented by the widespread belief that economic development is a national responsibility and by government determination to maintain tight control over economic, political and social development in Indonesia (Gerritsen and Situmorang, 1997). What these features add up to is an environment which is seemingly not conducive to decentralization.

It is therefore somewhat surprising to find that decentralization appears to be stressed in the three official principles guiding central–local relations: decentralization (*azas decentraliassi*), involving the transfer of functions to lower levels of government; deconcentration (*azas decontrasi*), meaning that some matters which remain the permanent responsibility of the central government will be carried out by the regional offices of central agencies; and co-administration (*azas tugas pembantuan*), involving the performance of certain functions under central government jurisdiction by autonomous regional governments (*pemerintah daerah*).

Despite these decentralizing principles guiding central–local relations, in reality the central state dominates. While sub-national governments in Indonesia have a significant role in the provision of services, financing and policy design remain securely under central government control (Gerritsen and Situmorang, 1997). Locally generated revenue plus shared revenue from land and property tax represent only 20 per cent of total local government income, while only between 10 and 20 per cent of activities performed at the regional level can be financed from the internal revenue of the region (Rohdewohld, 1995). Regional governments lack decision making powers on tax rates, and on raising new taxes, thus leading to the observation that 'significant fiscal autonomy does not exist at any lower level of government' (Ranis and Stewart, 1994, p. 45).

Regarding policy making, rules and regulations emanate from central government in a vertical direction downwards through the various levels of sub-national government. This has been captured in the image that 'Jakarta remains the one who enjoys the lunch while the regions still serve as its cooks and dishwashers' (Singha, as quoted in Rohdewohld, 1995, p. 85). While there are regional legislative bodies, decentralization has not strengthened their political role, and does not represent devolution. The central executive dominates in the regions through personnel from the line agencies, with one level accountable to the next, up to headquarters in Jakarta. Such centralization of politics and administration curtails local responsiveness to specific local conditions and inculcates a culture of risk aversion at the regional and local levels. The situation is compounded by weaknesses in the capacity of sub-national government. The shortage of qualified personnel in sub-national government is exacerbated by a career incentive structure in which advancement is gained in national agencies rather than in local government.

Like Indonesia, Bangladesh has introduced a variety of decentralizing reforms during the past few decades but 'service delivery in Bangladesh remains at exceptionally low levels and effective local governance is almost unknown' (Hulme and Siddiquee, 1997, p. 32). The rhetoric of the reforms has not been matched by their results.

In 1959, the Basic Democracies System of the military regime of Ayub Khan introduced a four-tier system of local government with councils at every level. Only the council at the top level actually had real authority and, in general, there was bureaucratic dominance over each tier. A planned reorganization in 1971 focused on making local government an adjunct of the highly centralized one-party state. A *coup d'état* ensured that this plan was never removed from the drawing board. Instead, General Zia introduced the Swanirvar Gram Sarker (self-reliant village government). Despite official recognition of disadvantaged socioeconomic groups, experience revealed the Gram Sarkers to be local extensions of the ruling Bangladesh National Party (BNP) rather than autonomous local bodies.

In 1982, General Ershad took over the reins of government and introduced a new and innovative decentralization policy. The 400 *thanas* (police post areas) were elevated to *upazilas* and responsibility for a large number of functions was transferred to the new democratic institution, the Upazila Parishad (UZP). Financial resources to sub-national government were increased considerably and authority over them and central government support staff was transferred to the UZP. Local political control undermined the former pre-eminence of appointed bureaucrats.

Unfortunately, the UZP did not live up to its billing. Instead of greater responsiveness to local problems, needs and issues, the *upazila* scheme increased the opportunities for patronage and corruption. Local representatives sought privileged access to resources for kin and clients. Budgetary allocation at the *upazila* level became skewed in favour of lumpy projects involving construction work. Large farmers and influential families became the main beneficiaries of UZP expenditure and the leakage of project resources. Popular participation was not enhanced as only the UZP chairman was directly elected by the *upazila* population. Even then, elections were characterized by malpractice and physical intimidation. When elected, the chairmen often spent considerable time in Dhaka cultivating relationships with national politicians. This derived from the almost total dependence of the *upazilas* on central government grants. Local resource mobilization was minimal.

In 1991, the new BNP government of Begum Khaleda Zia abolished the *upazila* government system without introducing an alternative. A deconcentrated system then started to replace the devolved approach, with the Thana Nirbah officer taking control of the defunct UZP. A review commission's recommendations for the stronger and more accountable local government was ignored and a system of Thana Development Coordination Committees (TDCC) was put in place. The TDCC gives greater authority to agents of the national government and makes no provision for participation of local people in the administrative and development activities undertaken by the various departments of government. The bureaucrats have regained some of the ground lost under the *upazila* decentralization.

The Bangladesh experience demonstrates how 'the concept of decentralization has been used as a rhetorical device rather than a genuine attempt to delegate power to lower levels' (Hulme and Siddiquee, 1997, p. 32). Reforms have been made to consolidate regime power. Even the *upazila* system can be interpreted as an attempt to win the support of local élites by legitimating their dominance of rural communities. Corruption and resource misuse at the local level was the price of political alliance and loyalty to the national regime. A further lesson of the Bangladesh experience is the lack of continuity in sub-national arrangements. A new national leader invariably entails a new sub-national system of government and administration, with local bodies being reshaped to suit political ends rather than promoting the welfare of the people.

Even when devolution has apparently taken place, the centre has ensured that it still retains important controls over local action. Rules and instructions ensured that local representatives were aligned to the national governing party and that the operation of the *parishad* was subject to central regulation. The centre has always maintained financial control so that channelling of national funds to local bodies can be used to secure a political support base in the countryside (Blair, 1989). Democratization has remained elusive, and in the current situation the Dhaka-focused bureaucracy is in control of most official sub-national activity. However, a new development in local governance has been the growth in number, activities, coverage, financial resources and influence of NGOs. The NGOs have shown an ability to engage with the poor and involve them in developmental and political activities. There is some 'decentralisation by default' (Hulme and Siddiquee, 1997, p. 32), with aid donors financing the expansion and proliferation of NGOs.

CATEGORY 3: RECENTRALIZATION

Despite the preference of NPM and good governance for decentralization strategies there is a group of countries whose central–local relations are currently moving in the opposite direction as they pursue far-reaching public sector, economic and social reforms. The recentralizers can be found among former socialist states such as Vietnam and Laos.

Conventional wisdom has emphasized the centralized nature of socialist states. This derives from the predilection of Western scholars to conflate the communist party with the administrative state; the assumption that the centrally planned economy is simply a one-way process of command from above; and an inappropriate focus on state–society conflicts with the concomitant neglect of conflicts within the state (Vasavakul, 1997). Such analysis is mistaken and overlooks the fragmentation and tensions *within* the administrative state.

Vasavakul (1997, p. 4) argues that the administrative state in Vietnam was in fact highly decentralized and 'the central planning system with its vertical economic structure of allocating and redistributing resources coexisted with a decentralized local administrative machine'. The economic reforms which commenced in the late 1970s ended with the abolition of the centralized planning system, 'further consolidating the power of local administrative agencies while undermining the centre's political and economic power' (ibid., p. 5). Thus, the socialist state had become the decentralized state, and middle-level cadres were using their administrative positions to support their economic endeavours.

The reform measures of the 1990s have reflected the central government's attempt to curb the rise of autonomous economic blocs within the state apparatus. The desired post-central planning state has been identified as an administrative state which is capable of representing public and national interests. Reformists have attempted to consolidate the central state's presence by linking it to the local state through imported concepts such as the rule of law and traditional concepts such as historical space. Despite such centralizing efforts Vasavakul (1997) maintains that the Vietnamese administrative state continues to be fragmented and diversified. Access to services may well have become more uneven. However, despite the advent of the market economy, the central government may have reduced, but has by no means abandoned, its role of allocating and redistributing economic resources.

Laos provides a further example of a country moving from a highly decentralized system of government and administration to a more centralized arrangement (Keuleers, 1997). Between 1947 and 1975, Laos was a mixture of centralized and decentralized elements. While the king appointed provincial governors, municipal mayors and district chiefs, the village chief and council were popularly elected. Coordination and control of local administration was the responsibility of the Ministry of the Interior. However, expenditure management was the responsibility of both the central ministries and their field offices, and of local authorities.

In 1975, the new socialist regime started to rebuild a highly underdeveloped economy after more than 20 years of political turbulence and civil war. Attempts were made to impose a centrally planned economy and unite an ethnically divided agrarian society, which was linked by the most rudimentary infrastructure and communications. Peasant resistance ensured the failure and abandonment of the centrally imposed cooperative farming model, thus questioning the capacity of the central state to determine local action.

At the political centre stood the Party Central Committee, the Government and the Supreme People's Council. At the three sub-national levels of province, district and commune, identical political and executive structures were set up. Popular participation was achieved through elections to people's councils at each of these levels. Governors, who were the leading party officials in the province, were no longer under the authority of the Ministry of the Interior but reported directly to the prime minister. But together with district chiefs, governors enjoyed considerable autonomy regarding their administrations and budgets. Local funding came from central state transfers and from operational surpluses of the state-owned enterprises under the local authorities' control. The situation was one in which apparent political centralization coexisted with a large amount of sub-national autonomy. The centre was in practice only loosely connected to the sub-national units.

With the abysmal performance of the Lao economy increasingly evident, Lao authorities proclaimed a 'new economic mechanism' involving the transformation of the centrally planned economy into a market-oriented one. With central planning abandoned, the relative autonomy of local government increased, and was deliberately strengthened to make provinces economically and financially self-sufficient. Provincial governments thus became responsible for planning and managing all local resources except externally funded projects. Even tax administration came under provincial and district control. Central ministries had no authority over technical services at sub-national levels, or over personnel matters. National policies could not be enforced.

Although beneficial effects of the economic reforms were being observed by the end of the 1980s, it became increasingly obvious that the decentralized administrative system was coming into conflict with the economic reform programme. Provincial autonomy had exacerbated interprovincial and even interdistrict inequalities; regulatory frameworks were absent, inefficient administration was characteristic; service provision was often extremely poor and sometimes non-existent; and ineffectiveness characterized much public service activity.

The Fifth Party Congress in 1991 determined that the highly decentralized state would be reconfigured into a 'unitary deconcentrated state' (Keuleers, 1997). This recentralizing direction was confirmed in the new Constitution and in the stream of decrees which began to emanate from the prime minister and Politburo. The central government reclaimed the authority to organize, direct and supervise the operation of state services in all sectors, including the local administration. People's councils were abolished, fiscal centralization was enforced and central institutions were established under the Office of the Prime Minister to issue guidelines on the organization of government and personnel matters for central and sub-national levels. Planning was made into a bottom–up and top–down system, but the bottom has proved to be the provincial level, thus indicating a *de facto* bias towards the top.

While the trend is undoubtedly one of recentralization, governors and district chiefs do in fact still have significant power. They have important coordinating roles, they are the leading party officials in their territories, and the local map of power and authority rarely, if ever, matches the idealized version drawn by the central state. There is also the consideration that the current recentralization is only a medium-term policy. Decentralization still remains an objective, but experience has shown that if it is not embedded in a legal and regulatory framework then budgetary anarchy and administrative chaos will result (Keuleers, 1997).

CONCLUSION

The three categories of central–local relation used in this survey of selected country experience in the Asia–Pacific are both loose and not exhaustive. Other modes of classification are possible, and other categories could be added. It is also evident that diversity exists within the categories. For example, there can be elements of centralization in what appears overall to be a case of decentralization. Despite these shortcomings the classification serves to emphasize the major finding of this chapter that divergence rather than convergence is still the dominant theme in central–local relations in the Asia–Pacific.

At one extreme are the devolving examples of the Philippines and Papua New Guinea, where considerable power and functional responsibilities have been awarded to sub-national units at the district or even community levels. At the other end of the spectrum are the recentralizing countries of Laos and Vietnam, making the transition from central planning to market economy. Paradoxically, central planning was complemented with decentralized administration. However, the early experiences with the market increased decentralization to the point of fragmentation, thus necessitating the assertion of central control. It is the market which apparently needs the imposition of central order and nationwide systems. Occupying the intermediate space are the centralized countries such as Indonesia and Bangladesh, where national authorities are reluctant to cede significant decision making powers to the local level. In instances where this has occurred, there is care to coopt local élites, or ensure strong regulatory control from the centre, and fiscal reliance on it.

While it is evident that there is no convergence towards one particular type of central–local relations, there is certainly a universal concern with the subject and it is mostly framed in a discourse of decentralization. The concept appears to be imbued with 'good' values and so, even in the centralized and recentralizing states, decentralization is seen to have positive virtues. Thus in Indonesia the current system of sub-national government and administration is labelled in terms of decentralizing principles and autonomous regions. In Laos, the recentralization is claimed to be a necessary precondition for planned decentralization. But such public acknowledgement of decentralization's virtues and desirability tends to obscure the political processes which in practice determine a country's form of central–local relations. The decision to adopt one or another form, to make incremental changes, or to maintain the *status quo*, is rarely, if ever, based on some evaluation of the technical superiority of the chosen mode. It is firmly grounded in the political interactions of stakeholders, all of whom will of course utilize technical arguments to justify their chosen strategy.

Another finding from the sample countries is that the nature of central–local relations can only be understood in relation to history. Each country has its own political trajectory which may span centuries and which will, in great part, influence the nature of central–local relations. Indonesia's preoccupation with national unity, the fragmentary character of Papua New Guinea, and the legacy of the British colonial administrative state in Bangladesh are features of historical and contemporary relevance. Policy is made looking forward, but with constant glances over the shoulder.

For this reason it is difficult to generalize about the nature of and trends in central–local relations. There are no straightforward correlations such that economic liberalization requires administrative decentralization, or that strong states demand a particular central–local configuration. Even where devolution is in place, questions can be raised about the nature of participation at the local level. There can be local centralization in which particular families and privileged classes monopolize decision making and resources. Conversely, centralized systems may sometimes need to accommodate regional strongmen and concede significant power to them in their own domains.

Finally, all the countries surveyed are publicly committed to or acknowledge the need for major public sector reform. They share the language of NPM and good governance, and in this sense there is convergence. A similar vocabulary is used throughout the region and there is a strong interest in others' experiences. However, the language is mediated by and refracted through a range of political structures, institutional frameworks, state–society relations and cultural distinctions. These will ensure that divergence rather than convergence will remain the overall characteristic of central–local relations in the Asia–Pacific region.

NOTE

1. This chapter presents some of the preliminary findings of a research project on central–local relations in the Asia–Pacific funded by the Australian Agency for International Development. It draws on some of the country papers presented at a Canberra workshop in March 1997. These papers include those of Patrick Keuleers, Ron May, Thaveeporn Vasavakul, David Hulme and Noore Alam Siddiquee, and Rolf Gerritsen and Saut Situmorang. However, the views presented in this chapter are my own interpretations of these papers, other data, and my own work in many of the countries surveyed.

REFERENCES

Associates in Rural Development Inc. (1996), *Synopsis of Findings: Sixth Rapid Rural Appraisal of Decentralization,* Manila: Associates in Rural Development.

Blair, H.W. (ed.) (1989), *Can Rural Development be Financed from Below? Local Resource Mobilisation in Bangladesh,* Dhaka: University Press.

Ferlie, E. et al. (1996), *The New Public Management in Action,* Oxford: Oxford University Press.

Gutierrez, E.U., Torrente, I.C. and Narca, N.G. (1992), *All in the Family: A Study of Elites and Power Relations in the Philippines,* Quezon City: Institute for Popular Democracy.

Gerritsen, R. and Situmorang, S. (1997), 'Central–local relations in Indonesia', paper presented at the workshop on 'Central–local Relations: Asia Pacific Experiences', University of Canberra, 21 March.

Hulme, D. and Siddiquee, N.A. (1997), 'Central–local relations and responsibilities in Bangladesh: experiments with the organisation, management and delivery of services', paper presented at the workshop on 'Central–local Relations: Asia Pacific Experiences', University of Canberra, 21 March.

Keuleers, P. (1997), 'Central–local relations in the Lao People's Democratic Republic', paper presented at the workshop on 'Central–local Relations: Asia Pacific Experiences', University of Canberra, 21 March.

May, R.J. (1997), 'Decentralization in Papua New Guinea: two steps forward, one step back', paper presented at the workshop on 'Central–local Relations: Asia Pacific Experiences', University of Canberra, 21 March.

Moore, W. (1963), *Social Change,* Englewood Cliffs: Prentice-Hall.

ODA (Overseas Development Administration) (1993), 'Good government', Technical Note, No. 10.

Osborne, D. and Gaebler, T. (1992), *Reinventing Government: How the Entrepreneurial Spirit is Transforming the Public Sector,* Reading, MA: Addison-Wesley.

Panganiban, E.M. (1995), 'Democratic decentralization in contemporary times: the new Local Government Code of the Philippines', *Philippine Journal of Public Administration,* **39** (2), 121–38.

Ranis, G. and Stewart, F. (1994), 'Decentralization in Indonesia', *Bulletin of Indonesian Economic Studies,* **30** (3), 41–72.

Rohdewohld, R. (1995), *Public Administration in Indonesia,* Melbourne: Montech.

Turner, M. (1997), 'The Philippines: from centralism to localism', paper presented at the workshop on 'Central–local Relations: Asia Pacific Experiences', University of Canberra, 21 March.

Turner, M. (1990), *Papua New Guinea: The Challenge of Independence,* Ringwood: Penguin.

Vasavakul, T. (1997), 'Rethinking the philosophy of central–local relations in post-central planning Viet Nam', paper presented at the workshop on 'Central–local Relations: Asia Pacific Experiences', University of Canberra, 21 March.

World Bank (1995), *Philippines: Public Expenditure Management for Sustained and Equitable Growth,* Washington, DC: World Bank.

15. Public services, complex emergencies and the humanitarian imperative: perspectives from Angola[1]

Ian Christoplos

SERVICES, WEAK STATES AND COMPLEX EMERGENCIES

A question which is increasingly asked regarding rehabilitation in weak and collapsed states is how *we*, decision makers at central levels and the aid community, should rebuild structures and processes of governance. This question is an inappropriate basis for action in weak states. It needs to be turned around to ask how *they*, the nurses, local administrators, extension agents and other staff of governmental and non-governmental organizations, perceive the challenges of reconstituting some form of public services in the face of a turbulent and hostile environment. Aid in war situations inevitably carries a shifting set of implicit humanitarian imperatives for people working in the field. These moral, ethical and practical aspects of humanitarianism are generally overlooked by donors, project planners and academics in the normative debate on the proper role of the state. Little attention has been paid to the various interpretations of the humanitarian imperative which emerge within the relationship between local field staff and their clients. There is a need to better understand the process of 'sensemaking' (Weick, 1995) which the staff of local service institutions engage in while struggling to sort out their roles as brokers between a strange aid bureaucracy and an array of desperate clients and predatory forces.

The factors arising in service provision as complex emergencies abate may shed light on processes under way in the margins of many other, seemingly far more stable nations. While the scale of the mess in Angola has few parallels, the state of affairs in specific areas in Angola is not so different from what can be found in the marginal areas and forgotten service institutions in countries which have not gone through similar trauma. In marginal areas, there are weak states within strong states. The 'rubble of development' in these places (Gould, 1996) is not easily distinguished from the ruins of war. A permanent emergency may be affecting a large proportion of the population even if there is no glaringly apparent crisis. There are places where the local population is (1) too poor and economically insignificant, (2) of the wrong ethnic group or nationality, or (3) too troublesome and well-armed to bother sorting out governance and public welfare. In marginal areas everywhere, there is no reason to assume that a salaried and supplied government nurse will show up, just because an NGO has rebuilt the local health post. But in lieu of any other broadly recognized goal, this 'developmentalism' remains the default assumption. No one has found a sustainable, unsubsidized model which will provide basic services for the poor and destitute in such areas. In these places, as in Angola, the micro-level discourse is not about development. It is about a scramble for survival, a human activity which has little in common with the constructs used in conventional development discourse.

Potentially, there is much to be gained by better linking lessons being learned in rethinking public services in 'normal' contexts of uncertainty and the collapse of state finance with the debate on the humanitarian imperative in complex emergencies. The discourse on disasters has not benefited from the lessons being learned regarding public services in turbulent situations. Even those calling for developmental relief often fail to realize that development specialists no longer have a clear notion of the ways in which public services should be delivered. The crisis in virtually all public services, particularly in poor and marginal areas, has meant that the underlying assumptions of linear development are questioned everywhere. The realization is growing that it can no longer be assumed that steady economic growth will produce a taxable surplus, which can be invested in basic public services for the poor and destitute. If this is correct, then, even without war and a consequent collapse of public ethics, it implies that we can no longer take for granted that a linear relief to development process will emerge in post-conflict situations. A possible way forward is to explore commonalities between the new non-linear concepts in organizational behaviour and the increasing awareness of the profound structural dysfunctions in complex emergencies. Finding out what the label of developmental relief might actually mean once it is shorn of the accompanying assumption of progress along a relief–development continuum demands a comparison of lessons learned in both arenas of action.

This is seldom done. The 'complex emergency' label has generally not led to a readiness formally to acknowledge the complexity of the social, political and institutional challenges of intervention in such situations. Rather than facing complexity, the relief definition of any emergency is usually automatically assumed simply to be the lack of items lost due to the war, drought, flood or other causes. Food aid so dominates emergency assistance that even health and other service-related emergency interventions are expected to function like food aid, to fill a temporary gap until everything is normal again. There is an inbuilt tendency to analyse programmes in terms of access to material resources rather than the sociopolitical dynamics of basic service provision. The differences between delivering a sack of food and managing a clinic are glossed over. Such thinking encourages projects designed to fix input delivery systems, even when the fundamental problem does not involve delivery. Donors force such analytical straitjackets on humanitarian interventions. Relief agencies have to claim that they can spend money, solve extraordinary problems and withdraw within a few months when things return to normal.

What is the 'normal' state of service provision in Angola? Even in the current post-conflict phase, Angola is an extreme case of the withdrawal of the state from provision of basic services, especially in rural areas. Officially 3 per cent of public expenditure goes to health, down from 6 per cent in 1992. Education has dropped from 12 per cent to 4 per cent of expenditure while social assistance has increased from 6 per cent to 9 per cent (UNICEF, 1996). These figures certainly overestimate actual expenditure since a significant proportion of government oil income is channelled directly to the military (Aguilar and Stenman, 1995). Of the funds allocated, few would dispute that at least half disappears through corruption. The majority of what is left goes to the urban areas. In sum, publicly funded rural services have all but disappeared (Sveriges Ambassad i Angola, 1996).

As in many countries undergoing economic crisis, this lack of financial resources does not mean that the civil service has been dismissed. Instead, the government's 'passive wage policy' on hyperinflation had caused salaries to shrink to insignificant levels (Aguilar and Stenman, 1995, p. 34). A year later Aguilar and Stenman (1996) reported that the situation was even worse and 'hyperinflation and lack of a consistent wage policy are destroying the state'. Staff still formally have jobs, but the meaning of public service employment has changed. Government institutions dealing with rural services are merely temporary employment agencies serving as an auxiliary to the NGOs. Staff are loaned to NGOs and UN agencies as and when required for their projects. For this the staff receive personal incentives, operational materials, and legitimacy in the eyes of the community. In between such secondments most staff are idle. They receive no real salaries and lack the logistical capacity even to visit the communities they are supposed to serve.

Angola does not lack the capacity to provide basic services. Rather, the government has decided to abandon its civil servants. It has turned over the responsibility for making use of the civil service to NGOs and donors. The basic subsistence of government functionaries has come to be seen as the responsibility of the international community. In the eyes of the people, the NGOs and the UN are assuming the legitimacy of the state. If an NGO rehabilitates a health post, it is *they* who are expected to pay the staff and stock it, not the government. As Duffield writes:

> The Emergency Programme of Government is tantamount to GOA [Government of Angola] consciously abandoning the social sector. After years of neglect and decline, it is being farmed out to the international community. This calls into question conventional development theory premised upon capacity building and handing over to government structures. GOA does not appear interested. Or, at least, what was previously seen as a lack of capacity, now appears as a conscious prioritisation. (1994, pp. 80–81)

The current state of affairs in service provision has not come about as part of government policy, but has developed within a policy vacuum (Duffield, 1994). The government has seen its development plans crumble, but has shown little interest in the emergency which has crept in to dominate the service agenda, as emergencies are seen as being NGO business. Both a cause and an effect of this policy vacuum is the conscious decision by many donors deliberately to promote a shift of responsibility for service provision from the government to the NGOs as part of their new policy agenda. Some donors are shifting their resources away from the government due to the ministries' lack of managerial capacity, while others promote the notion that services should be an arena for the private sector alone. There is also a reluctance to invest in capacity building in the turbulent post-conflict situation. Squeezed between donor pressures and a governmental vacuum, the NGOs are confronted by a massive humanitarian tragedy. In such circumstances many agencies feel a 'duty to scale-up' (Biggs and Neame, 1996), even if they harbour concerns about the sustainability and broader consequences of their actions.

Complex emergencies break down services, and service provision is complex even in stable contexts. Finding a way beyond the simplistic assumptions which shape the planning of support to service structures (such as health posts) demands uniting two realizations. The first is the realization that emergencies such as the one in Angola are complex, turbulent and ongoing occurrences. They are not just a matter of getting the relief inputs and the outside politics right. The other realization is that all service structures are about complex organizations which can only be supported through an understanding of their internal dynamics and how they deal with their environment. Fixing them is not just a matter of telling them what they should be doing and then giving them a package of training and materials. There are ample efforts to examine the complexities of emergencies and the behaviour of organizations, but few attempt to unite the lessons learned in these two disparate fields of study. The result is that simple clichés are put forth instead of considered analyses. Efforts waver between inappropriate relief projects and development programmes which reduce the capacity of local actors to adapt their activities to the turbulence, vulnerability and uncertainties of local reality. Awareness of complexity should not lead to calls for more complex planning. Rather, it means promoting effective decentralization. Aid to services in an emergency is about helping individuals with tremendous tasks at least to try to do a decent job. It is about helping them to feel they are at least partially addressing an overwhelming problem, and in so doing helping them attain a respected place in the community. It is about making space for local-level actors to search for synergy amid the ruins.

A currently popular concept to refer to the property needed for the evolution of governance and the meeting of welfare needs is 'social capital'. This is defined as 'features of social organisation, such as trust, norms and networks, that can improve the efficiency of society by facilitating coordinated actions' (Putnam, 1993, p. 167). At first glance, Angola does not appear to have high reserves of accumulated social capital. The lists of preconditions for development of social capital which Putnam and others present (democracy, trust, freedom of expression, stability, and so on) are depressingly absent. When I have looked for social capital in Angola, the properties I have found do not resemble Putnam's concept. His type of social capital is closely related to linear notions of development. For him, civil society is something which is steadily built up over time, implying a degree of stability and faith in the future which may not exist in weak and collapsed states where the arrangements are oriented toward day-to-day survival. Hirschman (1984) has proposed a different concept that fits better with what can be found in Angola. He correlates successful, but often ephemeral, collective action with the notion of 'social energy' which key actors 'mutated' in various changing organizational forms.[2]

An understanding of how nurses, extension agents and others choose to work and live (even the acknowledgement that they can choose at all) requires an awareness that subjective motivations shape their decision making processes. An illustration of this is provided in the case of Daniel (Case 1). One reason why this is not discussed in conflict situations is that political analysts are usually more interested in describing the environment of oppression and the structural limits to human agency. In decaying states the gross violations of human rights tend to overshadow the fact that totalitarian control has none the less usually been displaced. Terror does not necessarily lead to passivity. All local-level observers of the Angolan domestic economy note the inventiveness with which people (including civil servants) construct their livelihoods in the face of overwhelming adversity.

Case 1   Blood Donation, Photography and Latrines: A Red Cross Career

Daniel has been a Red Cross volunteer in Bie Province for 13 years. He started as an employee of the International Committee of the Red Cross (ICRC), travelling around the province, giving lectures about Red Cross history and sanitation. He also identified potential first aid volunteers and was active in recruiting blood donors.

During the 1980s the provincial Angola Red Cross (ARC) branch had a shop selling fish, primarily to blood donors. The supply of fish ceased in 1990, and a decision was made to turn the shop into a photo studio, which Daniel was appointed to manage. The studio was operated commercially, and produced identification cards for blood donors. During the siege of the city of Kuito (the provincial capital) the studio was bombed to rubble. A displaced family is now camping in the ruins.

Daniel was the leader of one of the underground refuges where people hid during the fighting. He organized food distributions and blood donations. He was appointed to this task due to his reputation as a community leader and a humanitarian. It was not a Red Cross position, and people did not see his role as being related to his work with the Red Cross. In his descriptions of how people survived during the war, he repeatedly mentions Red Cross volunteers, skills and values. The humanitarian imperative is overwhelmingly apparent, but the Red Cross's role is vague. People did what had to be done. The rest was not very relevant.

Currently Daniel survives on food-for-work payments he receives for managing a latrine construction programme for UNICEF. He sometimes rents photography equipment to continue his old profession. In the latrine programme he tries to involve Red Cross volunteers, but most of the work is done by food-for-work labourers. The youth and first aiders are not interested in digging latrine holes for very low wages ('That is the responsibility of the department of public works!').

Another reason why the survival strategies of local staff are not generally taken into account is concern over their abuse of power. It has been argued that the most profound underlying weakness in NGO operations is their inability to take into account how power manifests itself in local institutions (DeWaal, 1996; Duffield, 1996; Keen, 1994). Naïve and clumsy, NGOs are said to feed the forces of war and oppression due to their ignorance of the context, structures and channels into which their resources are absorbed. This criticism cannot be denied. The concern about power, however, often paints the local service staff as either simply part and parcel of the 'evil' power apparatus (as they sometimes are), or as victims of power (as they usually are). Such a structural view fails to explore their skills and capacities as survivors within a complex institutional structure. As brokers between the powerful forces and the communities, they have often found ways to deal with the violent chaos around them, skills which are essential to any relief or rehabilitation effort.

That is assuming they have stayed at their posts. Many (perhaps most) rural civil servants have long since given up. Even if prospects for peace are improving, one cannot assume that, just because the armies have pulled back and a clinic has been rebuilt, staff will show up to run it. Rebuilding hundreds of health posts is pointless if the nurses have given up nursing and are peddling tomatoes in the market. NGO and UN inputs such as training, medicines, household supplies, a bicycle, or a few months' salary may be the only means available to lure them back. Equally important is the presence of outsiders who see and acknowledge the importance of their work. Rehabilitation of services should be designed within an awareness of the decision making process by which these individuals choose whether or not to 'set up shop' in a highly threatening environment. Their commitment and creativity are the qualities which are going to be the basis for future rural service provision. There are very serious deficiencies in the ways that NGOs look for means to support the commitment and creativity of field personnel, as illustrated in Case 2. But these concerns should not overshadow the seemingly obvious fact that if staff are to find meaningful livelihoods in the rural areas they must first return to their posts. It is less important whether it is an NGO or the state which is providing the funds behind these individuals, than the fact that they are in the field in the first place. As Putnam (1993, p. 169) argues, social capital is a resource 'whose supply increases rather than decreases through use and which becomes depleted if *not* used'. Keeping some form of services going may be the way to preserve much of what is left of Angola's scanty reserves of social capital.

Case 2 Picking Up the Pieces

In the city of Kuito, in Bié Province, the Angolan Red Cross (ARC) is struggling to put in order what is left of its physical and human resources. Their office, looted and bombed during the conflict, has been replastered and the roof replaced. Furniture has been borrowed and locally constructed. Their bullet-riddled truck has been puttied and painted.

This office reconstruction has shown the volunteers that it is time to come back. Their city endured the most intensive siege of the war. During much of that period, the fighting was so fierce that the international NGOs could not operate. At that time the ARC sprang into life. First aiders, youth and other volunteers were at the forefront of relief efforts, distributing food, arranging blood transfusions and organizing sanitation in the refuges where the population hid from the fighting for months on end.

Afterwards the volunteers left the relief efforts. Their informal and ephemeral makeshift networks were replaced by the formal efficiency of the returning international agencies. The volunteers went back to struggling to re-establish their own lives, repairing their homes and finding a way to survive in the ruins of their city. Now, when a modicum of stability has been achieved, they are again starting to think about what the Red Cross should be doing. There are major differences, though. During the war they were helping their own community. Now it is a 'vulnerable group', the displaced in the camps on the edges of town. Before, the task was clear. Now they have to find a role which does not overlap with the many foreign agencies which arrived after the war, all of which have more material resources than they. For the volunteers, the emergency in their city has in some ways become more complex *after* the acute crisis; should they simply disappear now that the 'professionals' have returned?

Complex emergencies can inspire a pragmatic search for synergy at the local level. During the heat of the crisis inter-agency rivalries, egos, conflicting ideologies and competition for funds are often put aside to address the problem at hand. Hierarchies collapse (Lanzara, 1983). The debate over *who should do what* is put aside, as the important question becomes one of *who can do what.*

In Angola, this crisis mentality has in some fundamental respects carried over to the current rehabilitation phase. Local government sees the NGOs as being agencies which *can* do more than the civil service and Angolan NGOs. The international agencies also have the formal skills of logistics, reporting and dealing with donors that the ARC lacks. The natural course of action is therefore to establish a new hierarchy which hands over responsibilities to the strong international NGOs. The debate over *who should do what*, with respect to Angolan control over Angolan development, has only just begun.

HUMANITY AND SENSEMAKING

Exasperation is the emotion which overwhelms development planners in Angola. Their traditional goal of a Weberian ideal-type bureaucracy is so obviously impossible in the short and mid-term that despair takes over. A cloud of thinly veiled doubts about whether or not 'development' is on the agenda engulfs Luanda. If we abandon the hope that our projects will somehow 'cause' the emergence of a 'rational' bureaucracy, to what buoy do we tie our ship? Can humanitarian values provide us with an alternative? Is it possible to reverse the call for developmental relief, to think also about development efforts within an explicit framework of humanitarian concerns? Can humanitarian values bridge the objectives of relief and development, and if so, how do we describe and work within the ethical codes and moral judgements which these values suggest? The first item in the Code of Conduct for the International Red Cross, the Red Crescent Movement and NGOs in Disaster Relief declares that 'the humanitarian imperative comes first'. A problem with putting humanitarianism 'first', however, is that there is no clear definition for humanitarianism and it is sometimes used as a pejorative, to denote naïvety (Weiss and Minear, 1993). Isaac defines it in terms of altruism and solidarity, as 'a feeling of concern for and benevolence toward fellow human beings' (1993, p. 13). In current aid discourse, it is primarily associated with neutrality and impartiality (Walker, 1996).

Local and expatriate field personnel usually act within a combination of these interpretations. They construct their views of the situation and justify decisions based on overlapping but often different organizational and personal needs. Even though the Red Cross principles and mandate emphasize humanitarianism based on neutrality, local personnel cannot act within a pure notion of humanitarian neutrality simply because they do not have a choice about whether to stay or pull out if they find themselves contributing to the conflict. The current focus on this question of pure neutrality in the relief discourse potentially disempowers local humanitarians and their institutions by putting the humanitarian dilemma entirely in the expatriates' hands. Local staff have a humanitarian imperative too. It is different, however. If their perspective is added to the equation, this may turn the moral dilemma into a muddled dilemma. But to ignore their choices is to deny Angolan humanitarians one of the few means of self-determination they have left. For them the humanitarian imperative is primarily interpreted based on their image of their organization's role in the community, and the need to establish a trusting relationship with their clients. This means that, in a crisis, decisions put the alleviation of threats to survival before questions about the legitimacy of the state, before the sanctity of the market, and before the identification of sustainable solutions. It means that a concern for root causes can never be an excuse to ignore the net effects on dying people. The immediate survival crisis is given priority over broader economic and political crises.

This suggests that humanitarianism is a flexible and iterative process and not simply a clearly defined principle. Macrae (1996) refers to this socially constructed humanitarianism as the 'humanitarian impulse'. She restricts use of the term 'humanitarian imperative' to strict application of the rules and principles codified in humanitarian law. While this dichotomy is of some value in sorting out the muddle, the terminology carries some inappropriate connotations. 'Impulse' suggests a one-sided fleeting impetuosity, whereas this factor is rooted, at least potentially, in a complex and long-term relationship. Alternative labels for this imperative – impulse dichotomy might refer to the *ethical* imperative of humanitarianism (implying a code of conduct), and the *moral* imperative of humanitarianism (implying decisions based on individual values). Given the obvious and unavoidable lack of deep understanding of international humanitarian law (the ethical codes) at field level, these so-called impulses (the moral relations) are inevitably the most viable basis on which field personnel perceive the problems and dilemmas which confront them. Dissemination and training on ethical codes such as the Geneva Conventions are important ways to stimulate reflection on these questions, but such interventions should not be expected simply to instil a set of ethics among isolated nurses in the field. Moral impulses are the basis of their own cognitive imagery of their relationships and obligations to their clients and community. Once the projects have ended and the courses are a fading memory, the staff are once again left to their own devices. The balance tips from ethics to moral relationships. 'The crisis of ethics does not necessarily augur a crisis of morality' (Bauman, 1995, p. 42). We can undoubtedly restructure relief to make it more ethical, but the term 'developmental relief' calls for more emphasis on moral bonds.

Gut moral feelings about one's place in the scheme of things may naturally feed naïvety *vis-à-vis* the implications of one's actions for the causes of conflict. Malkki laments 'the idea of a universal, ahistorical humanity' (1996, p. 379) which she sees as dominating international humanitarian aid thinking. But it is from within the iterative processes by which street-level bureaucrats make sense of their social and organizational environments that new perspectives must emerge. If academic analysis is to be influential, it must be grounded in a far more nuanced understanding of the construction of practitioners' world-views. Malkki describes her own failure to find an opening in the administrative structures to apply her research on how refugees view their own situation. She berates the administrative staff for their refusal to listen to her presentations of the refugees' 'stories'. But she herself fails to look deeply into the organizational culture of the administrators (*their* stories) as it is here that the clues are to be found as to how the refugees' concepts may suggest to administrators new approaches for their work. Anthropologists such as Malkki frequently point out that refugees make sense of their current situation based on their historical experience of displacement. Individuals in organizations also make sense of their situation largely through a retrospective process (Weick, 1995). This emerges in stories because 'people think narratively' about their organization (ibid, p. 127). Outside of official meetings, practitioners (and even anthropologists) rarely argue directly about plans and structures. They make their points by telling each other stories ('When I was ...'), just as the refugees tell stories to an anthropologist whom they might want to bring into 'their' organization. This is particularly true in war situations, where complexity thwarts abstract rational explanation (Anderson, 1996). Bruner (1990) describes how the narrative process is used to handle the uncertainty which underlies moral dilemmas:

> Thus, while a culture must contain a set of norms, it must also contain a set of interpretative procedures for rendering departures from those norms meaningful in terms of established patterns of belief. It is narrative, and narrative interpretation upon which folk psychology depends for achieving this kind of meaning. (1990, p. 47)

If one is to understand how bureaucrats react to new information about clients' perspectives, one must first try to understand how stories have shaped the bureaucrats' view of their mission and relationships with their clients, and how little theoretical arguments and digestion of data have influenced their thinking (see Hulme, 1989). While the narrative process is gaining some respect in discussions of how organizations learn and address ambiguity in Northern contexts (Czarniawska, 1997), in the relief discourse, agencies are merely seen as ignorant about their clients, about international humanitarian law or about the politico-military situation. The solution is therefore to give them more information and to train them. Smothering them with information, however, is not the solution. Weick writes of this misconception:

> The important point is that retrospective sensemaking is an activity in which many possible meanings may need to be synthesized, because many different projects are under way ... The problem is that there are too many meanings, not too few. The problem faced by the sensemaker is one of equivocality, not one of uncertainty. The problem is confusion, not ignorance ... investigators who favor the metaphor of information processing often view sensemaking, as they do other problems, as a setting where people need more information. That is not what they need when they are overwhelmed by equivocality. Instead they need values, priorities and clarity about preferences to help them be clear about which projects matter. (1995, pp. 27–8)

Humanitarian values, as reflected in both informal stories and formal norms and procedures, are a touchstone by which most front-line staff and volunteers reflect on routines and priorities, and in turn consider their choice of action. It is important to bring this seemingly obvious basis for local decision making to the surface when addressing an issue which is otherwise generally perceived as being in the realm of international politics and humanitarian law. Recommendations for policy change usually prescribe new *formulations*. Mintzberg (1994) has pointed out that policy *formation*, the strategies which emerge as part of day-to-day practice, is a more accurate description of how sustainable change in organizations actually occurs. Particularly if one claims to believe in the principle of subsidiarity,[3] then the social construction of the humanitarian imperative cannot be written off as an example of the naïvety of field personnel. Subsidiarity implicitly suggests that their concerns must be the focal point of gently influencing emergent strategy. They should not be portrayed as the obstacle (Christoplos, 1996).

The motivations of field staff are, however, viewed as a problem in much of the literature on service institutions. Their rent seeking behaviour, where they only look to their own benefit, is described as leading them to working for the élite, or not working at all. The obvious answer is to constrain this rent seeking behaviour. Tendler and Freedheim lament that in our 'era of contempt for government' (1994, p. 1783) the emphasis has been on analyses of failed projects. In such dismal analyses field staff are presented as a source of failure. This inevitably brings about attempts to control their behaviour. Staff are no longer given leeway to do what they think is right, to listen to their clients and find solutions. Aid agencies are too worried about trying to avoid failure to allow people in the field the discretion to figure out how to succeed. This is despite the fact that in virtually all recent studies of service organizations the factor of discretion is highlighted as the key to developing quality services in turbulent environments.

This negative view of field personnel is even more pronounced in the relief discourse. An increasing awareness of the dangers of unprofessional and naïve relief agency practice has stimulated a growing concern with accountability. But this accountability is almost entirely framed as a problem of control. Anderson (1993) brings out the dangers of this control emphasis when she contrasts the trust which prevailed in post-World War II relief efforts in Europe with the single-minded focus on control in African and Asian relief operations of recent decades. She suggests that the readiness to build on trust is one of the central reasons for the success of developmental relief in the former and failure in the latter. Her research is one of the few pieces of empirical work which overcomes the prevailing negative bias and instead brings out how local dialogue helps people in the field to develop trust in a complex emergency (Anderson, 1996). Unfortunately, the implications of these findings are lost in the current calls for greater external control over the scramble of internationalized public welfare.

MORALS, MUDDLES AND MANAGEMENT

Field staff working in complex emergencies are increasingly confronted with moral dilemmas (Slim, 1997).[4] With *de facto* subsidiarity, they have assumed the moral dilemmas of those who must choose (Macrae, 1996), and they do so with the graphic and terrifying results of their decisions literally staring them in the face. An understanding of what constitutes a moral dilemma must start with attention to *mores*, meaning the guiding moral views of a group

(Donagan, 1996). Unpacking these *mores* is important to reveal the links between organizational culture and personal dilemmas in relief and rehabilitation practice. Bringing out the moral dilemmas is also a way to counter the idea that there is a simple rational institutional solution. Instead one must try to understand ambiguity, the alternative rationalities existing within a given agency which staff must reconcile in their work. Local and international NGO and UN staff in the field are unsure of themselves. They realize that the solutions that are bandied about at headquarters do not match the questions they face. They complain that in the capital there is the luxury of dealing with conflicting demands one at a time ('Our meeting to discuss that aspect is next week ...'). Even if moral dilemmas are identified, they can be deftly pigeonholed and ignored. At field level, project components and moral demands must somehow mesh in a working environment.

Much of the critique of relief and rehabilitation over the past decade can be summarized as a call to think developmentally in relief situations, and not to be blinded by immediate survival issues. This advice is valid and important, but at the same time the studies upon which the critique is based usually fail to take into account the nature of the humanitarian imperative at an operational level. This includes (1) the cruel choices which are required in following these recommendations, and (2) the tremendous uncertainty about what development might consist of in a turbulent environment. The limits to merely deciding to go out and implement developmental relief can be found in the fact that 'the technocratic belief that problems can be "thought through" is inappropriate for interventions in which knowledge is limited and uncertainty high' (Hulme, 1995, p. 226). The idea that we should first think things through and search for the developmental path that the relief operation should ideally take ignores the nature of organizational decision making in turbulent environments where adaptation and flexibility are essential for achievement. A more effective approach may be to delve into the question of rehabilitation, where the limits of both relief and development strategies are most glaringly apparent. Rehabilitation means that one need not and should not let go of the humanitarian imperative, as survival is still very tenuous, but that there is a clear need to make space for exploring the broader questions. In rehabilitation contexts a national Red Cross society can consider how far it is ready to go in addressing the root causes of an emergency without letting go of its humanitarian mandate and values. We have to accept that people may need both food aid and development assistance at the same time.

Strategic thinking is important, but it does not provide a sufficient handle for grappling with chaotic situations. Allowing for reflection on goals and duties is part of a shift away from faith in lock-step planning to a return to trust in competent management:

> When planning is placed amid continual adjustment to a changing world, it becomes hard to distinguish from any other method of decision. By making planning reasonable we render it inseparable from the techniques of decision it was designed to supplant ... Some call this adaptive planning; others call it muddling through. (Wildavsky, 1979, p. 128)

Muddling through may provide the space front-line staff need to listen to their clients, to consider the underlying nature of their problems, and to develop the trust required for moving forward together to formulate more appropriate strategies. Muddling through does not mean a *laissez-faire* attitude toward processes. It means a shift of focus from plan implementation to finding ways to build trust between field staff and clients. It means working within the structures by which service organizations make sense of their often bewildering environments. Wildavsky suggests starting with the muddles by constructing problem analyses based on the day-to-day routines, decisions and moral dilemmas of managers in the field. In the case at hand, this means keeping developmental goals firmly within a framework of humanitarian values, while providing space for finding a locally sensible mix of both.

During acute emergencies it is rare that outside assistance actually arrives in significant quantity (DeWaal, 1989; Schaanning, 1990; Walker, 1989). Public service institutions join with other local actors and react. Once the outsiders arrive the demand pressures on local institutions are reduced, as the better-resourced outside agencies take centre stage. Though frustration at this displacement of local institutions is justified, the horde of NGOs and donors showing up in a complex emergency can probably not be stopped (see Case 3 for an illustration of the actions of international NGOs). A more effective strategy may be to get some institutional back-up to local structures quickly, before they are trampled in the stampede of internationalized public welfare. The community trust, which was, it is hoped, developed by acting on earlier demand, can provide a basis for finding complementarity in a pluralistic environment. The starting point for this must be in acknowledging that these institutions exist, and that rehabilitation means that their resources of social capital must be used and strengthened.

Case 3 Whose Health Post is it? On the Fungibility of Social Capital

In 1992, when working for the International Federation of Red Cross and Red Crescent Societies (IFRC), I visited a nutritional rehabilitation centre/health post in Bailundo, Huambo Province. The head nurse, who was also the ARC municipal representative, eagerly told me about his history of working with the ARC, and how his post had repeatedly grown and shrunk over the years, at times becoming a major feeding centre with expatriate ICRC nurses, at other times hardly more than a first aid station. He was excited about the possibility that the IFRC might help him develop a real ARC branch in the town, and he offered a number of suggestions about how to proceed on environmental health issues. He was also happy to see that the IFRC might come to help, since he sorely missed contact with his own organization, the ARC, and felt that we could help him work more actively within the ARC. This was becoming particularly acute, as the ICRC had recently stopped funding his centre, and *Médecins sans Frontières* (MSF) had taken over responsibility. This had been done without any consultation with him. He felt very uncomfortable with the MSF requests to fly their agency flag.

When I brought up the topic of the Bailundo ARC Centre with the ICRC, they scoffed. As far as they were concerned, it was an ICRC organization which had now become an MSF organization. The proof of ARC's non-involvement was that ARC provincial and national staff had never even visited the place. The 'fantasies' of the head nurse were unimportant. He had been their employee, and now he worked for MSF; being an ARC municipal representative was unimportant.

When I brought up the issue with MSF, they explained that they were providing food, medicines, training and supervision. Beyond that, they were not really concerned with the long-term ownership of the centre. The business about the flags was tricky though. Maybe Luanda should decide about that ...

CONCLUSION

In a decaying state, civil society is seen as the guarantor of public welfare. Even if the ministry is crumbling, we can hope that the robustness of the social fabric can keep initiatives going. The concept of civil society in much of the development discourse rests largely on the assumption that stability can be established at the local level. This hope is in contrast with other observations that the strength of civil society lies in dynamic adhocracy (Tendler, 1993; Lanzara, 1983; Christoplos, 1996), the ability temporarily to pull together human and material resources in ephemeral organizations when confronting crisis. Social capital may emerge in unexpected places, mobilized through the ever-changing activities of entrepreneurial individuals endowed with social energy (Hirschman, 1984). Analysis of these two normative concepts of equilibrium and adhocracy requires more empirical study. These two approaches are certainly not mutually exclusive, but we perhaps need to pair a certain humility with our normativity. It may be possible to foster sustainable, trusting and productive relationships even if the linear development assumptions which usually accompany sustainability and institutional development are put on the back burner. Minter (1996, p. 113) borrows an Angolan concept in the exploration of these ephemeral forms of civil society:

> In Angola, the term *esquema* refers to the ingenious, creative and often devious 'schemes' individuals are forced to find to survive and, in the case of a few, to enrich themselves. In order for the peace process to succeed, both Angolans and their friends, official and non-official, will have to discover large- and small-scale *esquemas* for peace.

All organizations, including a Red Cross branch or a village health post, are 'socially constructed – and reconstructed – in everyday actions' (Czarniawska-Joerges, 1992, p. 34). An understanding of what rehabilitation may mean demands efforts to understand these processes. Humanitarianism and neutrality are social constructions of everyday life in a situation of everyday inhumanity. The fall of modernity has led many to conclude that morality has now become privatized (Bauman, 1991; 1995). The horrors of contemporary African warfare stem from the instrumental rationality behind the privatized immorality of the warlords. Even though this private immorality is terrifying, it is not an excuse to ignore the perspectives of those who have their morals intact. One way to do this is to realize that each health post or Red Cross branch is not a mere project implementation unit. It is a group of moral individuals with an *esquema* for peace. It is these sorts of individuals, and the institutions in which they run their *esquemas*, that will lead Angola out of its present mess and towards more effective governance, if anyone can do it.

NOTES

1. This chapter was prepared based on the author's research and experience as a practitioner working with the Angola Red Cross and the International Federation of Red Cross and Red Crescent Societies. Their support and hospitality are gratefully acknowledged. The views presented here are those of the author alone, and do not reflect the positions of the Angola Red Cross or the International Federation of Red Cross and Red Crescent Societies.
2. Hyden (1994) makes a similar distinction when he refers to fixed and moveable social capital assets.
3. Subsidiarity has been defined as the objective 'that decisions and actions should be taken as near to the people they impinge upon as possible' (Walker, 1996).
4. It may be argued, with some justification, that I am stretching the concept of moral dilemma in this chapter, since the actors in question may be either unaware or unconcerned about the negative impacts of relief on local institutions (from the relief side), or of the increase in human suffering from the triage which accompanies the delinking of aid from humanitarian concerns (from the development side). I suggest that this should be presented as a moral dilemma for two reasons: (1) in my discussions in the field, and in the literature, it is clear that awareness and concerns are increasing regarding the moral implications of these trade-offs, and (2) the conclusions of this report emphasize the need for critical reflection on practice. If this is acted upon, the moral dilemma should automatically follow.

REFERENCES

Aguilar, R. and Stenman, A. (1995), *Angola 1995: Let's Try Again*, Macroeconomic Studies, No. 63, Stockholm: SIDA.

Aguilar, R. and Stenman, A. (1996), *Angola 1996: Hyper-Inflation, Confusion and Political Crisis*, Macroeconomic Report, No. 11, Stockholm: SIDA.

Anderson, Mary B. (1993), 'Development and the prevention of humanitarian emergencies', in Thomas G. Weiss and Larry Minear (eds), *Humanitarianism Across Borders: Sustaining Civilians in Times of War*, Boulder, CO: Lynne Rienner.

Anderson, Mary B. (1996), *Do No Harm: Supporting Local Capacities for Peace Through Aid*, Cambridge: Collaborative for Development Action.

Bauman, Zygmunt (1991), *Modernity and Ambivalence*, Cambridge: Polity Press.

Bauman, Zygmunt (1995), *Life in Fragments: Essays in Postmodern Morality*, Oxford: Blackwell.

Biggs, Stephen and Neame, Arthur (1996), 'Negotiating room for manoeuvre: reflections concerning NGO autonomy and accountability within the new policy', in Michael Edwards and David Hulme (eds), *Non-Governmental Organisations – Performance and Accountability: Beyond the Magic Bullet*, London: Earthscan, pp. 31–40.

Bruner, Jerome (1990), *Acts of Meaning*, Cambridge, MA: Harvard University Press.

Christoplos, Ian (1996), 'Disequilibrium in ecosystems – disequilibrium in agricultural services: what role for the gardeners of the gardening state?', in Anders Hjort-af-Ornäs (ed.), *Approaching Nature from Local Communities: Security Perceived and Achieved*, Linköping: EPOS.

Czarniawska-Joerges, Barbara (1992), *Exploring Complex Organisations: A Cultural Perspective*, London: Sage.

Czarniawska, Barbara (1997), *Narrating the Organization*, Chicago: University of Chicago Press.

DeWaal, Alex (1989), *Famine that Kills*, Oxford: Clarendon Press.

DeWaal, Alex (1996), 'Contemporary warfare in Africa: changing context, changing strategies', *IDS Bulletin*, **27** (3), 6–16.

Donagan, Alan (1996), 'Moral dilemmas, genuine and spurious: a comparative anatomy', in H.E. Mason (ed.), *Moral Dilemmas and Moral Theory*, New York: Oxford University Press.

Duffield, Mark (1994), 'Complex political emergencies: with reference to Angola and Bosnia, an exploratory report for Unicef', School of Public Policy, University of Birmingham.

Duffield, Mark (1996), 'The symphony of the damned: racial discourse, complex political emergencies and humanitarian aid', *Disasters*, **20** (3), 173–93.

Gould, Jeremy (1996), 'Beyond negotiation: challenges of participatory projects for the anthropology of development', IDS Working Papers No. 9/96, Helsinki, University of Helsinki.

Hirschman, Albert O. (1984), *Getting Ahead Collectively: Grassroots Experiences in Latin America*, New York: Pergamon Press.

Hulme, David (1989), 'Learning and not learning from experience in rural project planning', *Public Administration and Development*, **9** (1), 1–16.

Hulme, David (1995), 'Projects, politics and professionals: alternative approaches for project identification and project planning', *Agricultural Systems*, **47** (2).

Hydén, Göran (1994), 'The role of social capital in African development: illustrations from Tanzania', in Henrik Secher Marcussen (ed.), *Improved Natural Resource*

Management: The Role of the State versus that of the Local Community, Occasional Paper 12, International Development Studies, Roskilde, Roskilde University.

Isaac, Ephraim (1993), 'Humanitarianism across religions and cultures', in Thomas G. Weiss and Larry Minear (eds), *Humanitarianism Across Borders: Sustaining Civilians in Times of War*, Boulder, CO: Lynne Rienner.

Keen, David (1994), *The Benefits of Famine: A Political Economy of Famine and Relief in Southwestern Sudan, 1983–1989*, Princeton: Princeton University Press.

Lanzara, Giovan Francesco (1983), 'Ephemeral organizations in extreme environments: emergence, strategy, extinction', *Journal of Management Studies*, **20** (1), 71–95.

Macrae, Joanna (1996), 'The origins of unease: setting the context of current ethical debate', Background Paper No. 1, Forum on Ethics in Humanitarian Aid, 9–10 December 1996, Dublin.

Malkki, Liisa (1996), 'Speechless emissaries: refugees, humanitarianism, and dehistoricization', *Cultural Anthropology*, **11** (3), 377–404.

Minter, Bill (1996), 'From war to peace in Angola: increasing chances of success', *Review of African Political Economy*, **23** (6–7), 111–18.

Mintzberg, Henry (1994), *The Rise and Fall of Strategic Planning*, New York: Prentice Hall.

Putnam, Robert D. (1993), *Making Democracy Work: Civic Traditions in Modern Italy*, Princeton: Princeton University Press.

Schaanning, Reidar (1990), *Study on Red Cross Disaster Preparedness in Southern Africa 1979–1989*, Geneva: League of Red Cross and Red Crescent Societies.

Slim, Hugo (1997), *Doing the Right Thing: Relief Agencies, Moral Dilemmas and Moral Responsibility in Political Emergencies and War*, Studies on Emergencies and Disaster Relief No. 6, Uppsala: Nordic Africa Institute.

Sveriges Ambassad i Angola (1996), 'Halvårsrapport Angola', Avdelningen för Östra och Västra Afrika, Stockholm: SIDA.

Tendler, Judith (1993), *New Lessons from Old Projects: The Workings of Rural Development in Northeast Brazil*, World Bank Operations Evaluation Study, Washington, DC: World Bank.

Tendler, Judith and Freedheim, Sarah (1994), 'Trust in a rent-seeking world: health and government transformed in Northeast Brazil', *World Development*, **22** (12), 1771–92.

UNICEF (1996), 'Angola: Economic Indicators Data Sheet', Luanda: UNICEF.

Walker, Peter (1989), *Famine Early Warning Systems: Victims and Destitution*, London: Earthscan.

Walker, Peter (1996), 'Chaos and caring: humanitarian aid amidst disintegrating states', *Journal of Humanitarian Assistance*, posted 13 October 1996.

Weick, Karl, E. (1995), *Sensemaking in Organizations*, London: Sage.

Weiss, Thomas G., and Minear, Larry (eds) (1993), *Humanitarianism Across Borders: Sustaining Civilians in Times of War*, Boulder, CO: Lynne Rienner.

Wildavsky, Aaron (1979), *The Art and Craft of Policy Analysis*, London: Macmillan.

16. Conclusions: looking beyond the new public management

Charles Polidano, David Hulme and Martin Minogue

Reformers in government often find that the journey from concept to practice, idea to action, covers treacherous ground. The relationship between intent and outcome can be extremely complex, ambiguous, and difficult to unravel. This may explain why researchers on governance can become preoccupied with conceptual issues in isolation from how those concepts translate, or fail to translate, into reality.

Nowhere is this more evident than in the debate about the new public management (or, in its universally known abbreviation, NPM). Proponents and critics alike tend to discuss the conceptual merits and demerits of the new public management without considering whether or to what extent reform programmes, particularly in developing countries, fit the mould. Yet as Minogue shows (Chapter 2, this volume), the implementation of new public management reforms in developing countries has been patchy at best – even where there has been a formal commitment to such reforms.

Issues of governance, including public management reform, need to be considered within a more balanced perspective. Almost two decades on, it is necessary to reassess the impact of NPM on public administration in both developed and developing countries; and to reconsider the conceptual model on the basis of a balanced critique of practice. The contributors to this volume have scrutinized both concept and practice. Following from the wealth of material which they have presented, we shall undertake a preliminary survey of the ground that would need to be covered by such a reassessment, signposting directions for other researchers to follow. We shall review the evidence for the success or otherwise of the new public management in developed countries; we shall look at the issue of its applicability to developing countries; and we shall also look at whether there are alternative approaches to improving the quality of governance. To begin with, however, we must address the issue of what makes a reform successful.

MEASURING SUCCESS: OUTPUTS VERSUS OUTCOMES

The keystone of the new public management arch is surely the definition of measurable standards of performance. Yet deciding whether NPM reforms themselves have been successful is a fraught process. What indicators can be used to judge the success or failure of new public management reform, or any administrative reform for that matter?

The practitioner charged with carrying out reform commonly takes implementation itself as the primary indicator of success. More detached observers would find this perspective too narrow. They would prefer to concentrate on what happens after implementation: whether the changes actually deliver on their promise of improved efficiency, effectiveness, responsiveness, or service delivery. Reformers should not be surprised at this, for it is a distinction which the new public management itself – at any rate, its New Zealand version – has fostered: that between *outputs* (measures to be implemented) and *outcomes* (end results). Kiggundu (Chapter 9, this volume) further elaborates on this distinction in his assessment of the success of reform.

The acid test of any administrative reform programme, NPM or otherwise, is the achievement of its promised outcomes. Yet the narrower perspective, the one which focuses on the implementation of outputs, should not be dismissed lightly. The practitioner's concern with implementation as a measure of success in its own right stems from the simple fact that most change initiatives fail at this stage. As Caiden (1991, p. 152) puts it, 'It appears that conception is easier than action and successful action is exceptional ... most reforms are blocked altogether or compromised into pale images. Implementation is the Achilles' heel of administrative reform.' For all the technocratic language in which reform is garbed, it is a highly political and very risky process.

The apparent ease with which reforms were pushed through in the heartland of the new public management – Britain, Australia and New Zealand – may lead some observers to lose sight of the inherent difficulty of bringing about change and to expect that like reforms should be implemented with similar ease elsewhere. But there was an exceptionally high degree of political backing for reform in these countries during the 1980s and 1990s. Moreover, reformers adopted innovative tactical approaches that helped minimize resistance (Polidano, 1995).

One need only look at the Public Service 2000 initiative in Canada to see how easily things can go wrong under more normal circumstances. Public Service 2000 contained many NPM elements; yet it ran out of steam in midcourse and was overtaken by other political developments (Caiden et al., 1995). The hurdles of implementation will be even higher in developing countries with their insecure governments, weak central policy institutions, and shortages of qualified staff. Discussing the success of reform in terms of outcomes is a luxury largely unavailable outside the heartland of the new public management.

NPM IN THE INDUSTRIALIZED WORLD: HAS IT DELIVERED?

Even in Britain, Australia and New Zealand, after years of successful reform, much of the evidence on outcomes remains anecdotal and difficult to verify. Hard evidence is still limited, and much of what there is remains subject to contestation. A good review is provided by Walsh (1995). He shows, for example, that the contracting out of public services to private operators typically yields savings of between 20 and 30 per cent in direct costs; but it is unclear whether these savings are sustained in the long run, or whether they apply to complex functions such as legal support as well as basic functions such as housekeeping or cleaning. In at least some cases the savings come directly out of the wages of those employed to provide the services. Transaction costs often go unreported but they can be huge, particularly in the case of major reorganizations such as the creation of agencies or the introduction of internal markets.

In the UK, some local authority and agency staff argue that the benefits of contracting out depend on the state of the economy. When the economy is weak, surplus private sector capacity leads to fierce competition and a drop in quoted charges. When the economy expands, the private sector places high premiums on its bids. In effect, the savings made during economic downturns are offset by the premiums paid during an upswing.

The British government claims that executive agencies have improved their productivity by an average of 3 per cent a year (Mountfield, 1997). Agencies and internal markets also appear to have led to a greater emphasis on service quality, particularly under the impetus of the Citizen's Charter initiative. Here again, however, it is not clear how the figures have been calculated; nor is it always easy to tell to what extent the 'greater emphasis on service quality' has actually led to tangible improvements.

On the other hand, those responsible for reform would complain that the goalposts are constantly moving. If cost savings are made, critics reply that the money is merely spent elsewhere; if performance targets are met, critics say that the targets de-emphasize intangible quality aspects (for instance, Walsh, 1995, pp. 232, 243). These criticisms may well be valid. But we must not confuse the issue of whether genuine results have been achieved with that of whether those results go far enough.

The debate is still in its early days, and it bears all the hallmarks. There remains too deep a divide between the proponents and the critics of NPM.

Some critics continue to deny any merit whatsoever in the reforms; they are still reacting to Osborne and Gaebler's equally one-sided *Reinventing Government* (1992) six years after it was published. Because of this it is too early for anything approaching a definitive assessment of the new public management in Britain, Australia and New Zealand, let alone more recent reformers.

To some extent, however, it will always be difficult to draw definite conclusions about the success of the new public management on the basis of observed outcomes. Where end results disappoint, is this due to defective outputs – that is, flawed reforms – or to intervening variables beyond the control of reformers?

Take, for instance, a letter which Peter Lilley, then British Secretary of State for Social Security, wrote to the Treasury in November 1995 (it was later leaked to the press). Complaining about the proposed budgetary settlement for his department, Lilley said that 'The impact on operations will be devastating. Quite apart from the fall-out as the service becomes more chaotic, I am convinced ... that we would be cutting off our noses to spite our faces' (quoted in Gray and Jenkins, 1997, p. 197). Gray and Jenkins say that the severe financial squeeze on central departments in the mid-1990s brought about growing problems of service delivery in the social security agencies, among others. In other words, budget constraints got in the way of adherence to service standards under the Citizen's Charter. Should we conclude from this that the Charter initiative is flawed and deserves to be discarded?

This much can be said about the success of reform in the heartland of the new public management. Many of the reforms, particularly those concerning the core civil service, have had all-party support (Aucoin, 1995, pp. 79–80). In New Zealand, reform did not flag after a change of government in 1990. In Britain, the Labour government elected in May 1997 has gone along with most of the changes introduced by its predecessor; even its intended reorganization of the National Health Service amounts to a modification rather than, as proclaimed, the abolition of the internal market (*The Economist*, 13 December 1997). New governments appear, so far, to have found it worthwhile to proceed with the NPM reforms instituted by their predecessors.

The Limits to Reform: Organizational Fragmentation

The experience of reform in the heartland of NPM throws up another issue for our attention: the limits of the new public management. How far can such reforms be taken? New Zealand and Britain, the countries which have run furthest with the baton, are the most instructive in this regard. We can look at three particular areas: the proliferation of single-mission agencies; the applicability of contracting; and the continuing salience of inputs as a tool of bureaucratic accountability.

In Britain and New Zealand, reforms have led to the proliferation of government organizations. Next steps agencies in the UK carry out discrete administrative functions which were formerly subsumed within large departments. The equivalent of agencies in New Zealand are known as state-owned enterprises (SOEs): unlike British agencies, they are no longer considered part of the civil service. But in addition to creating SOEs, New Zealand broke up its remaining government departments into smaller, more focused organizations. This was done not simply as a by-product of management decentralization, but in the express belief that fewer organizational objectives make for tighter accountability and better performance.

An issue this has thrown up is the risk of a loss of what Boston et al. (1996, p. 12) call 'strategic coherence': the ability to take coordinated, comprehensive action to deal with the complex problems of government. In 1990, New Zealand's newly elected prime minister expressed just such a concern with regard to what he called 'little islands' in public service, even though he broadly endorsed the previous government's management reforms (Aucoin, 1995, p. 195). And it should be noted that breaking up big organizations has not been on everybody's new public management menu. On the contrary, a concern with high-level strategic coherence in Canada and Australia led to departmental mergers and a reduction in the size of the Cabinet. Canada's experiments with 'special operating agencies' have been strictly limited (Aucoin, 1995).

There is a trade-off here between opposing principles: strategic coherence versus focused objectives; breadth of vision versus manageable spans of control. There is no ideal choice among these irreconcilables – only awkward compromises that fail to dispel a sense of restless dissatisfaction. That perpetual dissatisfaction leads to frequent shifts in one direction, then another. Public management reform has simply incorporated this process. We should by no means expect that the optimal organizational size has now been found and the pendulum has stopped swinging.

The Limits to Reform: Contracting

A newer concern emerging from public management reform is the applicability of contracting. Contracting has been applied in various ways: direct contracting out of public functions to private firms; internal markets and purchaser–provider relationships; and managing the performance of agency or departmental chief executives.

There are many questions still to be resolved with regard to the use of contracts, and some of them have particular relevance to issues of political accountability and governance. One is the extent to which such mechanisms can play a part in regulating the relationship between ministers and chief executives when policy priorities are shifting rapidly and ministers them-selves are frequently reshuffled between positions. The Derek Lewis case in the UK – in which the head of the prison service, an agency, lost his job following two high-profile prison breakouts notwithstanding that overall es-capes had declined sharply – raised fundamental questions about the viability of the model, though this case needs very careful interpretation (Polidano, 1997). Much more time must pass before this issue is resolved and we gain a clearer sense of the applicability of contracting at this level in government.

The question of the applicability of contracting arises in other areas. Take internal markets, for instance. A situation where one public organization depends on the services of another to fulfil its mission seems, on the face of it, ideal for regulation by inter-organizational contracting. But to draw up contract specifications and enforce them, the purchasing organization must develop some expertise in the provider's field of operations. A lack of such capacity could well be the reason why the purchaser procured services from the provider to begin with, and developing it may require too great a diver-sion of resources.

How would contracting work in the absence of such capacity? Mackintosh (Chapter 5, this volume) offers us a glimpse of the answer: contracting may remain a formalistic overlay on relationships that continue to be based on informal give and take. There is some similarity here with the situation in Ghana's Ministry of Health as described by Larbi (Chapter 11, also in this volume).

Another glimpse of the limits to contracting emerges from the provision of policy advice to ministers in New Zealand. The output–outcomes model of accountability requires ministers to specify the departmental outputs neces-sary to attain their desired policy outcomes, and to contract with departmen-tal chief executives for the provision of those outputs. For the sake of completeness it was decided to bring departmental policy advice to ministers within the framework of the output contracts. But the difficulty in predicting policy work is such that departmental policy outputs have been specified in a very general manner (Boston et al., 1996). This raises questions about the value of contracting for policy advice and the contribution that it makes to departmental accountability. It may well be that the contractual model has over-reached itself here. A more traditional approach to accountability may have more to offer in this particular area than a pseudo-contract.

The Limits to Reform: the Continuing Salience of Inputs

Finally, there is the question of the continuing political salience of inputs. In the core NPM reformers, centralized controls on inputs (that is, rules govern-ing the management of departmental resources) gradually developed over the hundred years up to the 1970s. This was a part of the bureaucratization of government – indeed, its defining feature. Until central controls were swept away by the reforms of the 1980s, a mainspring for their development was the recurring tendency for aspects of the management of public resources to generate public and political concern. Governments had to respond by setting out new rules for managers to follow.

Have the reforms laid this political dynamic to rest, or will it reassert itself in time? In New Zealand, for instance, responsibility for staffing and classification – including collective bargaining and pay settlements – has been delegated to departmental chief executives. Chief executives can award pay increases if they have money to spare in their budgets. Does this mean that the government has relinquished any concern for the size of the public sector wage bill? Or that it can manage pay awards at a distance simply by holding down departmental budgets?

It is too early to tell whether decentralized pay bargaining will prove sustainable in the long run. Elsewhere, however, there is a tendency for management to be seen as little more than a front for the government during pay negotiations in publicly financed organizations. In British universities, it is understood all around that staff pressure for higher pay is really directed against the government; the universities are happy to go along with this, notwithstanding their supposed autonomy, to gain added leverage in prising more money out of the Treasury. It is difficult to imagine this changing, even if the British government were to refrain from considering public sector pay settlements as a component of overall budgetary management.

More generally, there are indications that pushing management authority downward will not quite succeed in taking input-related issues out of the public eye. In Australia, says Shergold (1997, p. 303), there is still an 'underlying tension between the accountability standards of traditional public administration and contemporary public management'. Highly paid senior appointments, lavishly furnished ambassadorial residences, official travel junkets: these are bread-and-butter issues to which the public relates much more readily than all the talk of outputs, targets and efficiency dividends. The media would readily pick up any such issues that emerge. The British government, for instance, has had to prohibit civil servants from claiming 'air miles' for official travel following negative press coverage of this practice (McCourt, 1997, p. 29). This may be a nice perk for private sector executives, but not one that the public is prepared to see transferred to the public sector.

NPM IN THE DEVELOPING WORLD: STILL FALLING AT THE FIRST HURDLES

If examples of successfully implemented reforms outside the heartland of NPM are few and far between, they are even fewer and further between in developing countries. The contributions by Kiggundu and Larbi in this volume detail some of the difficulties involved. Reforms fail for numerous reasons: they may fall foul of vested interests, bureaucratic or political; they may be ambitious beyond the capacity of government to coordinate or implement; they may be no more than formalistic exercises in window-dressing in the first place; or they may be the brainchild of an overseas development agency, with local decision makers going along solely to avoid denying their country aid money. Caiden (1991) points to the unpalatable but inescapable paradox that reform initiatives must be at their most restrained and unambitious in precisely those countries where the need for change is greatest.

Administrative reform initiatives in developing countries are proceeding apace, as ever. Will these efforts prove more successful than previous ones? The signs are very mixed at best. McCourt (Chapter 10, this volume) offers evidence that retrenchment initiatives – however crudely designed and applied – have had some success in reducing staff numbers, though not necessarily costs. But reforms have made considerably less headway when they sought to encompass organizational and procedural change. This is well illustrated by the World Bank's costly efforts to reform agricultural extension (Turner and Hulme, 1997, pp. 110–12).

On the basis of past and present performance, it is not too pessimistic to imagine that in ten years' time current reform initiatives in many developing countries will resemble a landscape dotted with ruined edifices and abandoned skeletal structures. Researchers surveying the terrain may well conclude that the new public management was a failure: simply the latest in a long line of managerial fads that have had their day. Or they may conclude, as Common suggests in Chapter 4 of this book, that NPM reforms are an example of inappropriate policy transfer.

Is the New Public Management Appropriate for Developing Countries?

The question of the 'appropriateness' of the new public management in developing countries is a complex one. Both Minogue and Common in this volume survey some of the viewpoints that have been put forward on this issue. There is a school of thought which argues that Third World governments suffer not from an excess of bureaucracy, as advocates of the new public management might claim, but an *insufficiency* (Holmes, 1992; Evans,

1995). To draw an analogy with British administrative history, developing country governments are at the Northcote–Trevelyan rather than the 'next steps' stage of development. They still have to develop effective central control systems to restrain abuses of office and rationalize inchoate management structures, as Britain began to do in the late nineteenth century.

Talk of delegation is thus premature, according to this school of thought. Giving corrupt officials greater managerial discretion would merely offer them more opportunity for corruption. Weak control systems even affect contracting out and privatization: there is ample evidence from Pakistan, Sri Lanka and Russia, among others, that the processes surrounding the sale of state-owned enterprises are fundamentally different than those which are assumed to operate.

There is more than a little validity in this 'underdevelopment of bureaucracy' thesis. At the same time, it can be misleading. The typical problem of developing country administrations is not an absence of bureaucratic rules and regulations governing line management. Central controls are there aplenty, as line managers may attest, with all the consequences: multiple accountabilities, attenuated responsibility for operations, preoccupation with rules rather than results, delays. Recruitment processes lasting a year or more are by no means unknown. Shergold's reference to a 'culture of learned helplessness' (1997, p. 302) would be particularly apt in developing countries.

The true problem is that abuses of office continue to occur and management structures remain inchoate *in spite of* the rules and regulations. Developing countries incur the disadvantages of central controls in full force, yet they seem to gain few of the advantages. The well-meaning managers find themselves bound hand and foot. The ill-intentioned find their way round the regulations one way or another. The missing ingredients are not formal rules and regulations, but *norms of conduct*: bureaucracy in the classic Weberian rather than the everyday sense.

One person brought in to assess such a situation may call for the strengthening of central controls; another may call for a reduction. There is logic in both responses, contradictory though they are. This is precisely why the 'underdevelopment of bureaucracy' thesis can coexist alongside calls for the deregulation of management.

Agencification and Organizational Fragmentation

With this in mind, we can take another look at the question of management decentralization and 'agencification' or 'corporatization' in developing countries. We do not know to what extent this is really going on; but to the extent that it is, it is less of a new trend than might be supposed. Developing countries have been converting government departments into parastatals for decades. The difference is that whereas the old logic was to corporatize commercial functions, the new public management philosophy has legitimized the extension of this approach to non-commercial functions within the public service (while arguing that the commercial functions should be privatized).

The key word is *legitimized*. Notwithstanding Ghana's example (see Larbi, Chapter 11), it is arguable that corporatization in developing countries is happening less to improve managerial performance – as with British agencies or SOEs in New Zealand – than simply to allow a particular activity to carry on. This applies especially in the case of activities requiring highly qualified staff. In many countries, pay differentials between the civil service and the private sector have grown so great that setting up 'authorities' or other quangos able to set their own salary rates independently of the civil service is the only way to recruit and retain skilled staff. Corporatization is not a question of efficiency but effectiveness, in the most basic sense of remaining operationally viable. As evidence, few corporatizations are accompanied by efforts at performance measurement and target setting.

A partial, more surreptitious form of agencification occurs when public officials seconded to donor-financed projects are paid top-up allowances (sometimes amounting to more than their basic salary) out of project funds. This is another way to escape the constraints of the civil service pay structure. It can cause particular strains and stresses within the civil service (Wuyts, 1996). It can also lead to a misallocation of resources in that the best-qualified staff could end up managing donor-financed projects rather than, say, advising on economic policy in the Ministry of Finance – an area where their skills may be needed more (Cohen and Wheeler, 1997).

In a developing country context, where the number of specialists in a given field is limited and many of them may be employed in the public sector, corporatization has some very tangible disadvantages. Public bodies may end up competing for qualified staff not with the private sector but with each other. Capacity building in one part of the public sector becomes capacity demolishing in another as public bodies begin poaching staff from one another (Hirschmann, 1993). Intra-public-sector competition could also bid up salaries for a given specialization throughout the economy as a whole, quite unnecessarily, turning the private sector into a market follower rather than the market leader and making it harder for the civil service to catch up.

As in industrialized countries, organizational fragmentation in the public sector can bring about a loss of strategic coherence. Developing a capacity for coordinated policy making and implementation at the centre of government is already difficult enough in many Third World countries. Breaking the public sector up into 'little islands' may only make the problems even more insuperable. Uganda, like Canada and Australia, opted for consolidation in

1991 by reducing the number of ministries from 38 to 21 (Wangoto, 1995). In Zambia there is an aspiration to do the same, but the political difficulties are seen as too great (Borins, 1994, p. 19).

The obvious answer to all this is to raise civil service salary rates across the board to the point where they become competitive. That way, organizational fragmentation with its attendant problems of coordination and the poaching of staff would no longer be necessary. But the equally obvious rejoinder is that the money simply isn't available. And there is more. For all the drawbacks of corporatization, evidence is beginning to emerge that managerial autonomy is a factor distinguishing better-run from worse-run public organizations in developing countries (Grindle, 1997).

We are not yet sure how important this factor is in bringing about better performance (Grindle, 1997), or even whether it is better management that makes autonomy possible in the first place (Islam, 1993). Nor do we know whether performance improvements are simply due to the extra resources that are typically poured into newly corporatized bodies (Hirschmann, 1993). But in so far as the link is genuine, it places developing countries in a difficult dilemma. On the one hand, management decentralization is inextricably linked with the Balkanization of the public sector, and it also bears risks of greater corruption and abuse of office; on the other hand, it may be the only hope of improving the performance of sluggish public organizations.

More research is needed on the link between management autonomy and organizational performance in developing countries. There is some anecdotal evidence that the establishment of national revenue authorities in a few countries, including Tanzania and Uganda, has led to an improvement in tax collection. On the other hand, the Kenyan revenue authority appears to have had its teeth drawn by top political authorities (*The Economist*, 13 August 1997). But there is little published evidence as yet: here is an opportunity for some valuable research indeed.

More research is also needed on the link between management autonomy and corruption. The connection is by no means straightforward. Jeremy Pope of Transparency International argues that a high level of centralization is just as likely to generate corruption – as people seek to avoid delays and get around decision making bottlenecks – as a situation where there are few rules and decision makers have plenty of discretion (Pope, 1995). Pope also advocates the 'enclave' approach as a manageable way to reduce corruption: that is, corporatizing an organization, giving its staff higher pay, and concentrating reform efforts on it.

All this brings us back to the question of whether the new public management is appropriate to developing countries. There are valid arguments either way. The issue can be settled conclusively only on the basis of the *outcomes* emerging from successfully implemented reforms. Have NPM reforms in developing countries brought about efficiency gains, as their proponents hoped? Or have they simply led to more corruption and abuse of managerial discretion, as the critics feared? Is it possible to identify and set off the costs and benefits of particular reforms?

The poor record of reform initiatives to date means that we have next to no hard information on reform outcomes in developing countries. Current evidence points only to difficulties of implementation. And the failure, if such it is, of NPM reforms, if such they are, cannot be seen in isolation. As we have already indicated, it is merely a continuation of the pre-NPM record: over-preoccupation with labels can lead one astray. If we are to conclude retrospectively that the new public management is a case of inappropriate policy transfer on the basis of its record of implementation, then we may as well conclude the same about any kind of administrative reform in developing countries.

NPM AND GOVERNANCE: ALTERNATIVE ROUTES TO REFORM

Over-preoccupation with labels can also make us forget that there is more to public sector reform than the new public management/old public administration dichotomy. In what may turn out to be a seminal work, Tendler (1997) has argued for an alternative approach to thinking about the improvement of public management in developing countries. Rather than chronicling the poor performance of Third World bureaucracies, studying failure in detail, and then prescribing the NPM cure regardless of context, she argues for the analysis of service delivery *successes* through a framework derived from the literature on industrial performance and workplace transformation (IPWT).

Using this micro-level approach and, in particular, focusing on the field-level 'workers' themselves, she explains in detail why agencies in Ceará in Northeast Brazil have been able to achieve high levels of performance. Five main factors underpin achievements in Ceará: workers with unusually high levels of dedication; a government that has fostered the idea of 'mission' in its staff; workers that expand their roles and responsibilities, sometimes on a voluntary basis; the evolution of personal and community-based accountabilities (that is, downward accountabilities); and a central government that actively catalyses and seeks to 'create' civil society. Improving service delivery is not simply about state decentralization and the role of civic associations; rather, it involves a 'three-way dynamic' of central government, local government and civic associations.

Although the relevance of these findings in other contexts will no doubt be arguable, they are partly supported by the evidence in this volume (Robinson and White in Chapter 13 and Christoplos in Chapter 15), and provide alternative ways of conceptualizing the reform process. Pluralist service provision and partnership arrangements, rather than the NPM purchaser–provider model, may well be the best way to improve services in both urban (Mitlin and Satterthwaite, 1992) and rural (Tendler, 1993) areas of the developing world.

Tendler's work reminds us, as do several essays in this volume, how mistaken it would be to define public management reform too narrowly. Efficient management of structures and resources is necessary, but far from sufficient: how government performs must constantly be related to the underlying purposes of such performance. This directs attention to the fundamental nature of governmental systems and state–society interactions. It is in this context that public management reform merges with broader issues of governance and raises questions about the values which drive institutional change. Several contributions – notably Mackintosh (Chapter 5), Chambers (Chapter 7), Brown (Chapter 8), White and Robinson (Chapters 6 and 13), and Chauncey (Chapter 12) – are concerned with the issue of social inclusion and exclusion. If social exclusion may be increased by recent management reforms, costs of this kind need closer and more precise identification. If political power structures may be a primary factor determining the direction or feasibility of reforms, the political context in which managerial and financial reforms are designed and implemented needs to have a more central position in the research agenda. If bureaucratic and political self-interest threatens to capture the reform process, we need a more detailed understanding of these groups. If the central state is reluctant or unable to provide the services which society needs and demands, we need to explore innovative ways of institutionalizing the state–civil society relationship.

The need for better understanding in all these areas should drive the future research agenda in governance, and would help to construct the more radical and inclusive version of public management called for by Chambers. But research across these universal categories must always be sensitive to the cultural variations which determine precise state–civil society relationships in local contexts. As Turner (Chapter 14) reminds us, universalizing reforms must be adaptive rather than coercive, or merely rhetorical, if they are to have worthwhile effect. For this reason, the governance policies and strategies of aid donors, both multilateral and bilateral, deserve close and continued scrutiny.

CONCLUSION

By way of recapitulation, let us return to the new public management and its description by some of its proponents as a revolution. That description is apt in a select few industrialized countries. In the developing world, it is only one strand in a halting and uncertain process of change. There is no such thing as a single model of new public management reform, even in its industrialized heartland, though there are of course many common elements. The label, convenient though it is, can lead to the reification of the concept and the assumption that there is a greater degree of uniformity than is actually the case.

We are still a long way away from a definitive assessment of the value of the new public management. We have pointed out some gaps in our knowledge that need to be filled if we are to move closer to this goal. We need a greater understanding of, among other things, the outcomes of reform in industrialized countries; the limits and boundaries to the applicability of the reforms; the extent to which such reforms are actually being applied in developing countries; the impact of management decentralization in developing countries; and its relationship to organizational performance.

We also need to hear much more about *alternatives* to NPM, not simply critiques of it. How valid are Tendler's (1997) ideas about reforms driven by a 'three-way dynamic' in which workers and citizens, not only central authorities, shift supply-driven service delivery systems towards a more client-centred approach? Tendler's work relates to rural Brazil, but society-based initiatives using 'report card' surveys (Paul and Sekhar, 1997) have also helped to improve services in urban India.

Still, some limited and very tentative conclusions about the new public management are possible. First of all, the revolution is unlikely to fade away in its heartland. True, administrative reforms are never engraved in stone. Some elements of the reforms will erode under the daily grind of politics; others will become susceptible to pendulum swings; still others will be superseded by new reforms. Yet the changes are not likely to amount to a reversal of NPM. The label 'new' will have to be dropped at some point. But the new public management will take its place as part of the backdrop of concepts and principles against which public affairs are organized and conducted, if only because the ineluctable financial and political pressures which generated it are unlikely to diminish.

In developed and developing countries alike, though particularly in the latter, neither scholars nor practitioners should assume that NPM is – or should be – universal. It is no more than an extra set of ideas to draw upon, a new set of tools to add to the reformer's toolbox. Over-preoccupation with the label can lead us to ignore the variety of reasons why superficially new public management reforms are being carried out in developing countries, or the continuity with the past in terms of the poor implementation record of reform.

We should perhaps be more concerned with this continuity than the question of what label to pin on the reforms. By way of a final addition to the agenda for future researchers, we would suggest a need to revisit the longstanding questions of why reform fails and how the obstacles can be overcome. One particular issue within this field of inquiry needs urgent consideration: the scope of reform.

Most programmes in developing countries aspire towards a comprehensive approach – in part owing to the very centralization of government, in part because of the blueprint planning process that aid donors, the main financiers of reform, still use. But a more selective approach contributed to the success of the new public management in its industrialized heartland (Polidano, 1995). A suggestion emerging from the work of Pope (1995) and Tendler (1997) is that of using an organic approach which seeks to improve performance in only a very limited area (such as a single agency) and then diffuse the experience. This has much to recommend it, but it does not fit easily into aid-driven civil service reform projects.

Such strategic and tactical issues badly need consideration, particularly where developing countries are concerned. Past research into this aspect of reform is open to the accusation that there is an endless regurgitation of 'lessons' of varying degrees of practicality, coupled with a tendency to stop at prescription without asking *why* the lessons are ignored time and again. This may have led scholars away from tactical questions in recent years. But the current performance of reform in developing countries indicates that we have yet to come up with real answers.

REFERENCES

Aucoin, Peter (1995), *The New Public Management: Canada in Comparative Perspective*, Montreal: Institute for Research on Public Policy.

Borins, Sandford (1994), 'Government in transition: a new paradigm in public administration', Toronto: CAPAM.

Boston, Jonathan, Martin, John, Pallot, June and Walsh, Pat (1996), *Public Management: The New Zealand Model*, Melbourne: Oxford University Press.

Caiden, Gerald E. (1991), *Administrative Reform Comes of Age*, Berlin: Walter de Gruyter.

Caiden, Gerald E., Halley, Alexis A. and Maltais, Daniel (1995), 'Results and lessons from Canada's PS2000', *Public Administration and Development*, 15 (2), 85–102.

Cohen, John M. and Wheeler, John R. (1997), 'Building sustainable professional capacity in African public sectors: retention constraints in Kenya', *Public Administration and Development*, 17 (3), 307–24.

Evans, Peter (1995), *Embedded Autonomy: States and Industrial Transformation*, Princeton: Princeton Unversity Press.

Gray, Andrew, and Jenkins, Bill (1997), 'Public administration and government 1995–96', *Parliamentary Affairs*, 50 (2), 191–211.

Grindle, Merilee S. (1997), 'Divergent cultures? When public organisations perform well in developing countries', *World Development*, 25 (4), 481–95.

Hirschmann, David (1993), 'Institutional development in the era of economic policy reform: concerns, contradictions, and illustrations from Malawi', *Public Administration and Development*, **13** (2), 113–28.

Holmes, Malcolm (1992), 'Public sector management reform: convergence or divergence?', *Governance*, **5** (4), 472–83.

Islam, Nasir (1993), 'Public enterprise reform: managerial autonomy, accountability and performance contracts', *Public Administration and Development*, **13** (2), 129–52.

McCourt, Willy (1997), 'International assistance for the Human Resources Management Working Group: report on international comparative experience and benchmarking', report prepared for the Presidential Review Commission for the Transformation of the Public Service in South Africa, Manchester: British Council.

Mitlin, Diane, and Satterthwaite, David (1992), 'Scaling-up development in urban areas', in Michael Edwards and David Hulme (eds), *Making a Difference: NGOs and Development in a Changing World*, London: Earthscan, pp. 169–79.

Mountfield, Robin (1997), 'Organisational reform within government: accountability and policy management', *Public Administration and Development*, **17** (1), 71–6.

Osborne, David and Gaebler, Ted (1992), *Reinventing Government: How the Entrepreneurial Spirit is Transforming the Public Sector*, New York: Penguin.

Paul, Samuel and Sekhar, Sita (1997), 'A report card on public services: a comparative analysis of five cities in India', *Regional Development Dialogue*, **18** (2), 119–32.

Polidano, Charles (1995), 'Should administrative reform commissions be decommissioned?', *Public Administration*, **73** (3), 455–71.

Polidano, Charles (1997), 'The bureaucrat who fell under a bus: ministerial responsibility, executive agencies and the Derek Lewis affair in Britain', IDPM Public Policy and Management Working Paper No. 1, Manchester: Institute for Development Policy and Management.

Pope, Jeremy (1995), 'Ethics, transparency and accountability: putting theory into practice', in Petter Langseth, Sandile Nogxina, Daan Prinsloo and Roger Sullivan (eds), *Civil Service Reform in Anglophone Africa*, Pretoria: Economic Development Institute, Overseas Development Administration, and Government of South Africa, pp. 275–309.

Shergold, Peter (1997), 'The colour purple: perceptions of accountability across the Tasman', *Public Administration and Development*, **17** (3), 293–306.

Tendler, Judith (1993), *New Lessons from Old Projects: The Workings of Rural Development in Northeast Brazil*, Washington, DC: World Bank.

Tendler, Judith (1997), *Good Government in the Tropics*, Baltimore and London: Johns Hopkins University Press.

Turner, Mark and Hulme, David (1997), *Governance, Administration and Development: Making the State Work*, Basingstoke: Macmillan.

Walsh, Kieron (1995), *Public Services and Market Mechanisms: Competition, Contracting and the New Public Management*, Basingstoke: Macmillan.

Wangoto, Aneri M. (1995), 'Uganda civil service reform programme: implementation of the reform measures and lessons to be learned', in Petter Langseth, Sandile Nogxina, Daan Prinsloo and Roger Sullivan (eds), *Civil Service Reform in Anglophone Africa*, Pretoria: Economic Development Institute, Overseas Development Administration, and Government of South Africa, pp. 145–60.

Wuyts, Mark (1996), 'Foreign aid, structural adjustment, and public management: the Mozambican experience', *Development and Change*, **27** (4), 717–49.

Index